Virginity Lost in Vietnam
by Dave Lange

Dave Lange, an award-winning journalist and longtime newspaperman, shares the stories that helped to shape and define his character in this breathtaking collection of memoirs. From his childhood days in a tough steel valley of Pennsylvania to gritting it out in a war that no one could win, Dave recalls the trials and tribulations he endured that guided his life in becoming one of the most respected journalists I have had the pleasure of working with. His knowledge, commitment and passion for everything he does certainly come through in this book.

> *Bob Jacob, Managing Editor, Cleveland Jewish News*

Lange forcefully takes the rich and powerful to task for failing in their commitments to the public. His use of irony is masterful. Beautifully done!

> *First Place, The Press Cub of Cleveland*
> *Best Columnist in Ohio, 2011*

Out of a small notice concerning a gathering of Vietnam-era veterans, the Times developed a series of articles that helped lead to the formation of a local chapter of Vietnam Veterans of America. Interest from veterans nearly tripled, no doubt due in part to the Times getting the word out on the chapter. One story about a counselor dealing with post-traumatic stress disorder led to her offering free assistance to the VVA chapter. Another story covered the meeting of a local Vietnam vet with a Soviet vet from the Afghanistan conflict; it brought into focus the worldwide problems that ex-fighting men and women from unpopular conflicts have faced. Reporter Dave Lange puts a real feel for his subject into the stories.

> *Osmond C. Hooper Community Service Award, 1990*

Virginity Lost in Vietnam

Dave Lange

To Jeff:
May you find some
information + entertainment
in these pages.
Dave Lange

Act3 ▷

*To Linda Lange and all the other spouses
whose love and support have salvaged, fortified and
enriched the lives of their Vietnam veterans.*

Table of Contents

Part 2: Lost

Part 3: Ancestry at War

Introduction

This is an autobiographical coming-of-age compilation of stories set in and around the 1960s, one of the most tumultuous periods in American history. The Vietnam War is the consuming phenomenon hanging over the lives of those who grew into adulthood at that time.

I've been a troublemaker my entire life, and I've learned that finding truth makes big trouble for liars. Pursuit of truth led me to a career in journalism. Causing trouble by exposing lies made opinion writing my most favored application of that honorable craft.

As the double-entendre title of this book, "Virginity Lost in Vietnam," suggests, it is much about the war in which I and many of my contemporaries served but also about adventures and frustrations associated with male pubescence. No true story about the 1960s and Vietnam would be complete without the ingredients of drugs and rock 'n' roll.

This book also is about race. It's about a white kid from an all-white, working-class neighborhood who, through his military experience, came to know the true brotherhood of all races.

Of course, this book is about politics. War is always about politics. War and politics always are overshadowed by lies, about power and privilege and about contempt for the powerless and unprivileged. It is about unlearned lessons that disconnect the present from the past.

Every story in these recollections is true. That means they really happened. It does not make this a journalistic enterprise. Truth and factuality are not imperatively consummate.

Fifty-year-old memories are imprecise. Without a tape recorder at my continuous disposal – actually never – the dialogue contained herein is anecdotal, intended to convey the spirit of the recollections. Some of the communication I can recall verbatim. Mostly not.

The majority of the characters with whom I shared my early life are scrupulously depicted in these multifarious actions and reactions. But not all of them and not always. In group engagements, especially, the numbers, the faces, the positions, the sequences and the environs are matters of inexactitude. Not being a diarist, I only hope that, in balance, I have given credit where credit is due.

Facts are facts, regardless of what ideologues and narcissists may claim. The historical context of my stories is the product of documentation and research into numerous reliable sources. The vast majority of those sources are cited within the text, but this is not a scholarly work.

Most of the key individuals profiled in these true stories are identified by name. However, some names have been changed to protect the guilty, as well as the innocent. Also, there are those whose chance encounters in the distant past leave my memory at a loss, which resulted in the application of some random appellations. Pseudonymous assignations are listed alphabetically at the end of this work.

Acknowledgements

This book is a labor of love. And no one has labored more over my telling these stories than the love of my life, Linda Lange. She is the one who brought order to a life of disorder. She also is the one who provided studious proofreading of these chapters.

Additionally, I owe debts of gratitude to our son and scrupulous editor, Tony Lange, and my longtime friend and colleague, Carole Vigliotti, who provided an insightful review of the text. Several dear friends who played roles in these true stories offered critical feedback, most notably Keith Ball, Jeff Murphy and my brother, Danny Lange.

Foreword
by Ken Douthit

The late Hal Douthit, who founded the Photojournal Press newspaper publishing company in 1957 and served as president of the Ohio Newspaper Association, called Dave Lange "the best weekly newspaper editor in the country."

Hal, my father, a U.S. Army veteran who was the first communications major at Yale, earned his master's degree from Columbia University's Pulitzer School of Journalism and published some 30 newspapers and magazines, knew all about editors.

As Hal Douthit's successor at the helm of Photojournal Press, which evolved into Douthit Communications Inc., I've known Dave Lange as a journalist and a friend for 40 years. Together, we've fought to uphold the freedoms that the Founding Fathers established in the First Amendment. We've persevered for the citizens' right to know against political leaders who sought to deny it. We've stood fast for government that is "of the people, by the people, for the people."

Many of these battles have not been easy. Yet Dave has engaged them with an unyielding pursuit of the truth and a commitment to fairness.

So it comes as no surprise that his autobiography, "Virginity Lost in

Vietnam," exemplifies these journalistic qualities. He doesn't just tell his own story about growing up in the turbulent 1960s, graduating from high school, beginning college but losing his draft deferment and then going to Vietnam. He puts his experiences in the perspective of the news that impacted our generation.

As he did throughout his newspaper career, Dave conducted meticulous research for his book. He doesn't just call out government leaders who lied to the American people about Vietnam. He credits the great journalism of the era that exposed those lies.

After completing his military service and becoming a journalist, Dave never wavered in his loyalty to fellow veterans. From the issues surrounding Agent Orange and post-traumatic stress disorder to disparagements from the Department of Veterans Affairs and trumped-up attacks by the so-called Swift Boat Veterans for Truth, his articles have dug into the real facts.

As early as 1990, Dave was honored with an Ohio Newspaper Association Community Service Award for a series he wrote on the formation of a local Vietnam Veterans of America chapter. "Interest from veterans nearly tripled, no doubt due in part to the Times getting the word out on the chapter," the judge wrote. "Reporter Dave Lange puts a real feel for his subject into the stories."

During his 25 years as editor of the Chagrin Valley Times, Dave led our staff to win the ONA's General Excellence Award in the Osman C. Hooper weekly newspaper contest 19 times.

In awarding Dave Lange more than 60 statewide contest honors individually, here are just a few comments made by the judges:

"Lange forcefully takes the rich and powerful to task for failing in their commitments to the public."

"Sarcasm and irony put to good use, shades of Twain. ... he can make you laugh or get angry."

"He fulfills the watchdog responsibility of the press with energy, and his work shows a good deal of research behind the opinions he expresses."

"The writing is of superior quality, as is organization and clarity."

"He is an entertaining writer who isn't afraid to take a stand."

That's the kind of writing Dave Lange is known for, and it's the kind of writing that flows through the pages of "Virginity Lost in Vietnam." This book is loaded with all of the above – sarcasm and irony, force and energy, laughter and anger, research and clarity.

Whether the reader is a product of the 1960s, the 1990s or another decade, whether he or she served in Vietnam, protested against the war or both, these stories are stimulating, provocative and, best of all, the truth.

Ken Douthit is CEO of Douthit Communications Inc., publisher of weekly newspapers across Northern Ohio and a past president of the Ohio Newspaper Association.

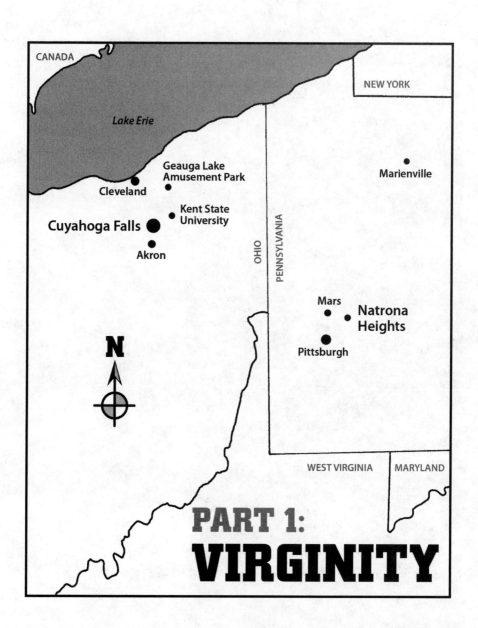

PART 1:
VIRGINITY

Chapter 1 | # A Child of Refugees

"Take this," my dad told me. "You're gonna need it." It was the reliable wristwatch that had gotten him to the factory floor on time, day after day, year after year. He had slipped it off his wrist and was handing it to me. I put it on my left arm. Dad grasped my right hand. We looked eye to eye. Our days of turmoil were past. The memories of world war that he never shared lie beneath that hard-nosed exterior somewhere. Then I embraced my mom. I saw the worry in her eyes. Her firstborn child, still a child to her, the one she had conceived as an unsettled 17-year-old bride was leaving her, maybe forever. But the tears she shed during her own war-torn childhood were drained. She had no more.

After one, last, two-day visit at my family's home, it was time to board a plane at Cleveland Hopkins Airport. This was it. Uniformed in my dress blues, I was leaving my boyhood behind.

Why war? Why Vietnam? Why me? For half a century now, I keep asking myself. Maybe the answer lies in my genes. Who knows?

Nearly 21 years earlier, on March 26, 1948, Charles Garfinkel, officer in charge at the United States Department of Justice Immigration and Naturalization Service office in Pittsburgh, received a letter from my father, World War II U.S. Army veteran Charles M. Lange, of Natrona Heights, Pennsylvania.

This is what he wrote: "For your information it is my intention to bring to the United States a young lady whom I met while in the service of my country in Germany, and I will be deeply grateful if you will mail to me at your earliest convenience the necessary application, also affidavit forms as to my finances and other evidence as to my ability to support a wife."

That wasn't entirely true. Chuck Lange had been in service to his adopted country in his native Germany, all right, and the decorated U.S. Army infantryman did intend to bring a young German lady, 17-year-old Helga Hingst, to the United States. But he had never met her.

Garfinkel responded with a list of requirements for "Visa Applications of Alien Fiancees and Fiances of Certain American Citizens," among them: evidence of availability of transportation to the United States; sworn statements of both parties to the proposed marriage; evidence of honorable discharge from the military; fiancee's birth certificate, four photographs of the fiancee; and "Fuhrungszeugnis," a police dossier.

Indications in the documents were that, if the applicant was under the age of 18, execution of the affidavit was required by signature of a parent or guardian.

On June 18, 1948, a letter from Garfinkel to the U.S. Visa Office in Berlin advised that a $500 bond had been posted by Emy Lange on behalf of her son for the proposed temporary admission of his fiancee to the United States in accordance with the War Fiancee Act of 1946. The 1946 act was an amendment to the War Brides Act of 1945, which authorized the admission of alien spouses of American military veterans and their minor children. The War Fiancee Act temporarily admitted aliens who were engaged to be married to those who had served in the armed forces, based on the expectation that official matrimonial rites would be held within three months.

Arranged marriages were common around the world until the 18th century. Often they involved very young women – girls, actually – marrying much older men – not necessarily willingly – and many were matters of aristocratic mutuality. In 1533, for example, 17-year-old Emilie of Saxony, daughter of Henry IV, duke of Saxony, became the third wife of 48-year-old George of Brandenburg, the future Margrave of Brandenburg-Ansbach and duke of Silesia.

Saxony is the far eastern German state where my father's mother, Emy Lux, endured an unpleasant living arrangement with her much older half brother, Ernst, in the city of Dresden before the outbreak of World War I and where she visited her other half brother, Alfons, festering with battle wounds on his death bed in the city of Leipzig shortly after the war. Brandenburg is the state surrounding Berlin, where my other grandmother, Gertrud Zeyssig Hingst, gave birth to my mother prior to divorcing the hard-drinking, abusive Ewald Hingst and her subsequent marriage to Heinrich Meyer. Silesia is the state southwest of Berlin where the women and girls of my mother's family found temporary refuge from Allied bombing in World War II.

Emilie of Saxony blessed twice-widowed George of Brandenburg with the heir that his first two wives had failed to produce. Emilie and George were active in advancing the Protestant Reformation that Martin Luther began by challenging Pope Leo X with the Ninety-Five Theses that he posted on the door of the church in Wittenberg in 1517.

The marriage of Emilie and George was arranged, but it wasn't a consanguineous one, which involves spouses from common ancestors. Those also have been common throughout history. Rock 'n' roll icon Jerry Lee Lewis, for one, at the age of 22, married his 13-year-old cousin Myra in 1957. Writer Edgar Allen Poe, who was 26 at the time, married his 13-year-old cousin Virginia in 1839. Other famous men who married first cousins have included author H.G. Wells, naturalist Charles Darwin and outlaw Jesse James. Composer Johann Sebastian Bach, physicist Albert Einstein and former New York Gov. Rudy Giuliani married second cousins.

Consanguineous marriages are frowned upon by Christianity today. Thirty-one of the 50 states in the United States prohibit marriage between first cousins, as do Buddhist-Taoist Taiwan and China and the mostly Catholic Philippines. Ethiopia, where Christians outnumber Muslims by nearly two to one, bans consanguineous marriages out to the sixth cousin. South Korea, where Christians and Buddhists account for more than half of the population but where agnosticism is the largest single belief, prohibits them out to the third cousin. Nonetheless, such marriages remain common in the Middle East, West Asia and North Africa.

According to a 2012 account by Hank Pellissier, an affiliate scholar and former managing director of the Institute for Ethics and Emerging Technologies, 70 percent of the marriages in Pakistan are consanguineous today. Other predominantly Muslim countries have high rates as well, including Saudi Arabia at more than 50 percent, Iran and Afghanistan between 30 percent and 40 percent and Iraq at 33 percent.

Genetic defects have long been associated with intermarriage. According to a 2005 BBC report, Pakistani-Britons, 55 percent of whom marry first cousins, account for 33 percent of Britain's children with genetic illnesses, even though they represent just 3 percent of the country's births.

Muslims are not the only religious group to experience such consanguineous consequences. As Pellissier wrote, "This dire prognosis is duplicated" in Geauga County, Ohio, 30 miles east of Cleveland, "where the Amish population represents 12 percent of the citizenry. After inter-breeding for 300 years, Amish total 50 percent of the county's special needs cases. Additionally, there's a debilitating seizure disorder that's so rare only 12 individuals worldwide are afflicted with it; the infirmity is exclusively Amish."

The Amish, many of whom continue to speak German among themselves today, originated in Switzerland amidst the splintering religious orders that divined varied interpretations of Christianity in the bloody years immediately following Martin Luther's bold breakaway.

As for "the deleterious risks of consanguineous mating" exemplified by the Geauga County Amish experience, Pellissier pointed to quite a list, including schizophrenia, congenital heart defects, cystic fibrosis, albinism, central-nervous-system anomalies and mental retardation plus greater likelihood of infant and child mortality.

Unbeknownst to my mother, Helga Hingst, in the spring of 1948, my two grandmothers – her mother, Gertrud Meyer, and her grandfather's half-sister, Emy Lange – were plotting a consanguineous marriage. Helga had just graduated from high school and had hopes of continuing her education, but those prospects were bleak and getting bleaker.

In the aftermath of World War II, the four Allied powers – the United States, the Soviet Union, the United Kingdom and France – divided Germany into four occupation zones. Unfortunately for Gertrud and Heinrich Meyer, my mother, her younger half-sister and some 2.8 million other Berliners, the capital city also was divided into four sectors. Worse yet, it was wholly embedded 100 miles deep inside the country's Soviet zone. The Meyers, whose Tempelhof area seemed somewhat secure within the American zone, were not among the some 11 million refugees who made their way from the communist-controlled areas to western Germany before the Soviets decided that the old counsel about "love 'em or leave 'em" would not apply to the peoples unwillingly enveloped by Marxist infatuations.

On June 24, 1948, six days after the U.S. Visa Office in Berlin received notification that the $500 bond had been posted for Helga's American wedding maneuver, the Soviets blocked off all highways, railways and canals connecting the city's American, British and French zones to the Western World. In what became known as the Berlin Blockade, the Soviets impeded freight deliveries, including water, and conducted bellicose military exercises just outside the city limits.

Although the Potsdam Agreement of 1945 neglected to grant Allied ground routes across the Soviet zone to Berlin, it did establish three 23-mile-wide air corridors to the city. That enabled the American and British governments to undertake one of the most monumental and ambitious acts of humanity in history, one in which conquering powers reached out to save the subjects of a defeated fascist state that itself had so recently inflicted so much human misery on the world. My own life very well may be indebted to the Berlin Airlift and to the American and British people who supported it.

During the airlift, which lasted more than a year, Allied supply planes made nearly 300,000 flights in and out of West Berlin and delivered more than 2.3 million tons of cargo, eventually averaging about 8,000 tons a day. It provided enough food to prevent my mother and her fellow Berliners from starving, but the comforts afforded by fuel and electricity were in short supply. Even before the blockade, Berlin was not a place for a college-age girl to fulfill her aspirations.

So Gertrud Meyer wrote to her Aunt Emy in Pennsylvania about the possibility of advancing Helga's education in the land of opportunity. What precisely transpired in their communications was not known to my mother. But it's evident from the immigration service's documentation that the simple desire for an American education didn't swing the doors wide open to postwar refugees.

Five months after the $500 bond was posted, on Saturday, the 13th of November 1948, they received notice that a seat had opened up on a flight out of Berlin that very afternoon. Helga had one hour to get to the airport. There was no time to pack a suitcase or bags. With nothing but the clothes on her back, she was whisked into the terminal, kissed her mother and sister goodbye and was off to a new life of freedom – sort of.

She changed planes in Frankfurt and made refueling stops in Shannon, Ireland, Gander, Newfoundland, and Boston before arriving in New York, where, upon debarkation, she was handed another airline ticket and $20. The English she had learned in school was good enough to be understood by New Yorkers, but the New York dialect was as foreign to her as the skyscrapers she could see through the windows towering toward the clouds. Fortunately, written English has no accent, and Helga learned that she needed to catch a cab to a different airport for the final leg of her scrambling journey to Pittsburgh.

It was there that she met for the first time her mother's Aunt Emy and her mother's cousins, Charles Manfred "Nook" Lange and Helga Lange Klemzak, both of whom were Helga Hingst's first cousins once removed and were 12 years and nine years her senior. A month later, on Dec. 17, 1948, 17-year-old Helga Hingst was married to her 29-year-old cousin, Charles Lange.

The consanguineous marriage was not contested by the Pennsylvania legal authorities, perhaps because it did not come to their attention, and it was a well-kept secret from its offspring for many years.

For my mother, the situation had been painfully clear. She could become the child bride of her much older cousin, a man she didn't even know, and perhaps get an opportunity to attend college. Or she could be compelled within three months to head back to the battered and partitioned city of Berlin, where her prospects at the germination point of the looming Cold War were much gloomier. And who knows how complicit her own mother was in facilitating this betrothal anyway? After all, Trud Meyer did have to sign that affidavit in the visa application certifying the intent of her teenage daughter to marry the U.S. Army veteran in Pennsylvania. Helga couldn't just pick up the phone and say, "Hey, Mom, could you pick me up at the airport?"

As for my father, the motive for hooking up with a German girl he had never met is one of those great mysteries. His relationship with Signe, the young woman who apparently found alternative romantic connections while Nook was stationed in Panama, was long past. According to accounts that surfaced many years later, that fling had concluded with a well-advised annulment. The war had captured a few of the most virile years of his life. His hairline was receding too fast for his fancies. Nook's body was still young, even though the dreams of his youth had vanished in the frozen foxholes on the Siegfried Line, but he wouldn't be getting any younger.

Then his mother received some black-and-white photographs of that pretty young cousin in the mail. Her fair-skinned face had a sprinkle of freckles, soft lips that curved in the right places, a gently shaped nose of proportionate size and eyes that shined with more reflection than sparkle. Nicely formed ankles protruded from a long gray skirt, which gripped tightly around her recessed waist, and a woolen blouse fit loosely around her ample bosom. Nook learned that she was 5-foot-2, eyes of blue, and that wavy hair atop her head was as auburn as an autumn maple grove at sunset.

With the 30-year benchmark of maturity waiting in the wings upon his next birthday in the coming spring and with the convention of marriage and parenthood settling upon the generation of world warriors, Nook knew that a man could do worse. The age differential might be unconventional for 20th-century Pennsylvania, but that would narrow over time. And the consanguinity, well, who would know?

The marriage itself came unceremoniously. Consummation of the marriage came rapidly. By the time my mother reached her 18th birthday on March 16, 1949, her slender waist had transitioned to a life-giving and life-changing bulge – the first of four pregnancies that supplanted girlhood with motherhood over the next six years.

Early baby-boom member

My arrival came as an early member of the baby-boom generation at Allegheny Valley Hospital nine months and 27 days after the wedding. A child of refugees, I weighed in at 6 pounds, 4 ounces. I was the first of the von Selhorst or Hingst bloodlines to be born on American soil, but I carried neither of those surnames. Helmut von Selhorst, the World War I German soldier who impregnated my grandmother out of wedlock in 1918, soon vanished on the Western Front. Gustav Lange, who married my grandmother, adopted my infant father, fathered my aunt and delivered them from their war-ravaged homeland to America, is the only grandfather I ever knew. His name is mine.

Personally, I cannot describe the pain of circumcision. I don't remember a thing about it. Older males who undergo the ancient surgical procedure that amputates the foreskin from around the head of the penis describe it as quite excruciating. In modern times, the use of analgesia has been recommended in conjunction with it.

I suppose I can thank the book of Genesis in the Old Testament, which describes the circumcision of Abraham and his descendants, for making it a religious obligation as part of the brit milah for newborn Jews and somehow eventually subjecting me to it as well. The New Testament does not recommend it for Christians, but neither does it forbid it. Even today, circumcision is uncommon in Europe. It has been condemned by the German Society of Pediatrics and Adolescent Medicine, and a court in Cologne outlawed it in 2013, ruling that it causes "bodily harm." During the Holocaust, the Nazis routinely examined male genitals to root out the Jews from the uncircumcised "master race."

In the early part of the 20th century, circumcision became prevalent in the United States, as well as Britain, based on the puritanical notion that it would discourage masturbation. Therefore, I became the first in my bloodlines to suffer the indignity. My parents wanted me to be all-American, complete with a butchered penis head. Besides, the physician who delivered me, Dr. Hymel Fishkin, was Jewish. What could go wrong? I imagine I screamed. Who wouldn't?

The Langes, Charles and Helga, carried me home to their little one-bedroom trailer jacked up on a patch of weeds behind the cinder-block garage in my grandparents' backyard at 1200 Pennsylvania Ave. We were just a half block northeast of Freeport Road, Route 28, which follows the Allegheny River from Pittsburgh, cuts through the heart of Natrona Heights and then up to Kittaning and beyond. There was an unpaved alley on one side of our lot, which gave access to our garage, as well as those behind the homes facing Freeport Road. Another cinder alley ran across the back of our property. In the house next door, sitting on a similar narrow and deep lot with ample foliage to the rear, lived my aunt and uncle, Helga and Eddie Klemzak, and my 7-year-old cousin, Jill. The shopping plaza on the opposite side of Freeport Road was not yet built, and no one dreamed of minimum-wage workers someday flipping burgers at a McDonald's restaurant on the next block.

On a cold winter day, after his shift with a couple thousand other laborers at the Alcoa plant in New Kensington, my dad would plop onto the sofa in our intimate living space and bury his head in the Valley Daily News until my mom would serve up some hot potato soup, cabbage stew or whatever else they might afford for dinner. It didn't matter to me. I was still sucking milk from her teenage breast and pooping in my diaper whenever I damn well pleased.

After dinner, with the moon casting shadows over the valley, Mom would dump that dirty diaper into the same portable potty they squatted over to relieve their bowels and bladders. Dad would pull on his heavy jacket, slip a narrow-brimmed cap on his head and lug that smelly pot of slop out the trailer door, down a couple steps and onto the frozen ground. He'd grab his pick and shovel and head around the back, where, under the shroud of darkness, he'd chop a hole deep enough into the bone-hard earth to contain a day's worth of our oozing bodily waste.

On most days when Dad was at work, even in the throes of winter, Mom would tuck me in a stroller and head out for a walk or a visit with a neighbor. Occasionally, Mom would get a little time for herself, thanks to Mrs. Samuelson, a Jewish lady who lived around the corner from my grandparents and who kindly watched over me for a couple hours. My own grandmother couldn't be bothered with babysitting, according to my mom, but the Samuelsons, who had every reason to turn their backs on a German girl and her baby, were warm and welcoming.

I didn't spend much time with my Papap either. Each evening when Gus Lange got home from his job at the PPG plant, he'd head down to the cinder-floored cellar with a bottle of whiskey and work on mechanical inventions that never made it to the patent office. Mom said his wife drove him to drink. I don't think she was too fond of her mother-in-law.

It's probably a good thing we didn't spend another winter in that shit hole of a trailer, because the rear yard was running out of dumping ground. Years later, whenever we'd visit the relatives on Pennsylvania Avenue, my dad would warn us kids to watch our step behind the garage, and I noticed that the weeds were growing pretty well.

It was not such a good thing that work was less than steady at Alcoa, and, apparently, trained welders like my dad were not in high demand. For a short time, he found work in a lumber mill about 60 miles up north in the town of Marienville on the edge of the Allegheny National Forest. My grandparents and their best friends, the Hoaks, had a tiny cottage there, where they could get away for weekends of drinking and card playing. Although the cottage included a single-seat privy out back and cold spring water was available from a communal pump a quarter mile up the road, we opted for a heated apartment above the hardware store in town instead.

By the time my sister Yvonne arrived in December 1951, we were back in Natrona Heights, where we rented a regular apartment with indoor plumbing and all, which I was old enough to appreciate. Mom appreciated the laundry room in the basement of the building, where we kids could play and she could perfect her comprehension of American English while socializing with other young mothers.

At the age of 22, Mom was pregnant with child No. 3, and Dad was collecting a regular paycheck again, so they were able to pull together a down payment for a little house on Saxonburg Road, not far from the cemetery where my Papap soon would rest in peace. My brother, Daniel, was born in December 1953. Things were looking up. We could pick up our telephone receiver, recite a few digits to the operator, and she'd connect our calls, assuming that the folks next door weren't already yakking on the party line. We got our very own black-and-white television set, so we could watch "Lassie" and "The Adventures of Rin Tin Tin." Best of all, we had a little dog named Prince, who followed me everywhere. He'd catch rats in the usually dry stream bed that separated our house from the nicer ones on the side street. Then he'd bring them home and plunk their bloody carcasses on the kitchen floor, which made my mom mad and made me giggle.

That didn't last. In the mid-1950s, Pittsburgh and Allegheny County were still "the steel capital of the world," but signs of a long, steady decline were evident, and my dad was one of the early casualties. This time his chances of regaining employment in the industry were pretty dim. He got a job for a while in the town of Mars up in Butler County, but that didn't last. My mom got a job too. She'd catch a ride to work with a guy from town, and he'd bring her back home late in the evening. My parents began to argue over money and other matters that I didn't quite understand. They'd get loud, and I'd hold my pillow over my head as I lay in bed at night. One night my mom called the cops. They threatened to haul my dad away, but he calmed down, and they left.

Not long after my father's stepfather, my Papap, died in 1954, our family's fortunes took a turn for the better. Dad learned through a friend that the Ford Motor Co. was hiring at two of its stamping plants – one just outside of Buffalo, New York, and the other just outside of Cleveland. Buffalo being about 220 miles from his hometown and Cleveland just 140 miles away, Dad took the job in Ohio.

At the time, Cleveland was the nation's third-leading steel maker and second-largest producer of automobile parts, not to mention the fact that nearby Akron was the "rubber capital of the world." Industry was booming in the postwar years on the southern shores of Lake Erie.

Ford's brand new Cleveland Stamping Plant in the village of Walton Hills on the southern edge of Cuyahoga County, just above the Summit County line, covered about 2.2 million square feet and employed 2,400 people. With the exception of some cafeteria and office workers and nurses, they were all men. They were of different colors and had different places of origin, including Europeans like my father and a heavy dose of transplanted West Virginians. They worked in three shifts on production lines of stamping presses and welding machines to fabricate bumpers, hoods, roofs, quarter panels and other parts for Ford automobiles. The cavernous plant was sooty and fumy and hot as hell on summer afternoon shifts. The hulking machines were thunderously loud and could chop off an arm as effortlessly as a finger and eject it down a scrap shoot along with steel trimmings to a dumper in the basement. The welders fired off sparks that could spin through coverall collars to sizzle some chest hairs or sear a little skin.

The Ford plant was the American dream for families like mine that could count on weekly paychecks to cover the rent or make mortgage payments, put hot suppers on the kitchen table, buy the kids new shoes every year or so and imagine that they were getting a fairer slice of the pie.

For the first few months, Dad found a bed in a rooming house in nearby Bedford, from which he was able to scope out the area, and he'd return home to Natrona Heights during an occasional weekend off work. Sometime around my fifth birthday, we packed up and made the move to Cuyahoga Falls, Akron's most populous suburb, 20 miles south of the Ford plant.

World-shaking developments

The life-changing events of 1954 were much too unsettling for the Lange family to pay much attention to world-shaking developments in Southeast Asia. The French had indeed recaptured Vietnam in 1947, but the emboldened Viet Minh communist nationalist revolutionaries fought for their country and finally defeated the colonial occupiers in the decisive battle of Dien Bien Phu on May 7, 1954. The Geneva Accords that followed temporarily divided the country in two, with the North led by the communist Ho Chi Minh and the South by dictator Ngo Dinh Diem. The accords called for elections to be held in two years to reunite Vietnam. But when that time came, Diem, knowing that the exercise in democracy would not work in his favor, refused to abide by the agreement. He found a willing ally in the United States, whose Truman Doctrine viewed communism as the greatest threat to the world and saw democratic elections in Vietnam as the first "falling domino" in a fearful theory.

Chapter 2 | # It Really Did Stink

Drivers on Route 8 between Cuyahoga Falls and the Ford plant in Walton Hills would want to be on the lookout for the notorious "Boston Strangler," whose propensity for handing out speeding tickets helped the town of Boston Heights pad its budget. Also, Sportsman Park, which opened as a greyhound track in 1934 but quickly found midget auto racing more sustainable, and other commercial enterprises in the village of Northfield, with its 25 mph speed limit, could slow traffic to a crawl. The racetrack was torn down in 1956 and rebuilt as Northfield Park for harness racing the following year. It became an even better bet for the owners when the state government twisted Ohio law to allow the addition of slot machines there in 2013.

About 30,000 people, most of them blue-collar families, called Cuyahoga Falls their hometown in 1950. It was growing fast when we arrived. The city's population reached nearly 48,000 by 1960 and topped off at about 50,000 in 1970.

When it was founded in 1812, the town was called Manchester, but the name later was changed in honor of the "crooked river," or Cuyahoga, in the language of American Indians. The Cuyahoga River descends a total of 800 feet over its twisty course of 100 miles between its headwaters in Geauga County 30 miles due east of Cleveland and its mouth at Lake Erie in the industrial center of the city. Much of that drop occurs at the southernmost point of the serpentine journey, where the river roars over two falls and a series of rapids at the bottom of a 100-foot-deep gorge through the middle of Cuyahoga Falls. According to the city's own historical account, during its 2-mile surge from one border to the other, the river's plunge is greater than the height of Niagara Falls.

That isn't the Cuyahoga River's claim to fame, however. Almost from the time Moses Cleaveland arrived to survey the area known as the Connecticut Western Reserve in 1796, the river attracted settlers and then gave birth to industry. Industrial growth took place in towns like Mantua and Kent in Portage County, Cuyahoga Falls and Peninsula in Summit County and Cuyahoga Heights and Newburgh Heights in Cuyahoga County. Most significantly, it occurred near the river's mouth in Cleveland's Cuyahoga River Flats. Over the next century and a half, those industries were given virtual free rein to use the river not just as their sewer but also as the dumping ground for their toxic, combustible wastes. It really did stink.

According to Case Western Reserve University Law Professor Jonathan H. Adler's 2003 book, "Fables of the Cuyahoga: Reconstructing a History of Environmental Protection," the first of at least 13 fires to ignite in Cleveland's poisonous river occurred way back in 1868. Sooty flames from the biggest one, which broke out in 1952, reportedly caused more than $1 million in damages to boats, a bridge and an office building. The blaze that finally caught the attention of the national media and the Environmental Protection Agency in 1969 was much smaller, causing an estimated $50,000 in damage, mostly to a railroad bridge.

Reliable city services, including its own water supply from deep artesian wells and its own electricity company, well-regarded neighborhood schools, comparatively low taxes and an ample supply of cheap housing attracted working-class families to Cuyahoga Falls. Many of the breadwinners worked in Akron's nearby rubber plants, and more than a few, like my father, were employed at Ford's Cleveland Stamping Plant.

One more thing attracted people like my dad to Cuyahoga Falls. While folks of just about every European extraction – Italians, Poles and

Irish among them – plus plenty of transplanted West Virginians and even a couple Jews could be found in the city's various neighborhoods, they were all white. America of the 1950s and 1960s was a very segregated country, to be sure, but few places were as lily white as Cuyahoga Falls. Black people did not live there, and they did not work there – except for an occasional cement job for a patio or driveway. Even that was frowned upon and complicated by the city inspectors. In fact, Cuyahoga Falls became commonly known as Caucasian Falls to outsiders with minds more open toward the virtues of integration. But it is home to the Black Tigers, mascot for the high school's athletic teams. According to the 2010 U.S. Census, the city's African-American population had burgeoned to 3.3 percent.

My parents found a place to rent in a two-story duplex on one of the numbered streets a few blocks west of the river and downtown, just off of Portage Trail, one of the city's main drags. There was a small shop run by a blind broom maker at the corner, but we brought our own factory-made broom with us from Pennsylvania. My mom enrolled me in kindergarten at Redeemer Lutheran Church on Fifth Street, but I didn't pay much attention to that.

They tied Prince up to a doghouse in the backyard, next to the heavy-gauge wire basket where my dad burned the trash. I think trash-burning days were the only times when Prince got any warmth that winter. There weren't any good places for us to go exploring together and for him to catch rats, so Prince stayed tied up in the yard all the time. More often than not, his barking sounded like whining to me. The landlord didn't like the barking, but he wouldn't let Prince move into the apartment with us.

Finally, on a cold January day, Mom said, "We gotta take Prince to the pound," so that's what we did. Vonnie, Danny and I waited in the back seat of the Chevy coupe while they took my four-legged best friend inside a very unfriendly building in Akron. Fifteen minutes later they came back out with uneasy smiles on their faces. "Good news," Mom told us. "Just as we walked in, there was a nice couple with a young boy waiting at the counter. They took one look at Prince and said he was the perfect dog for them. All they have to do is fill out some paperwork, and they'll be taking him home." I believed her.

The next day my Dad took the Chevy to the nearby Sunoco station for an oil change. He let Vonnie and me stay in the front seat with the windows halfway down while the car was elevated on the lift and 10 minutes later took a tummy-tickling dive back to floor of the bay. That always cheered me up. I was 5 years old, and she was 3, but year-old Danny was too young for such fun.

Planting roots in the woods

The west side of Cuyahoga Falls was the bigger side of town, and just about anybody who's familiar with it would tell you it's also the nicer side of town. Much of the area between downtown's Front Street and the commercially active State Road, about 1.75 miles to the west, was residentially built out before World War II. After the war, a developer named Ray W. Heslop bought up land a bit farther west to provide housing for veterans, their brides and the baby boom. Altogether, he built more than 500 cookie-cutter homes and apartments, which, according to the Cuyahoga Falls Historical Society, was believed to be the largest housing development in the state at the time.

In 1949, Heslop shifted his attention to the east side of the river, where he put up nearly 300 somewhat smaller bungalows, most of them on cement slabs. Each one included two bedrooms, a living room, bathroom, kitchen and utility room crammed on the first floor plus an unfinished attic with enough headroom to create two children's sleeping areas. If it weren't for different hues of exterior paint, you could hardly tell one house from another. They originally sold for $10,250 and didn't cost much more when we bought ours on East Bailey Road in 1955. Elizabeth Price Elementary School was just one block away off of Myrtle Avenue. Bailey Road is a well-traveled through street. There was a shopping plaza directly across from us, complete with an independent grocery store, drugstore, hardware, bakery, variety store, doctor's office and shoemaker. How convenient.

On one side of our house, at the corner of Myrtle Avenue, lived the Little family. The Littles had one daughter, who was much older than me. They called her Doodie. They were from West Virginia. At least they sounded like it, which wasn't unusual at all in our neighborhood, or in most of the working-class neighborhoods within smelling distance of Akron's rubber factories. The Littles didn't talk to us much, and they seldom used their back door, which was just a few feet from the edge of our driveway. Maybe they didn't like us. One day I heard old man Little yelling to my mom as she was walking past his house toward the grocery store, probably something about me taking a shortcut across his yard to Myrtle Avenue. She yelled back and called him "numb nuts," which was unusual for her, because she didn't talk like that. I didn't comprehend the connection to his one-child family.

On the other side, our neighbors were the Williamses. Mr. Williams worked at one of the rubber plants. I don't know if it was Goodyear, Goodrich, Firestone or Seiberling. Their son, Gary, was in first grade when we moved in, a year ahead of me, and he had an older sister. The Williamses weren't particularly friendly, but they weren't necessarily unfriendly either. Mostly, Gary and I got along fine, although he did call me a Kraut once or twice. I heard that word spoken by GIs in TV programs about the war, and it wasn't a term of endearment.

Most kids in the neighborhood didn't call me names other than David or Dave, though. Except for Mrs. Little and Mrs. Williams, my mom didn't have any trouble making friends with other mothers in the tight-squeezed neighborhood.

Prince would have liked it there. A block away, between Curtis Avenue and North Moreland Boulevard, just before the Lawson's food store at the corner, where I'd trade an empty gallon milk jug and a dollar bill for a full jug and some change every couple days, was the Little Woods. You had to watch out for the poison ivy, which I occasionally forgot to do, but there were lots of good climbing trees there. Plus, a narrow creek that you could jump across in some spots was teeming with tadpoles, salamanders, water bugs and other good stuff. You could catch toads along the banks and lift up rocks to snatch garter snakes by the neck. I liked to bring little creatures home to show Mom and Dad, but they'd make me let them go. If Prince were still around, I imagine he'd bring some dead rats home too, but I never could catch those critters.

I made friends with a kid my age named Raymond Cooper, who lived on the next block, a few houses closer to the Little Woods. Sometimes when we'd get tired of catching toads and snakes, we'd lug scrap lumber that people had dumped in the woods back to his house and set to work with a saw and hammer to build an airplane which we hoped to fly away one day. Other times we'd play games like hide-and-seek or tag with other kids on his block, most of whom were girls.

One summer evening after supper, as the Lange family sat in the living room to watch television, there was a knock on the front door. My mom let a man in whom I did not recognize but who apparently knew me, because he kept pointing his finger in my direction. Although I couldn't quite hear what he was saying to my mom and dad, he was quite animated. Eventually, he calmed down. I heard my parents say they were sorry and would take care of it. Then the man left.

My parents called me into the kitchen, where Dad looked me straight in the eyes and asked, "Did you make kuckuck in Janie's sandbox?" I did my best to remember the events of that day and had to admit that I was playing in a sandbox after Raymond went home and Janie got called inside for dinner. It's quite possible that I had to go, I told them, "but I covered it up real good." "From now on," Mom told me in no uncertain terms, "you'd better come home and use the bathroom." I promised that I would, which was preferable to getting a good smacking, but I thought doing so would be most inconvenient. Clearly, my parents were a lot more embarrassed about the whole thing than I was with my 5-year-old sense of social graces.

The next day, back at Raymond's house, as some of the other kids looked on with haughty glares of superiority, three mothers confronted me and said, if I didn't change my antisocial behavior, I would no longer be welcome on their block. Not only that, Janie's sandbox was off limits to me. From that day on, if I had to poop when I was playing outside, I'd just head over to the Little Woods. Peeing outside, on the other hand, could be accomplished with a great deal more expedience, at least for boys.

As anthropologist Alan Dundes claimed in his 1984 "Chicken Coop" book, Germans historically seem to have a hang-up about excrement. It seems that my father did a better job of burying shit in the weeds behind our Pennsylvania trailer than I did in Janie's sandbox. But as Thea Dorn, co-author of "The German Soul," said in her 2012 interview, Germans do have a historic affinity for the woods. That being said, I most fervently advise against wiping your ass with poison ivy.

Early elements of education

With the approach of autumn 1955, not long before my sixth birthday, I entered first grade at Price School. Among the other kids in my class were a few that I already knew from the neighborhood, including Marjorie Frazee, who was one of the witnesses to my sandbox admonishment, and Glen Barnhouse and Mike Kensinger, who became close friends of mine through our growing-up years. Several of the boys wore bow ties for our class picture that November, including Tim Meyer, who later became the first baseman on my baseball team, Terry Everhart, whose last name later changed to Gray and who became one of my partners in crime during junior high school, and Ronnie Drope, who damn near knocked my eye out with a snowball in seventh grade.

There was Donny Mathew, who became the star player on my baseball team the summer after sixth grade, not to mention a co-captain and all-district halfback on our high school football team. Donny's twin brother, Danny, who was in a different class, played catcher on our baseball team but was not similarly destined for athletic stardom. Bob Heacock, who was born the same day as me, and I became competitive swimming teammates from the time we were 11 years old through high school, when he won the state butterfly championship our senior year.

One of the girls in our class, Alauna Redfern, also shared my birthday. I learned from her that President Dwight David Eisenhower had been born on Oct. 14 as well, but that had occurred in the previous century. She had recently sent the president a birthday card, and he returned the favor. The next fall my mom helped me do the same thing. When I received his bulk-printed and sincerely wished greeting for our mutual birthdays, I tucked it away in a safe spot at the back of my top dresser drawer and became a loyal Republican.

Another boy in my first-grade class, Bobby Kohler, was Jewish, and everybody knew it, which made him different, we were told, but I didn't fully understand why. Other kids were Catholic, Lutheran, Methodist, whatever, but that didn't make any difference. We couldn't care less. I liked Bobby Kohler. My parents, the German immigrants, and his parents, the Jews, got together socially.

Standing right next to me in the top row of that first-grade picture was Kevin Golub, who probably had the biggest head in the class, except for maybe a chubby girl named Bonnie, and he seemed to be pretty smart to me. Other than reading groups, where I was assigned to the lowest of three levels, I sat next to Kevin in class. He didn't seem to mind when I copied from his lesson papers.

I don't know whether Mrs. Penn was a good first-grade teacher or a bad one, because I didn't listen to her much. But I can say she was a mean one. She was big and bulky, had close-cropped dark hair with bulbous earrings poking out below the curls and thick red lipstick that seemed to hold her mouth in an interminable snarl. Not only did she stick me in the third reading group, which was a bit humiliating, even for a first-grader, but she sent me to a special room to meet with a speech therapist, as if I had an accent like my mother or something. One time when she was yelling at the class, which she was prone to do, I snuck past her and hid behind the door. All of a sudden, Mrs. Penn's crackly voice got even louder. She reeled around and said, "I can smell you back there, David." She grabbed hold of my earlobe and yanked me clear across the room before slamming my skinny ass back into my chair. It was nearly as bad as the sandbox inquisition.

I did like recess, though, even the time when one of the littler girls in our class skipped around and kissed me and Bobby Kohler right on the lips.

That February, my second sister, Heidi, was born. Our Mamam came to stay with us while Mom and Heidi spent some extra time in an Akron hospital and Dad worked overtime at the Ford plant. Mamam made us donuts in a deep fryer. I had never tasted anything so good. When Heidi came home, I paid about as much attention to her incessant whining as I did to Mrs. Penn's yelling. Mom told us she wouldn't be having any more babies. I didn't care to have another sister anyway.

Kevin Golub had a younger brother but no sisters. That was a good reason to play at his house, which was the spitting image of ours. He kept an empty glass jar hidden in a corner of one of the two bedrooms that had been sectioned off upstairs. He showed me how handy it was to pee in the jar and then spill the contents out the window but not to toss it so far that it would splatter the car in the neighbor's driveway. By peeing in the jar, we didn't have to walk downstairs to the bathroom. His mom probably thought we both had pretty good bladders.

One spring day after school, Kevin and I were walking toward the gas line to cut over from Myrtle Avenue to get to his house on Curtis Avenue, where we intended to play in his backyard. A second-grader ran up to us and said we best not go that way, because another kid was running around and flashing a pocketknife. I didn't think much of it, even though I didn't have a pocketknife myself, but, when we got to his house, Kevin told his mom, as if it was some big deal. Apparently, she or some other nosy mom reported the incident to the principal, because Kevin got called to the school office the next morning.

After the school secretary ushered Kevin back to Mrs. Penn's classroom, she called out my name and proceeded to lead me down to the office, where I met the principal, a tall, lanky man named Mr. Ferguson, for the first of numerous times during my primary-school career. He asked me if I knew about the alarming episode involving the flashing pocketknife, and I said I did – which really was a stretch of the facts, because it was only hearsay to me.

"Wait here a minute, and I'll be back," Mr. Ferguson said, and he went to the outer office. He returned a few minutes later with a boy from one of the other two first-grade classes in tow. The boy was somewhat bigger than me, which wasn't saying much, because my growth already was falling below average, and he was wearing glasses and looking quite sheepish. "Is this the boy who had the knife?" Mr. Ferguson asked me.

Truth be told, I had never seen the knife, if there really was one, and didn't see that particular boy, or any boy at all, flashing a pocketknife. But he looked mighty guilty to me, and why else would the principal have him in tow? "That's him all right," I said.

"Are you sure about that?" Mr. Ferguson said, his voice sounding even more serious than before, his imposing frame leaning over me and his eyes piercing into mine.

"Yep," I replied.

"All right then, get on back to your class," he said. Something told me that my testimony was less than convincing. But that was the end of that.

Matters of truce and consequences

During the summer of 1956, a lot of people were sporting buttons that said, "I Like Ike." I liked Ike. President Eisenhower was 66 years old when he was re-elected that fall, and there was some concern about his health. He was still a war hero, though. The country was tired of wars but not tired of the president. People would just as soon forget about the Korean War, and Eisenhower helped them do that by negotiating a truce in 1953. Nobody really paid much attention to the fact that the president had sent a Military Assistance Advisory Group of up to 350 members to Vietnam in early 1956. The U.S. Temporary Equipment Recovery Mission to Vietnam was not an issue in the American presidential election campaign. Neither was the announcement by recently elected President Ngo Dinh Diem that a new constitution had been established for the Republic of Vietnam, which solidified the political division of South from North and trashed the Geneva Accords of 1954.

What happens when boys get excited

For me, second grade was an improvement over first grade. I'd estimate that Mrs. Conley was a smarter teacher than Mrs. Penn, and not half as mean. Before I knew what was happening, she moved me up from the third reading group to the second one and then right on up to the first one. I still didn't listen much, but at least I felt smarter about it. Never once did Mrs. Conley yank on my ear.

It was in second grade that I first realized I was heterosexual. Not that I knew what that meant, of course, and not that I had any suspicions whatsoever that anyone else had homosexual inclinations. What I do know is that I spent more time gazing at the pretty little girls in my class than I did paying attention to what Mrs. Conley was teaching us. I had no interest in playing with girls, just admiring their pretty faces and curly hair.

Also in second grade, perhaps coincidentally, I became more acutely aware of my penis. Prior to that time, I had mostly appreciated the convenience it presented when it was necessary to relieve myself behind the garage, in the bushes or wherever. Although I was quite proud of possessing that little tool, I had no clue that there was any connection whatsoever between having a penis and gazing at pretty little girls.

It's perfectly normal for newborn baby boys to get erections. Some of us were born with our penises sticking up like pencil stubs, and that had nothing to do with the exit from our mothers' wombs. I'm quite certain we just wanted to get the hell out of there. Erections occur quite frequently in our early years, long before we're ready to use them for any sexual purposes.

You might say that penises have minds of their own. One day in Mrs. Conley's classroom mine apparently did. Normally, reaching my fingers through the open zipper of my trousers and negotiating the overlapping aperture in the front of my Fruit of the Loom briefs to access my equipment for bodily functioning could be a bit of a challenge. But on this day, as I feigned attention to the reading lesson – something about Alice and Jerry, I suppose – I could feel my expanding penis wending its way past the gantlet of those cotton briefs all by itself. Unbeknownst to me, a nickel-sized hole had somehow worn through the crotch of my corduroy pants, and, to my surprise, my penis managed to squeeze its way through that little hole. Naturally, I quickly reached under the desk and cupped the protruding intruder with a concealing fist, lest any of my classmates dropped a No. 1 lead pencil on the floor and began crawling around to find it.

I can't say that I found displeasure in this predicament until Mrs. Conley announced that it was time for recess. As the other kids lined up by the door to head outside, I just sat there. What else could I do?

"Let's go, David," Mrs. Conley said. "Don't hold up the whole class now."

"I don't feel so good," I told her in a whimper as I held up something else. "Can I just lay my head down on the desk for awhile?" I missed recess, my favorite class, that day, but eventually my penis receded back to where it belonged, so I could concentrate on other things, like the fluttery eyes of a girl named Gail whose father was a doctor and lived next door to Donny and Danny Mathew, the glistening smile of Patty, whose mom was the school secretary, or the beetle stuck in a spider web at the corner of the ceiling.

That evening I asked my mom why a bone sometimes sticks out in my peeper when I least expect it. She told me not to think anything of it. "That happens to boys when they get excited," she said. Well, I had to go with that explanation, even though I didn't think there was anything exciting about second-grade reading lessons.

Another memorable day occurred when our class took a field trip to a farm, where we got to see chickens sitting on eggs and clucking around, some goats standing with their front legs hanging over the fence, trying to get us to share our peanut-butter-and-jelly sandwiches, and cows getting milked. As we were following the farmer from one barn to another, we couldn't help but notice as a big cow with horns climbed on the back of another cow and started jumping and dancing around. The entire class thought it was about the funniest thing we had ever seen. When Kevin and I went to his house after school that day, we told his mom all about it, laughing through the entire story. She explained to us that the two cows were mating, whatever that meant. Mrs. Golub was pretty smart.

Kevin Golub and I were best buddies in and out of school through third grade, when, at the end of the last day of classes on an early June day, Mrs. McKinney had an announcement. "I have some good news," she told us. "Everybody in this whole class, except for only one, will be staying together next year in fourth grade. I hope you all have a wonderful summer." That was fine news, I thought, better than when Mike Kensinger left us to repeat first grade or when that little kissy girl moved after second grade.

My mom was waiting for me when I got home. She told me she had some sort of meeting with the principal, Mr. Ferguson, and my teacher, Mrs. McKinney, and it was decided that I would be better off switching to a different class for fourth grade. She said I had gotten too close to Kevin, following him around all the time, mimicking his behavior and such, and maybe that was holding me back from learning as much as I should. Well, I figured I could daydream about climbing trees, catching snakes and playing baseball with or without Kevin Golub in my class, and there would be cute girls to gaze at other than Gail and Patty.

I joined a Cuyahoga Falls Recreation Department F League baseball team called the Angels that summer. In addition to me, there were a couple other 8-year-olds on the team, including Ronnie Sayers, but most of the boys were older, including my next-door neighbor Gary Williams, who was 10 already. The best players were 11 and 12 years old. Our coach was Mr. Goshorn, whose son, Junior Goshorn, was a pitcher and one of the best players. Mr. Goshorn showed up for practice two or three times but then stopped coming around, even though the baseball diamond at Sill Junior High School was practically in his backyard.

Suddenly, my dad became the Angels coach. Under his leadership, we won game after game that summer, beating teams with names like the Beavers and the Seals, until we went up against the Stars, who were the perennial league champions and who brought their own umpire to the games. It seemed like our pitchers couldn't throw many strikes that day and the Stars pitchers didn't throw many balls. They won. We cried. I learned how to be a poor loser. There was a hubbub about the umpiring in that game, so the next time the Angels were scheduled to play the Stars the league assigned a "neutral" umpire to call balls and strikes and safe and out. The Stars didn't show up. The Angels were declared league champs. I didn't play hardly at all in the games that summer. Mostly, I watched from behind the backstop. But at least I got to practice.

When I wasn't practicing baseball that summer, I took swimming lessons in the giant outdoor pool at the city's Water Works Park. Built during the Great Depression in the 1930s, the pool was 100 meters long. A bulkhead was constructed in the middle of the pool to separate the deeper half, which included a 12-foot-deep diving area and had eight marked lanes for 50-meter, Olympic-sized competition swimming, from a shallower half, where even little kids could splash around in a 2 1/2-foot-deep section without getting in over their heads. I was a lot better at learning to swim and play baseball than I was at paying attention in school.

Also that summer, my pal Kevin and I did some extensive exploring of the Big Woods, which we accessed at the dead end of Myrtle Avenue. Not only did the Big Woods have a tangle of trees with low-hanging limbs where you could hide away from the outside world, it had a much larger creek than the one in the Little Woods and a murky pond where slinking black water snakes competed with us to snag frogs. We called it the Frog Pond. Next to the Big Woods was a desert-like sand pit where you could take a flying leap, sink into a soft landing 10 or 15 feet below and then somersault another 20 feet or so to the bottom. Near its western rim, there was a scratchy but delicious blackberry patch. If you ventured through the Big Woods, there was a rifle range with a steep earthen backstop where we would collect leaden projectiles, plus there was an old town dump along one section of the creek where we could throw stones at rats. My dog, Prince, would have liked it there.

One sunny day at the pond I caught two frogs that were stuck together, which I thought was quite interesting, so I decided to carry them up the Myrtle Avenue hill and through the Littles' backyard to my house. Along the way, they made quite a grubby mess, which not only got all over my shirt and trousers but somehow oozed into my ears and clung to the short-cropped hair on my head. I began to fear that the mess I had gotten myself into would deserve a good whacking from my mom, but, when she saw my situation, she could hardly stop laughing. She directed me to relocate the over-friendly frogs to the crick in the close-by Little Woods and then made me take a bath.

Fourth grade was a whole new ballgame for me. Miss Pinkel was my best teacher yet, and most of my new classmates tolerated me, especially the girls. Donny Mathew's twin brother, Danny, was in this class. My new classmates also included K.C. Roberts, who later became the top backstroker on our swim teams. Don Graham and Gilbert Rice, two of the taller guys, Marty Harrington, who was about my size, and Ronny Chadwell, the smallest kid in the class, all became part of the gang that I hung out with in high school. I thought some of the girls, like Janet, the smart one, Rosie, the feisty one, and Phyllis, the daughter of the shoemaker, were quite fetching.

I guess you could say I came out of my shell in fourth grade. Miss Pinkel told my mom I was smart, and the grades on my report cards seemed to confirm that, although, to tell the truth, I'm not sure why that happened.

I went out for the Price School Blue Devils touch football team for fourth-through-sixth-grade boys that fall. At the first practice, the head coach, who played in the marching band at Cuyahoga Falls High School but told us his mom wouldn't let him play tackle football, asked us which positions we wanted to play. Not knowing anything whatsoever about the sport, when he came to me, one of the smallest kids on the team, I wanted to play quarterback but said, "Center," thinking that must be the center of attention, you know, the player who gets to call the shots. I didn't get to call any shots. I learned how to hike the ball and to throw blocks, which worked best if I stayed low, about thigh high to opposing linemen, so I didn't immediately get knocked flat on my rear, and to try to get my hands on the guy with the ball when playing defense.

My dad bought me a helmet and shoulder pads, and he showed up for all the games, even though we lost most of them and I stood on the sidelines the whole time. Finally, near the end of the last game of the season, the coach put me in on defense for a couple plays. On the final play before the referee's whistle, I managed to elude the offensive center's block and touched the other team's running back for no gain. Needless to say, I was pretty damn proud of making that play and bragged to my dad about it on the ride home. "I think the lineman on the other team felt sorry about you being so small and didn't want to block you too hard," he said with a chuckle. "Besides, you're supposed to fight your way into the other team's backfield, not wait for the ball carrier to come to you." That was the end of my inglorious football career. But at least I had a helmet to keep.

For some reason I cannot recall, I invited one of the larger boys in my class, Jim Richards, to a fight after school one day, and then I challenged another kid, Ted Lusch, who was ahead of me on the football team's depth chart and knew some dirty tricks, to settle our differences the following week. Six or eight of the other boys stood around in a circle as Jim and I rolled on the grass of a front yard just off the school grounds. He soon sat on top of me with his knees pinning my arms down and wouldn't let me up until I said "uncle." Much the same scenario played out between me and Ted until Pam LaCroix's father parked his car at the curb, got out, separated us and lectured Ted that he should pick on somebody his own size. Ted didn't tell him it was me who was picking fights with the bigger boys.

At noon one winter day when Miss Pinkel told our class to line up for lunch with the usual admonitions against running, pushing or cutting in – a concept that baffled some of us – little Ronny Chadwell and I banged our heads together and bounced off the block wall. He let out a yelp and spit a chunk of his tooth onto the floor. From the next day on, Ronny had a shiny gold front tooth that everybody admired.

During the fall and winter of fourth grade, several of the boys in our neighborhood joined the Young Men's Christian Association in Cuyahoga Falls, which enabled us to advance through swimming lessons in its indoor pool. In the 1950s, nude swimming was the rule of thumb at YMCAs and other indoor pools. We young boys didn't think much of it, but it was an eye-opener when the Y held father-son open swims. The justification was that woolen suits, which were commonplace in those days, could harbor unhealthy bacteria such as typhus and cholera, plus those suits tended to shed, which would clog up the pool filtering systems.

There were rumors about a hidden window at the bottom of the pool where girls could spy on us from the basement, but I never did find it, even though I was darn good at holding my breath underwater. There also were reports from the YMCA staff that a certain chemical was added to the pool that would cause the water to turn bright red if it mixed with urine. I didn't believe that for a minute. When the YMCA opened its membership to girls in the early 1960s, the prohibition against wearing swimming suits was discontinued, which seems sexist, in retrospect. With or without suits, swimming came quite naturally to me.

Thus began a life of crime

In fact, by the summer of 1959, not only had I advanced through every one of the swimming-lesson levels at the Y – minnow, fish, flying fish and shark – but I was beyond the top level of the American Red Cross lessons at Water Works. So my mom signed me up for a Junior Lifesaving course and told me to tell the instructors I was 12 years old, which was the cut-off age for the class. Even though I was on the small side for 9 years old, I had no problem passing the swimming test, so they let me take the course. Everyone in the class was assigned to a buddy, and mine was a sandy-haired kid named Tom, who was 12 years old.

Sometimes when she took my brother and sisters home from their swimming lessons, my mom would let me hang out at the pool after it opened to the public in the afternoon. My buddy Tom couldn't teach me anything that I didn't already know about swimming, but he taught me a few other things.

When we took a break from splashing other kids and then swimming off to the 8-foot-deep section of the pool, where they couldn't catch us, he told me to keep an eye on three teenage girls lying on a blanket near the snack shop. "Did you see where that red-haired girl in the polka-dot suit put her wallet after she bought that Nutty Buddy?" he asked me.

"Yep, she slid it under her rolled-up towel next to her friend's swim bag," I said.

"OK," he said, "let's wait till they take a dip," and, soon enough, they did. "Grab our towels and follow me," Tom said. So I did. We took a carefree walk over to where the three girls had been sunbathing, Tom bent down and, in a flash, snatched the wallet from beneath the rolled-up towel. I handed him his towel, which he wrapped around the wallet, and we headed to the dressing room. After making sure nobody else was around, he removed two dollar bills plus some change and then tossed the wallet into a toilet stall. He handed me my share of the loot, and we went our separate ways toward home.

It all happened so fast I was practically dumbfounded, but that buck and a couple dimes were the most money I'd ever had of my own, and I wasn't about to give it back. Thus began my life of crime – if you don't count pooping in a sandbox.

Even though some of the older boys on the Angels baseball team sat on the bench most of the time that summer, I became the starting second baseman. That probably had something to do with my connection to the coach, but I was pretty adept at snagging ground balls and making the short throw to first base, plus my short stature enabled me to draw more than my share of bases on balls.

The pitchers tended to be the older, most athletic boys on the teams, and one of them had a mighty rapid fastball that might have stuck in my left ear, if I hadn't been wearing a helmet that snapped around the back and sides of my skull but didn't cover the top of my head. I flopped down in a heap on top of home plate, and, by the time stars blinked away in my clattered brain, my dad had me up on my wobbly feet and was steering me to first base. "Shake it off," he said, "and be ready to steal second."

After that experience, I became apprehensive in the batter's box, especially with the faster pitchers on the mound, much to my father's consternation. A couple weeks later, he and I were watching a men's softball game at Harrington Field when we ran into Mr. Goshorn. So Dad told him about my encounter with the baseball practically stuck in my ear and how I subsequently was stepping back from the plate as though I were scared of the ball hitting me instead of concentrating on my bat hitting the ball. "What do you suggest we should do about that?" Dad asked him.

"Well," Mr. Goshorn said, "you just lay six or eight bats on the ground behind him next to the batter's box at practice and then throw the ball at his head a few times. He'll learn real fast to duck out of the way of those bean balls, because, if he backs up, he'll slip on those bats and fall flat on his rear." My father thanked him for the good advice, and that's exactly what he did at practice the next day. I think it worked.

When I wasn't on the baseball diamond or in the swimming pool, I still found time to hang out with my pal Kevin. Late one afternoon in August, after recreation department activities in the Price School gymnasium closed down for the day, Kevin and I plus my little brother, Danny, were riding our bikes around the school parking lot. We stopped by the front entrance to the building, which was situated beneath an overhang that kept us kids from getting wet on rainy mornings before they opened the doors. "Look at me," said Kevin, grabbing onto the 4-inch-thick iron pipe that supported the overhang and angled to the concrete patio. "I can shinny up to the roof," he said, and, sure enough, he did. Well, if he could do it, so could I, and I did. And then little Danny did it too.

That lofty vantage point afforded us a fine panorama of the parking lot, with its basketball court, plus the backyards of the little bungalows separated by a cyclone fence from the schoolyard. We wandered about the chip-and-seal rooftop to check out the scenery, including the line of crabapple trees to the west and the grassy field where I had practiced touch football with the Blue Devils the previous fall. Then we spotted the attached ladder leading up to the gymnasium roof. Of course, we couldn't pass that up, not even little Danny. Talk about a view. We looked over the asphalt-shingled roofs of houses two streets away. The backstop behind home plate on the baseball diamond seemed pretty high when we climbed it the other day, but it was way down below the gym roof. We could spit and quickly count to five or six before it splattered in a little speck on the sidewalk.

Suddenly, our childish euphoria over being so high above our world was interrupted by a stern, deep voice crackling through some sort of loudspeaker. "This is the police," the voice said. "You boys better come down off that roof right this instant."

Our excited chatter came to a screeching halt, and the happy smiles on our faces turned to grim looks of dismay. Silently, the three of us descended the ladder from the gymnasium roof, where our antics must have been too obvious to one of the nosy neighbors, most likely that Mrs. Mc-Cormick, whose house on Delmore Circle was closest to the schoolyard. We crept along the gym's high wall farther from the front of the school, instead of toward the loudspeaker, and found what we figured was a good hiding spot behind a brick chimney. "Let's just wait here until they leave," Kevin said as we hoped the Cuyahoga Falls Police Department would soon be called to the scene of a more heinous crime.

That didn't happen. "All right," came the gruff voice through the loud-speaker. "If you boys don't get down here now, we're going to have to take your bikes."

That was it. If we went home without our bikes, what was I going to tell Mom and Dad? That somebody swiped them? "Who would do such a thing?" they were sure to ask. They'd probably call the police about that. And then what? I didn't want to think about the consequences. Reluctantly, sullenly, we trod across the roof to the front of the building and slithered down the iron pole to where two police officers were waiting. They took down our names and addresses, informed us of the seriousness of our offense and advised us not to be repeat offenders, or else! With our sworn statements that we would not return to the roof of Elizabeth Price School, the police released our bicycles to our custody, and we were on our way.

Not only did I now have a rap sheet on top of my previous criminal activity, but my little brother, who was just 5 years old, had one too. "Danny," I said to him. "You better not say anything to Mom about this, or she'll take the paddle to both of our butts." Wide-eyed, he promised he wouldn't, and he didn't.

Chapter 3 | **Warning to a Free People**

It was summertime, early afternoon. Swimming lessons were over for the day, and we were back at home from the pool. Vonnie was playing in the backyard with a couple friends from the neighborhood. Heidi was out there too, probably eating dirt or dandelions. The windows were open. I could hear the silly girls giggling about something, probably nothing. Danny was at Butch and Johnny McCulley's house, three doors down on Myrtle Avenue. Our dachshund, Gretchen, was curled up in her box in the utility room, next to the kitchen, between the furnace, which hadn't been needed since early May, and the washing machine, which also was quiet but was overdue for my dirty underwear. I was trying to decide whether to head over to the school for a game of four square in the gym or ride my bike down to the trails around the sand pit.

"Hold on there," Mom said as I reached for the knob on the screen door. "It looks like you're ready for a haircut. Have a seat here while I go get the clippers." She was back in a flash. "Well, take your shirt and pants off so we don't get them all full of hair," she said.

"No, Mom, I'll just leave them on today." Normally, it wouldn't bother me much to sit there in my briefs with a barber's cape tied around my neck and hanging below my bellybutton. Unfortunately, when I opened the top drawer of my dresser to grab some undies after getting home from Junior Lifesaving and stripping off my swimsuit, I remembered that I'd tossed my last pair in the hamper the previous night.

"Don't talk back to me, buster. Now get your clothes off," Mom said, her patience wearing thin.

"I can't, Mom, 'cause I don't have any underpants," I replied.

Smack! Her right hand caught me full force across the face. "You what!?" she hollered. "Take those pants off right this instant."

I feared the worst, which was that Vonnie and her girlfriends, who were just outside the kitchen window, heard the commotion and would peek inside and see me sitting there with my naked crotch, which I was doing my best to cover with my hands. The slap in the face would have been humiliating enough, if anybody had witnessed it, but getting my hair cut while sitting there bare-assed added insult to my injury.

In 1989, the United Nations adopted the Convention on the Rights of the Child, which generally is considered a discouragement to such corporal punishment as slapping children across the face. By 2015, 193 countries around the world had ratified the treaty. Slapping isn't directly addressed by the convention, although it calls upon the ratifiers to protect children from "all forms of physical or mental violence" and acknowledges children's rights to life, protects them from abuse and exploitation and forbids capital punishment of those under the age of 18. Only three members of the United Nations – Somalia, South Sudan and the United States – refused to ratify it, even though the administrations of President Ronald Reagan and President George H.W. Bush took part in writing it.

In early 2015, Pope Francis stirred up controversy by saying it's all right for parents to smack their children if they misbehave, but he allowed that slapping them across the face might be counterproductive. The American Academy of Pediatrics opposes corporal punishment, and a 2012 study in the Pediatrics publication found a correlation between harsh physical punishment and an increased risk of mental problems. It is a general consensus in the medical establishment that corporal punishment is not an effective form of behavior modification, and slapping in anger is generally frowned upon. Although studies have shown that 80 percent of American parents whack their children sometimes, the presumably enlightened ones have come to condemn face slapping.

During the 1950s and '60s, though, face slapping was commonplace, parents generally displayed visible signs of anger when they slapped their kids, and there was no reprobation when it occurred in public places like church, the grocery store or around the swimming pool.

Sitting in the balcony before services at Redeemer Lutheran Church one Sunday, I was stunned when a tall blond girl in my Bible study took a sudden facial wallop from her mother, who loudly let it be known that yawning in church would not be tolerated. Just to be on the safe side, I made sure that I never yawned in church. So, yes, corporal punishment can be effective.

Our mom routinely would leave Vonnie, Danny and me in the car while she wheeled Heidi around in a shopping cart at the A&P or Kroger on Saturdays. If we didn't snitch on each other, the three of us wouldn't get smacked when she was done shopping, whereas arguing or running around inside the supermarket was sure to have consequences.

Mom was the disciplinarian in our family, mostly because Dad spent much of his time at the Ford plant or planted in his living-room chair with his head buried in the pages of the Akron Beacon Journal. Sometimes we might catch a swift kick from his foot, if we made too much commotion and carelessly got within range, but his temper was as quick to cool down as it was to flare up.

There was no cursing in our house. Aside from that incident involving the assumed lack of production out of Mr. Little's testicles, the worst thing to come out of Mom's mouth was "son of a sea cook." That expression was given popularity by the censors who refused to allow the character of Mortimer Brewster, played by Cary Grant, refer to himself as a "bastard" in the 1944 Hollywood production of "Arsenic and Old Lace." I'm quite certain that horn-dog von Selhorst, who impregnated my grandmother, was not a sea cook, and, therefore, my father was no son of a sea cook.

Outside of my parents' earshot, I was prone to speak of bastards at an early age, although I had no concept of illegitimacy and may have applied the word to my dad on occasion in a more vernacular sense. I also learned about "shit," "piss" and "tits" from the boys in school and around the neighborhood. The other four words that comedian George Carlin hilariously outed in 1971 among the seven that "you can never say on television" didn't become part of my lexicon until junior high school.

Except for my father's occasional reference to the "Hunkies" who monopolized the caddy jobs at the local golf club when he was growing up in Pennsylvania, no ethnic slurs were spoken in our house on East Bailey Road. That was not true of the neighborhood. In our backyard, it was acceptable to recite the counting rhyme about "Eenie, meenie, miney, moe, catch a tiger by the toe." In preparation for playing tag or hide-and-seek down at the schoolyard, though, "tiger" sometimes was replaced by the N-word. Either way, "If he hollers, let him go." Also, if you were the last one in at the swimming pool, it could qualify you as an N-word. But our family did not talk that way.

I cannot say we were less prejudiced than other white people in Cuyahoga Falls. When I ticked him off, which was not unusual, my father would threaten to give me away to "Big Black Joe," one of the men who worked with him at the Ford plant and who probably lived someplace in Cleveland that would not be so tolerant of a bratty white kid like me.

United Automobile Workers Local 420, which represented the unionized employees at the Cleveland Stamping Plant and supported civil rights, along with less-hazardous working conditions, overtime pay, pensions and other so-called liberal ideals, hosted Christmas parties in early December and picnics at Geauga Lake Park in the summer. Those family events not only were great fun, but they made me realize that black kids enjoyed the same things we did, like getting presents from Santa Claus, roasting burgers and hot dogs on the grill and riding on the swinging rocket cars at Geauga Lake.

Sure enough, as I was licking an ice-cream cone after lunch in a pavilion at the amusement park on the perimeter of the 49-acre lake, my dad struck up a conversation with a large Negro, as we called African-Americans then and whom I figured must be "Big Black Joe." I didn't think I had caused enough trouble to be given away that day, but, to be on the safe side, when the two men looked my way and smiled, I scooted down the bench at the picnic table close to my mom. Just then I noticed a couple black boys – one about 7 years old like me and the other one a little younger – who were watching the same two men with nervous looks on their faces. I could tell they were as frightened of "Big White Charlie" as I was of "Big Black Joe."

As the oldest of the four kids in our family, I was the one who got to go on the bigger rides at Geauga Lake with my dad. There was one ride that loomed above the rest – higher, steeper, faster and more screaming than anything I had ever seen. And my dad was going to ride it. "Take me with you," I begged, my eyes and bravado bulging while my feet were firmly planted on the ground.

"I don't think so," he said, as my mom shook her head in agreement.

But, being a normal child of great persuasion, I soon was in line for the Clipper roller coaster. Unlike latter-day precautionary excesses, a parent's presence and permission superseded any height requirements or apprehension about amusement-park rides in the 1950s. Undeterred as I watched the preceding train of cars being yanked up to the summit and heard the blood-curdling shrieks that quickly followed in rapid free-fall, my anticipating grin widened as the safety bar slammed shut across my dad's lap but several inches above my skinny legs.

Knots tightened in my abdomen with each reverberating clack of the steel wheels over the track during our ascent. My eyes widened as people on the midway shrank to the size of mice, the parking lot resembled colorful pieces on a game board and the big lake became a mere puddle below. Then we reached the apex. The track vanished. The coaster lurched forward like a pebble flung from a slingshot. My stomach flew into my throat. And my little body slid under the restraint bar in a reflex of horror. I felt my dad's big hand grab the shoulder of my shirt and hang on for my dear life as I bounced around on the floor of that roller-coaster car for the most terrifying flash of time in my young life. I didn't stop quivering for the rest of the day. And I didn't set foot on another roller coaster until I was 13 years old.

The Clipper, which originated as the Sky Rocket in 1925 and became known as the Big Dipper in 1969, was the 10th-oldest coaster in the United States and the 14th-oldest in the world when Geauga Lake Park was closed down in 2007.

Aside from riding the roller coaster together, my dad and I did some other bonding. I especially enjoyed catching a passenger train at the station in downtown Cuyahoga Falls along with other fathers and players in our baseball league for an annual excursion to Cleveland for an Indians game at the gigantic Municipal Stadium next to Lake Erie. Despite my hearty cheering for Rocky Colavito, Minnie Minoso and Jimmy Pier-sall, the visiting team from New York City spoiled my celebration. My dad seemed to enjoy himself, even if he did miss the Pirates game on radio-station KDKA that day. Another treat was watching professional basketball games in the gym at the Goodyear plant, where the Akron in-dustrial-league team matched up against the likes of the Bartlesville Phil-lips 66ers, of Oklahoma, the Cleveland Pipers and the New York Tuck Tapers.

'Slave-labor bill' be damned

In late summer of 1958, my father brought home some disturbing news from Walter Reuther. The son of a German immigrant who worked in a West Virginia brewery, Reuther followed in his father's socialist-unionist footsteps and rose to the presidency of the United Auto Workers. My dad was no socialist, but he knew which side his bread was buttered on. It sure as hell wasn't spread by the Red-baiting McCarthyists and the politicians who had passed the Taft-Hartley Act "slave-labor bill," as union leaders called it, a decade earlier. Reuther had big enough balls to stand up to the anti-union forces, and he was about to call a strike to prove it.

It was tough enough to keep up with mortgages and grocery bills when "Big White Charlie" Lange and "Big Black Joe" were on the assem-bly line seven days a week. If it was Ford workers' turn to strike and their steady paychecks weren't deposited in the bank each week, families like ours would be in dire straits in a hurry. Sure enough, it was our turn. On Sept. 17, 1958, 100,000 Ford workers at plants in 24 states walked out. Fortunately for us, Ford management learned that Reuther wasn't bluffing and settled within six hours.

With the pay increases hard won by union workers, the median American family annual income was $5,100 in 1958. The average chief executive officer was earning about 20 times as much as the typical work-er, although my father, being a member of one of the more robust unions and being one who put in more than his share of overtime, did somewhat better than that. We thought of ourselves as middle class.

Accounting for inflation, that $5,100 income in 1958 was worth around $41,000 in 2015 buying power, when the median family income was more like $52,000. Even that figure was $5,000 lower than the $57,000 median that was reached in 2007, before the Great Recession took a heavy toll on working people but not so much on Wall Street crooks. Nonetheless, by 2015, the average CEO was making 275 times as much as the typical American worker. During the economic expansion of the Eisenhower presidency in the 1950s, the top federal income-tax rate was a whopping 92 percent. Fifty years later, during the Barack Obama presidency and the struggling economic recovery, the top federal income-tax rate was a fraction of that at 35 percent, yet it was roundly assailed as an unfair redistribution of wealth.

Behavioral idiosyncrasies

Both of my parents were smokers. Cigarettes were cheap. Pall Mall was my dad's brand, "outstanding ... and they are mild," according to the TV commercials, providing "the pleasure of smooth smoking." He went through a pack or two a day. My mom preferred Salem, a filtered cigarette flavored with menthol. She only smoked a half a pack or so each day. After either one of them would crush their last butt in the ashtray, they'd send me scurrying across the street to Stutzman's Foodliner with a couple dimes to buy a fresh pack of Pall Malls or Salems. The cashiers didn't question me or other kids who ran into the store to replenish their parents' nicotine supplies.

That was convenient for kids who got the notion that it was a sign of maturity to experiment with the drug which nobody thought was a drug and an addiction that everybody thought was an easy habit to break but few people did. For an extra nickel a pack, cigarette machines beckoned in just about any gas station or vestibule.

My friend Kevin introduced me to the habit in one of our favorite hiding spots amidst a thick clump of trees in the Big Woods during the summer between fourth and fifth grades. He showed me how to stick the filter end between your lips and light the other end with a match then blow out a puff of smoke that momentarily hung above our heads before dissipating through the low-hanging leaves. He didn't warn me about inhaling. I clenched a cigarette in my mouth, fired it up with the second or third match and gave the noxious fume a strong draw into my lungs, just like I'd seen my dad do so many times, except he seemed to take pleasure in it. I felt like my chest was on fire and my brain was about to explode.

I damn near coughed myself unconscious. As soon as I was able to stop choking, I said, "Mmmm, that was pretty good." The next puff didn't get past where my tonsils used to be, and I blew the smoke out in a satisfying display of grownup accomplishment. It probably was a good thing that the Golubs moved to California the next year.

In fifth grade, I had my first male teacher, Mr. Eisemon, a fit man with a flat-top haircut and a 5 o'clock shadow that showed up around noon. It was my second year with new classmates, and they had adapted to my behavioral idiosyncrasies fairly well. I was generally recognized as one of the smarter kids. Mathematics and spelling came especially easy for me, but I was even better at drawing attention to myself.

When Mr. Eisemon had to leave the room for some pressing reason, I was prone to do things like grab a rubber-banded bundle of well-sharpened pencils from the desk of a seriously studious boy named Stuart and redistribute them among those who were less well supplied. As you might imagine, Stuart did not appreciate my redistribution of wealth and, in a fit of uncharacteristic rage, flipped my desk onto its side – with me in it. Not one to take such an indignity lying down, I picked myself up and popped my clenched fist onto the bridge of Stuart's nose just as Mr. Eisemon returned to the room. The sniveling Stuart, with a mere speck of blood dribbling out his nostril and salty tears rolling down his cheek, managed to avoid any further consequences, but Mr. Eisemon hauled my ass down the hall and laid a couple wicked whacks on it with a sturdy wooden paddle. That was a new experience for me, as the reverberating sound of wood slamming against skinny butt cheeks was for the entire class.

I couldn't prevent myself from spilling the beans about the whole thing to my mom after school, especially how it was that rat Stuart's fault, although her subsequent cross-examination most likely established that the punishment fit the crime. Nonetheless, she paid Mr. Eisemon a visit the next day, at which time I assume they shared proper whacking techniques. There was no further need for Mr. Eisemon to fetch his wooden paddle from his bottom desk drawer on my behalf for the remainder of the school year, and Stuart's nose was better off for that.

It was a different story with our health and gym teacher, Mr. Lipinski, a hefty man whose face turned red and whose nostrils flared like a wild boar's snout at the slightest provocation and who kept score on his wooden paddle. Mike McCullough and I had our names recorded on that paddle for the minor infraction of breaking up the boredom of health class by ejecting spittle across the aisle at each other. I must say, though, the chunk that Miss Pinkel made me chew from a slippery bar of Dial for committing a similar offense in fourth grade left a nastier impression. A stinging butt recovers quicker than a sudsy mouth.

My new best friend in fifth grade was Jeff Cain, who lived with his mother and sister near Little League Park and a satellite fire station before moving a year later after part of the Big Woods was bulldozed over to make room for fancy new tract houses with basements. There was a patch of woods behind Jeff's first house where we built an evening campfire, puffed on filtered cigarettes that I'd bought at Stutzman's and exchanged tidbits of sophistry.

"I built a fire back here by myself a couple days ago," he said. "A strange man came sneaking through the woods and all of a sudden was standing right where you are now."

A chill shuddered down my spine as my eyeballs peered for any sign of movement in the darkening spaces between the trees. "Well, what did he want?" I muttered.

As Jeff's face glowed orange and yellow from across the flickering flames, his voice lowered, and he said, "He came over to where I was sitting on this log here, unzipped his pants and pulled his peter out. Then he grabbed my head and tried to stick it in my mouth."

I'd never heard anything so revolting. Why in the world would anybody want to do something like that? "What the hell?" I yelled.

"I was so scared," Jeff said. "I just kicked him in the balls as hard as I could and then ran across the yard into my house."

I asked Jeff if he told his mom about it. He said he didn't, but he wouldn't be making campfires out there by himself anymore. It was the kind of story I wasn't about to share with my mom either, or anybody else, for that matter.

On another occasion, Jeff told me he saw a guy in the Big Woods pissing on his hands to warm them up on a cold winter day. Sometimes you don't know what to believe.

Some of the boys my age were more sophisticated than I was about the facts of life. At the age of 10, I had no idea that sucking on a penis had anything to do with sex. Actually, I knew nothing whatsoever about sex. Nobody talked about it in our house.

Also at the age of 10, I was not yet addicted to nicotine, probably because I had no desire to choke on the smoke. Plus, I wasn't made of money and had better things to do with 20 cents than buy cigarettes, such as buying four packs of baseball cards for 5 cents apiece, including the bubble gum. So I quit smoking after one pack.

That probably was good for my athletic career. I joined the swimming team at the YMCA that winter. After a few swim meets in places like Dover, Alliance, Canton and Akron, our coach, Mr. Stewart, noticed that I had a genetic inclination for the frog kick, as opposed to the flutter kick, and decided I should be a breaststroker, as opposed to a freestyler or a backstroker. The frog kick also was permissible in swimming the butterfly, so I did some of that as well, although the kids who could do the dolphin kick were faster. Mr. Stewart could be grumpy, like when he told us he wasn't getting paid to coach swimming, so he didn't have to listen to kids whining about practice being too hard. But he must have been a pretty good coach, because, by the end of the season, I was winning most of my breaststroke races in the 10-and-under age group.

English as an only language

Our family had lots of friends. In the summertime, we went on picnics to places like Munroe Falls Park and Wyoga Lake with the Von Guntens. Mr. Von Gunten was our insurance man. Their son, John, who was a year younger than me, had contracted polio as an infant and walked with a limp, but he didn't let it bother him much. The Kensingers frequently took us boating on a 1,685-acre reservoir near Youngstown called Lake Milton, where I learned to water-ski. Mike Kensinger was my age and had been in my class when we started school, but somebody decided it was a good idea for him to take first grade over again. Mike's sister, Joanie, was my sister Vonnie's age. One time when we were splashing around in the shallows near the edge of the lake, she stepped in a hole, slipped underwater and got all panicky, which gave me an opportunity to use my lifesaving skills. She had long, dark hair. I liked Joanie.

Many of our family friends were German immigrants, some of them arriving by way of other countries like Argentina or Canada. The Fried-richs, who lived on Myrtle Avenue, had two sons, Peter and Thomas. They had python skins hanging on their living-room wall.

The Kaspers, Ted and Katie, who lived in a duplex off of Munroe Falls Avenue and then moved to a new tract house near Jeff Cain in the subdivi-sion that wiped out part of the Big Woods, had three daughters. Margaret was in my grade, and Kathleen was in Vonnie's grade. Katie, who had performed in a gymnastics exhibition as a child at the 1936 Berlin Olym-pics, was my mom's best friend. The two of them would sit at the kitchen table for hours, speaking German and drinking coffee. Katie smoked like a chimney.

My mom told me I should partner with Margaret for square dancing during sixth-grade gym class at Price School. I preferred dancing with Phyllis Prinzo – until I saw her and Ronnie Chadwell kissing during a birthday party for one of our classmates. Since we had to dance with girls anyway, Margaret turned out to be a fine partner.

Sometimes our parents would drop me and Vonnie and Margaret and Kathleen off at the State Theater for a Saturday matinee. On one of those occasions in 1960 – sometime around my 11th birthday – we called home and got permission to stay for the main feature, an Alfred Hitchcock mov-ie called "Psycho." The bloody shower scene scared me shitless. I told the girls I had to go to the bathroom, but, actually, I didn't want them to see me cover up my eyes in terror.

Ted Kasper was a skilled tradesman at the Ford plant. I think he was a little nuts. Maybe a lot. After his daughters grew up and moved out, he shot his brains out. When Katie returned home one day, she was treated to the sight of his blood and brain tissue splattered on the wall.

We met another family through the German-American Club, Wolf-gang and Gisela Heigelmann and their little boys, Volker and Michael, who lived in Akron. I was fascinated by their city neighborhood, where the houses were even closer together than ours in Cuyahoga Falls. In 2008, Michael, who grew up to be an avid outdoorsman, according to his obit-uary, was bowhunting in Rootstown when he slipped from his tree stand and was caught by the harness around his waist about 25 feet from the ground. He may have survived the fall, but the position in which he was suspended prevented his lungs from expanding. He was reported missing by his wife at about 9:15 p.m. on a Friday. Searchers found his body at 2:30 the next morning. He was 48 years old.

The Friedrich and Kasper kids spoke English as a second language. We Lange kids spoke English as our only language. Our mom was fluent in German, of course, and she was more than willing to raise bilingual children. Our dad used his native language when they got together with German-speaking friends, but he wanted English spoken in our house – unless he and Mom had something to discuss that was none of our business. He might not have been born in the United States, but he was an American, for damn sure, and so were his kids.

When our grandmother came over from Germany to pay us a visit, she was not pleased about her grandchildren's inability to carry on a conversation with her. After I accidentally knocked her toothbrush into the toilet, I thought twice about conversing with her about that, but, overwhelmed by guilt, I confessed to my mom. She broke into laughter before translating the news to Oma, who failed to see the humor in it. Her initial anger seemed to be mollified by the realization that I could have fished the toothbrush out, shook off the yellow water, replaced it on the sink and kept my mouth shut about it.

Dad decided that, with two adults and four kids – plus Oma or Mamam spending some time at our house – it was a good idea to add a half bath on the second floor. He appreciated my assistance with his upstairs building projects and didn't mind my brother, Danny, looking over my shoulder as I fished out various items from his toolbox. But when our dog, Gretchen, came up to check on our progress, Dad ran out of patience. "Throw that mutt downstairs," he said. Danny, who got all excited about his opportunity to be helpful, did just that. Gretchen screeched as she bounced to the bottom of the stairs. We rushed her to the veterinarian, and she had to wear a splint on her leg for a few weeks.

There were 13 steps up that staircase, which had a see-through shadow box with porcelain figurines overlooking the living room and a bulkhead part way up that connected to the ceiling above the front door. When Mom and Dad weren't around, Danny and I had a daring contest to determine who could jump down from the highest step without falling over or chickening out. At just 6 years old, he was proud of his ability to leap from the fourth or fifth step and nail the landing. Being four years older, I easily topped him from the sixth or seventh step.

Emboldened by my high-soaring achievement, I decided to go for the ultimate test from the very top. I would have made it too, if my forehead hadn't conked into the bulkhead, which resulted in the back of my skull bouncing off the fifth step as my heels slammed onto the main floor. Fortunately, my body was more flexible than Gretchen's. Slowly, I gathered myself together, began to pick myself up and saw Danny looking at me in utter awe. "You win," he said.

Military-industrial complex

Anticipation spread across the country in the autumn of 1960 because of the upcoming presidential election. The upper three grades at Price Elementary School were pretty excited about the fact that we were going to hold our own mock election on Monday, Nov. 7, one day before the adults, those age 21 and over anyway, would be doing the real thing. I voted for the Republican, Richard M. Nixon, of course. If he was good enough for President Eisenhower to trust as his vice president, he was good enough for me. My sister Vonnie, being only in fourth grade, liked the young, clean-shaven senator from Massachusetts, John F. Kennedy, and so did a lot of the other girls, who, in my estimation, valued appearances above substance.

The fact that Kennedy was Catholic had a lot of people in a tizzy, being that the country had never thought much about having that kind of president before, but that didn't make any difference to us. I believe our mom and dad nullified each other's votes, just like Vonnie and I did.

After they counted the paper ballots at Price School, a couple hundred of which were cast, Kennedy won by a single vote. If I had been able to talk some sense into my sister, things would have been different. When they counted up the votes for the national election, it ended up being the closest presidential race in U.S. history – 49.7 percent for Kennedy and 49.6 percent for Nixon. Even though most states, including Ohio, went for Nixon, heavily populated eastern states like New York and Pennsylvania and just about all of the Dixiecrat states, including Texas, gave Kennedy the Electoral College victory, 303 to 219.

Prior to leaving office, President Eisenhower delivered his farewell address on Jan. 17, 1961. He affirmed the necessity of the United States maintaining a mighty military to meet the threat of "hostile ideology" and of "the conflict now engulfing the world." It was the damned commies' fault that we had to conduct nuke drills by kneeling down and covering our heads in the halls at school and pay attention to where the bomb shelters were located in public places. That much I knew about hostile ideology.

Eisenhower's speech is best known for its warning to a free people: "This conjunction of an immense military establishment and a large arms industry is new in the American experience. The total influence – economic, political, even spiritual – is felt in every city, every statehouse, every office of the federal government. We recognize the imperative need for this development, yet we must not fail to comprehend its grave implications. Our toil, resources and livelihood are all involved; so is the very structure of our society.

"In the councils of government, we must guard against the acquisition of unwarranted influence, whether sought or unsought, by the military-industrial complex. The potential for the disastrous rise of misplaced power exists and will persist."

Eisenhower didn't speak of it that day, but the war in Vietnam was well underway. The president knew it, and the military-industrial complex he warned us about was itching for it. The Ho Chi Minh Trail, the communist supply route along the Vietnam-Cambodia border, which was to become very personal to me in 1969, had been laid out by the North Vietnamese Army in 1959. In July of that year, the first American military men, advisers Maj. Dale Buis and Sgt. Chester Ovnard, were killed by Viet Minh guerrillas.

As early as 1954, Eisenhower had expressed fears about Vietnam becoming the first falling domino in the theory that communism would spread from there to Burma, Thailand, Malaya and Indonesia and ultimately threaten Japan, Formosa, the Philippines, Australia and New Zealand. The utterly irrational fear of dominoes gave great cheer to the military-industrial complex.

The Vietnam War was the last one for which the Jeffersonian concept of citizen-soldiers substantially connected the American public to the life-and-death brutalities and realities of engaging in interminable global military excursions. During our Afghanistan and Iraq wars of the early

21st century, fewer than 1 percent of the country's citizens were called upon to put their lives on the line in military uniform.

Meanwhile, the privatization and increasing secrecy of the military-industrial complex consumed greater and greater portions of our unbalanced budget. In 2011, we had 45,000 moderately paid American soldiers in Iraq but were covering the much more handsome salaries of 65,000 private-contract workers there with money borrowed from communist China.

Eisenhower's warning that "unwarranted influence" would lead to "the disastrous rise of misplaced power" that absolutely "exists and will persist" has proven to be expensively and deadly accurate.

Chapter 4 | **A Real Kick in the Ass**

Aside from the 1960 presidential election, which I got over much more readily than did the loser, Richard M. Nixon, sixth grade was pretty good to me. One of my teachers, maybe Mrs. Allison or Mr. Hibbard, recommended me for the safety patrol. I suppose it was a sexist assignment in which some of the sixth-grade boys assisted the younger children in safely crossing Myrtle and Center avenues and Wichert Drive before and after school. While on duty, we, the privileged members of the safety patrol, got to wear distinctive sashes and wield aluminum poles with flags that said, "Stop," which commanded kids to wait for any cars to pass by and to alert any drivers who approached while kids were in the crosswalk. Better yet, we got to cut out of class five minutes early in the afternoons.

Twice, the school principal threatened to remove me from the patrol due to minor disciplinary infractions, such as refusing to sing in music class. But he cut me some slack.

For me, safety patrol was a learning experience in itself. Most of the sixth-grade boys – and no doubt some of the girls as well – were more knowledgeable about the facts of life than was I. While we stood with our flags on opposite sides of the street during lulls in pedestrian traffic, some of my duty partners would share jokes, the risque likes of which I had never heard and which I found to be gut-splitting hilarious. What could be funnier to an 11-year-old boy, for instance, than the woman who, after ordering her sixth "bartini," is informed by the "martender" that she is mistaken about having heartburn, because her "tit's in the ashtray"?

One evening, after dining on my mother's tirelessly prepared and supremely nourishing green-bean soup flavored with chunks of slab bacon for the third straight day, a regular routine for our family of four children living on one autoworker's paycheck, I called my parents aside. "I heard a very funny joke today," I told them with a grin.

They looked at each other in amusement, and my dad said, "Well, let's hear it."

"It's about Santa Claus," I said, barely able to contain a giggle. They nodded and smiled.

"He's going door to door in an apartment building, and a young lady wearing a negligee answers her door. 'Oh,' says Santa, 'I guess there aren't any children here.' 'That's OK, Santa, she says as she unbuttons the top of her negligee.' 'Ho, ho, ho, I gotta go and deliver toys to girls and boys,' Santa tells her. 'Please, Santa, come in and stay for a while,' the lady says, and she unfastens another two buttons. 'Ho, ho, ho, I gotta go and deliver toys to girls and boys,' he says again. All of a sudden, the lady unbuttons the whole thing, and she's standing there practically naked. 'Come on, Santa, you can stay for a few minutes, can't you?' she tells him. Then Santa says, 'Hey, hey, hey, I gotta stay, I can't get up the chimney this way.'"

I knew it was pretty funny, but, to hear my mom and dad laugh so hard, that joke must have been funnier than I realized.

Even for us happy-go-lucky elementary-school kids, world affairs were no joke in the 1950s and early '60s. Black-and-white film showing mushroom clouds from atomic-bomb testing over the Pacific somewhere was shown on the evening news. Signs directing people to fallout shelters were displayed in public places everywhere.

Every month or so, the public-address system at school blared out a directive to take shelter against a nuclear attack from the evil Soviet Union. Unlike the fire drills in which students were lined up in orderly fashion and paraded outside to the schoolyard, many schools conducted the so-called "duck-and-cover" drills right in the classrooms, where kids ducked under their desks and covered their heads with interlocked fingers. At Price Elementary School, we were herded into the hallway, where we crouched down along the solid block walls, which presumably were sturdier than our flimsy desks, and covered our heads with interlocked fingers. The joke was on us.

But in Hiroshima and Nagasaki, where American atomic bombs had vaporized some 100,000 human beings, the vast majority of them civilians, on the spot in August 1945 and where more of them continued to drop dead from radiation poisoning even as we huddled in our school hall, Japanese children were not laughing.

A strange thing happened in the early spring at Price School – even stranger than the message surreptitiously written in backwards lettering with a bar of soap on the outside of a classroom window: "Fuck Mrs. Jensen." Mrs. Jensen was not one of my teachers, but I heard that she broke into tears when she arrived in her room that morning. Some of the kids were aghast, my younger sister Vonnie among them. I wasn't quite sure what "Fuck Mrs. Jensen" meant, but I knew it wasn't good.

Anyway, Mrs. Allison told me and several other kids in my class that we had to meet individually with a lady she called a psychologist and take some sort of IQ test, which meant about as much to me as "Fuck Mrs. Jensen." My mom told me it meant "intelligence quotient," which still didn't mean much to me. The psychologist asked me a bunch of questions that didn't seem to have right or wrong answers, and she had me describe what I saw in random blotches and images on a set of cards. Whatever. Several weeks later Mrs. Allison told me that I had been selected for a special new "accelerated" seventh-grade class the next fall, when we were to move up to Edward Rowland Sill School, which was the junior high school for the east side of Cuyahoga Falls.

I didn't realize it then, but it was not the best turn of events for my young life.

A new Amateur Athletic Union team called Water Works Swim Club was started in the summer of 1961 by Tod Boyle, a young coach who recently had graduated from Ohio University. Among the dozen or so swimmers who ventured into the chilly Water Works pool for a couple hours early each morning were Bob Heacock, whom I'd known since first grade, Lou Garcia and his younger sister, Roseann, whom I took a liking to, Mike and Janie Bachtel and Jeff Weiss, who was a couple years older than me. Our workouts were significantly more intense than the ones I'd been accustomed to at the YMCA, and they seemed to pay off with some pretty respectable races in AAU meets around Northeast Ohio.

An unwarranted walk on the backside

As usual, with my dad as the manager, the Angels baseball team was leading the Cuyahoga Falls Recreation Department F League that summer. It sure didn't hurt that Charlie Lange convinced Donny and Danny Mathew's dad, Bill, to be assistant manager, which ensured that his twin sons would be on the team. We also managed to get my friend Jeff Cain, another top-notch player, on the Angels that season, so our lineup was pretty formidable. Playing second base, I was at the top of my game. Hitting second in the order, my batting average was well above .500, and what I lacked in power I more than made up for with a God-given talent for base running.

It would be untruthful to say that my father was a good loser. It was a typical hot and muggy late July evening on the dusty diamond at the bottom of Newberry Hill on the west side of town, between Newberry Elementary School and Bolich Junior High School. The Angels weren't doing much right that day, and the Padres took a three-run lead in the bottom of the third inning. With sweat slopping the armpits of his T-shirt and dribbling down the crook of his nose, Charlie was not happy. The hanging heads of his players after we finally ended a Padres rally and headed for the bench did not lighten his mood. "You guys better get your heads in the game," he yelled at us. "You're playing like a bunch of losers."

When Danny Mathew, our catcher, led off the top of the fourth with a double and Jeff followed with a single to right field that put them at the corners, it looked like the momentum could be turning for the Angels. But then the bottom of the order gave the Padres two easy outs with a weak pop-up to the pitcher and a strikeout on three straight swings and misses, the third one way off the plate. Our leadoff hitter, Donny Mathew, coaxed a base on balls with a full count, which loaded the bags.

I stepped to the plate with the weight of the game on my shoulders, not to mention my father's stony silence getting inside my head. The first pitch was high, and the second one was in the dirt. Then I watched one fly right down the pipe. "Come on, David, what are you looking at?" I heard him loud and clear, but I didn't acknowledge him. I fouled the next pitch off and then took ball three up high for the full count.

The pitcher wound up. He lifted his left leg off the mound. I just knew it was ball four even before he let the payoff pitch sail. It came my way belt high, but I just knew it was going to be inside. I backed away from the plate. There was no row of bats lined up in the dirt behind the batter's box like there used to be at practice. Nothing at all to trip me up and tumble me over. No, sir. I saw myself trotting down to first base with a free pass. Danny would be heading home to score, and our come-from-behind rally would be well underway. I watched the pitch fly past me and into the catcher's mitt.

"Strike three!" the umpire yelled. The Padres in the field leapt up in glee. Their teammates on the bench cheered. My heart sank. My chin dropped to my chest. My eyes focused on the dirt under my sneakers. I tromped over to our bench, grabbed my glove and began my beaten trek back to second base. Midway across the infield, I heard the clumping of heavy footsteps rushing up behind me. There was no other warning, just the sudden crunch of my father's shoe in the crack of my butt. I felt myself lifted off the ground. I stumbled but regained my footing. I knew what it was. The son of a bitch added that demeaning insult for all to see on top of my inglorious letdown to the team. I didn't look back. I didn't look up. I didn't see the jaw-dropping faces of moms and dads and siblings seated in their lawn chairs behind the team benches. I didn't catch the wide-eyed disbelief of my teammates in the outfield. I just kept on walking.

I was still in a silent brood on the back seat of our Ford Falcon station wagon when my dad opened the tailgate and tossed in the canvas equipment bag. My brother and sisters crammed in beside me. My mother took her spot at shotgun, turned around and let me have it. "You really let the team down, David," she said. "They had a chance to come back in the sixth inning and needed you to get back in there and pinch hit. So we lost the game."

Hard to believe she was taking his side after he kicked me in the ass in front of the whole damn world. I looked right in her steamy blue eyes. "That just goes to show what you know, Mom," I shot back at her. "Once a player comes out of the game, that's it. He can't go back in to pinch hit or do anything else." That shut her up. My dad didn't say a word.

We didn't lose many more games that summer and went on to win the league championship again. Donny Mathew and I were named to the all-star game at the end of the season. I started at second base, singled to right in my only at-bat. After the third inning, I was replaced by Rick Morgan, the star second baseman for the Seals. Rick and I became buddies several years later.

The boys at Sill Junior High School had a ritual that they called "initiation," which was conducted after classes were dismissed on the first day of the new school year. Eighth- and ninth-graders would chase down the seventh-graders, hold them down and smear their faces with lipstick. If an initiate put up a struggle, he was likely to get it smeared in his hair and ears as well. Mostly, it was all in good fun and was accepted as a sort of coming-of-age rite of passage. Girls were allowed to witness this tradition from a safe distance, but they did not participate. After I was thoroughly initiated in several encounters with the older boys, my well-decorated face was greeted with laughter from my mom, who assisted with the cleanup.

By seventh grade, most of the other boys were outgrowing me physically in more ways than our height and weight might indicate. That became evident to me in the wide-open shower room at the YMCA and the one next to the gymnasium at school. I had never backed down from a fight with anyone in elementary school, but many of the guys at Sill School towered over my skinny frame, their voices were changing, and I learned quickly to stay out of their way.

The inaugural accelerated class, which included a few kids I knew pretty well from Price School, along with those from the district's other east-side elementary schools, had a few nerds, but most of us were pretty typical kids. They stereotyped us based on our IQs, after all, not necessarily by our established records of academic performance. There tends to be a strong correlation between the two, and our class had a goodly portion of high-performing students, but there also seemed to be a few of us with behavioral inconsistencies.

One of our nerds, Jeff Steinwedel, whom we dubbed "Einstein," was among the kids in our class who had attended Silver Lake Elementary

School. Although it's part of the Cuyahoga Falls School District, the village of Silver Lake is populated by a higher class of people than most of us who lived in the city of Cuyahoga Falls. Their parents tended to be doctors, lawyers and business owners, as opposed to automobile and rubber workers. Einstein's physical attributes were especially noteworthy in gym class, where he would spastically hop around like a marionette on steroids as far as possible from the center line of the dodge-ball court. He was easily picked off, and the rest of us were thoroughly amused.

Except for gym and shop, where the boys from two classes were combined – because the girls had separate gym classes and home economics – our accelerated class was segregated from the normal students. That caused me to develop some new friendships with a couple of fellow Price School alumni. Harry "Kip" Keller was a thin, athletic boy who was an inch taller than me and had a stock of sandy hair that swooped down over his forehead. Terry Gray, a freckle-faced kid with red hair, was an inch taller than Kip and stockier but not as quick on his feet. They must have had pretty high IQs but were disinclined from applying them to academic pursuits.

Another Price School product, Bob Berdella, who was one of the tallest kids in our grade but was uncoordinated, hung around with us sometimes, even though he tended to be more studious than we were. Bob was the boy I had falsely fingered as the pocketknife-flashing first-grader in the principal's office six years earlier. I don't think he remembered that earlier encounter, at least he never said anything about it.

Despite my general lack of attentiveness and tendency toward disruptiveness, my grades were among the best in the class.

Kip's father was a professional baseball player and wasn't around much. I never saw him. Terry's mother was divorced from his father and in the process of divorcing her second husband. I saw the stepfather once or twice and heard him trying to bust the front door down once when I was at their house. Eventually, he gave up and left. Mrs. Gray laughed it off. Bob Berdella's father worked at the Ford plant. For some reason, my dad couldn't stand the guy. He was never around when I visited the Berdellas' house.

Battles at home and abroad

On Oct. 3, 1961, 120,000 members of the United Auto Workers union walked out on strike at 88 Ford Motor Co. plants in 26 states. Following the settlement of the General Motors strike with substantial increases in wages and benefits, Ford quickly agreed to a 7-cent hourly pay hike, raising the average to $2.85 an hour, plus full health-insurance coverage and an improved pension plan. But the Ford employees wanted more, including a slowdown in the assembly lines and less stringent production standards, so my father was out of work and on the picket line. Union benefits put oatmeal on the table in the morning, peanut-butter-and-jelly sandwiches in our lunch sacks and green-bean and potato soups in our dinner bowls, but I could sense the stress mounting for Mom and Dad when the mortgage payment came due and the electric bill arrived in the mail.

The UAW and Ford reached an accord on Oct. 11, but 25 local bargaining units, including my dad's Local 420, refused to go back to work until other grievances such as overtime rotation and wash-up time were settled. We hoped for mild fall weather and kept the thermostat set to off. Twenty-four of the union locals reached agreements over the next week, but Local 420 at the Cleveland Stamping Plant in Walton Hills still wouldn't budge. Finally, the phone rang with good news. My dad returned to work on Oct. 20.

My mom took me into the doctor's office the next day. She hoped it wasn't too late for a tetanus shot. We told the doctor I stepped on a rusty nail while playing tag after dark the previous evening, but it actually had occurred a week earlier. My dad's health insurance covered the shot.

It was around that time that President Kennedy ordered increased support, including U.S. helicopters and more than 3,000 American military advisers, for the South Vietnamese government of the authoritarian Premier Ngo Dinh Diem in its war against communist guerrillas. That was important news for Kip Keller and me and many other boys in Cuyahoga Falls, especially Rick Morgan. But we didn't pay much attention to such things. I don't know that our parents did either.

Learning about birds and bees

For one thing, we were paying more and more attention to girls. This inclination was greatly enhanced by Charles J. "Charlie" Boyd, a towering, nimble man who spoke with an unmanly lilt and was the proprietor and head instructor of the Charles Boyd School of Dance. He was into his 50s at the time and had returned to Cuyahoga Falls, the place of his birth, in 1935, after spending his younger years studying dance in New York City and working in the nightclubs there. On Monday evenings, he offered dance lessons in the Sill School gymnasium at a bargain price, and more than 100 of us students, including many in our accelerated class, took advantage of them.

We learned the steps to the waltz, cha-cha and other ballroom dances and switched partners throughout the lessons so that we became acquainted with girls of various sizes and shapes. Many of them were developing breasts of various sizes. We boys took notice of those protrusions and, while waltzing, sometimes had the opportunity to nudge our chests against them. Actually, the boobs on some of the taller girls were somewhat higher than my chest, which I really took notice of.

Behind Charlie Boyd's back, he was known to us as "Twinkletoes," which was a tribute to his light-footed demeanor and effeminate characteristics. Our classmate Bob Berdella displayed similar peculiarities, but we didn't hold that against him.

Being in seventh grade and one year shy of becoming a teenager, my parents thought it was about time that I learned about the birds and the bees. So they bought me a book titled, "Being Born." By the time I got through the first chapter, I was thoroughly bored with "Being Born," and it just didn't make much sense to me. I much preferred reading books like Jack London's "Call of the Wild," which I concealed inside my textbook while ignoring the teacher in English class.

"So, David, did you finish your 'Being Born' book?" my mom asked one day after school.

"Yep." I lied.

"Now you know all about the birds and the bees then?"

"Yes, I do, Mom. Everything I ever wanted to know." I lied again.

"Well, do you have any questions about it?"

"Nope. Can I go up to my room now?"

"I was just wondering," Mom said. "I was talking to Mrs. Horstler the other day, and she told me Bruce has been having nocturnal emissions. Have you started those yet?"

What in the hell are nocturnal emissions? There must be something about them in the second chapter of that stupid "Being Born" book, which I didn't read, and now my mother was giving me a quiz. Bruce Horstler, who lived on the next block, was in my grade but a few months older than me. He and I knew each other well but were not what anyone would call friends. Not that we were unfriendly, but he sure wouldn't be telling me about nocturnal emissions, and I didn't care to know about his damn nocturnal emissions. "Uh, maybe, Mom. I gotta go do my homework now." Jeez, I'd rather do that than talk about nocturnal emissions, whatever they were.

I got two pairs of boxing gloves for Christmas that year, which was a complete surprise. They weren't on my gift list. I suppose they were better than lumps of coal, which had been promised to me more than once.

On the following Saturday, which happened to be New Year's Eve, my mom was out grocery shopping with my brother and sisters in tow. My dad was sunk in his living-room chair reading the Akron Beacon Journal sports section and probably looking for some good news about his Pittsburgh Steelers. I was outside fully engaged in a neighborhood snowball fight. Glen Barnhouse, Mike Kensinger and Kenny Chrzanowski were on my side. My next-door neighbor, Gary Williams, plus Bruce Horstler and a couple other boys were on the other team. It was a good fight and all in good fun until I nailed a kid named Carl Hoddle in the back of the head from 40 feet away with a well-packed snowball, and he ran home bawling.

"What did you do that for?" Bruce yelled at me.

"Because we're having a snowball fight, that's why," I yelled back.

All of a sudden the two snowball-fighting squads were facing each other down in my driveway and throwing wild accusations about snowball sportsmanship back and forth.

Suddenly, my 6-foot-tall, 200-pound father stormed out the side door, beaming from ear to ear. He was holding up one pair of my brand new boxing gloves in his right hand and the other pair in his left hand. "Why don't you two guys follow me into the garage and settle this the old-fashioned way?" he suggested, pointing to me and Bruce.

"That sounds good to me," Bruce, the kid whose mom liked to brag about his nocturnal emissions, said with a toothy grin.

Bruce wasn't the most athletic kid in the neighborhood, but he wasn't the least athletic kid around either. I knew I could whip him in a snowball fight any day, because I had better aim, coordination and reflexes. However, while we were nearly the same below-average height at about 5 feet, his stocky frame carried a good 110 pounds, compared to my skinny body that was still a bit shy of the 100-pound mark. My past experience with pushing, shoving and rolling around on the ground wasn't quite the same as actual boxing, and I wasn't too keen on getting my nose bloodied or my lip fattened. But my father and Bruce weren't the only ones in favor of the two of us lacing up the gloves. Even if I were chicken, I didn't want the whole neighborhood, much less my old man, calling me "chickenshit."

So into the garage we went. And then we went at it, trading punches to each other's faces and the sides of our heads but not landing too many body blows as the rest of the snowball-fighting group cheered us on. Using his 10-pound advantage, Bruce backed me into the corner several times, at which point my father, acting as the referee, would move us away from his shovels and rakes and shift us to the middle of the garage, where we'd start whacking each other all over again.

I was pleased to realize that, with the padded gloves, even Bruce's best punches didn't hurt all that much, and, after about five minutes of wild flurries, I thought I detected some exhaustion on his part. His jabs were falling short, and his guard was dropping, so I thought. I went on the offensive and had him backtracking toward the open garage door, at least for the moment.

Just then I heard a car horn. I looked up and saw our station wagon pulling in the driveway. My mom jumped out of the car like a mad woman, yelling at us in English and tossing some German in my dad's direction.

That was the end of the boxing match. My father told me later that I'd won, which was uncharacteristic of him. My neighborhood pals insisted that I'd lost, but who could believe them? Bruce Horstler told everybody he knew that he beat me. We never boxed each other again, never talked about nocturnal emissions either.

I continued my competitive swimming that winter, both with the Cuyahoga Falls YMCA team and with Tod Boyle's AAU team, which practiced a couple evenings each week at the Goodyear Tire and Rubber Co.'s indoor pool in the basement of one of its monstrous Akron plants.

The next summer our Water Works Swim Club boasted a pretty good 11-and-12-year-old boys medley relay with Casey Roberts leading off in the backstroke, me swimming the breaststroke leg, Bob Heacock doing butterfly and Carl Schmidt bringing it home in the freestyle. Tod was so encouraged with our success that he and his wife, Sally, took the four of us plus Jeff Weiss on a swimming and camping excursion to Western Ohio and Indiana. The two adults slept in the back of their station wagon, and the five boys camped out in a tent.

Our first stop was Delaware, Ohio, the home of Ohio Wesleyan University. We set up camp in a nearby park, which happened to include a small zoo on the grounds. Between afternoon competition and dinnertime on the first day, three of us watched in amusement as a male monkey fiddled quite enthusiastically with his penis, which quickly became erect. He soon received some assistance from one of his caged cohabitants, which I assumed to be a female, as she was not similarly equipped. It was all quite hilarious.

From Delaware, we headed across the state line and on to Indianapolis, where we competed in a very large swim meet at the Miramar Club and camped near some trees on the far side of the parking lot. Our final stop was at a lake in Huntington, Indiana, which was the site of the nationally known open-water Huntington Mile. Some of the other Water Works swimmers made the trip for the distance competition and met us there.

A couple of 13-year-old girls sneaked into our tent that night. There was some giggling and shushing. By this point in my life, I had a pretty good idea about the meaning of "Fuck Mrs. Jensen," even without reading "Being Born," and, like my friends, had become accustomed to tossing the word around rather impetuously myself. Also, I'd heard stories about the connection between penises and vaginas, but I still wasn't quite clear about the reason for Santa's inability to "get up the chimney this way." Penises and vaginas weren't getting connected in our tent, I was quite certain of that, so the giggling just a couple feet away from my sleeping bag might have had something to do with the girls' titties. As I lay there with my eyes open but seeing only hazy shadows in the darkness, I wondered how bare breasts might feel. But I was not a participant in that monkey business.

Minds and more in the gutter

By eighth grade, it was apparent that I wouldn't be making a living as a professional boxer and probably not as a professional baseball player either, so it would have made sense to pay attention in school. Instead, my mind drifted from the teacher's lesson about verb tenses to girls in their Speedos at swim practice, to "The Adventures of Huckleberry Finn" hidden inside my English book, to Little Joe and Hoss on the "Bonanza" show, to soaping some neighbors' windows on Halloween night.

"Lie, lay, lain," I heard the teacher say, although I wasn't really listening. "Lay, laid, laid."

Daryl Lucien, the dark-haired smart aleck who sat near the front of the class, cracked up.

Mrs. Hendrickson lost her cool. "Daryl, I'm sick of your filthy mind," she yelled. "Get out of this class, and come back when you're ready to apologize."

"I'm sorry," he said sheepishly.

At least I learned something that day. I didn't put much stock in the teacher's assignment for the next week, though.

"OK," Mrs. Hendrickson announced on Monday morning. "I assume you're all prepared to give a two-minute presentation in front of the class on a subject of current interest. David, you can go first."

"Uh-oh," I thought to myself as I slowly stood up from my desk near the back of the room and headed toward the front, feeling the eyes of the entire accelerated class upon me. "Well," I stammered, trying to think of something to say. Anything. "I just had my 13th birthday last week. And now that I'm a teenager, I don't think it's fair to charge a higher admission for us at the State Theater. I mean, after paying 75 cents on Saturday, I didn't have any money left for popcorn or jujubes. Then there were these young kids in the front row, who only paid a quarter to get in, and they're making a bunch of noise. Me and the girl sitting next to me weren't making hardly any noise, and we were too busy to even watch the movie, so I don't think we should have to pay so much." That was all I had. So I stepped past Daryl, who was chuckling under his breath but not laughing out loud. I trudged to the back of the class and plopped back in my desk chair.

Truth is, I didn't make that stuff up. Kip Keller, Terry Gray and his seventh-grade brother, Randy, knew some girls our age from Stow who met us at the bowling alley in the State Road Shopping Center on Route 8. The eight of us walked about a mile along the busy four-lane road lined with stores and restaurants to the State Theater together, puffing on some cigarettes as we went. I don't know whether the little blond girl named Becky took a liking to me, but I sure liked her. Her three friends hooked up with my three friends, so she and I ended up sitting next to each other. It was my first experience with almost necking, which I was pretty happy about. I put my arm around her, and we leaned our heads together rather passionately for the entire feature film, although we did not swap spit or connect our lips in any other way.

Based on the D-plus grade Mrs. Hendrickson gave me for my impromptu presentation, my English teacher wasn't very impressed with the performance.

About half the boys at Sill Junior High School presented themselves as Greasers, which basically meant that we applied a greasy tonic to our hair so that we could slick it back in a cresting wave like Elvis Presley, Ricky Nelson and other early rockers did. Many of us also fit the genre, dressed in buttoned shirts, black turtlenecks or both, tight-fitting stovepipe slacks and black loafers with pointed toes and Cuban heels.

True Greasers, of course, smoked cigarettes – preferably without filters and absolutely without menthol. Cigarettes were still easy for kids to acquire, either from the machines that could be found in any gas station or at the hole-in-the-wall store just across Tallmadge Avenue from the school. The proprietor, who made a nice profit off junior high school boys' lunch money, didn't mind his shop being choked full of smoke every weekday at noon. I could have bought my cigarettes at Stutzman's Foodliner across the street from my house but didn't want to raise unnecessary suspicions. Although I had previous smoking experience, it was mostly a charade for me, as I held the nicotine-besmirched puff in my mouth long enough to create the illusion of inhaling but couldn't stand to suck it down into my lungs.

Kip and I spent many after-school hours and weekend days with the Grays upstairs in their bungalow, where they had a pool table. Their mom usually was not at home. We'd play eight-ball, smoke cigarettes and say "Fuck" a lot, so we didn't have much time for homework. After dark, we'd head out into the neighborhood for the usual kinds of mischief like setting a paper sack filled with dog shit on somebody's front stoop, lighting it on fire, knocking on the door and running for cover. Or we'd swipe a carton of eggs from the Lawson's store and toss them at cars from behind some trees on Bailey Road. Sometimes Bob Berdella, who wasn't much of a Greaser and who didn't play pool, would go out with us.

Our most incendiary ploy was to buy some saltpeter at Hanna Pharmacy, which was almost next door to Stutzman's, and mix it with sugar, which was abundantly available in our mothers' kitchens. We'd spread an inch-wide line of the powdery concoction across Northmoreland Avenue, which did not have streetlights and wasn't well-traveled. We'd wait until we saw headlights approaching from the opposite side of a low rise in the road and then put a match to the powder, which erupted in blue, red and orange flames shooting 6 to 8 feet high from one edge of the pavement to the other. Invariably, the vehicle would screech to a halt, the driver would leap out hollering and try in vain to locate the hidden culprits.

On a chilly February night, our vaporized breath must have given us away, and a guy in his 30s left his wife and kids in his idling Dodge to give chase. The fleet-footed Kip ran off in one direction with Terry following him, while Bob and I headed through neighbors' yards and toward his house on Curtis Avenue a couple streets away. Nobody was home, and the house was dark. We scooted inside the screened back patio, hitched the dead bolt on the door and crouched behind a glider with leather cushions. We heard footsteps closing in and heavy breathing just outside the screens. The door handle jiggled, but it didn't give. "I know you're in there," the man yelled. "What you guys are doing is dangerous, and you better not do it again, because next time I will catch you, and you will be sorry." Then he left, and we breathed sighs of relief.

The summer of 1963 was a relief from my declining educational performance, but my life was going downhill in other areas as well.

I moved up to the E League in baseball. The team was mediocre, and the manager showed up for practice about half the time. I decided to give up baseball just about the time that my father was ready to take over the manager's job. I figured he had done enough baseball managing.

My performance in the swimming pool also was disappointing. Most of the other boys were hitting full stride in the maturation process. Not me. Tom Morton, a tall, blond guy who previously had been the backstroker on our YMCA medley relay, transitioned to breaststroke and knocked me off the Water Works Swim Club relay.

When I wasn't swimming that summer, I'd be wandering around downtown Cuyahoga Falls, through the woods or around the spacious, treed picnic grounds between the pool and the river at Water Works Park with Kip Keller and the Gray brothers. In addition to smoking cigarettes, we liked to throw stones at the cabooses on the trains speeding toward Pittsburgh or Toledo along the railway that dissects the park.

The trestle that spans the park access road was fortified with a spiny thicket of shrubs at every corner of the sheer embankment that made it virtually impossible to scale up to tracks at that location. We were familiar with every alternative steep, winding path through the low canopy of maples and oaks within a half mile east or west of the crossing. But most drivers heading to the picnic grounds with their families or to play games on one of the baseball diamonds were not. That made it convenient for us to drop pebbles onto the hoods and roofs of vehicles passing under the trestle and laugh as we made our getaway and heard the futile cursing of angry motorists.

Despite its beckoning, meandering course along the back edge of the park, we knew better than to venture into the filthy Cuyahoga River, and we learned quickly to avoid getting sucked in by its mucky bank, where more than one kid had lost a tennis shoe. On one steamy July afternoon, though, Kip and I became curious about a bowl-shaped excavation where water had risen up during the past couple weeks. It was approximately 30 yards in diameter, which was no distance at all for a swimmer like myself, and Kip, ever the adventurer, suggested that we ditch our clothes, hop in and cool off. The water was over our heads within a few feet of shore, but Kip was confident that he could make it to the other side. I swam slowly so that he could keep up, and, within a couple minutes, our feet could touch bottom at the far side. We took a few steps to reach a waist-high depth.

"Hey!" a man's voice shouted from a mound of dirt overlooking the pond. "What the hell are you guys doing in there? You know, that's overflow from the sewer. It's full of piss and shit. Now, get out of here before I call the cops." We scampered out the best we could with our bare feet on the stony ground, each of us shielding our penises and testicles with one hand. We saw the guy get back in his city pickup truck and drive away. Hoping nobody else would come by and see us walking around naked, we made it around to the other side of the sewage pit and put our clothes on.

I knew something didn't smell right about that place. Like that damn anthropologist Alan Dundes put it, we Germans are repeatedly getting ourselves in deep shit.

Chapter 5 | **A Mass Murderer in Our Midst**

It was the second day of school at the beginning of ninth grade. The authoritative voice of the principal, Clinton Emmerich, a no-nonsense educator with piercing eyes and receding grayish hair, thundered over the public-address system. "Harry Keller, David Lange and Michael Mooney, come down to the office at once."

Mike Mooney, a red-haired Irish kid who loved to fight and otherwise cause trouble, was a grade behind us, but we knew him well and sometimes smoked cigarettes in the same hideouts. Kip Keller and I had done our fair share of initiating seventh-grade boys by smearing them with lipstick after school on the previous afternoon. We figured Mike was doing much the same, but that was no reason to be called to the principal's office. Initiation was a school tradition, after all.

Kip and I, from one direction, and Mike, from another, arrived in the main office simultaneously. The secretary motioned Kip and me to have a seat. She ushered Mike into the inner office and closed the door behind him. We heard Mr. Emmerich's voice rise, but his words were muffled. Then we heard some mumbling and sniveling. A couple minutes later Mike came out. His eyes were red and watery. He didn't look our way as he exited the office and headed back to class.

The secretary directed the two of us into Emmerich's office, and we stood at attention in front of his oak desk. He was fuming. "I got a call this morning from Mrs. Stemley," he said with a scowl. "She tells me you two smeared lipstick all over her son, Ricky, yesterday. Is that so?"

We nodded, figuring, so what?

"Well, it got all over the collar of his brand new white jacket, and it won't come out. It's ruined."

We thought it was pretty dumb to wear a white jacket when he knew it was initiation day.

"That behavior will not be tolerated by this school," Emmerich shouted with veins popping out on his temples. He rose up from his swivel chair and pulled a wooden paddle out of his desk drawer. "Both of you bend over and put your hands on your ankles." Out of the corner of my eye, I saw Emmerich rear back with a firm grip on the handle of his paddle and take a mighty swing at Kip's skinny rump. Wham! Man, that was loud. Again. Wham! Then it was my turn. Wham! Wham! Boy, did that sting. "Now you two get back to your class, and I better not see you here again."

Gingerly, we stepped out through the main office and into the hallway. "That Mooney sure is a fuckin' crybaby," Kip said. That made me smile.

Our lipstick caper did not occur inside the school building. It did not occur on school property. It did not occur during school hours. So how was it the principal's business anyway? And what gave him the authority to inflict corporal punishment on us for something that wasn't any of his damn business?

Another problem was that the entire school heard Mr. Emmerich's announcement over the PA system, including my sister Vonnie, who had just started seventh grade. Here she was in a new school filled with older kids, most of whom she did not know, some of whom could be quite intimidating, and, before she knows it, her new teacher and her class of accelerated students hear the principal angrily calling her brother to the office.

Needless to say, my mom heard all about it before I got home that afternoon. "So why did Mr. Emmerich call you and Kip down to the office this morning?" she asked as I walked in the back door and set down the homework assignments that I didn't intend to do.

I gave Vonnie, who was sitting at the dining table and starting her homework, a scornful glare. "Ahh, he just wanted to ask us a couple questions, Mom."

"What about?"

"You know, it was initiation day yesterday, Mom, and he wanted to know whether we were involved with that."

"Yeah?"

At least she knew that the junior-high lipstick initiation was all in good fun, unlike the ignorance of Emmerich and old-lady Stemley, and I caught a glimmer of amusement cross her face.

"We said yes, but we didn't hurt anybody, and he told us that the school wouldn't be putting up with initiations anymore. So we told him OK. Anyway, initiation is over for this year, and we'll be in high school next year, so we're done with it."

Mom nodded at me. I gave Vonnie another glare. That was that.

Sinking into 'bottomless quagmire'

On the afternoon of Nov. 22, 1963, a Friday, less than a week before our four-day Thanksgiving break, Mr. Emmerich's voice broke over the PA system. This time he didn't sound angry. His voice was quivering. "Can I have your attention, please?" Our classroom went silent. "I have some bad news. Our president, John F. Kennedy, has been shot. He's been assassinated. He passed away."

A few minutes later the bell rang, and we shuffled out to our lockers. A lot of kids were crying.

By the time of President Kennedy's death, distant rumors of war in Vietnam had evolved to whispers in the halls of government and then to rumbles in the newspapers. Soon after his historic election, the young American leader had paid a visit in May 1961 to French President Charles de Gaulle, whose country was all too familiar with the sucking swamps of Southeast Asia. The United States will "take our place" in Vietnam and re-ignite "the war which we brought to an end," de Gaulle warned Kennedy, and "you will sink step by step into a bottomless quagmire, however much you spend in men and money."

Experience be damned. The United States does not take advice from losers. In January 1963, 10 months before Kennedy's assassination, five American helicopters were shot down by communist guerrillas in the Mekong Delta, killing 30 Americans in action. That was six years before I began flying over the delta and other arboreous wildernesses in Navy and Army helicopters, and 13-year-olds don't do a lot of newspaper reading. No one I knew was among those 30 dead Americans.

In June 1963, a Buddhist monk, Thich Quang Duc, sat in the middle of a busy Saigon intersection, where a fellow monk drenched his body with a jug of petrol. He lit a match above his head and set himself ablaze. Malcolm Brown, bureau chief for the Associated Press in Saigon, snapped photographs of the flesh-burning protest against religious oppression by the Catholic president, Ngo Dinh Diem. Brown won a Pulitzer Prize for the photo that emblazoned front pages across the country. Kennedy said, "No news picture in history has generated so much emotion around the world as that one." It opened my young, inattentive eyes to a place called Vietnam, but it still was far, far away.

On Nov. 1, three weeks before the Kennedy assassination, a group of Vietnamese generals conducted a well-planned overthrow of President Diem. Although he and his brother, Ngo Dinh Nhu, were promised safe passage if they agreed to surrender, they were brutally murdered instead. President Kennedy expressed surprise over Diem's death, but he was hardly surprised by the coup. Henry Cabot Lodge, his ambassador to Vietnam, congratulated the generals on a job well done. It was not the last military coup inspired by France's trailer sinking into de Gaulle's "bottomless quagmire," but it was the last one for Kennedy.

Lyndon B. Johnson was sworn in as our 36th president shortly after the assassin Lee Harvey Oswald took deadly aim from the sixth floor of the Texas School Book Depository Building in downtown Dallas.

With an unforgiving game of musical chairs being played by generals in South Vietnam and with our presidents yanking those chairs from the constricting circle of death, we Americans were supposed to believe that freedom was at stake and that our young men would need to sacrifice their limbs and lives for its sake.

It wasn't until 1971 that a secret U.S. Department of Defense study known as the Pentagon Papers was exposed to the American public in an explosive freedom-of-information battle between the government and the press. The "encyclopedic history of the Vietnam War," as it was lesser known, wasn't compiled until Secretary of Defense Robert McNamara created a task force consisting of 36 analysts, half of them military officers, in 1967. The comprehensive analysis made it clear that our country's infiltration of Southeast Asia never was about helping a friend in need, South Vietnam. It always was about containing the communist menace, China. That was not an empty objective, to be sure, but it surely was different from the one being sold to the American people, who were expected to send their sons to spill their blood in faraway jungles and rice paddies.

As Daniel Ellsberg, the U.S. Marine Corps veteran and defense analyst who worked on the secret project and later leaked the Pentagon documents to the New York Times and Washington Post, revealed, every president since Harry Truman had been advised by military leaders that a war in Vietnam was not winnable.

Charles de Gaulle was not full of crap. The liberal media did not cause the United States to lose the war. Anti-war protesters on college campuses across the country didn't cause any military demise. Those of us who didn't burn our draft cards never lost a single major battle in Vietnam. But Kennedy, Johnson and Nixon all knew the truth. Yes, it was all about politics, the politics of acting tough and lying to the American people.

By the end of 1963, 16,300 American military advisers were in Vietnam. Plans were being hatched to put mercenaries in the cockpits and bomb bays of old U.S. warplanes and conduct secret raids on the Ho Chi Minh Trail inside Laos. Gen. Duong Van Minh, who had succeeded the assassinated Diem just a couple months earlier, was ousted in another coup in late January 1964, this one without bloodshed.

Catholic school to the rescue

My January surely was less turbulent than that of the generals in Saigon, but it was not an object lesson in stability either. Our dachshund, Gretchen, was diagnosed with cancer and was put down on the same day that I flunked a science test in school. My prayers hadn't helped. I blamed God for the early death of Gretchen, who never hurt anyone – except for the Peeping Tom my mom supposedly spied outside the kitchen window. But I knew who was responsible for my academic deceleration. I had become more interested in the smutty paperbacks I swiped from the bookstore on Portage Trail than boring textbooks, and the biology lessons imprinted on my brain didn't show up on any tests.

"Who's the Shadow?" my mom asked after cornering me in the kitchen while the rest of the family watched "Ben Casey" on the black-and-white RCA television in the living room.

"I don't know," I replied, wondering if she'd heard about a new mystery program on one of the three network stations that we could pick up with the rabbit ears on top of the console TV.

"I hear that's what some of the kids are calling one of the boys in ninth grade at Sill," she said. She must be hearing stuff from Mrs. Kasper again, I thought, because Margaret probably blabs to her mom all the time. Girls are like that. "Wherever one of the boys in his class goes," Mom continued, "that boy follows him around like a shadow."

Then it hit me. She was talking about me hanging around Kip Keller.

"Your dad and I have been talking about your grades and thinking maybe your teachers aren't getting through to you so well at Sill," she said. "We let you drop out of French class, because you didn't like the teacher, Mrs. Rouleau. And Mrs. Hendrickson called the other day to tell me she's had to send you out to the hall three times in the past few weeks, because you were disrupting her language-arts class. So I called the principal at Hoban High School and asked about transferring you there for next semester. I told him you're in the accelerated class, and you could be on their swim team. He said they have space for you in the freshman class, and we decided that it's the best thing for you right now."

That hit me like a ton of bricks. But I had to admit, if Margaret Kasper told her mom about me being the Shadow, other kids might be saying things behind my back too, and I didn't take that as a compliment. Plus, other than my math and gym teachers, I really wasn't all that impressed with the faculty at Sill School, and probably the feeling was mutual.

"But Hoban's a Catholic school," I said, "and we're Lutheran."

"I explained that to Brother William, the principal. After we talked for a while, he said they have a few other Protestant students, and they get along just fine," Mom replied. She happened to be a pretty persuasive woman. She probably could get a Jewish kid into a Catholic school, if she wanted to.

"But Hoban's way down in Akron somewhere," I said. "How would I get there?"

"You know Allan Carlini, who lives over on Curtis Avenue. He's in 10th grade this year at Hoban," Mom told me. "Well, on his way to work early each morning, Mr. Carlini drops Allan off at the bus stop at the corner of Broad Boulevard and Fourth Street. A special city bus goes right to the school, and it drops you off at the same place in the afternoon. You can walk home from there. It's only about a mile away."

I knew Allan Carlini from the neighborhood, and he had begun to learn competitive swimming with Water Works Swim Club the previous summer, but he wasn't very good at it. He was a tall, lanky kid with dark hair.

When I knocked on his front door in the Monday-morning darkness, his mom let me in, smiled and directed me to a cushioned chair in the living room of their older colonial. Allan was still getting ready for school, and so were his younger sisters, exactly how many I wasn't quite certain. All of them were dark haired like Allan. They ranged from the quite cute youngest one to the downright stunning oldest Carlini girl, who was a couple grades behind me. As the girls ran up and down the stairs to fetch one item or another, they did their best not to look me over, and I did my best to reciprocate. They all wore the plaid Catholic schoolgirl skirts and white blouses that were required for students at St. Joseph Elementary School on Second Street.

Mr. Carlini led me out to the driveway, where he started his car and told me to wait in the backseat as it began to warm up. The sun had yet to break above the peaks of the Heslop bungalows lining the streets to the east. I watched my breath float across the car's interior and bounce off the foggy window. I listened as Kenny Halterman announced the local news on the WAKR AM radio station. The temperature might reach 15 degrees by the afternoon, he said. Allan and his father hopped in the front seat, and off we went. A few blocks to the west, we picked up two other boys, Tony, a 10th-grader like Allan, and another Dave, a ninth-grader like me, outside a tavern on Main Street. Tony's father owned the place, and his family lived upstairs.

Just as the car began to feel warm, Mr. Carlini dropped us off at the bus stop. About 15 minutes later, when I thought my toes were about to crumble like the crunchy snow under our stomping feet, the Akron city bus arrived. We each plunked a couple dimes in the coin drop. In those days, public school districts were not yet required to cover the transportation costs of students attending parochial and other private schools. We paid our own way to ride the city bus on the Hoban route.

As we grabbed seats on the bus, a couple guys wondered who the new kid was. "His name's Dave. He's my neighbor," Allan said. I didn't say much. My toes were killing me, and the heat blowing out of the floor vent wasn't helping much.

The bus made several stops along Sackett Avenue as we headed west, turned south on State Road and crossed the high-level bridge where you could look through the unpaved, checkered steel surface into the deep Cuyahoga River valley below. As we crossed into Akron, State Road became North Main Street. We turned onto Iuka Avenue and wound our way through the North Hill neighborhood, where the bus filled to standing room only by the time we reached Tallmadge Avenue and got on the Akron Expressway. About 5 miles to the south, we exited at Johnston Street, cut over to Inman Street and then lurched up the 5th Avenue hill to Hoban High School.

My new school was founded by the Brothers of Holy Cross not far from the center of Akron in 1953 in honor of Archbishop Edward F. Hoban. The Brothers of Holy Cross trace their founding to Le Mans, France, in 1837. Their order of priests and brothers is devoted to the mission of spreading the Gospel around the world, including many areas stricken by dire poverty and danger. The brothers also are committed to educational excellence in the Catholic tradition and probably are best known for their establishment of and continuing association with the University of Notre Dame in Indiana.

The school itself is situated on 34 acres at the crest of Sumner Hill. It was an all-boys school upon its founding and remained so when I arrived. It had four grades, ninth through 12th, as opposed to most public high schools of that era, which did not include ninth grade. There were more than 350 boys in my freshman class. Four of them were black, which was four more than I had ever seen in Cuyahoga Falls. The educational staff included 40 Catholic brothers, half of them products of the University of Notre Dame, and 12 lay teachers. The brothers knew their subject matter well and took a genuine interest in their students. They resided in a monastic building attached to the east side of the school.

Although the tuition was not exorbitant, it posed an additional challenge for my working-class parents, including my mom, who was supplementing our family income by providing day care for the two preschool children of a single mother. My father condescendingly referred to the lady who dropped her kids off each morning and picked them up in the evening as "Thusnelda," an ancient German name that gave rise to the term, "Tussi," which refers to a woman who wears revealing outfits and treats her face to heavy doses of makeup.

Hoban High School was the best thing that could have happened to me at that point in my life. I am indebted to my parents for that opportunity, and Thusnelda's situation was a contributing factor.

The parking lot was at the backside of the building. But that became the main entry after the state constructed an east-west freeway right through the middle of school property several years earlier, which, in turn, relegated the architecturally inviting building front into an under-appreciated afterthought.

Inside the main hallway, I found the school office. Proudly displayed just outside the door was a large portrait of our country's one and only Catholic president, the late John Fitzgerald Kennedy. The Brothers of Holy Cross called him "The Admirable President of Equality." Inside the main office, the principal, Brother William Fitch, a powerfully built man with a warm smile, welcomed me and three other transfer students to the school. I was directed to my locker, where I, like most of the students, would stow my sports jacket and snap-on necktie to be worn religiously each school day. I got my textbooks and class schedule then headed for homeroom.

Brother John Patrick Lahiff was the prefect of discipline. He also taught geography. I heard that he had been a wrestler in the days before he joined Holy Cross in 1947. He was not a tall man, but he was broad across the shoulders. He was said to be "a proud Bostonian Irishman." Following his death in 1990, the Legacy Project noted that "John was tough but fair, with a twinkling Irish eye and happy smile for even the loneliest student." Being new to Hoban and not yet knowing any of my classmates, Brother John immediately made me feel welcome. "His pug nose and rapid-fire

Bostonian accent were his trademarks," according to the Legacy Project. That was accurate. For those in need of discipline, the prefect was well equipped to dish it out. As suddenly as I had changed schools, though, my need for disciplinary measures in the classroom had vanished.

At the beginning of each class, we all stood and recited the "Hail Mary" prayer. We Lutherans did not hail Mary. Hardly anyone at Hoban knew about my Lutheranism, and I wanted to keep it that way. I adapted quickly. "Hail Mary, full of grace. The Lord is with thee. Blessed art thou among women, and blessed is the fruit of thy womb, Jesus. Holy Mary, Mother of God, pray for us sinners, now and at the hour of our death. Amen." In the name of the Father, the Son and the Holy Spirit. Amen to that. Freedom of religion was alive and well in America.

It still is. Even a half century later, when certain Christians were whining about being persecuted by a so-called secularized society, nobody was stopping them from praying in their parochial schools, their churches, their homes or just about anywhere they wanted. Nobody was stopping them from displaying the Nativity or posting the Ten Commandments at their parochial schools, their churches, their homes and their places of business. Some Christians' notion of freedom of religion is being able to shove their particular set of beliefs down the throats of everybody else anywhere they damn well please and have the government enforce their subversion of the First Amendment. Even so, they claim that they want less government. What hypocrisy.

I never got that impression from the good Catholics at Hoban High School. I was excused from religion class there, which was OK, as I was getting plenty of that each Saturday with an hour of catechism at Redeemer Lutheran Church, not to mention Sunday school and regular church services there as well.

"Go to hell!" bellowed the Rev. Ronald R. Zehnder, scaring the crap out of me and everybody else in my catechism class as he rambled in the door. Silence. "I'm talking to the devil," he clarified with a lower volume of his baritone voice. Whether it was catechism class or Sunday sermons, Pastor Zehnder knew how to get your attention. I actually paid attention some of the time.

In the Lutheran Church, Missouri Synod, we did not take Communion until after completing two years of catechism and then officially being confirmed in a ceremonious ritual at the age of 13 or 14, which was not going to occur for me until that March. For Catholics, confirmation and first Communion occurred at an earlier age.

I did not know that when the entire school was called to Mass on Friday of my first week at Hoban, and I joined the crowd that settled into folding chairs in the gymnasium. Most of the service was in Latin, and I mumbled some recitations along with everybody else. I sat when everybody else did. I stood when they did. And I knelt when they did. But when they began to file up front to receive the body of Christ row by row, I didn't know what to do but follow along. As we approached the priest who was distributing Communion, I saw my fellow students bowing their heads, making the sign of the cross, which I had learned to do, and saying something, but I couldn't hear exactly what. Just before my turn, I panicked, scooted around the kid ahead of me, felt blood rush to my face and hurried back to my seat.

"What was that all about?" the kid asked as he kneeled back down next to me.

"I was gonna sneeze," I said, "and didn't want to get any on him."

I soon got word from Brother William that I should report to the office with the other Protestants instead of going to Mass from then on. That's how I figured there were five other Protestants attending Hoban High School that year.

Brother Joseph Tobin, one of the Notre Dame products, was my art teacher. He was a soft-spoken, very gentle man. I loved art class, because it gave me the kind of freedom that I couldn't find in math, English, history and sure as hell not French class. I just wasn't a very talented art student. Somehow, with Brother Joseph's guidance and support, my mosaic of a helmeted football player won an Award of Excellence in the Cleveland Diocese Catholic High School Art Festival.

New learning experiences

My physical-education teacher at Hoban, one Paul R. Baldacci, who also served as the school's athletic director, was another story. My introduction to his gym class was assignment to the worst among a half dozen volleyball teams. Initially, that was a good thing, as, despite being one of the smallest ninth-graders, I clearly was the most athletically coordinated player on my team. My teammates seemed pleased that we became more competitive and only lost our game by five points. But it wasn't good enough.

With time running short on third period, Baldacci bellowed, "All right, winning teams line up for the paddle machine." Amidst chuckles and smiles, about 30 boys got themselves in formation several feet apart along the sideline of the basketball court. "Losers, get ready to grovel," Baldacci ordered.

"What the hell?" I murmured as I joined my teammates and the other losers lining up to face the winners, who were bending over with their legs spread apart.

"Go!" yelled the gym teacher. In disbelief, I watched my fellow losers crouch down on all fours and begin scurrying between the legs of the winners. Reluctantly, I followed suit. Wham, bam, the whacking began. The quicker we scurried, the less we got whacked, mostly with open hands on the buttocks but also with a few closed fists to our ribs and thighs. It was not a good idea to lose volleyball games in gym class at Hoban High School.

"That's enough fun for today, boys," Baldacci quipped when we finished. "Now take your showers and get dressed for your next class." Talk about adding insult to injury, the communal shower room made it all too evident that I was one of the few ninth-grade boys who had not yet reached puberty.

On Feb. 9, 1964, the Beatles, a British rock 'n' roll quartet, made its American television debut on "The Ed Sullivan Show," which was a regular Sunday evening experience for the Lange family. An estimated 73 million viewers tuned in for the show, which was a record for that time. We already were familiar with Beatles songs like "I Want to Hold Your Hand," which was No. 1 on the pop charts, and "I Saw Her Standing There," because all the AM radio stations were playing them. And we were hearing plenty about their revolutionary long hair. I don't think I knew anybody who missed that show.

On Monday morning, everybody on the bus was talking about Paul McCartney, John Lennon, George Harrison and Ringo Starr. "Can you believe that hair?" one guy said. "Yeah, that's pretty crazy," another replied. "Never saw anything like that," a junior from North Hill said. "Let's see you comb yours down like that," his buddy said. "Nah, it's too short. Somebody else should do it. I know, look at Lange, he's got longer hair. Hey, Lange, comb your hair like the Beatles."

I still had a big wave greased back to the center of my head. I pulled my comb out of my pants pocket, smoothed the wave down and swept it across my forehead. Apparently, that was close enough, as the entire bus load erupted in laughter. "That's it!" one guy shouted. "Lange looks like a Beatle." Thanks to the Beatles, I gained acceptance to my new school.

Mom always packed our lunches for school, even when they were just 25 cents apiece in our early years, and she continued to do so when I was in high school. The next Friday, when I pulled the sandwich out of my paper sack in Hoban's cafeteria and unwrapped the wax paper, I just about fainted. Clear as day, sticking out from the crust of the two slices of white bread was a mustard-slathered slice of bologna. The horror. Quickly, I smashed it into a ball and tossed it back in the sack. I contented myself with an apple for lunch that day, didn't want anyone to think I wasn't a fish eater. From then on, I reminded my mom to make peanut-butter-and-jelly sandwiches on Friday.

One afternoon a kid in my homeroom convinced me to stay after school and join the chess club. I fancied myself as a pretty good checkers player, so I thought I'd give it a try. That turned out to be a mistake but not so much due to the fact that I didn't know the difference between a pawn and a rook. It caused me to miss the regular bus back to Cuyahoga Falls.

The west side of Sumner Hill, up from Inman Street, was a predominantly white working-class neighborhood, much like my own, which I determined from the people I could see in their yards and on their porches though the bus windows. But the city buses heading downtown, where I could make connections to the Falls, did not regularly run along Inman Street. The east side, where there was a bus stop on South Arlington Street, was a different world.

As I trudged down the hill lugging my books, I encountered more black people than I had seen in my entire life. Most of them didn't speak a word to me, but, when they looked my way, I knew they could tell what color I was. I passed a group of girls about my age standing on a corner. "Hey, white boy, watchya doing here?" one of them asked. I didn't answer. "Yeah, you better walk faster, whitey." I did. I arrived at the bus stop unscathed. The bus arrived about 10 minutes later. It felt more like an hour. I was relieved to see that the driver was white, and so were some of the passengers. I grabbed a seat about halfway back next to a chubby white lady who smelled like garlic.

Turning away from old friends

In early spring, I got together with my buddies from Sill School one more time. Shortly after my transfer, the Grays moved from Cuyahoga Falls on the north side of Akron to Norton, a less populous suburb southeast of the city. Kip Keller's mom picked me up on a Saturday morning and drove us down. The Grays' new place was similar to the house they left in the Falls, although there was no pool table upstairs. Mrs. Gray dropped the four of us off in downtown Barberton, where we spent the afternoon wandering through some stores for five-finger discounts, smoking cigarettes on street corners, cursing like lowlifes – although I, for one, did not use the name of the Lord in vain – and otherwise acting tough. We didn't talk about school.

A new subject came up. "Hey, Lange, are you jacking off yet?" Terry asked with a grin that widened across his freckled face. His brother Randy laughed out loud. Kip chuckled.

I knew a bit about ejaculations from the paperback books I had swiped and read in the privacy of the bedroom I shared with my brother. But those carnal accounts always involved a man with a woman, or two women, or young boys under the table at an all-male banquet in some exotic Arabian kingdom, or maybe a sheep on the outskirts of a Himalayan village. I was not yet aware of self-induced sexual gratification. Sure, I got erections while reading those books that I kept hidden from my mom, but they were nothing new. Unlike Bruce Horstler, whose mother was bragging about his nocturnal emissions more than a year earlier, I still hadn't experienced my first wet dream. Truthfully, I didn't know anything about jacking off. Nevertheless, I responded, "Are you kidding me? Fuckin' aye, I am. Doesn't everybody?"

"Ha-ha, we'll see about that tonight," Terry said.

After dinner back at the Grays' house, which was followed by a couple TV programs, we headed upstairs to the bedroom – Terry and me in one double bed, Randy and Kip in the other. Pretty soon I heard some muffled pounding sounds from both beds, then heavy breathing, gasping and finally hushed moans. "Oh, yeah, that felt good. I got it all over my undies," Randy said. "Me too," Kip said. "What about you, Lange?"

"Yep, I did it," I whispered.

"Oh, yeah? Let me see your underpants," Terry told me.

It was pitch dark. He wouldn't be able to see anything. I quietly spat in my left hand as I pulled my underpants down with my right hand and then smeared the crotch with the frothy saliva before handing them over to Terry. He gave them a quick inspection and then announced, "Guess what, Lange can do it after all. Not much, but some." For me, puberty had not yet arrived. My masculinity was vindicated nonetheless.

That was the last time I ever saw the Gray brothers. It also was the end of my friendship with Kip Keller, although we eventually ended up in the same high-school graduating class. After graduation, Kip served with the U.S. Army in Vietnam. The oddball in our little clan, Bob Berdella, also graduated with our class, but I never spoke with him again.

Bob's life took a more notorious course that made headlines in newspapers across the country. A front-page story in the Akron Beacon Journal on Nov. 5, 1989, by Lisa Austin, of Knight-Ridder Newspapers, told it this way: "Jailed for life without the possibility of parole, Bob Berdella considers himself repentant. After all, the former Cuyahoga Falls native says, he was only a murderer for four years."

"In those years from 1984 to 1988," Austin wrote, "Berdella killed six men, ages 18 to 25, in the bedroom of his midtown Kansas City home. Berdella tortured and drugged them, then took snapshots of them in agony. After they died, he dismembered their bodies and mixed the parts with his trash."

"So they found a head in my backyard. That doesn't show that I killed the person," Berdella told the reporter. He confessed "so I could get my new life ahead of me and try to accomplish something," he said.

His story was told after some 20 hours of interviews conducted over six months in two Missouri penitentiaries. He recounted that, during his teenage years, he turned away from his friends in Cuyahoga Falls. "At that point, when I stepped back out, was when I looked at the kids I was running with and figured that isn't where it's at and started looking at the direction I wanted to take." Apparently, he didn't mention our saltpeter-and-sugar escapades and the angry driver who chased him and me through our neighborhood on a cold winter night. Other than me, Kip and the Grays, Berdella didn't have any friends.

He told the reporter how he began frequenting gay bars in Akron and became disillusioned with the Catholic Church. I knew Bob Berdella was strange, but who in the hell could be that strange?

On the day before Easter 1988, the reporter Lisa Austin wrote, "a captive in Berdella's bedroom squirmed to reach a book of matches, set fire to ropes binding his wrists, then jumped from a second-story window. Dazed and wearing only a dog collar, he asked neighbors to call police. He said Berdella had bound, drugged and tortured him for four days."

Chapter 6 | # Handshake with the President

John Ferguson lived with his parents on Myrtle Avenue, around the corner and two houses away from us. The Fergusons' Heslop bungalow was just like ours and all the others in the neighborhood – the main difference being a variety of pastels on the ceramic shingle siding. As an only child, John had the entire upstairs of his house to himself, and his parents didn't feel the need to bust open the roof to add a half-bathroom dormer. He was a year older and a grade ahead of me in school. He was a giant of a boy whose buzz-cut head reached the 6-foot mark in the Price School gym by third or fourth grade and topped off at 6-foot-4 by junior high school.

His dad, Elbert Ferguson, worked at the Ford Motor Co.'s Cleveland Stamping Plant, as did my dad. They were friendly but not buddies. El Ferguson fancied his son being a football star, which he wasn't.

John and I hung out together often. Sometimes we dug up projectiles embedded in the hillside at the rifle range on the opposite side of the Big Woods, brought them home, melted them down on his back porch and created leaden figures. Other times we'd capture scads of honeybees as they zipped amidst the dandelions that proliferated in our yards. We'd apply a variety of techniques to annihilate them. An ounce of gasoline poured inside a lidded jar worked best. Often we'd play P-I-G or H-O-R-S-E at the basketball hoop attached to his garage or home-run derby, slugging a whiffle ball with a wood bat over the wire fence into the Mc-Culleys' backyard. In early July, his mom, Margie, let us set off firecrackers in their yard.

My mom called John and me "Mutt and Jeff," a reference to cartoonist Bud Fisher's classic comic-strip characters, Augustus Mutt, a tall, greedy, dimwitted racetrack gambler, and Jeff, a half-pint insane-asylum inmate who shared a passion for horse racing. I assume she was joking about our widely disparate statures, as opposed to our wits and sanity.

John introduced me to sleeping out under the stars, first in his backyard and then with Boy Scouts of America Explorer Post 2164. El Ferguson was assistant Scoutmaster of the post that was hosted by the Methodist Church on a treed city block known as Church Square near downtown Cuyahoga Falls. Although Explorer Scouts opened membership to boys upon their 14th birthdays, my connection to John and his dad enabled me to join the post at the age of 13 1/2, which I celebrated on April 14, 1963.

Post 2164's main Scoutmaster was Jerry Zrelak, a much younger man who had risen through the ranks to become an Eagle Scout when he was a teenager. El and Jerry knew a farmer, J. Dalton Williams, in Carroll County, which is situated more than an hour south of Cuyahoga Falls in the Appalachian foothills. The farmer let our post set up camp in a wooded area beyond his cow pasture. To reach the camping spot from the farmhouse at the end of a dirt road, we bumped along a deep-rutted, muddy tractor trail for about a half mile.

Jerry drove a pickup truck. He towed a small trailer that opened up into a tented cooking unit on one end and a two-man, covered sleeping compartment with mattress for the Scoutmasters' comfort on the other. The truck carried our sleeping bags, backpacks and other gear, along with a 10-man canvas tent, in the bed and a couple Explorers inside the cab. El's car followed with six boys crowded in as passengers. I was the youngest and smallest of the bunch.

Before heading for the woods, we filled a couple 10-gallon metal milk cans with well water from the farmer's pump house. There were no facilities at the campsite. Upon arrival, we dug a hole amidst some trees at a downwind distance from our group tent. We'd squat over the hole when necessary. Not far from our site was an old barn where the farmer stored some equipment.

With the exception of that one field trip back in elementary school, when my whole class was amused by two cows "mating," as Mrs. Golub explained it to me and Kevin, this was my first visit to an actual farm. I liked the wooded hills of Carroll County and did my best to sidestep cow pies in the pasture.

Most of the Explorers in our post were 15, 16 and 17 years old. A couple of them previously had spent some time away from home in juvenile detention. Several were known as troublemakers in our neighborhood. Others were just regular roughnecks who generally stayed out of trouble. It was not your usual group of Scouts, to be sure, but Scouting was a welcome diversion from school and the schoolyard. I liked my fellow Explorers, and they all tolerated me just fine.

El and Jerry, the Scoutmasters, gave us the opportunity to get away from our cramped little houses and postage-stamp yards so we could wander through the woods during the day and play mumbletypeg with our jackknives around campfires at night. We were lucky to have their leadership, and we knew it. About half of the guys smoked cigarettes, and the leaders paid it no mind. Although I had given up the habit the previous winter, I wasn't averse to taking a few puffs when the adults weren't looking.

For my inaugural Carroll County camping trip, our post had invited another Explorer post from Akron to join us. They arrived in their separate vehicles. After dinner and cleanup, most of us headed into the woods for flashlight tag. An hour or so later we returned to sip on cups of hot chocolate around the campfire.

John Ferguson, who had warned me in advance about an initiation ritual that I should avoid, pulled me aside. "See that pot bubbling on the right side of the stove," he whispered to me. "That's the safe one." The adults from both posts had already filled their cups. John reached in his pocket and pulled out a half dozen packets of Ex-Lax chewable tablets, which he proceeded to stir into the pot on the left. "This one's for the other post," he said.

The shit hole got plenty of use that night. Our camping guests were not amused when they learned why from big, laughing John the next morning.

Gulf of Tonkin Resolution

Being white boys growing up in an all-white, blue-collar town in Northeast Ohio, we didn't pay much attention to growing unrest spreading across the South in the 1960s. The murder of three civil-rights workers by white supremacists in Mississippi in June 1964 was of little concern to us. When President Lyndon B. Johnson signed the Civil Rights Act of 1964 in July, it was a big deal to racial minorities, but we working-class white kids thought we were part of the privileged majority. Riots that erupted in the black ghettos of Harlem, Bedford-Stuyvesant, Chicago and Philadelphia were a long way from the cheap bungalows of Cuyahoga Falls.

The Gulf of Tonkin, which swoops off the South China Sea between the coast of North Vietnam and Red China's Hainan island, was in another world. We didn't know it then, but what occurred there in the early days of August 1964 had the same profound impact on the lives of white teenage boys in suburban Akron as it did on black teenage boys in Harlem. It wasn't that the Tonkin Gulf showdown between U.S. Navy destroyers and North Vietnamese PT boats in and of itself altered the course of history so much as it was distorted and contorted into concocted legitimacy.

Democrats, led by President Kennedy, who had sent thousands of American ground troops into Vietnam the previous year, and President Johnson, who had been mounting clandestine military attacks against the North and putting plans together for bombing it, were sick and tired of being painted by Republicans as soft on communism. All Johnson needed to seal the deal was some sort of equivalent to a declaration of war.

According to the Pentagon Papers – you know, the U.S. government's official accounting of the war that we, the people, were not supposed to know about – one week before the USS Maddox was attacked by North Vietnamese boats, Hanoi Radio charged that Americans had fired on a North Vietnamese fishing craft. Three days before the attack, Hanoi accused the South Vietnamese of raiding fishing boats in the Tonkin Gulf and, with the protective cover of an American destroyer, bombarding two North Vietnamese islands.

The Pentagon report notes that, when the attack occurred, apparently, the North Vietnamese had mistaken the Maddox for a South Vietnamese vessel. Hanoi later charged that the Maddox had violated its territorial waters, an assertion that the U.S. denied.

Whatever the case, the North Vietnamese made a fateful mistake, because the Maddox sustained no serious damage, while one communist craft was sunk and two others were hit by U.S. aircraft. After this first incident, the Maddox was joined by a second destroyer, the Turner Joy. Within 24 hours, both destroyers reportedly were attacked by North Vietnamese torpedo boats.

There was some dispute over whether the second attacks actually occurred and questions over whether they were provoked. In 2005, after top-secret documents were declassified, John Prados, a National Security Archive research fellow, thoroughly examined the ones relating the Tonkin incident. Among his findings was a 1988 statement by U.S. Air Force Lt. Col. Delmar Lang, who said, "There was no question that the second attack a couple of days later was not an attack."

Nonetheless, within six hours of that supposed second attack – one hell of a fast response, to be sure – retaliatory bombing strikes were ordered against the North. As the Pentagon Papers later revealed, the target list for those strikes had been drawn up three months earlier.

On Aug. 7, Johnson got what he wanted – passage of the Gulf of Tonkin Resolution by the U.S. Congress. It authorized the president to take "all necessary measures to prevent further aggression." Given the anti-communist tenor of national leaders in general and, more particularly, the sword-rattling politicking of Sen. Barry Goldwater, the Republican challenger to Johnson's presidency that fall, whether the Tonkin incident was even needed to expand the war is debatable. Only two senators voted against the resolution, and many among the majority were most willing to believe the Tonkin tale.

It didn't mean diddly to me. I was just as anti-communist as any red-blooded, 14-year-old American boy would be expected to be. Not only that, I was a loyal Republican, even though we didn't talk much politics in my union household, and I would have voted for Goldwater, if I could have. Sharing a birthday with Dwight D. Eisenhower was as good a reason as any to formulate a kid's political ideology.

Major and minor developments

It was around this time that the Lange family became a foster family. My mom said she did it because she just loved little babies. Her four children – me and Vonnie and Danny and Heidi – each had our own beds in the two bedrooms our father had finished upstairs, and we even had our own half bathroom up there. Summer nights could get mighty hot and sticky for us, but nobody had air conditioning. Anyway, there was an extra bedroom on the somewhat cooler main floor. The lady from children's services gave the arrangements her approval, and a few days later she delivered a tiny little thing wrapped in newborn jammies fresh out of the maternity ward. Mom named her Valerie.

Before we knew it, a second one arrived. We named her Melanie. And then a third one – Gregory, I guess. Babies cry a lot. Sometimes they scream for no apparent reason. Even in the middle of the night. They drink a lot of formula from bottles with rubber nipples on them, and they burp and puke and pee and poop, which stinks. When you're 14 years old and learn how to feed them and burp them and try to avoid getting puked on and remove crappy diapers, the contents of which you have to dump in the toilet, and then put fresh ones on while doing your best not to prick the babies' hips with safety pins, which would make them scream – well, I can tell you, I'd rather go to school.

But it was for a good cause. Not only did Mom love babies, but she also got paid for being a foster mom. It wasn't much, but she began saving some money for that college education she had been promised 16 years earlier when her mother put her on a plane out of Berlin.

I headed back to Hoban High School by way of Allan Carlini's house for my sophomore year with a different outlook on life. I liked my teachers. I paid attention some of the time. My grades were looking up. I had disconnected from junior high school's "accelerated" classmates and reconnected with the neighborhood boys I had known since first grade and who had joined the Explorers not long after I did. After a solid summer of workouts and improving times with coach Tod Boyle and Water Works Swim Club, I was looking forward to earning a varsity letter on the Hoban swim team. And sophomores didn't have gym class with Baldacci's damn paddle machine.

Unfortunately, in early October, less than two weeks before my 15th birthday, my mother just had to deflate my high spirits. "I'm taking you to see the pediatrician tomorrow," she told me.

"Who?"

"You know, the children's doctor that has already seen your brother and sisters and given them good checkups," she said.

"I don't need no kids' doctor," I told her. "I'm gonna be 15. I'm not a kid anymore. If I need a shot or stitches or something, Dr. Lewis across the street is fine with me."

"We have an appointment, and you're going after school tomorrow, whether you like it or not."

I didn't lose any sleep over it. The pediatrician's office was on Portage Trail, close to Bolich Junior High School. The physical exam was just fine, other than having to pull my trousers down for the doctor to give an extra checkup to my private parts. Afterward, I was told to have a seat in the waiting room while Mom went into the office for a chat with him.

When we got back to her car out in the lot, she had some bad news and some more bad news for me – although she didn't quite put it that way. "Well," she told me, "the doctor says you haven't started puberty yet." Great, just what I wanted to hear from my mother. My sister Vonnie, on the other hand, who was two years younger than me and who had her physical checkup a week earlier, had indeed reached puberty, Mom informed me. But that was just fine, she said, because girls tend to develop at a younger age than boys. No, it wasn't fine with me.

"Another thing," she said, giving me a look that I suppose was intended to convey comfort and compassion but did no such thing. "Dr. Carlson says you need to have a minor procedure done on your penis."

"What the hell!? I told you I didn't want to come here, Mom."

"It's not a big deal," she said, "and watch your language. When you were first born and got circumcised, the doctor in Pennsylvania didn't quite finish the job. You need another half inch or so of your foreskin snipped."

"The hell I do, Mom! That guy isn't touching my peter again."

"He said it's a good idea for hygiene, especially as you do reach puberty and become more mature," she said. "But you'd think a Jewish doctor like that Dr. Fishkin would have done it right."

Damn it, they should have taken me to a rabbi.

'What Asian boys ought to be doing'

With the presidential campaign in high gear, President Johnson scheduled a stop in Akron on Oct. 21, 1964, and the brothers in charge of Hoban High School decided to let us students out early that day. Being good Catholics who valued our country's first Catholic president and who probably had some partiality toward the policies of inclusion being expanded by his successor, that seemed reasonable.

Because I had been singled out by Brother Donan Johnroe as the second-best student in his French I class, Leo Landoll, a genius who had skipped a grade in elementary school and was the top student in that class and probably all of his classes, had befriended me. Although we both considered ourselves Republicans and surely would have cast our votes for Barry Goldwater two weeks later, if only we could, we thought it would be interesting to catch a glimpse of the president. So we hopped on a city bus on Inman Street, at the foot of the mostly white side of Sumner Hill, and arrived to a bustling downtown in advance of Johnson's arrival. The temperature was 42 degrees, and clouds hung overhead.

According to reports in the Akron Beacon Journal, the leader of the free world and his entourage, including Lady Bird and Texas Gov. John Connally, were greeted by Akron Mayor Edward Erickson, who had declared the date "Lyndon B. Johnson Day," and a crowd of 4,000 at Akron-Canton Airport. Leo and I were part of a much larger throng that made way for the motorcade as it rolled up South Main Street. Johnson himself rode in the very same limousine that had carried John F. Kennedy to his death 11 months earlier in Dallas and in which Connally had been wounded. The newspaper report said the limo "had been refurbished, armored, painted black and topped with a roof."

I had never experienced such a spectacle. As the limo reached our position in the shoulder-to-shoulder gathering outside the six-story O'Neil's department store where my mother had taken me and my siblings to admire the Christmas windows when we were younger, I could see the president inside. Squeezing between some spectators and bouncing around others, I kept pace with Johnson's vehicle. Suddenly, it stopped, and I was right there. I could reach out and touch it, but I didn't. As I stood there in awe, the roof of the limo slid open. The president stood up, waving to the cheering crowd. Then he reached out and began shaking hands, mine being one of them. OK, it wasn't exactly a handshake, but he touched our hands, which was good enough for me. One of the Secret Service guys who had been pacing alongside the motorcade handed me an "LBJ" lapel pin. Not only did I shake the president's hand, but I had proof of it.

From there, the guest of honor headed a few blocks east to the University of Akron, where a thunderous crowd awaited him in Memorial Hall. "I can assure you that your country is the mightiest nation in all the world," Johnson told those who had managed to get inside. "But we do not intend to use that might to bury anyone. And we want all to know and read us loud and clear: We do not intend to be buried, either." No doubt he was referring to our communist adversaries in China and the Soviet Union.

"Sometimes our folks get a little impatient," the president continued, apparently referring to the political rhetoric of his adversaries. "Sometimes they rattle their rockets some, and they bluff about their bombs. But we are not about to send American boys nine or 10,000 miles away from home to do what Asian boys ought to be doing for themselves."

That might have been reassuring to me, if I had Vietnam on my mind, but it was not yet a concern of mine. Johnson went on to repeat the caution by Gens. Dwight Eisenhower and Douglas MacArthur against getting sucked into a land war in Asia. He fantasized about Vietnamese troops being able "to resist aggression," just as long as they could receive proper training from American advisers.

On Nov. 3, two days after four Americans were killed, 72 others were wounded, five bombers were destroyed and 15 others were damaged in a communist mortar attack at the U.S. air base in Bien Hoa, just 20 miles from Saigon, Johnson went on to defeat Goldwater in a presidential election landslide.

Assault in the shower room

At about that time, the Hoban Knights swim team began training for the upcoming season in Akron U's 25-yard competition pool, which happened to be below the hall where Johnson jabbered about not sending American boys to war in Asia. Memorial Hall, including the pool, was built in 1954 and named in honor of the 1,534 GIs from Summit County who had died in World War II. The building was torn down in 2010.

Since Hoban did not have its own pool, the university was one of three places where we traveled for workouts under new swim coach Donald Lippert. I say new, because he had never coached swimming before, nor had he been a swimmer himself. He was built like a football lineman, big and bulky, and his blond hair was cut short like a Marine's. He was a jovial sort and needed only a fake white beard and red suit to take a part-time job as Santa Claus in the middle of swim season. He apparently was reading up on our sport, and it was apparent to me that he had a lot to learn. Under experienced coaches, high school swimmers did not practice their flutter kicks for 10 minutes straight while hanging onto the gutters on the edge of the pool.

The Akron U pool in Memorial Hall, where we practiced twice a week, was less than a mile and a half northwest of Hoban High School, as the bird flies. One day a week we used the pool in the basement of the nursing school at Akron City Hospital, which was about the same distance, only directly north and just east of the Route 8 expressway. When we arrived there early, we could wander into a paneled conference room where human fetuses in various stages of growth floated in large glass jugs of formaldehyde. It was a long walk to either the university or the nursing school, so, more often, we'd ride city buses or catch a lift with somebody's parent.

Our third practice location, two days per week, was at Harvey S. Firestone High School, named after the founder of one of the Rubber City's major corporations. It had opened just a year earlier and had a beautiful swimming pool, complete with stadium-like spectator seating along one side. Located on Akron's far northwest end, getting there involved making a bus connection downtown. The surrounding neighborhood is the city's most affluent section. The school is just a few blocks from Stan

Hywet, originally a 3,000-acre estate where F.A. Seiberling, founder of the Goodyear Tire and Rubber Co., built Ohio's largest mansion between 1912 and 1915.

Prior to the opening of Firestone High School, many of the city's best swimmers had attended the more urban Buchtel High School, which had won the state team swimming championship in 1963. More state championships were about to go Firestone's way in 1966 and 1969 and then again in 1982 and 1983.

About 25 guys went out for the Hoban team that November. As a sophomore, I was the shortest and skinniest guy on the team, even smaller than the freshmen, including John Sullivan, a red-headed kid whom I knew quite well from Water Works Swim Club. A freestyle and backstroke specialist, John stood out as the team's best swimmer from the get-go. Dave Belitsky, a tall, well-muscled junior who also swam the backstroke, wasn't far behind. John Ragsdale, a senior who had a phenomenal start off the blocks, was our top sprinter.

With my versatility in all four strokes, especially the breaststroke, coach Lippert penciled me in as our top competitor in the individual medley. That gave me a good deal of respectability among my teammates, even though I was the only one whose voice hadn't at least started to change and probably the only one whose pediatrician recently informed his mother that he hadn't yet reached puberty.

At least I wasn't the only one who kept his Speedo on in the showers after workouts. The showers at Firestone were much like those adjacent to the gyms at Hoban and Sill schools, the Falls Y and others that I knew well. They had about a half dozen shower heads lined up on each of two facing tiled walls. There was nothing private about them.

Allan Carlini, also keeping his private parts covered with his swimsuit, and I were soaping ourselves down under hot streams of water. We were alone for a couple minutes before two seniors, Mark Barnett and Ron Finney, stepped into the steamy room, twisted their faucets to the hot settings and whipped off their trunks.

"Hey, Car-peni," Barnett said with a snicker to Allan, who was about 6 feet tall and had hints of dark whiskers sprouting from his chin and upper lip but was not the aggressive type. "You swim like a little girl. You ought to get a girlie tank suit and cover your nipples up. Ha-ha-ha!" Allan didn't respond. Sheepishly, he shut off his shower and turned toward the locker room. But Finney blocked his way. Barnett knocked him onto the shower floor, kicked him back down as he tried to get up, put a foot on his chest and then urinated on him. Allan was bigger than they were, but he was physically overwhelmed as he wriggled to escape from the humiliating assault.

I just stood there in disbelief, didn't lift a finger to defend him, didn't call out for help, never told the coach or anybody else.

Allan and I didn't speak as we walked past sprawling ranch houses and sturdy colonials with pillared entryways between the pool and the bus stop on West Market Street. I had never been inside a house as large as every one we passed. We were quiet when we got off in front of the O'Neil's store on Main Street. Fifteen minutes later, our bus to Cuyahoga Falls arrived. We sat together in silence as the bus traveled north, crossed the high-level bridge to State Road, turned east at Broad Boulevard and dropped us off at Fourth Street, where it headed toward Sackett Avenue and its return route to Akron. Not a word was said about the ugly incident on our walk across Front Street and the downtown business district, over the Cuyahoga River bridge and railroad tracks, past the Summit County Receiving Hospital for mentally ill patients and back to our neighborhood.

There would be no more swim practices and no more showers afterward at Firestone High School or anywhere else for Allan Carlini. I don't know whether he told his parents why he quit the team. I never asked. I just tried to forget about my failure to stand up for him.

Aside from my early competition in the YMCA league and 11-and-12-year age group in AAU, before most other boys quickly outgrew me, my sophomore season at Hoban was the epitome of my swimming career. Other than Firestone, Cuyahoga Falls and Buchtel, the Akron City Swimming League was not packed with state-caliber competition. The best inner-city athletes tended to excel on the floors of basketball courts and grass of gridirons rather than in the chlorinated water of swimming pools.

In our first meet, we overwhelmed Akron North, 70-6, winning both the freestyle and medley relays and taking first and second places in all seven individual events. I won the 200-yard freestyle and 200 individual medley, which consists of 50-yard legs for butterfly, backstroke, breaststroke and freestyle.

The following Monday, my health teacher, James Haines, who also was an assistant track coach, asked at the beginning of class whether I was the Lange listed as a double winner in the results reported in Sunday's Beacon Journal. I nodded and said, "Yes," my voice crackling into a high pitch, which brought laughter through the room. "That's me all right." This time the words came out in an undulation of high and low tones, causing more snickers. I could feel my face redden with a torrid rush of blood. Chuckling, Haines congratulated me on my success, which seemed to impress some of my classmates and eased my embarrassment.

The Hoban Knights went 7-5 that swim season, also knocking off Akron Garfield, Hower, East, Kenmore, Central and Coventry – with me winning the IM all but once in our victories. Our losses came against Firestone, Falls, Buchtel and two exclusive private schools, Western Reserve Academy in Hudson and Gilmour Academy in Gates Mills.

Among our team losses, I still won the IM against Buchtel and Firestone – the latter being a result of legendary coach Dick Wells taking us too lightly and letting his top swimmers sleep in that Saturday. After my IM victory and our sprinters' wins in the 50 and 100 freestyle events pulled us within eight points against the team that was gearing toward a state championship, a worried Wells dispatched his assistant to a pay phone in the hall. With the city league running five dual meets concurrently, that gave two of Firestone's better swimmers living close by enough time to grab their suits and hurry over to the pool. They won the backstroke and breaststroke events and built a 12-point cushion before we took the final event, the freestyle relay, and pulled within 41-36 for the final score. Despite swimming against mostly backups, coming that close to Firestone and putting my name in the victory column for Hoban made me proud.

That night I awoke from a strange yet pleasurable dream and encountered a sensation akin to the one I had felt on the roller coaster at Geauga Lake Park, my stomach lurching to my chest and my breath aerating my brain. Only this one emanated from below my abdomen, ejected a warm quiver between my legs and sent a ravishing shiver to my extremities. I felt the front of my pajama pants, which was slobbery wet and reminded me of those oozing frogs that were stuck together and which I had carried home from the pond in the Big Woods some years earlier.

I just had an unusual dream, and I was wet. I put two plus two together. So that was one of those nocturnal emissions my meddling mother had questioned me about after gossiping with Bruce Horstler's mom. Maybe I was two or three years behind schedule, but, yes, puberty was coming on. That pediatrician could go fuck himself. I went back to sleep with a smile on my face.

Uppercut of global reality

On the other side of the world in early 1965, there were no moral victories. On Feb. 6, eight Americans were killed and 126 were wounded in a Viet Cong attack at the U.S. military base in Pleiku, located in South Vietnam's Central Highlands. That prompted President Johnson to order bombing in North Vietnam the next day. On Feb. 10, the VC blew up a U.S. barracks, killing 23 Americans in the coastal city of Qui Nhon.

Like most high school boys, I was more interested in the upcoming heavyweight boxing rematch between the world champion, Muhammad Ali, and Sonny Liston, from whom he had won the title a year earlier and subsequently shucked his given name, Cassius Clay. It would be another two years before Ali's refusal to be conscripted into the military jolted kids like me with an uppercut of global reality. The confluence of sports, which always had our attention, and a war that was killing American boys not much older than us but had been raging below our misdirected radar, soon would be coming into focus.

Chapter 7 | **Misadventures Near and Far**

It was spring 1965, a warm, sunny Saturday morning in Carroll County. Jerry Zrelak and John Ferguson were filling the metal water jugs in Farmer Williams' pump house. Glen Barnhouse, Mike Kensinger and I were goofing around outside, circling the pickup that was parked in the dirt driveway between the farmhouse and barn, hopping in and out of the truck bed. Mimicking chickens clucked, strutted and fluttered nearby. Ronny Hughes sat in the cab. There were no seat belts. Nobody would have worn them anyway. Patience being his virtue, Ronny waited for the return jaunt across the pasture to our campsite.

Ronny didn't say much. He was developmentally disabled, although we didn't use such terminology in 1965. He had a flat nose and squinty eyes on a round head that was connected to his shoulders with a short, thick neck. He was hefty and not too tall. He lived on Myrtle Avenue near Price Elementary School, but we never saw him in school. When we'd first known him as a fixture in the schoolyard during city-run summer recreation programs, he had been taller than the other kids, but we outgrew him. He watched us play but didn't join in. He wasn't very mobile. We didn't know for sure how old he was.

We knew Ronny was retarded, but we were more likely to call each other retards than direct that offensive term toward him. Not unlike the unconventional Scouts who had been welcomed to Explorer Post 2164 in the past, for Ronny, camping was an experience he otherwise could not have had. That was a tribute to the leadership of Jerry Zrelak and El Ferguson.

The post had changed dramatically since I joined two years earlier. Other than John Ferguson and the Shumway brothers, Kenny and Billy, the older guys had moved on. John liked to say, "There's the right way, the wrong way and the Shumway." With the addition of Glen, Mike, Kenny Chrzanowski and Roger Smith, Post 2164 was going strong. The five of us worked on merit badges and were advancing through the Scouting ranks.

For Glen and me, it was another chapter in a long history of competition. Our frequent wrestling bouts as disagreeing 6-year-olds in front yards along Suncrest Drive generally ended in reluctant truces as we lay out of breath in interlocking bear hugs and then went our separate ways in grass-stained trousers and T-shirts. Our alternating assignments on the pitchers' mound as 12-year-olds for the Angels baseball team ended with Glen being voted to the all-star team but not me.

Leaning against a rear fender of the pickup truck in Farmer Williams' long, dusty, sloped drive, I felt a sudden lurch. I stepped back, glanced through the driver's side window and saw Ronny Hughes' eyes widen. I looked down the rutted driveway behind the truck, which started to roll. A straight shot in that direction would take it some 100 yards downhill toward a clump of trees, where it surely would meet with a metal-and-bone-crunching thud. The slightest turn of the wheels would swerve the truck into a lumpy pasture, where it surely would roll over and eject its terrorized passenger through the windshield or side window before he was crushed beneath three tons of twisted steel.

"Holy shit!" I yelled and turned toward the driver's side door. Glen was already there. Yanking the door open, he leapt onto the driver's seat and stomped his foot on the brake. The truck had moved no more than 10 feet before it stopped. Jerry came running out of the pump house, quickly reached inside the cab to put the stick shift back in first gear, scooted Glen aside and yanked the emergency brake into the position where it was supposed to be. After watching his life heading toward a violent end, whether he knew it or not, Ronny sank back in the passenger seat.

I knew it was Glen's heroic reaction that saved the day. Jerry and John finished filling the water jugs. We lugged them into the bed of the truck. John, Glen, Mike and I held onto them as we took the jerky ride back to camp.

After eating lunch cooked on the white-gas-fired stove, the guys from our neighborhood, minus Ronny Hughes, headed down a trail that took us to the old barn. We climbed up to the rafters, tiptoed over sturdy wooden beams and went airborne into the hayloft.

"You're it!" Glen said, tapping Mike on the shoulder and then scurrying over to a ladder, where he descended to the main floor. I straddled a beam well out of reach on the opposite side of the barn. Roger made a run for it, but Mike caught up and tagged him "it." Eventually, Roger found Kenny hiding in one of the stalls on the lower level, and Kenny managed to corner Glen in the hayloft. I was still up top, observing from a safe perch, but Glen was determined to put the tag on me. I managed to elude him as we maneuvered from one narrow beam to another and back and forth across the upper reaches of the barn – until I found myself at a dead end. "I got you now," he said, closing in fast.

There was nowhere to go but down. I saw some bales of hay stacked below and took a flying leap. What I didn't take into account was the rusty old manure spreader parked next to those bales, which is where I tumbled after making a cushioned landing. I felt a sharp twinge as a metal tine gouged my right thigh. I saw another one of the pointed protrusions barely an inch from my groin. A third one pressed against my abdomen. Delicately, I dragged myself out of the stationary machine and stumbled out of the barn into the sunlight. A small patch of blood oozed onto my upper pant leg, but there was no hole in the material. With my arms spread across Glen's and Mike's shoulders, I limped back to our campsite.

It wasn't until then, with both Scout leaders and eight or nine Explorers gathered around, that I dropped my trousers to assess the damage. There were a few gasps, but nobody looked away. The gash was 4 inches long and three-quarters of an inch wide. Through the slushy conglomeration of mangled muscle and fat, we could see the bone. Fortunately, there was no gush of blood. El went over to the supplies, opened the first-aid kit and grabbed a package of gauze to cover the wound.

"We need to get you into town and find a doctor to stitch that up," Jerry said. He told Billy Shumway to go with us. We hopped in the front seat of El's car for the 5-mile drive to Carrollton. With two hands, Billy kept pressure on the gauze. "Don't worry, Dave," he said as we negotiated the bumpy trail through pasture and headed toward the road. "You're not going to die." I was not particularly relieved to hear that optimistic prognosis.

We located a doctor with an office in his house on a residential street in Carrollton. His waiting room was empty, so he took me right in. I pulled off my trousers but not my underwear. He applied antiseptic and injected my thigh with anesthetic. A few minutes later, I watched his sturdy needle pull a thread from one fleshy side of my wound to the other 13 times. Lucky for me, other than numbness, I didn't feel a thing. The doctor bandaged me up, collected our data on the Boy Scouts insurance policy and sent us on our way. I didn't play any more tag on that camping trip.

Our Sunday-morning ritual was always the same. Not long after sun-up the Scoutmasters would open the flaps to our group tent and yell inside, "Rise up, Explorers. Let's get ready to roll." Moaning and groaning, we'd respond, "Go away. It's too early." We didn't know what time it was, only that it was too early. Ten minutes later that scenario would be repeated. On the third or fourth go-round, Jerry, with some assistance from Kenny Shumway, would grab the feet of our sleeping bags and drag them outside, one by one, leaving the human contents to slide out onto the tent's floor. With sleeping bags strewn on the bare ground and us Explorers still lying inside in various stages of consciousness and undress, the tent stakes would be pulled, and the canvas enclosure would collapse upon us. It was time to get up for pancakes and bacon.

After breakfast, we packed up our gear and headed to town, smelly and dirty but smartly attired in our Scout uniforms. Jerry drove the pickup truck, carrying a handful of Catholics, including Kenny Chrzanowski, to a church named for one of the saints. The rest of us crammed in a couple cars with El and Kenny Shumway at the wheels and arrived at a Methodist church. We never missed church on Sunday, although we Protestants experienced some variety. It could be a Presbyterian church in Loudonville when we camped in the rocky river valley of Mohican State Park or a Lutheran church in Wellington after we pulled up stakes beneath towering pines at Findley State Park.

More often than not, the Williams farm in Carroll County was our camping destination. Friday night treks with our flashlights into the woods for "snipe hunts" or other investigations were a highlight. Usually, we'd be back to camp in time for hot chocolate, but not always.

The sun was sinking toward the treed hills in the west as Glen, Mike, Kenny, Roger and I hiked down the dirt drive where Ronny Quinn had nearly met his maker two months earlier. We skirted Tabor Lake, a small reservoir encircled with tiny cottages, as hazy darkness enveloped our surroundings. Onward we went into densely grown forest. The crescent moon and stars in the unclouded sky above were obscured by a thick canopy of stately oaks and their broad-leaved brethren. Prickers grabbed at our trousers. Low-hanging branches snapped at our faces.

The beams from our flashlights revealed splintered stumps and downed limbs whose crashing falls had gone unheard but were ready to trip up unwary intruders. Poison ivy clinging to tree trunks was itching for some human contact. Aside from the in-and-out glimpses of the moon, our gradually dimming beams were the only signs of light in our wooded world.

"I think maybe we better turn back," Kenny said after an hour of our slow and disorienting hike. "Did anybody bring a compass?" Afraid not. We made an about-face, at least we thought we did, with Mike leading instead of bringing up the rear. Another hour passed as we kicked away prickers and dodged branches. Still no lights in sight, only the flashlight beams straining for juice from weakening batteries.

"We're like that Indian tribe, the Fockowwee," Roger said. "Right, we're the Fockowwee. Where the fuck are we?" Kenny replied. "We're the Fockowwee, we're the Fockowwee," we all chimed in as we trudged onward, who knows where.

Finally, we saw a glimmer in the distance. Twenty minutes later we found the porch light at an otherwise dark, solitary house next to a paved country road. It was well after midnight. There was no traffic. None. We followed the pavement, a sure sign of civilization, for about a mile before we recognized the narrow lane that passed the small lake and led to Farmer Williams' dirt drive.

It was 3:30 a.m. when we got back to the campsite. A few embers flickered amidst the ashes of what had been the campfire. A cold pot of what had been hot chocolate sat on the stove. The Scoutmasters were fast asleep in the relative comfort of the trailer. Our fellow Explorers were still as the night inside the tent. Quietly, the five of us crawled into our sleeping bags. We were the last ones to wake up Saturday morning. The sausages were cold, but plenty of eggs were left to be fried – over easy for me. Roger and I had cleanup duty.

In addition to camping and working on merit badges together, the five "We're the Fockowwee" hikers from my neighborhood began connecting in social get-togethers that included members of the opposite sex. The girls were Mike Kensinger's sister, Joanie, who was two years younger than us, and four of her friends. The parties were held periodically in our group's various living rooms, where potato chips, pretzels and Lawson's chip dip were provided, music was played on the phonograph, and we took turns slow dancing with each other – except Mike did not dance with his sister. Although there was no making out, not even kissing, at least not that I knew of, the significance of this, to me, as I headed toward my junior year of high school, was that I definitely liked girls, and I was convinced that they liked me back.

Fairways and rough ways

Also that spring, my Hoban buddy Leo Landoll told me that Lake Forest Country Club in Hudson, which was about 10 miles from my house in Cuyahoga Falls and about half that distance from his house in Stow, could use some more caddies. It was my first real opportunity to earn some money. My mom drove me to Lake Forest on Saturday and Sunday mornings. She'd pick me up at the end of the day, after I signaled her from a pay phone with collect calls that she declined to accept. After school let out in June, I spent most afternoons after swim practice on the golf course. On a good weekend day, I could earn as much as $13 or even $14 for lugging a pair of golf bags on two 18-hole rounds.

Lake Forest was known as a Jewish country club. I heard that, even in the 1960s, anti-Semitic exclusions were common in some of the other clubs. Regardless, club memberships tended to come from the professional class. Wednesday was known as "Doctors Day," being that many men of the medical profession took that afternoon off. The golf course was plenty busy each Wednesday. Lake Forest members had names like Manny and Marvin. In fact, a "Mannys Day" tournament with several foursomes was held each year.

Most of the caddies at Lake Forest Country Club came from white, working-class families in neighborhoods like mine, and some of them I knew from growing up in Cuyahoga Falls. A few guys came from the small enclave north of Hudson known as Twinsburg Heights, which was settled by African-Americans in the 1920s and where residents had been intimidated by the Ku Klux Klan in its early years. Homes there didn't have running water until the 1970s. Some black kids who earned money caddying also came from towns like Oakwood Village and Bedford, which are closer to Cleveland than to Akron.

The two races tended to stick to their own kind, but we couldn't avoid each other in the caddy shack, where we waited to be called up front by the caddy master in the morning and took breaks around lunchtime. It was the first time in my life that I had actual interracial interactions. Some of them were better than others. When a loud, spiteful black kid grabbed the bologna-and-mustard sandwich my mom had made for me, I got a bad taste for race relations.

On another day, I was assigned to the same foursome as a black kid named Roosevelt Barnes. I learned that we both were Cleveland Indians fans and both had been serious baseball players prior to our teenage years. Our fathers were factory workers. Neither one of us figured that we'd ever become members of an exclusive country club. I had more in common with Roosevelt than I did with the Mannys' and Marvins' kids who arrived at Lake Forest in Lincoln Continentals, lounged around the club's swimming pool, played on the tennis courts and had dinner served by black waiters onto white tablecloths in the clubhouse.

As a caddy, I learned about the game of golf, distinguished the good players from those with high handicaps, got to know the pine-treed 150-yard markers and observed the swings that tended to slice and those that hooked. I determined which men could reach the green of a 150-yard par-3 hole with a 7-iron and which women would need a driver from the closer tee. I could judge which way and how much the ball would break on the putting greens. I was happy to caddy for couples who gave me a dollar tip. And I knew which "schmucks" – a term I picked up from the male club members – had no appreciation for good caddies.

Monday was "Caddy Day." The club was closed, and caddies were welcome to play as many holes as we wanted for free. I figured I'd give it a try. My dad arranged for me to borrow a set of clubs from one of his friends at the Ford plant, and my mom agreed to drop me off. When I arrived, I joined some of the other caddies on the practice green and got a feel for actual putting, which had some similarity to miniature golf. When a couple guys invited me to join them on the first tee, I declined, thinking I'd better get some practice without witnesses. After all, I'd never swung a wood or an iron before.

So I headed by myself to the 10th hole, a relatively short par 4. The tee was elevated from the fairway. About 20 yards to the left but off the course itself, Lake Forest, covered in lily pads, measured about three-eighths of a mile from one end to the other.

I teed up one of the golf balls I had collected from the weeds that gobbled up errant shots from the tees and fairways on the front nine. I wrapped my fingers around the driver's rubber grip, took a stance like I had seen so many golfers do, swiveled my hips for my backswing and let the club head rip. Whoosh! I whiffed. I tried it again. Whump! The club hit the closely clipped turf and dug up a hefty chunk of sod that flew up in the air as my ball dribbled off the tee and into the rough below. I scurried downhill, retrieved the ball from the shaggy, damp grass and set it back on my tee.

"Good thing nobody's here to see this," I said to myself, but I was determined to send that golf ball straight ahead to the well-groomed fairway. So I took another mighty swing. Another whiff. This time the grip slipped from my moist hands. The driver went flopping through the air like the blades of a helicopter, not straight ahead but off to my rear. Splash! I watched it sink into the lake 10 yards from shore.

Laughter erupted behind the tee. "Lange, that was the worst shot I've seen all summer." It was Rick Morgan, a kid I knew from baseball, with two other guys from the Falls. I didn't have time to disagree or even explain that I'd never played the stupid game of golf before. I ran down to the lake, kicked off my tennis shoes and waded in amidst the lily pads, tadpoles, frogs, lizards, snakes and whatever else might be slithering below the surface. My bare feet shuffled through the muck, my toes feeling for the sunken club. I squatted down into the murky, 3-foot depths to pull up sticks and other hard objects, but no driver was to be found.

I had some explaining to do at home that evening, and, to my surprise, both of my parents found some humor in my woeful tale. "It's just a cheap set of clubs that Sam bought used," my father told me, "and he doesn't play much golf anyway." Dad took me to Miracle Mart, the bargain store with cluttered aisles and stacked shelves on State Road, where I was able to replace his friend's driver for one day's caddy pay.

Inconvenient facts exposed

In July of 1965, President Johnson announced that the U.S. military would be increasing its presence in Vietnam from 75,000 to 125,000 men and that the military draft would be more than doubled from 17,000 to 35,000 men per month. With news of the war being delivered to our doorsteps every afternoon and pictured on the black-and-white television screens in our living rooms each evening, even a 15-year-old kid who liked camping trips, dancing with 13- and 14-year-old girls and, yes, pleasant dreams could no longer ignore its unpleasantness.

In August, CBS television correspondent Morley Safer and his Vietnamese cameraman reported on a raid by U.S. Marines on a village called Cam Ne, which intelligence sources had identified as a base for Viet Cong fighters. By the time the Marines arrived, according to the report, which was visually confirmed by the camera work, the enemy was gone. The total absence of resistance did nothing to forestall an onslaught of rockets, machine-gun fire, grenades and flame throwers. As sobbing old Vietnamese men and women begged for mercy, their huts and rice supplies were torched and destroyed.

"This is what the war in Vietnam is all about," Safer reported to the nation. "The Viet Cong were long gone. The action wounded three women, killed one baby, wounded one Marine and netted four old men as prisoners. Today's operation is the frustration of Vietnam in miniature. To a Vietnamese peasant whose home means a lifetime of backbreaking labor, it will take more than presidential promises to convince him that we are on his side."

Johnson, who told the Akron crowd 10 months earlier that he was "not about to send American boys ... to do what Asian boys ought to be doing for themselves," was incensed, not about what he had sent American boys to do but that the American citizens learned about it. He ordered an investigation of Morley Safer as a possible communist – apparently because reporting inconvenient facts was a matter of disloyalty.

I knew nothing then about the frustration that American boys were experiencing in Vietnam. How could I?

As the start of school approached, I told my parents that I wanted to transfer to Cuyahoga Falls High School. My best friends all were there, I told them. I had known them since first grade. They were not juvenile delinquents. They were different from the guys I'd hung out with in junior high school. My grades were good, and I promised to keep them up. It went without saying that Hoban was an all-boys school. I didn't mention that I liked girls. My parents relented. A year and a half of Catholic schooling had been good for me, but I was returning to public education.

As I marked my 16th birthday and thought about learning to drive that October, anti-war protests were mounting across the country and getting attention from the news media. Tens of thousands of people, many of them college students, marched in Berkeley, California, and downtown New York City. Other mass protests were held in Philadelphia, Boston and Ann Arbor, Michigan, home to the University of Michigan.

On Oct. 15, the day after my birthday, David Miller, a 22-year-old member of the Catholic Worker Movement, conservatively dressed in a gray suit, burned his draft card in a public display of opposition in New York City. He was the first person to be prosecuted under a new law that made destruction of Selective Service registration certificates a federal crime. He was arrested and sentenced in early 1966 to three years in prison. His appeal to the U.S. Supreme Court on the grounds of freedom of speech was denied.

On Nov. 2, Norman Morrison, a 31-year-old member of the pacifistic Quaker religion and a graduate of the College of Wooster, 25 miles southwest of Akron, handed his 1-year-old daughter to someone in the crowd outside Secretary of Defense Robert McNamara's office in the Pentagon. In apparent emulation of the self-immolation by Buddhist monk Thic

Quang Duc in downtown Saigon 2 1/2 years earlier, Morrison doused himself from a gallon jug of kerosene and lit himself on fire. In a letter to his wife, he had written, "Know that I love thee ... but I must go to help the children of the priest's village."

One week later, Roger LaPorte, a 22-year-old member of the Catholic Worker Movement and former seminarian, set himself ablaze in front of the United Nations building in New York City. Asked the question, "Why?" before dying in the hospital from second- and third-degree burns that covered 95 percent of his body, he replied, "I'm against war, all wars. I did this as a religious action (against) all the hatred of the world."

Apparently, Buddhists, Quakers and Catholics, at least some of them, held common religious beliefs in their opposition to war, at least this one.

By the end of 1965, America had 184,000 men in Vietnam. More than 1,900 of them died that year, nearly five times the number that had been lost since Richard B. Fitzgibbon Jr., a member of the Military Assistance Advisory Group, was the first one killed there nine years earlier. He wasn't KIA, killed in action, though; he was murdered by a fellow American serviceman. America had seen nothing yet.

Better news on home front

Despite the shocking news that seemed to get worse by the day, junior year was going well for me. Not that I paid much attention in class, but I did complete most required assignments, and I made the high honor roll at school.

Ohio High School Athletic Association rules penalized me with a year of ineligibility because of my school transfer. I still was able to train before and after school under my longtime coach Tod Boyle, who somehow was able to work a squad of 30 high school boys into top competitive shape in the undersized 20-yard, four-lane Falls Y pool, the only indoor swimming facility available to us.

Because the men's locker room there was being cleaned during our 6 a.m. workouts and because the Y wasn't open to the public at that early hour, we used the women's locker room. Unlike all the wide-open shower rooms I had known in my young life, it was interesting to note the individual shower stalls with curtains that were provided for the other gender. Apparently, women and girls had greater privacy rights than men and boys.

During Explorer Post 2164's Court of Honor that winter, Glen Barnhouse and I received our Eagle Scout awards. My mom had sewn 27 merit badges on my sash. According to the National Eagle Scout Association, only about 5 percent of all Boy Scouts earn the organization's highest honor. Glen and I joined the likes of then-future President Gerald Ford, astronaut James Lovell, actor Jimmy Stewart and television anchorman Walter Cronkite.

In early 1966, after being a loving foster home to more than two dozen babies, some of them for four or five months before we had to give them up to their adoptive parents, who would give them new names and new lives, my mother said she couldn't take it anymore. She loved them too much. She wanted to keep each one of them, watch them learn to walk and talk and go to school and someday grow up, but she had to let them go. So Mom and Dad quit being foster parents and adopted a cute baby girl that February. They named her Wendy. About 15 months later they would adopt a second baby girl and name her Tammy. My brother, Danny, and I wondered what they had against boys.

Collateral damage hits close to home

One of my mom's closest friends was the mother of Alauna Redfern, who was born the same day as me and had been in my class at Price Elementary School. Not only did Helga Lange and Wanda Redfern get together in each other's kitchens to drink coffee and gossip about who knows what for hours on end, but the Langes and Redferns both were avid members of local square-dance clubs. Wanda and her husband, Bill, whom my mother said was prone to answer his phone, "Joe's Whore House" or with some other quip that amused her, had three sons. The oldest was Ken, whom I didn't know very well. Tom was two years ahead of Alauna and me in school, and I knew him as the best fastball pitcher in town. Playing catch with him during my baseball days was a real thrill. Mike Redfern, a nice kid, was my sister Vonnie's age.

"Oh, my God!" my mother practically screamed a few seconds after the phone rang. "Is he alive?" she asked. "Where is he?" She listened for a few more seconds. "Is Wanda there with him?" Then she hung up.

I went into the kitchen from the living room, where I had been reading "Black Like Me." The diary was written by journalist John Howard Griffin, who had his white skin temporarily darkened and traveled through Southern states to explore what it was like to be a black man in segregationist society. "What's the matter, Mom? What happened?"

"Bill Redfern shot himself, and it doesn't look good," she said. Her face had turned whiter than usual. She shook her head.

Shot himself? I wondered. Why would he do that? My dad kept two guns in his closet, the 12-gauge shotgun and the military rifle he had confiscated from Germans after World War II. But they were never loaded. He didn't keep shotgun shells or any other ammunition in the house.

I went back to reading about how the writer Griffin's disguise, effected through rigorous dermatological ingestions and extensive ultraviolet exposure, had gained him the trust of black people, Negroes, as they were called in polite society. It also invoked the condescension and scorn of white people and a ban from public restrooms. As horrible as that experience being conveyed to me in black ink on white pages was, the horror of a man we knew in the flesh and whose red blood had been gushing from a hole in his chest was all too real.

The headline on Page A2 of the Tuesday, March 29, 1966, Beacon Journal read, "Dad Hurt As Deed For Son Backfires." Date-lined Cuyahoga Falls, the story, without a byline, carried this account:

"A father's concern for his soldier son's sore shoulder put Dad in the hospital today in critical condition.

"Army Pvt. Thomas E. Redfern, home on leave before shipping out for Vietnam Sunday, had complained that firing his rifle made his shoulder sore.

"His father, William E. Redfern, 47, of 1436 Anderson (Road) bought Thomas a rubber butt plate for his rifle – but forgot to give it to him before Thomas left.

"Writing Thomas a letter Monday, the father mentioned the butt plate and then apparently decided to try it out.

"Police said Redfern was trying to pull the butt plate onto a 20-gauge shotgun when the gun discharged into his chest. Redfern is in the intensive care unit at St. Thomas Hospital, Akron."

That Friday, three days later, again on Page A2, in reporting Bill Redfern's death, the Beacon Journal recounted the events that led up to the terrible end that came on April Fool's Day.

A follow-up story headlined, "How Red Cross Helped In Tragedy," came a month later. A photograph above it showed Tom Redfern and his older brother, Ken, with an American Red Cross caseworker. "Thomas, on his way to Vietnam, was en route to the Army Terminal in Oakland, Cal., when the Red Cross reached him," the Beacon Journal reported. "He is now being routed to Fort Hayes for processing of discharge because he is needed at home. Kenneth, his brother, in the Air Force, was in Puerto Rico when reached by the Red Cross. He has been home on leave and will return to Puerto Rico this week."

I did not yet personally know anyone who had died in the Vietnam War, but now I knew someone who died because of the Vietnam War.

I thought about my friend and neighbor Kenny Chrzanowski's older brother, Ed, who just a year earlier had been camping with the Explorers in Carroll County and now was one of those American boys President Johnson was drafting to do what Asian boys were supposed to do. I wondered when he'd come home. I wondered if he would come home.

Chapter 8 | **Grandpa's Boys**

Leroy Albert Stutzman began his meat-selling business from the back of a truck in the 1930s, at the height – more accurately the bottom – of the Great Depression. With the economy struggling to rebound under President Franklin D. Roosevelt's New Deal, as reported by Steve Wiandt in the Cuyahoga Falls News-Press upon the business's closing in 2010, Stutzman opened a store in his house on Newbury Street, two blocks east of the Cuyahoga River. After operating a couple of small shops – one near the high school and the other near Sill Junior High School – he moved to East Bailey Road and formed a partnership with his son-in-law, Al Marconi, in 1952. That was three years before my parents bought our Heslop bungalow directly across the street from Stutzman's Foodliner.

While it was homey by the standards set by the gigantic supermarkets that came to dominate the grocery business a half-century later and even compared to the A&P and Kroger chains of its time, Stutzman's offered a full line of foodstuffs. Before they quit smoking, it was a convenient place for my parents to replenish their cigarettes and continued to be for me to exchange my dad's empty cases of Blatz beer bottles for full ones. Stutzman was always a meat man, and his store was best known for its butcher department.

From my point of view, Leroy Stutzman was a grumpy old fart who mostly sat around the small, partially enclosed office situated in a front corner of the market, between the cash registers and the produce aisle. But everybody liked his cheerful, outgoing son-in-law. It seemed as though the entire neighborhood was grieving after Al Marconi died of a heart attack in 1965. Al's wife and Leroy's daughter, Dorothy Marconi, took over the store's management for about a year. The Marconis' son, David, fresh out of Mount Union College in Alliance, where he graduated with a degree in sociology, joined his mom in 1966 and pretty much assumed the business leadership.

The biggest news for me that spring was my purchase of a 1960 Volkswagen Beetle for $550, with some assistance from my parents, who arranged for a loan through First National Bank of Akron. Dad helped me learn to operate the transmission with the four-on-the-floor shifter and left-foot clutch pedal. The Beetle, with its four-cylinder, air-cooled engine in the rear, regularly transported me and two or three fellow caddies to Lake Forest Country Club, where I earned enough money to make monthly loan payments and taught myself to play golf with the staggered set of Fernwood clubs I'd received for Christmas.

Knowing that caddying is seasonal work and that those loan payments would be more challenging during the school year, my mother returned from Stutzman's early one evening carrying a paper sack filled with unsalted butter, a slab of unsliced bacon, a gallon jug of milk, fresh green beans and some other items. "Good news," she told me. "You've been hired as a packer. Dave Marconi says you should stop in tomorrow, fill out an application, and you'll start at 4 o'clock." Mom had her ways of getting what she wanted. She didn't even ask me whether I wanted to work at Stutzman's.

I did. I liked earning money, and the minimum wage of $1.25 an hour wasn't all that bad for a kid.

Fifty years later, the notion of increasing the minimum wage was a subject of great political debate. Many liberals, as those who fight for the working class tend to be labeled, favored significant enhancements. They argued that, with the decline of good-paying manufacturing jobs, many heads of households were collecting welfare subsidies from the government at the same time that they were paid pittances for full-time work as fast-food burger flippers, big-box-store cashiers and the like. Conservatively speaking, the opponents of decent wages said, "Tough shit!" Based on inflation, the $1.25-an-hour I was paid as a 16-year-old bag packer converted to nearly $9 an hour in 2016, when the federal minimum wage was a stingy $7.25 per hour. So it goes with corporate welfare. And good luck finding a dependable 6-year-old VW for $550.

I could say that car ownership changed my life. It certainly gave me some independence, much more than I could have had without it. Not many teenagers in my neighborhood had their own cars. It enabled me to go pretty much wherever I wanted and return home at later hours of the night. I could say that beer, to which I was introduced by my old neighbor John Ferguson, who had graduated from high school and turned 18 years old, the legal age for buying the watered-down 3.2-percent-alcohol variety in Ohio, changed my life.

I certainly could say that the Stutzman's job, which enabled me to pay for that car and for beer purchased for me by various 18-year-olds, changed my life. More to the point, perhaps, the Stutzman's job connected me to several fellow part-time workers whom I had known since elementary school. Not only did Ron Chadwell, Gilbert Rice, Marty Harrington and Don Graham pack grocery bags and stock shelves at the grocery store, but they all were members of a group called "Grandpa's Boys." Cuyahoga Falls school officials and police called the group a gang. If it hadn't been for the car and the beer and the job, I suppose I wouldn't have been drawn to Grandpa's Boys. But it was my life, and it was my choice to change it.

Or maybe it wasn't really changing at all. It was the same life of the kid who defecated in a neighbor's sandbox when he was 5, picked fights with classmates and got nabbed by the cops for climbing on the school roof when he was 9, punched Stuart in the nose just as the teacher walked into the class when he was 10, smoked cigarettes and tossed stolen eggs at cars when he was 12. It wasn't rogues who got me into trouble. It was me who was drawn to trouble.

Worst day of my life – so far

Led by future hall-of-fame fullback Jim Brown, the Cleveland Browns had won the National Football League championship in 1964 and lost in the title game the next year. Unfortunately, Brown called it a career after that, but I still had great hopes for the 1966 season.

It was 20 minutes before kickoff on a Sunday in October. My mom was out shopping with the younger kids. My dad, who was reading his paper, sister Vonnie and I were in the living room with the television on. Vonnie's youth group at Redeemer Lutheran Church was scheduled to meet at 1:30 p.m. I was expected to drive her there, but I wasn't about to miss the Browns game.

"Let's get going," I told her.

"Not yet," she said. "It's too early."

"Dad, tell Vonnie that she needs to get going now, so I don't miss the football game," I pleaded.

"No," he said. "The church is locked, and there's nobody there yet to let her in." He was a Pittsburgh Steelers fan. Losers.

"Well, then she'll have to find somebody else to take her," I said.

"The hell she will," Dad growled.

I was steaming. I watched the coin toss. The Browns elected to receive. After a runback near the 30-yard line, the offense went to work and picked up a couple first downs.

"Time to go," Vonnie said.

"Tough luck," I replied. "I was ready to take you before but not now."

"Listen to me," my father yelled. "You get your butt out to your car and drive your sister to the church right now."

"Not gonna happen," I said, standing up in front of the TV with my back toward him and watching the Browns fall short on third down.

I heard the hefty Sunday paper, loaded with advertising, hit the floor. Two footsteps bounded across the room. The fingers of two solid hands latched onto the shoulders of my shirt and ripped it apart down my back. I'd always had quick reflexes and good hand-to-eye coordination, which were ideal for playing second base on my dad's team. They also occurred without consciously thinking through the impending results. I whirled around in the blink of an eye, clenched my right fist and swung a roundhouse that caught my father's nose broadside. I felt a crunch. Blood spurted out like the flush of a urinal. It splattered on the carpeted living-room floor.

Vonnie screamed. I looked at Dad in horror. His jaw dropped in disbelief as he cupped his hand under his chin and tried to catch the gurgling fountain of blood.

I ran up to my bedroom, changed my shirt and grabbed my wallet and jacket. I charged back downstairs, out the front door and across the street to Hanna Pharmacy, where I took a stool at the lunch counter next to Bill Roach. Bill, a well-constructed guy who already had stubbles of whiskers back in ninth grade at Sill School, was widely recognized as the roughest guy at Cuyahoga Falls High School and as leader of Grandpa's Boys. You didn't want to tangle with him.

"Hey, what's going on?" he said.

My body was shaking, but I hoped it wasn't noticeable. "Not good," I replied. "I just had a fight with my dad, and I think I broke his nose."

Bill just shook his head.

If it wasn't the worst day of my life, I didn't know what was. Sure, my father had kicked me in the ass in the middle of the infield after that called strikeout when was I was 11 years old, but I shouldn't have taken that pitch. Besides, it never would have happened if he hadn't cared enough to manage my baseball team. Sure, he made me box with Bruce Horstler in front of my friends, but he did that to instill some confidence in me. And, yes, he had just ripped the shirt off my back, but it was me who had provoked him, and I knew he had a short fuse.

Hell, I knew I should just get out of his way when he was mad – like the time he chased me across the backyard, I jumped over the 4-foot-high, wire fence with him in hot pursuit, but, when he landed behind the neighbors' garage, he slipped in the dewy grass and fell flat on his back. When I sheepishly returned home three hours later, he was sitting in his living-room chair and reading the Beacon Journal as if my lucky escape were ancient history. Something told me, though, that this incident wouldn't be so easily forgotten. And my mom wouldn't be too happy about it either.

Charlie Lange fought the Nazis in World War II. He came back with nagging pains in his lower legs from poor blood circulation that followed haphazard treatment for the severe frostbite he'd suffered in the brutal winter of 1945. Like too many veterans in western Pennsylvania, he bounced from job to job in the struggle to support his young family, as privileged industrialists tossed workers around like so much raw material. After he found steady employment with the Ford Motor Co., he often worked 10 or 12 hours a day, sometimes seven days a week to pay the mortgage, put food on the table and make life better for his children than his was.

I loved my parents. And this was the thanks they got from their rotten son. As I sat there next to Bill, I wondered whether I could ever go home again. I ordered a fountain drink, sipped it slowly through the straw.

We talked about this being our final year of school. He was going out for the wrestling team and wondered whether I'd be on the swim team this winter. I said yes. We were the only two kids among our east-side confederates, including the "We're the Fockowwee" guys, to be varsity athletes.

With the autumn sun setting, Bill left for home. Soon, Mr. Hanna and his employees prepared to close up for the evening. It was time for me to go home and face the music. With his nose heavily bandaged, Dad was watching TV. He didn't speak. The doctor said his nose was broken in two places, Mom told me, her eyes sunken in sadness, not anger. She had cleaned the blood out of the living-room carpet. "There's some spaghetti left over from supper," she said. "Do you want me to heat you some up?" I did.

My parents got over it. I never did.

'Clean-cut, nice-looking boys'

By the time I was inducted into National Honor Society on Nov. 2, 1966, I was involved in some less honorable affairs. Some of them were exposed beneath a 60-point banner headline, "Teen-Age Gang In Falls?" atop the tabloid front page of the Dec. 1 edition of the weekly Falls News, which some years later merged with the competing City Press. "Police, School Officials Had Trouble With Group," the subhead read.

The story recounted "a fight at the Hullabaloo between Falls youths and Cleveland teens" a few weeks earlier and "two fights at Lions Park which resulted in one boy going to the hospital with a broken jaw." I was present for both altercations, although I hadn't thrown or been hit with any punches before the Cleveland teens high-tailed it back north on Route 8 and had only cheered on one fighter at Lions Park.

"The common denominator in each case is a teenage gang, most of whom are students at Cuyahoga Falls High School," the story continued.

"They go by the name of Grandpa's Boys."

According to the account, to which no byline was assigned, the name of the group came from the deaf and blind grandfather of one of the members and in whose east-side home the grandson and some friends had partied and played hooky from school. Cuyahoga Falls truancy officer Malcolm Anderson told the paper the group had given him plenty of headaches the previous year. After Grandpa died over the summer, those problems had diminished, he said, but he was aware of the group's involvement in fights and heavy drinking.

"You would never realize some of these boys are part of the gang," Anderson said. "They're clean-cut, nice-looking boys that you would probably like if your daughter brought one home. They are not the typical hood element."

However, more than a half dozen students were interviewed about Grandpa's Boys by the reporter. "And many of them are frightened." One boy said he went to a Catholic Youth Organization dance at Lions Park and left as soon as he saw some of the gang members there. Another told the reporter that they carried knives, and some even had guns. A girl said they were "bad actors" who could be identified by their green-and-black flannel jackets.

The distinctive jackets were being sold for about $5 apiece at the JC Penney store in State Road Shopping Center. All the Grandpa's Boys who worked at Stutzman's had them. Nobody else in the Falls would dare to wear one around town and certainly not to school.

Bill Roach didn't have a job yet. But, as he and I again sat at the lunch counter sipping Cokes and sniffing the greasy aroma of a burger frying on the griddle at Hanna Pharmacy, he said his prospects were good. "Hey, Dave, can I borrow five bucks so I can buy me one of the Grandpa's Boys jackets?" he asked. "I got my application in here, and Mr. Hanna says he'll have a job for me in a few weeks. I can pay you back after I start working."

Having Bill Roach as your friend gave you a good deal of respect at school, at least in my mind, and being associated with Grandpa's Boys struck fear in the hearts of some students, at least according to the front-page newspaper story. I'd been hanging out with the boys, drinking beer with them, standing around, cracking jokes and looking tough at the Hullabaloo and Lions Park dances and otherwise having the kind of fun that other teenagers expected from "bad actors." But I had not been one of the guys that attracted the truancy officer to Grandpa's house, and nobody told me that I was actually a member of the gang. "Sure, Bill," I said. "I'll lend you five bucks. So, can I get one of those jackets for myself also?"

"Yeah," he said.

So I did.

Mom woke us up for school the next morning. Dad was long gone for the day shift at Ford. The AM radio was on, as it was every morning.

"Fighting soldiers from the sky. Fearless men who jump and die. Men who mean just what they say. The brave men of the Green Beret." Staff Sgt. Barry Sadler's hit single, "Ballad of the Green Beret," was playing, as it had been every day for months.

I poured myself a bowl of Cheerios. Mom cooked a pot of Quaker Oatmeal for my brother and sisters. I hated hot cereal. I spilled some cold whole milk over my Cheerios.

"Back at home a young wife waits. Her Green Beret has met his fate. He has died for those oppressed. Leaving her his last request."

"Put silver wings on my son's chest. Make him one of America's best. He'll be a man they'll test one day. Have him win the Green Beret."

Barry Sadler was nine years older than me. He had earned his silver wings as a U.S. Army Special Forces Green Beret. He was on patrol in the Central Highlands of South Vietnam in 1965 when he slipped off a narrow trail and encountered a feces-covered punji stick, one of the various booby traps that Viet Cong guerrillas planted for their unwelcome visitors. The spearhead-sharpened bamboo stake sliced a nasty gash in his knee, which resulted in a virulent infection and his evacuation to the Philippines, where military doctors saved his life. During his recuperation, Sadler collaborated with writer Robin Moore, a World War II veteran, to pen the lyrics in honor of Army Spc. 5 James Gabriel Jr., who had been killed by the VC in 1962.

Moore also wrote a book called "The Green Beret," upon which the 1968 film of the same name, starring John Wayne, was based.

The mournful harmony of the music, coupled with the gallant lyrics of the song, was uplifting to the American spirit of sacrifice "for those oppressed." It made boys like me dream about heroism. It made refugees like my mom, who knew too well the horrors of war, proud to be American.

I didn't have a green beret. But I did have a green-and-black Grandpa's Boys jacket. I wore it to school that day.

On Saturday night I sat in the middle of the back seat of a Pontiac sedan, with Gilbert on one side of me and Marty on the other. Don was behind the wheel, and Bill rode shotgun. We pulled into the gravel lot at Shiflett's beverage store just north of town on Route 8 and slowly proceeded around to the dark rear of the cinder-block building. Don turned off the headlights and cut off the engine. "OK, Dave," Bill said to me. "That garage door up front should be unlocked. Open it as quietly as you can, and you'll find plenty of beer stocked inside. Now, go get us some."

Gilbert opened the car door and let me out. The sky was clear, and the temperature was falling. My green-and-black plaid flannel jacket wasn't made for December nights in Northeast Ohio. Wearing gloves wasn't cool. I stuffed my bare hands in my trouser pockets and stepped lightly along the block wall. I looked around the front corner, close to the garage door. I waited as a middle-aged man carried out a six-pack of P.O.C. – which formerly stood for Pilsner of Cleveland but was altered to Pleasure on Call after being sold in 1963 to the Duquesne Brewing Co., which shut down the Cleveland brewery and produced it in Pittsburgh. The man got in his car and drove away, leaving the small parking lot empty. Other cars sped by on the road, but nobody looked my way.

I skulked over to the door, grabbed the handle and, sure enough, was able to slide it up slowly, silently, just high enough for me to roll underneath it. A smidgen of hazy light from the store's front door bounced off the ground to reveal beer cases stacked against the wall. I hoisted one case of Stroh's from one stack and carefully set it down under the door. Then I did the same with a case of Rolling Rock. I scrunched my 5-foot-5, 125-pound frame back outside, lugged one case by the handle with my left hand, the other with my right hand and ran around to the waiting car.

Two doors opened. Bill grabbed the Rolling Rock. Gilbert grabbed the Stroh's. I hopped back in my middle seat. "Way to go, Dave," Don said as the rear tires of his car flung loose cinders behind us and we headed south toward the Hullabaloo.

At about 2 a.m. I sneaked in the back door at home, at least I thought I was being sneaky. I tiptoed through the kitchen, stumbled across the living room and made it to the staircase. With my head spinning, my wobbly foot missed the fifth step, I sprawled forward, and my benumbed body slid down to the landing. As I rolled over, my stomach wrenched, my esophagus throbbed, an acidic fluid erupted through my throat and down the front of my shirt.

"Have you been drinking alcohol?" I had woken my mother but, fortunately, not my father. She gave me a scornful glare.

"No, Mom, it was the milk," I said. "I think milk makes me sick."

"I'll give you milk, buster. Help me clean this mess up, and you better be ready for church in the morning."

She made sure that I was. As I sat in the pew, my head aching, my belly churning and my shoulders drooping, I knew God's punishment.

But my mother figured I needed some more. After we got home from church, I hung my dress slacks, sports coat, collared shirt and necktie in my closet, threw on my regular clothes and went downstairs. "I'm going to teach you to get drunk," she said, setting a half-full fifth of bourbon and an empty glass on the kitchen table. "Drink this," she said. It seemed like a strange form of punishment for getting drunk, but I sat down and poured myself a glass. Straight bourbon didn't taste anything like beer, and the first few sips didn't go down easy, but I finished the glass in a few minutes. "Pour another one," Mom ordered. I did. I drank it one sip at a time and could feel myself getting lightheaded.

"Mom," I said, "this is pretty good stuff. I think I like it." Actually, I didn't.

"All right, that's enough," she grumbled, apparently realizing that this punishment didn't exactly fit my crime. She grabbed what remained of the fifth and put it back in the cupboard. "Go up to your room," she said. "You're grounded for the rest of the day."

It was the week before Christmas. A spongy snowfall covered the grass and coated the shingled rooftops. Unburdened by schoolwork, children had visited various Santas in the department stores and had visions of Erector Sets or Barbie dolls dancing in their heads. Heartened by frosty flakes floating in the shimmering glow of streetlights, they anticipated the jolly, old elf's return in a sleigh soaring across the sky behind flying reindeer.

Shoppers with fresh-cut rump roasts, canned mixed vegetables and bagged noodles waited to check out. Altie's mom, Julie Taylor, a war bride from Belgium who lived two doors down from us on the far corner of Myrtle Avenue, and Margie's mom, Betty Frazee, who hopefully had forgotten my odorous sandbox caper on the next block, ran the registers. They greeted shoppers with cheery "Merry Christmas" wishes, to hell with "Happy Holidays." Old man Stutzman stood up from the desk where he had been farting off and on for the past three hours and slipped on his winter coat. I weighed a sack of apples and marked down the price for the last customer on the produce aisle, where I had been promoted without a pay raise a month earlier. I misted the green vegetables with a retractable hose and covered the bins with rectangular metal plates as I prepared to close up for the night.

Gilbert, the tall, lanky Grandpa's Boy who had played basketball for the junior-high team but gave it up for other interests, stopped by after stocking shelves with canned goods on the next aisle. "Are you up for throwing some snowballs as soon as we get out of here?" he asked.

"Sure," I said.

"OK, meet me out back."

Dave Marconi waited for the crew to clock out and exit the front door. Then he shut off the lights and locked up.

Gilbert and I crouched behind the hefty container of unfrozen, rotting garbage next to the rear parking lot and waited for Dave to get in his car then drive away. It was all clear, nobody else in sight. From the top of the container, we were able to latch onto a metal pipe and shimmy up about 20 feet, where we could grab the edge of the flat, tar roof and pull ourselves on top. We trudged through several inches of heavy snow to the front of the store, where we looked over the slushy intersection of Bailey Road and Myrtle Avenue. I could see the traffic light at the corner from my sisters' bedroom window, but this was a better view.

We packed up several good, hard snowballs and waited. As a blue-and-white Ford Fairlane approached slowly from the south, we readied our frozen ammo. The driver had a green light and kept moving. Bam! Bam! We both nailed the roof over the chassis. The car didn't stop. We laughed. A yellow Chevy Impala came our way from the north and stopped for a red light. The light changed, and the car passed between us on the Stutzman's roof and my house across the way. Gilbert powdered the Chevy's hood, and I hit the trunk lid dead center. This time the driver hit the brakes, pulled into the parking strip in front of the pharmacy, stopped and got out. Concealed in the relative darkness above, we ducked out of sight behind the extended facade. After a minute, we heard the car door slam shut, the engine rev up, the tires crumble the crunchy snow and the rumble of the exhaust muffle into the distance.

After five or six cars were pelted without incident, we saw the same yellow Impala that had stopped previously return from the south. Bombs away, we hit it again before it turned right onto Myrtle Avenue and pulled over to the curb. Soon a police cruiser arrived and parked on Bailey Road, facing north. A woman got out of the Impala, and the cop met her on the sidewalk. She pointed toward the Taylors' house. He scoured the back-yards for some sign of movement in the still darkness.

Looking down at them with their backs toward us, Gilbert said, "What do you say?"

I knew what he meant. I nodded and smiled.

We each picked up a snowball. The cruiser was a sitting duck. Bam! Bam! The woman jumped. She and the cop turned around. We ducked back down behind the facade. "We better get the hell out of here now," Gilbert said.

We scurried across the roof, climbed back down the pipe at the rear of the store, hopped onto the garbage container and then to the ground. We could see the red flashing light reflecting off bare tree limbs and heard the siren of a second cruiser getting louder. We ran across the back lot to Curtis Avenue and then a block west to Deming Street, where Gilbert headed north to Shubert Street and toward his house on Munroe Falls Avenue, which was almost next door to the B&K Root Beer drive-in. I made a circuitous escape over to Broadway Avenue, through the Little Woods, which I knew like the back of my hand, to Anderson Road and then across some backyards and safely to my own back door.

"I heard a siren, and now there's two police cars out front, David," my mom said after I took off my shoes and went into the living room. "Do you know what that's all about?" Vonnie and Danny looked at me. Dad didn't.

"I think some lady has a flat tire around the corner by the Littles' house," I said. I did my best not to laugh out loud.

Sports prospects fall short

Inspired by Bill Roach, I held my alcohol consumption to a minimum during the winter sports season. Our swim team, the Black Tigers, went 16-2 in dual meets, losing only to state powers Akron Firestone and Upper Arlington, the latter 49-46 loss being the result of two disputed calls by the home team's officials. We didn't have home meets in our undersized YMCA pool. These were the days before touch pads recorded finishes to within hundredths of a second and when the hands on stopwatches, subject to inconsistent human fingers, pointed to tenths of a second.

I generally was the team's No. 2 swimmer in the 200-yard individual medley, which put me on the travel squad, as opposed to the second team that prevailed over most of the Akron City Swimming League competition. Coach Boyle gave me some hope of qualifying for states, but I let myself down in both the 100 breaststroke and IM at the district meet held at Firestone. Bob Heacock, whom I'd known since first grade and had swum with since we were 11 years old, was the state butterfly champion. Tom Morton, who had been the backstroker on my YMCA medley relay but switched to breaststroke and knocked me off the Water Works Swim Club relay, took second in the breast. Our medley relay, with my longtime teammate and fellow Price School alumnus Casey Roberts leading off in the backstroke, Morton in the breast, Jim Gable in the fly and my former baseball teammate Greg Hileman bringing it home in the freestyle, took first in the state. No thanks to me, Cuyahoga Falls was fourth in the team standings.

I didn't attribute my athletic shortcomings to beer drinking. After all, I had only gotten shitfaced a half dozen times in my entire life. It couldn't have been the cigarettes. I'd quit smoking and didn't inhale when I did. It was that damn puberty that came so late and let those boys whom I used to beat grow shoulders above me and leave me in their wakes.

Even so, I had scored enough points to earn my varsity letter. I ran into Bill in school on the day of the winter sports banquet. He had gotten that job at Hanna Pharmacy and bought a car, but he told me his fuel gauge was on empty and wondered if I could give him a lift that evening. When I picked him up at his house on Munroe Falls Avenue, across from the railroad tracks and a few doors down from Portage Trail, he grabbed a gas can and a 5-foot section of rubber hose from his trunk.

I was one of 17 swimmers to get our varsity letters. Bill was one of 16 wrestlers to get their letters. The wrestling team, undefeated in seven dual matches and three tournaments, had won the district championship and sent four members to state but, unlike the swim team, brought home no crowns from Columbus. Twelve basketball players earned their letters. Their varsity team, led by all-state forward Jim Thorne and center Roger Evans, had gone 19-6 for the season and advanced to the elite eight in the state tournament. Basketball was named our school's "1967 Team of the Year," because, naturally, eighth best in the state is better than fourth best in the state.

After collecting our awards, Bill and I drove to the three-story brick building that had given School Avenue its name and where old timers remembered learning American history and biology. Hauntingly, the grimy glass set inside tall, arched window wells glowered down from the neglected structure that cast a foreboding moon shadow over the dozen school buses parked in what once was a lively schoolyard.

I parked on the street, turned out my headlights and switched off the motor. Bill grabbed his gas can and hose from behind the passenger seat. We surveyed the surroundings and then stealthily made our move to the buses, where we settled out of sight between two of them. I removed the gas cap and shoved one end of the hose into the tank. Kneeling down with the other end inches from the ground, Bill sucked on the hose until he got a mouthful of the pungent liquid. He spat it out and pointed his end of the hose into the 2-gallon can, which quickly filled to the top. I yanked out the hose and twisted the gas cap back on.

At 32.9 cents a gallon for gas, we had earned half an hour's worth of our pay in about two minutes. We understood the principles of crony capitalism, in which government is always there for those who have connections. Our connection was a rubber hose. I dropped Bill off at his house and watched him lug the gas can to the back, where his car was parked.

Chapter 9 | **Looking for Trouble**

Much like the world also known as Earth, my world was twisting, turning and being pulled apart by rivalrous, compelling forces as the bone chill of winter reluctantly yielded to the buds of spring 1967, my final stretch of secondary education.

I was confident that college lay ahead for me, although not for most of my contemporaries. Seven miles from home, Kent State University, an easy commute for the typical Cuyahoga Falls product with the bare wherewithal for tuition at $170 per quarter but not for dormitory room and board, was my destination. Architecture school was my destiny, because my parents convinced me that it was a reasonable pursuit. Our class adviser at school was impressed by my mathematics score in the 99th percentile on aptitude tests, even though the trajectory of my grades in other subjects left an oppositional impression. For some reason, algebra, trigonometry and the basics of calculus came easy to me, regardless of how little I paid attention in class, but my inattention in other classes had a negative impact.

Conscientious objections

By that March, Operation Rolling Thunder had been dropping bombs toward military and industrial targets in North Vietnam for two years. Our real enemy being communism, of course, China and the Soviet Union provided unified assistance to their evil brethren in constructing a highly sophisticated defense system against the air assault. The effectiveness of our strategy – which, by the end of the United States' combat engagement in 1972, had jettisoned about 4.6 million tons of bombs and extinguished the lives of an estimated 2 million Vietnamese – will always be a matter of debate for historians, not to mention clueless babblers.

Apparently, President Johnson believed the bombs would help bring peace, as he offered to halt the offensive and the buildup of American combatants, if only North Vietnamese President Ho Chi Minh would call off the insurgency in the South and sit down for talks. It was unconvincing to Ho, who simply repeated his earlier demand that the United States must stop the bombing and withdraw its troops from Vietnam before there would be any talk of peace. Bombs away!

At about that time, the Rev. Dr. Martin Luther King Jr., the most noteworthy leader of the civil-rights movement, argued that, proportionately, blacks accounted for twice as many combatants and twice as many battle deaths as Caucasians in Vietnam. It is a claim that reverberates among the misinformed decades after King's untimely death.

When the accounting was done by the 1973 Office of the Assistant Secretary of Defense report, "Negro Participation in the Armed Forces, 1965-1972," the facts were that 88.4 percent of those who served in Vietnam and 86.3 percent of those who were killed as a result of hostile action there were Caucasian. Blacks accounted for 10.6 percent of those who served in Vietnam and 12.1 percent of those killed in hostile action – a pretty fair reflection of the population of black Americans of military age. To be fair, the proportionate numbers prior to 1967, before the height of the war and before American deaths became much more statistically significant, may have been somewhat different.

In King's April 4, 1967, speech, "Beyond Vietnam," delivered before 3,000 people at Riverside Church in New York City, he bemoaned "the cruel irony of watching Negro and white boys on TV screens as they kill and die together for a nation that has been unable to seat them together in the same schools. So we watch them in brutal solidarity burning the huts of a poor village, but we realize that they would hardly live on the same block in Chicago. I could not be silent in the face of such cruel manipulation of the poor."

I was not familiar with the poor neighborhood blocks of Chicago, or even those in Cleveland, but I had seen different colors on opposite sides of Sumner Hill in Akron. I had only seen white people in the working-class neighborhoods on both sides of Cuyahoga Falls. Nevertheless, Martin Luther King Jr. was correct about the newsreels from Vietnam befouling our black-and-white television screens. The death of war was nondiscriminatory.

"I am as deeply concerned about our own troops there as anything else," King said.

Later in his speech, he offered his solution. "As we counsel young men concerning military service, we must clarify for them our nation's role in Vietnam and challenge them with the alternative of conscientious objection," he said, drawing a sustained applause in the church of Christians.

That term, "conscientious objection," was unintelligible to me and had no place in my particular Christian religion.

But it did ring a bell 24 days later, when Muhammed Ali, the heavyweight champion of the world, showed up for his scheduled military induction in Houston but refused to step forward when his name was called. He previously had said that his religious beliefs as a black Muslim made him a conscientious objector.

Not only was he arrested and stripped of his boxing title, but Ali was roundly reviled for his anti-war stance. Among the most brutal revilers was television host David Susskind, who said, "He's a disgrace to his country, his race, and what he laughingly describes as his profession ... He is a simplistic fool and a pawn." Susskind, a World War II veteran himself who had seen action at Iwo Jima and Okinawa, typified the attitude toward conscientious objectors, black or white. Unfortunately, just a few years later, many World War II veterans became similarly disdainful toward those who did not conscientiously object, who did not refuse to be inducted and who did serve their country.

I was 17 years old. What did I know?

Stealing for that first kiss

Glen Barnhouse, Mike Kensinger, his sister, Joanie, and a couple of her friends were going to pick me up after work, maybe cruise the Hungry I on Portage Trail or check out the Hullabaloo on State Road. I was in the Stutzman's stockroom sorting soft-drink-bottle returns and couldn't help but notice a grocery cart filled with bottles of wine. One of those could liven things up, I thought. So, at closing time, after misting the vegetables and covering the produce bins, I made a quick return visit to the stock-room, where I loosened my belt, shoved a bottle of white wine with a screw-off top in the rear of my trousers, refastened my belt around it and covered up with my Grandpa's Boys jacket, which I also figured would impress the girls.

Dave Marconi, who was waiting up front as the cashiers emptied their registers, gave me the eye as I walked past and headed for the door. "Good night," I said. He nodded.

My ride was waiting. Glen, at the wheel, and Mike, riding shotgun, had a pretty girl I did not know seated between them. I hopped in the back and quickly found myself between Joanie and her friend named Barb. We drove to the picnic grounds of Water Works Park, which were dark and still. I opened the wine and passed it around.

Joanie pulled me toward her and kissed me on the lips. I liked it. Her friend pulled me to her side of the seat and kissed me on the lips. I liked that too. Joanie kissed me again. She slipped her tongue into my mouth. I really liked that. She laughed. Her friend did the same thing. I really liked that too. The longer we did it, the more I liked it. Everybody laughed. Evidently, they were experienced French kissers. I wasn't, but I was deter-mined to get as much experience as I could that night.

After I got home and went to bed, I had pleasant dreams.

The next morning my mom told me Dave Marconi, my boss, had called and wanted to see me. I got dressed, went across the street to Stutz-man's and found Dave in the office. "There's a bottle of wine missing from the cart that I left in the stockroom," he said. "I know you stole it."

Somebody had been pilfering bottles from the wine shelves next to the produce aisle, so he set up a trap to find out who it was, he told me. But it wasn't me, I said. I'd never stolen anything from the store before, which was the truth, and I only took that one bottle, well, because it was practically asking to be stolen. I was fired, Dave said, and not only that, I had to pay for the wine – nearly a full hour's wages, before taxes. He should have known it was against the law to sell alcohol to minors.

I went back home, told Mom I had a disagreement with my boss, and I quit. She shook her head but didn't ask any questions. She had her sources. I poured myself a bowl of Cheerios for breakfast. Fortunately, golfing season would be starting soon. I could keep up with my car payments.

Having that VW Beetle and having my connection with Grandpa's Boys, especially Ron Chadwell, who did not have a car but did have a girlfriend, who had girls as friends, gave me some opportunities to practice French kissing and related activities. There were numerous locations where we would park my car, turn out the headlights and enjoy those activities. Galt Park, just a few blocks from our homes, a stone quarry next to Munroe Falls Park, east of Cuyahoga Falls, Sand Run Park, not far from Firestone High School in Akron, and Virginia Kendall Park, which was a major component of what later became Cuyahoga Valley National Park, were favorite destinations.

Making out with girls, beer drinking and fighting were common occupations for testosterone-infused teenage boys – probably still are. They were especially popular for Grandpa's Boys, some of whom were a lot luckier with the girls than I was.

Reputation for better or worse

It was about an hour before sunset. A half dozen of us were standing outside the barbershop between Stutzman's and Hanna Pharmacy, smoking cigarettes, tossing butts into the parking strip and shootin' the shit. Bill Roach ended his work shift and joined us. "Did you guys hear what the North Hill Boys have been saying about us?" he asked. I hadn't, but a couple of the others nodded their heads. "They say Grandpa's Boys are just a bunch of punks. We gotta set them straight," Bill said, spitting the words out in disgust.

The seven of us crammed into Don Graham's car, three in the front, four in the backseat. We drove up to State Road, turned south, crossed the high-level bridge to North Main Street in Akron and continued to

Cuyahoga Falls Avenue, where we turned left and parked on the side of the street.

"They'll be hanging out in the diner around the corner," Bill said. "I'm going inside to scope it out. They won't think nothin' of one guy going in and having a seat. If I'm not back in a couple minutes, you'll know they're in there. So then you head around the block and park right in front of the diner. They'll see you, and they'll know who you are. That's when the shit will hit the fan." He took off his green-and-black flannel jacket, stepped out of the car and vanished around the corner back onto North Main Street. We waited a couple minutes and then followed Bill's instructions.

Almost as soon as we pulled over in front of the diner, in full view through the wide storefront windows, a group of 10 or 12 guys who were gathered around two booths took notice. In the booth at the far end of the shop, Bill was biding time. One guy pointed out the window at us, shook his finger and said something to the others. They all stood up and stomped toward the front door. We jumped out of the car and spread out on the sidewalk, ready to rumble. As they began to squeeze out the door, two or three at a time, Bill Roach, the toughest guy at Falls High, stormed up behind them and smashed into their backs like a bowling ball knocking pins every which way. The element of surprise sent the North Hill Boys stumbling our way with fear in their eyes. Our fists flew into their faces and our feet into their groins. Those who didn't fall to the sidewalk writhing in pain ran down North Main Street in horror from the flurry of flying fists and kicking feet. A few more punches pummeled bloody faces into the pavement.

"We better roll before the cops get here," Gilbert shouted. We all jumped back in the car and sped up Cuyahoga Falls Avenue, across the bridge over the gorge, past Ohio Edison's mounds of coal and onto Front Street.

"Damn it!" I said. "My fucking shoe flew off back there."

It was an amusing culmination to some serious business.

For better or worse, the Grandpa's Boys' reputation got around.

With Glen behind the wheel of the old Chevy that his father had spent many months restoring, four of the five "We're the Fockowwee" guys stopped for burgers and Cokes at the PDQ drive-in restaurant on Kent Road in Stow. We thought the name stood for "pretty damn quick," and it was. Glen backed into a parking spot, and the four of us placed our orders through the speaker. Four good-looking girls parked next to us. They looked over, and two of them flashed intriguing smiles. I smiled back. They ordered their food and initiated a conversation through the open car windows on a seasonable spring evening.

"Where are you guys from?" one of them asked.

"The Falls," Mike said. "What about you?"

They were from Hudson, high school seniors like us, except for Mike, who had been persuaded to attend first grade twice back at Price School.

After we ate, it was decided that Mike and I would take a ride with two of them, and the other two girls would take a ride with Glen and Kenny. Soon after we pulled out of the PDQ, the driver asked if we were familiar with Grandpa's Boys. That brought a hearty laugh from Mike, who was in the front seat. "He's one of them," he replied, pointing to me in the backseat.

The Hudson girls were delighted to be in my company, especially the one sitting next to me. Her name was Lynda. She had long brown hair and a nice face. After driving around Stow and Kent for an hour or so, during which time I took a liking to her, and then meeting back up with our friends, I asked her if we could get together again. She said yes and gave me her phone number.

Having a date to the junior-senior prom was a big step for me, as I'd never had the nerve to ask a girl to any of the previous big dances. Bill, Don, Gilbert and I arrived at Summit Mall west of Akron to pick up our tuxedos. We heard a ruckus in the parking lot and moseyed over to see what it was all about. A couple dozen guys wearing white karate garb with green, blue and purple cloth belts around their waists stood in a big circle. I figured they were getting themselves organized for some sort of demonstration inside the mall.

Inside the circle, we saw the focus of the disturbance. A redheaded, freckle-faced kid was hopping and twisting around, wildly kicking his legs up in every direction and loudly challenging the karate guys to some sort of physical engagement. It was Mike Mooney, which came as no big surprise to the four of us, because his crazy behavior was well known in our neighborhood and our high school. The dumbfounded karate guys, whether through the restraint of their instructors or just plain disbelief, maintained their distance.

"Wouldn't you know," Bill said. We went inside the mall to get our tuxes.

Mike was the kid who had been called to the office with Kip Keller and me in connection with the lipstick-initiation tradition at Sill Junior High School and whom Kip had labeled a "fuckin' crybaby" after he weaseled his way around the principal's wooden paddle. But Mike, who was a grade behind us in school and wasn't much bigger than me, was no "fuckin' crybaby." He didn't back down from fights, and he knew how to use his fists and feet to win them. His quick kick to the testicles of a brutish motorcycle guy after class earlier in the school year had sent a message to other adversaries. He liked hanging around Grandpa's Boys more than some of them liked hanging around him.

I was assigned to classes taught by two of our high school's new English teachers my senior year. One of them, Mr. Birdy, taught creative writing. "Yep, tweet, tweet, tweet," he had said in introducing himself on the first day of school in the fall. He told me I had a talent for writing, something no teacher had ever noted before. Apparently, it was something I could do well despite my wandering mind during class.

The second semester had me in an English literature course taught by Miss Kimball, who seemed to be somewhat intimidated by a bunch of high school seniors, especially those who couldn't care less about William Shakespeare's "The Merchant of Venice" or Homer's "Iliad," despite the greed and the blood. Even during her lectures, if you could call them that, Miss Kimball seldom looked up from her desk.

That gave one kid in particular the opportunity to get up from his desk in the back of the room, walk out the door and roam around the hallways. My locker was just around the corner on the second floor of the school's old section. My brother, Danny, had picked up a sack containing several nudist magazines that some pervert had dropped in the parking strip outside Hanna Pharmacy a couple days earlier and shared them with me. So I went to my locker, where I'd stowed a half-dozen of the steamiest photo pages, along with a roll of Scotch tape, and proceeded to post them on the walls of the halls. Then I returned to class, apparently unbeknownst to the unobservant Miss Kimball.

After the bell rang to signal the change of classes, congestion and boisterous behavior ensued. Myself unassumingly among them, boys guffawed and pointed fingers at the copious display of nipple-crested mammary glands and pretentiously exposed pubic regions of both sexes. Girls covered their eyes in simulated chagrin as they squeezed through gatherings of gawking guys. Even after the starting bell for the next class sounded, many of us continued to survey the exhibit.

Drawn from his classroom by the hullabaloo in the hall, one of the male teachers evaluated the spectacle. "You guys better get to your classes right now," he shouted. "Now!"

In no big hurry, we dispersed. On my way to the stairway heading to Mr. Sharpnack's advanced social studies class, I looked back to see my prurient attraction being mercilessly ripped from the wall and wadded up into crumbled balls of trash.

Some afternoons while sitting through Miss Kimball's boring analyses of literary exceptionalism with her eyes glued to the notes on her desk, I'd light up a Marlboro just to prove that I could. That would bring some chuckles from the back of the class. Not everyone was amused. When I chose to puff on a cigarette during a student presentation by John Schumm, a spindly, awkward kid whom I knew from church, he had the audacity to break from his prepared spiel and say, "Please don't smoke while I'm speaking." As if taken by complete surprise, Miss Kimball looked up and quickly surveyed the classroom. Then she resumed her examination of her desk. I put the cigarette out on the sole of my shoe.

When the bell rang, I hurried out the door and waited. When John Schumm exited the room, I grabbed him by the front of his shirt and shoved him against the wall. "Don't you ever talk again while I'm smoking," I growled. Then I pushed him away. Stunned, he didn't say a word.

"Whoa, Dave." I heard a voice behind me. I turned around. It was Mike Mooney with a wide grin across his face. "I guess you told him," he said. John Schumm was a pushover, and I knew it, but Mike probably didn't.

Mutually beneficial friendship

Mike and I found each other's company to be mutually beneficial. He didn't have a car, but I did. After splitting up with my prom date, Lynda,

I didn't have a girlfriend. Mike knew how to fix that. And we both knew how to drink beer.

To my great enjoyment, certain girls were attracted to bad boys like us. A 10th-grader named Marcia was attracted to Mike, as well as to other guys. Marcia had a friend named Cindi, and the four of us got together. Cindi was a cute blond girl with a substantial pair of breasts, a physical quality that I had eyes for but one that I hadn't put my hands on. Cindi and I became acutely interested in each other and took advantage of numerous opportunities to spend time together.

On June 8, I received my diploma along with 801 other graduates in the class of 1967 at Cuyahoga Falls High School. Through little fault of my own, an asterisk next to my name in the commencement program signified that I was a member of the upper 10 percent of my class.

Our commencement was held at the Cathedral of Tomorrow, the only place in town large enough to hold all of us and our guests. The huge worship hall, with seating for 5,400 people, was built in 1958 for the ministry of the Rev. Rex Humbard, a television evangelist whose show was aired on more than 1,500 stations around the world and reached up to 20 million viewers. Ten years after my graduation, Rex Humbard officiated at Elvis Presley's funeral.

On a sunny June afternoon, Daryl Lucien, whom I'd known since our accelerated class in junior high school and who worked at Stutzman's but did not usually hang out with Grandpa's Boys, pulled into my driveway with his convertible top down. Ron Chadwell and his girlfriend, Brenda, were in the back seat. "What's going on, Dave?" Daryl said. "Want to go for a ride?"

"Hell, yeah." I hopped in the front seat.

Daryl asked if I'd like to go pick up Cindi for a spin in his convertible, which I did, and he thought maybe she could hook him up with Marcia. It was a well-laid plan. The six of us cruised around the Falls, basking in the warm sunshine and cooling with the breeze that flowed through our hair and stroked our skin.

After awhile, Daryl drove into a driveway next to a duplex on Munroe Falls Avenue. He knew a more mature chick, 20 years old or so, who was house sitting for a couple while they were on vacation, he said, and she was there with her boyfriend. After letting us in, the house sitter said

Daryl and Marcia and Ron and Brenda could go upstairs and Cindi and I could use the main bedroom.

French kissing and passionately embracing were usual proceedings for Cindi and me, but this was the first time we'd done it in the comfort of a bedroom, as opposed to the bucket seats of my Beetle. Sensing an unprecedented opportunity, I was able to slip my hand under her blouse. I put my right leg across her midsection, and she could tell that I was thoroughly aroused. She told me she'd never gone all the way before. I didn't reciprocate with any such acknowledgement. She assisted with the removal of her pants and panties. I pulled off my slacks and briefs. We were naked from the waists down. Carefully, I slid my body on top of hers.

I knew what was supposed to happen from there, because I'd read about it in paperback books, but none of them had given me detailed instructions. I felt that my equipment was properly aligned with Cindi's, but there was no magnetic force to accurately pull mine into hers. I needed some assistance, but none was forthcoming. My heated excitement was doused by a flush of frigid fluster. My big chance petered out.

It was a quiet ride as we dropped the three girls off at their homes. After Marcia got into her front door and Daryl backed out of the drive, the silence was broken. "Wow, that was all right!" Daryl boasted as the night air whooshed through the open car and rushed past our ears. He went on to describe his ability to manipulate a sweet spot that arouses a girl's intimate desires. "How did you guys make out?" he asked.

"Good," Ron replied. "Real good."

I just smiled. Nobody needed to know the details of what went on in that bedroom. Let them think whatever they want, I figured. Besides, I had gone where I'd never been before, and that was something to smile about.

On the wrong side of the law

A 1967 article in Time Magazine traced the roots of the countercultural hippie movement that was spreading across the country to ancient Greece and noted that it was heavily influenced by peace lovers like Jesus Christ, Buddha, St. Francis of Assisi and Mahatma Gandhi. It also had been advanced by restless German youths known as Der Wandervogel prior to World War I. Naturally, it was whimsical wandering German immigrants who can be blamed for bringing their alternative lifestyle to the United States. I'm quite certain that my grandparents had nothing to do with that.

The term "beatnik" gave way to "hippie" around the time of the 1967 "Human Be-In" gathering in San Francisco's Golden Gate Park. Disciples of the movement embraced freakish back-to-nature behaviors such as getting stoned on God's gift of marijuana and refusing to cut their hair.

Hippies were not welcome in Cuyahoga Falls, at least not yet, and guys like Mike Mooney and me did not embrace such behaviors.

We were stopped for a red light at the intersection of Broad Boulevard and Second Street. Two guys that I recognized from school but didn't really know pulled up in a car next to us. Both of them were overdue for haircuts.

"That hippie faggot just gave me the finger," Mike said. "Did you see that?"

Actually, I hadn't noticed an extended middle finger, but I nodded nonetheless. "Why, that long-haired son of a bitch," I said.

Mike flung open the passenger door, hopped onto the pavement and strode over to their car. Surprised, the driver looked at him just in time to get plugged in the face by a fist flying through his open window. He yelped as his head jerked backward. His buddy gasped. Mike got back in my car. The light turned green. I hit the gas pedal, proceeded past the Lawson's plant, smelled the fresh bread baking, and continued to Mike's house. I parked on the street, and we smoked our Marlboros on the front stoop. He went inside and returned with a couple glasses of lemonade.

The phone rang inside. His mother picked up the call and seemed to be answering some questions, but we couldn't tell what it was about. She hung up and came outside, shaking her head. "That was the Cuyahoga Falls police," she said. "Some boy reported that he was assaulted, and the police want you guys to go to the station."

The cops had been to my house the previous summer, after I'd held Mike McCormick down on the ground in a chokehold, because he'd lost his temper and was taking wild swings at one of my teammates in a sandlot football game. Other than Mrs. McCormick, though, nobody called the cops about teenagers choking or punching each other. At least that's what I thought. I'd never been in the police station before, but I knew where it was.

When Mike and I got there, we were ushered into an interrogation room. Two officers soon walked in the door and closed it behind them. They told us a complaint had been made and that the victim of the unprovoked assault had recognized Mike Mooney, the assailant, from school. One of the officers said he remembered going to my house in connection with the McCormick incident and that he had warned me to stay out of trouble.

"I know," I said. "But that crybaby McCormick started trouble then, and so did this guy now."

"So, do you admit that you punched him?" the officer asked Mike.

"Well, yeah," Mike said. "But, like Dave told you, those long-haired hippie creeps gave us the finger, calling us names, and both of them were shaking their fists at us."

"I didn't like the looks of that kid either," the officer said, "and he probably deserved what he got. However, if you go up to somebody who's sitting in his car and punch him through the window, the law says he's defenseless, and that is a criminal act. I'll tell you what, though, we'll have a talk with the victim. It's you guys' word against theirs. I'm going to tell him that I gave you a good talking to and warned you that it better not happen again. You got that?"

We nodded.

"Now get out of here. We don't want to see you two again," he said.

Mike knew a kid who had just finished his junior year and had been a member of the first class of freshmen to attend the all-boys Walsh Jesuit High School when it opened in 1964 on Route 532 in Northampton Township, just north of the Falls. Rick Wilson was the star quarterback at Walsh until he got kicked off the team for drinking beer or some other petty infraction, Mike told me. Rick knew some girls in Tallmadge, east of Akron, and they wanted me to drive them there.

It was a substantial house in a newer development of similarly sized homes. The girl who lived there opened the door and let us inside. The living room was larger than the entire main floor of my house and all the other ones in our neighborhood. The color TV in a separate room was twice the size of our black-and-white set. One of the girl's friends was the only other person there. I had hoped there would be at least one more.

After a few minutes of chatter and giggles, the four of them went upstairs and left me alone in the living room. I heard bedroom doors close and decided to check the place out. I got up from the plush upholstered sofa and went to the dining room, where a hardwood table with seating for 10 sat beneath a crystal chandelier. There were wide marble counters, a center island and matching appliances in the kitchen.

Not wanting to disturb whatever was going on behind closed doors, I quietly climbed the staircase that switched back at a landing halfway up. I slipped down a long, carpeted hallway. One of the bedrooms was open. Inside were a double bed, one tall dresser, a shorter one with full-width mirror and a desk. A picture of a girl in her graduation cap and gown sat in one rear corner of the desk. A pile of "Congratulations, graduate" cards was stacked neatly in the other corner.

Next to them was a bulging, unsealed envelope. I picked it up. Inside were no fewer than 20 crisp greenbacks, at least half of them featuring the face of Andrew Jackson. Nobody I knew received graduation gifts like that. My dad was earning about $4 an hour at the Ford plant. More than a week's worth of his wages, including overtime pay, was in that envelope. It would take me a couple days of caddying at the country club to earn one of those 20-dollar bills, if I were lucky. I figured she'd never miss just one of them.

I heard a car pull into the driveway and hurried back down to the living room. The graduate in the photograph walked in the front door.

She was startled to see the thief sitting on one of the sofas. "Who are you, and what are you doing here?" she demanded.

"I'm Dave. We're just visiting," I replied.

"Where is Sheila?" she said, her voice rising.

"They're upstairs."

I watched her go up and disappear around the bend. Then I heard a scream. "Oh, my God! What are you doing, Sheila? How could you? I can't believe I'm seeing this." The door slammed shut.

The girl in the photo didn't come back downstairs. I hoped she wasn't counting her graduation cash. Mike and Rick did come down, in a hurry. "Let's get out of here," Mike said.

We did.

With my newfound wealth, we met up with one of our 18-year-old pals, and I sprang for six quarts of 3.2 beer at about 50 cents apiece later that day. We joined the usual clientele parked at the Hungry I. The drive-in restaurant didn't make a big profit on soft drinks, as many young customers supplied their own beverages. Business was pretty good, though, with steady sales of burgers, hot dogs, french fries and chips delivered to car windows on metal trays by Benny Linnen and other young carhops earning less than minimum wage.

Since the establishment had no indoor seating, we didn't use the restroom, although the girls might have, when necessary. More conveniently for the guys, there was a small parking lot on the opposite side of Schiller Avenue, which ran diagonally between Portage Trail and State Road and cut behind the Hungry I. After taking care of that business, several of us were standing around when someone saw a police car approach from the west. Before the cruiser made the sharp turn onto Schiller Avenue, several beer bottles were tossed into the bushes next to the building.

The cruiser's spotlight was directed at us as it pulled into the lot. Two cops climbed out and walked over to where we were standing. Thankfully, I didn't recognize them, and they didn't know me.

"What are you guys doing here?" the taller one of the two asked.

"Nothing. Just talking," Bill Roach said.

"Really?" he said, with more than slight skepticism. "So what's all this wet stuff on the pavement?"

"No idea," Bill replied.

"It hasn't rained here in a week," the cop said. "Maybe you guys dumped your beer out when you saw us coming, huh? Hey, Charlie," he said to his partner. "Dip your handkerchief in that liquid and tell me what it smells like to you."

Charlie squatted down, swabbed up a sample, stood up and held it to his nostrils. "It's piss!" he stammered. "You little shits!"

"It wasn't us," Bill said.

"We'll be watching you guys," the taller cop said. They got back in their cruiser and drove off.

That was worth a good laugh. "Chicken-Shit Charlie just stuck his snot rag soaked with our piss back in his pocket," Marty Harrington howled. We laughed some more.

We returned to our cars to drink some more beer. We did not hire an attorney to file a lawsuit against the police for that disparaging remark about us being "little shits."

Mostly, it was just us boys who had run-ins with the law. But sometimes we dragged girls down our path of criminality.

At one of the Lions Park dances, Mike and I hooked up with a couple girls who attended Our Lady of the Elms, an exclusive all-girls Catholic school in Akron. We took them out to the parking lot and had a few swigs from the quarts of low-powered brew that were waiting in my VW Beetle. After properly acquainting these sweet things with our warm affections, we drove westbound on Graham Road and then south on State Road, swigging down our beer, smooching and laughing along the way. A police cruiser traveling in the opposite direction passed us by on the four-lane road. The flashing red lights were switched on, which caught my attention. In the rearview mirror, I saw the brake lights brighten. The cruiser veered into a U-turn.

"Uh-oh," I said. "Here comes trouble."

"Quick. Put the cap on your beer bottle and give it to me," Mike said. I did. "Lift your butt up off the seat for a second, Lisa," he said. She did.

I pulled off the road into a plaza parking lot, and the cops pulled in behind us.

The battery for those old Beetles was underneath the rear seat, which was easy to unhitch, if you knew how. I had shown Mike how. He stowed the evidence next to the battery and snapped the seat back into place.

One officer stepped up to my side of the car. His partner went to the other side and aimed his flashlight through the rear window. "Let me see your driver's license," the first cop said.

I fumbled for my wallet, found the license and handed it to him.

"OK, all four of you, out of the vehicle, now!"

We complied. The girls were a little wobbly and more than a little frightened. I can't say I wasn't. We did our best not to breathe in the cops' direction.

Both officers poked their heads inside the car. With flashlights shining, they searched under the front seats. They kept looking. Finally, they stepped back and gave us all a visual inspection. There were no bulges in our pockets or even the fronts of our trousers, no irregular humps on the girls' bellies.

"I swear to God I saw them drinking beer," the first cop said to his partner. "And I know they didn't throw anything out the window." He glanced back up the road. There was no broken glass in sight.

"Well, what can we do?" his partner said.

"All right, get back in your vehicle, and you better be careful," the first cop told me. "We'll be watching you punks."

I breathed a sigh of relief as I turned the key in the ignition, lifted my left foot off the clutch, hit the accelerator with my right foot and proceeded to steer my car over the curb with a clunk. As I turned left onto Sackett Avenue, I lost sight of the flashing red light.

"Holy shit!" Vicky sputtered from the front passenger seat. "That was a close call."

"Glad you had fun," Mike said. "We should do this again."

We got their phone numbers.

Fortunately for all of us, perhaps, a 17-year-old white boy like me – the son of a factory worker who was scratching out a living, often doing it from one paycheck to the next, a boy who had only once seen the inside of a swanky home where kids had their own bedrooms, a boy whose family had never eaten in a fancy restaurant where diners tipped the waitresses – knew what to do and what not to do when he saw the flashing lights of a cop car.

I knew that we were breaking the laws against drinking and driving, underage consumption and open container and that we could face serious consequences. But I didn't step on the gas with the foolish notion that we could make a clean getaway. No, I quickly pulled off the road in a safe spot. And when the cops told us to get out of the car, I didn't make a run for it between the retail buildings and toward the trees that could provide cover in the backyards of the nearby neighborhood. I didn't have the idiotic idea that the police would just let me escape. My parents didn't have to teach me such things. I figured it all out by myself.

I can't say what would have happened if my skin were a different color. Some people might call our experience that night the benefit of white privilege. I just thought we were pretty damn lucky and not too dumb.

Chapter 10 | **Fanciful Sexual Heroics**

Prior to passage of the National Minimum Drinking Age Act of 1984, which coerced all 50 states and the District of Columbia to deny adults between their 18th and 21st birthdays the legal right to consume alcohol, Ohio was a place where prohibition was at least partially evaded. In the 1960s, 40 states were of the mindset that 18-year-old males were mature enough to be drafted into the U.S. military and die for their country in Vietnam but they were too young and immature to be trusted with even low-powered beer.

Ohio was one of the few exceptions. The city of Kent, full-time population approximately 20,000, was known locally as "where the action is," and Kent State University, which doubled the town's population during the school year, was recognized as one of the country's top party schools. The lively bar scene, in which many establishments were licensed to serve 3.2-percent beer to 18-, 19- and 20-year-olds and in which some were rather lax in checking consumers' identifications, was the main reason for that notoriety.

Numerous kids in my neighborhood, including myself, my sister Vonnie and our friends, were most familiar with Kent through the recycled school bus that collected us one afternoon each week during the summer and delivered us to the Moon-Glo Roller Rink just east of town.

When the summer of 1967 arrived, Mike Mooney and I and many of our pals made the 7-mile trip one evening each week, when the Dome nightclub in downtown Kent shuttered its liquor cabinets and hosted teen nights. No matter. We'd stop along the way at the Bee-Line drive-through beverage store in Munroe Falls, where at least one real or fake 18-year-old ID could be produced, if necessary. We'd get fairly well looped by the time we forked over a token cover charge at the door. The Dome regularly featured some of the region's top rock 'n' roll bands, which attracted dance-loving girls from near and far.

Our rhythmic arm-swinging and hip-pumping talents were more than adequate to hook up with some of those girls on the dance floor, which would lead the way to some extracurricular activities – as much as could be accomplished anyway in the Dome's darker corners and crevices.

On one steamy night, I connected quite favorably with a petite girl who had big brown eyes and long black hair and called herself Deborah. She said she was from Ashtabula, which was unfamiliar to me, and that this was her first visit to Kent. Her family had rented a couple cottages for the week at Punderson State Park, which also was unfamiliar to me but was somewhat closer to Kent. Her older sister's boyfriend from college had driven the three of them down for the evening, she explained, but she didn't know where they went, so would I mind giving her a lift back to Punderson? The way things were going, of course I wouldn't mind. So I told my buddies that I thought I'd be getting lucky and that maybe they could hitch a ride back to the Falls. Under the circumstances, of course they could.

The drive out to Ravenna, the Portage County seat, and then north on Route 44 took us through the small town of Mantua, where a kid named Jack Lambert was growing up and soon would play football for Crestwood High School. After high school, Lambert would become a star linebacker at Kent State University and then go on to become a nine-time All-Pro in the National Football League and win four Super Bowl championships with the Pittsburgh Steelers, which brought great cheer to my father.

As we crossed into Geauga County, the maple-syrup-producing and horse-raising capital of Ohio, I could see the moon reflecting off the surface of LaDue Reservoir just east of the highway. The 1,477-acre reservoir had been created by the City of Akron several years earlier by damming Bridge Creek, a tributary of the Cuyahoga River, whose headwaters lie farther north in Geauga County. Water from LaDue is piped about 25 miles south to supply the showers and drinking fountains in places like Hoban High School, where I'd found its taste not much better than that of the filthy river itself. I was spoiled by the artesian wells near Water Works Park that supplied the good people of Cuyahoga Falls with delicious, thirst-quenching water.

The trip was much longer than I had anticipated, but, as we turned into the park entrance and proceeded along the tree-lined, curvy parkway, my hopes grew that it would all be worthwhile.

The state park is named after the 101-acre Punderson Lake, which was formed by glaciers during the Ice Age. With its depth at 85 or 90 feet in some places, it is one of the area's deepest glacial lakes. Its name is taken from Lemuel Punderson, who ventured to Ohio from Connecticut in 1806 and had a grist mill and distillery built near what was then called "the big pond."

I couldn't see the lake in the darkness, but I couldn't help but notice the huge Tudor-style mansion that had been built on its shore by a pair of wealthy families from Cleveland and Detroit in the 1920s and '30s. Due to fortunes lost, the property was sold to the state of Ohio in 1948, and the manor later was converted to a lodge with 32 guest rooms.

Unbeknownst to me, eerie tales of horrible deaths, disappearances and apparitions have been associated with Punderson Lake and Punderson Manor throughout their history. According to legend, Lemuel Punderson decided to float out into the lake one day in a "golden bathtub" then pulled the plug and sank into the cold, unforgiving depths. Another story has it that campers have seen the shadowy ghost of a young woman who drowned in a boating accident emerge from the lake before returning to her watery grave. Guests in the manor have reported children running up and down the halls, even though no children were registered. Others have heard loud laughter in unoccupied rooms. Staff members have reported numerous sinister encounters, including one with a man dressed as a lumberjack hanging by his neck from the rafters in the dining room.

As we approached the cottages, I had a different kind of encounter on my mind. After we went into a wood-paneled outer room with two love seats facing a fireplace on one side and a table with four chairs at the other, Deborah's sister and her boyfriend came out of the bedroom. Their disheveled appearances were encouraging. The sister gave us a nod toward the bedroom. Deborah squeezed my hand and smiled. I was eager to continue what we'd started back at the Dome, and my confidence was solidifying.

Then came a knock on the exterior door. It was their parents, who were staying in the adjacent cottage, and they wanted to check on the two girls.

They knew the sister was there with her boyfriend but seemed surprised to see me. "This is, ah, Dennis," Deborah stammered.

Jeez, she didn't even remember my name.

The mother said hello. The father nodded coolly in my direction.

"It's getting pretty late," he said. "You girls need to get your sleep so we can get up and go fishing in the morning. And I think it's time for you two boys to be heading home, don't you?"

It was a long, lonely drive back to Cuyahoga Falls.

Our summer evenings were filled with dances, parties, beer drinking and, most importantly, the pursuit of girls.

John Mitchen, who lived a couple blocks from Sill Junior High School, was a dancing machine. He told Mike Mooney and me that we should check out the Starlight Ballroom at Chippewa Lake Park. It had been a lively destination spot during the Roaring Twenties, when the U.S. economy was booming, jazz music was hopping, sexual inhibitions were flopping, and Prohibition inspired speak-easies and gangsterism. In our day, the park was well known for its coasters and other amusement rides along the shore of the 385-acre glacial lake.

Chippewa Lake is in Medina County, about 10 miles west of Akron. Pressing the throttle to the floor in his rusty, eight-cylinder Dodge sedan, John gleefully pointed out that the needle on the speedometer was edging past the 120-mph mark as we zoomed out Route 224 and crossed the county line in the blink of an eye. Arriving at the park an hour before the band was scheduled to take the stage, we grabbed hot dogs on the midway, splattered them with mustard and sat on a bench to gobble them down while kids screeched for joy on the Tumble Bug behind us.

When the sun set over the lake and the flashy lights went out on the carousel and Ferris wheel, we joined the crowd of teenagers lining up to pay the cover charge at the ballroom entry. The band played Brenton Wood's "Gimme Little Sign" and other energetic numbers. Out on the dance floor, John's gyrations were especially enticing to good-looking girls, but I didn't see any guys' overtures being rejected.

Four or five dance partners into the evening, I felt a special connection to a nicely figured girl with curly brown hair from the Cleveland suburb of Parma. Kathy and I ventured outside for some privacy, which we believed we found under the moonlit sky on some soft grass near the edge of the beach. In passionate embrace, we rolled on the ground, and I pulled her chest close to mine. Once again, I felt my confidence rising. Stealthily, I moved to second base and then made a dash for third.

"Oh, my God," she whispered in my ear. "Dave, we gotta stop."

"What's wrong?" I said. "I thought you wanted to."

"I do, I do. But look up there." She pulled her hand away from my unfastened belt, slid it up my side and extended her forefinger past my eyes.

I followed it to the balcony on the second floor of the idyllic Hotel Chippewa located on a rise between the beach and the ballroom. The moonlight revealed an elderly couple leaning forward from two Adirondack chairs in which they were seated, evidently being entertained by the performance unfolding below them. Kathy may have been experienced, but she didn't care for an audience. Stage fright got the best of me. We did not take a bow. We took our fevered bodies back to the dance floor.

In its centennial season, the amusement park at Chippewa Lake closed down in 1978. The rides were left to rust, rot and crumble, and Mother Nature gradually enveloped them into oblivion. In 2002, the ballroom burned to the ground. According to news reports, a young girl from the area who was playing with matches in the building accidentally started the fire.

John Mitchen had some acquaintances who attended Ellet High School on Akron's east side and got himself invited to some parties in their neighborhood. It seemed to me that there were friendly girls wherever he went, so I was happy to tag along.

Even after downing several beers, I was surprised when asinine twaddle seemed to work in my favor. "Why don't you sit on my lap, and we can talk about the first thing that pops up?" I'd ask, expecting a chuckle, as just about everyone had heard that line. An attractive brunette with glistening lips named Denise took me up on the invitation. We enjoyed each other's company for the rest of that night and several times afterward.

At another house party in Ellet, I encountered the most beautiful blonde I'd ever met. "You're the best-looking girl here," I told her, "and I'm the best-looking guy. We should hook up." Her name was Pam Lowe. We spent time together that night, and I visited her at home a few days later. She told me she was going to be a flower child and move to California. She and some of her friends were going to get together that Sunday at Goodyear Park, kind of like "Itchycoo Park," she told me, and I should join them.

The song "Itchycoo Park" originated from an open space ridden with stinging nettles outside of London, England, and the British band that played it was known as the Small Faces. Neither the song nor the band were well known on our side of the Atlantic, certainly not among my companions, and the song's message about psychedelia was as foreign to me as were rice paddies and jungles in Southeast Asia.

But I sure had an attraction to Pam Lowe, so I picked up Mike Mooney and Rick Wilson and took a drive down Darrow Road to the park. We pulled into a parking lot next to a picnic pavilion. There were a half dozen cars in the lot but no picnickers in sight. Looking across a grassy field, we could see some movement at the crest of a hill, so we took a walk in that direction. At the hilltop, we encountered a group of about a dozen teenagers who were frolicking in some sort of dance gesticulation but without any music. Some of them were unusually attired, and a couple guys had hair growing over their ears. When they saw us, they took a break from their activity. Pam greeted me with a smile and embrace. We introduced each other to our friends, after which she and hers resumed what I assumed was the "Itchycoo Park" routine.

Mike, Rick and I decided against joining in their frivolity, choosing instead to observe and whisper disparagement.

"These guys are freaks," Mike said. "The three of us could easily kick the shit out of those six fuckers."

"Yeah, I'll take out that tall, skinny kid wearing a blouse and a neck-lace with one punch," Rick said.

Despite her hippie friends and "Itchycoo" inclination, I still was itch-ing for an extended relationship with Pam Lowe. "Come on, guys," I said. "These pussies aren't worth our effort. If we start beating the crap out of them, the girls will be screaming their heads off. The cops could be here before we get back to my car. Besides, I want to get in that girl's pants later, so don't fuck it up for me."

I knew I wasn't going to get in her pants, or even try, but my point was well taken by the two guys who had left me alone in that Tallmadge living room while they went upstairs to the bedrooms. I waved goodbye to Pam, and we went back down the hill.

Greenbacks on the golf course

Most of my summer days were spent at Lake Forest Country Club, and I was saving some of that caddy income for my upcoming freshman year at Kent State. I regularly played golf on "Caddy Day" with several guys from my neighborhood, including Rick Morgan, whom I had known from the baseball all-star team. I didn't fling any more golf clubs into the lake, and my scores became respectable.

In late June, I was one of the caddies from our club who were selected to tote bags for the pros in the Cleveland Open golf tournament, which was held that year at Aurora Country Club.

The city of Aurora lies in the northeast corner of Portage County, with the city of Twinsburg in Summit County to its west, the city of So-lon in Cuyahoga County to the northwest and Bainbridge Township in Geauga County to the north. The golf course, which straddles the Aurora Branch of the Chagrin River and gently rolls with the surrounding ter-rain, is 3 miles southeast of Geauga Lake Park. The iconic amusement park is where I'd survived my first harrowing roller-coaster ride, thanks to my dad, and shivered in my briefs at the sight of "Big Black Joe," also thanks to my dad. About three-quarters of the 49-acre Geauga Lake and most of the amusement park, which closed down in 2005, are in Geauga County, which probably accounts for their shared name. The park's last remnant, the 91-year-old Big Dipper coaster, was demolished in 2016, after local police responded to repeated reports of trespassers seeking thrills by climbing around on its towering scaffolding and rickety tracks.

The world's top golfers, including "the Big Three," Arnold Palmer, Jack Nicklaus and Gary Player, were in town for the big tournament.

I was assigned to caddy for Dan Sykes, which I considered a pretty lucky draw, because he had won the tournament and taken home the $25,000 first prize two years earlier. He was at the top of his game in 1967 and tied with Nicklaus for third place in the PGA Championship held in Colorado the following month. I'd heard that tournament winners sometimes paid their caddies as much as $500 for five days of comparatively easy work. The four competition rounds were preceded by a practice round. Carrying one golf bag, as opposed to two, for just 18 holes a day, as opposed to 27 or 36, and for one great golfer who hit mostly straight shots, as opposed to a couple duffers smacking their golf balls every which way, was indeed easy work.

A good caddy can get a good feel for his golfers' club selection pretty quickly. I, like most of the other caddies in the tournament, had stepped off the course in advance, so I knew the 150-yard markers and could judge the distances from every spot on every hole. By the time Sykes finished five or six holes in his practice round, I knew his game well enough to point out the correct club to knock his Titleist golf ball pin high. He agreed with my selections until I put my finger on his 7-iron after a drive that found the center of the fairway on a par-4 hole midway through the front nine on the first round. He grabbed his 6-iron instead and hit the ball perfectly. It landed on the rear fringe and kicked into a patch of trees behind the green. That's how a 17-year-old caddy gains the trust of a seasoned pro.

Dan Sykes finished the first round at 2-under-par and in second place, which got my hopes up for a repeat of his 1965 performance, when he'd sunk a 35-foot putt on the final hole for the victory at 12 under par. But he faltered in the second round and ended up finishing back in the pack. He paid me $100 in cash. I didn't tell the Internal Revenue Service.

My financial situation took another turn for the better in August, when the Cleveland District Golf Association Caddie Foundation announced that I was one of 19 caddies to be awarded college scholarships. I was the only caddy from Lake Forest Country Club to be so honored. The $100-per-quarter scholarship came as a great relief to my parents.

With good reason, as it turned out.

As the golf season was winding down and I was ready to begin my college career as a commuter student, my mom spoke with the manager of the Click store in the Stow-Kent Shopping Center on Kent Road, just west of the Kent and Portage County line. He was hiring several part-time bag packers at the big-box store that sold groceries on one side and everything from hardware and sporting goods to toys and apparel on the other. With my grocery experience – excluding the reason why I'd left my previous employment – I was hired. My friend Mike Kensinger already was employed in the department-store side of the Click operation.

I would be working a couple four-hour evening shifts during the week and one six- or eight-hour shift on Saturday or Sunday. Owned by the Fred W. Albrecht Grocery Co., based in Akron, Click was a union shop, so I was required to pay dues to the Retail Clerks International Association. That got me a 10-cent-an-hour raise above what I previously earned at the nonunion Stutzman's Foodliner. The hours for this new job enabled me to continue my caddy job on one weekend day each week into the fall, and, who knows, maybe I'd have some time left over to study.

The bad news for me was that I got pulled over for driving 70 mph in a 35 mph zone on North River Road after a night of partying in Kent. Fortunately, though, the Breathalyzer device for determining blood-alcohol content had not come into common use, or the consequences in juvenile court would have been greater than the loss of my driver's license for 90 days. Despite my mother's advice to the magistrate in Akron, "Throw the book at him," he granted me permission to drive to work and school during the license suspension. A major disadvantage, as I saw it, the driver's license was my only valid identification. Without it, many of the bars in Kent would continue to deny me entry even after my 18th birthday on Oct. 14.

Much worse news came on Sept. 6, 1967, when some 160,000 members of the United Auto Workers, my father among them, walked off their jobs in what was to become the longest strike in Ford Motor Co. history. According to a June 16, 2003, review in Automotive News, the strike lasted 68 days and cost the company the lost production of 500,000 vehicles. A three-year agreement was reached on Oct. 22, but many workers did not return to their jobs until mid-November.

On Friday, two days after the walkout, one of the so-called "liberal media," the Chicago Tribune, whose credo was to "present the news of the day, to foster commerce and industry, to inform and lead public opinion, and to furnish that check upon government which no constitution has ever been able to provide," assailed the UAW and its president, Walter Reuther. The "conspiracy" predicted by Reuther of General Motors and Chrysler Corp. locking out their workers to blunt the union's "usual option of striking a single target company and using that tactic to whipsaw its competitors ... failed to materialize," the sneering Tribune reported.

"Reuther seasoned his charges by accusing the industry of 'monopolistic practices,'" according to the Tribune's assessment. "Even the most myopic can see that the real crunch is monopoly unionism, extended thru an industry and unchecked government."

The newspaper went on to lambaste President Lyndon B. Johnson, a liberal Democrat, by gosh, for his failure to take firm action against labor strikes that imperil the "national interest." Decent wages and working conditions, presumably, were not in the national interest.

The UAW strike fund helped my family get by for a couple weeks, but it didn't take long for our ability to pay the mortgage, the utility bills and the grocery store to be in jeopardy.

With my tuition covered for fall quarter, my textbooks purchased and my monthly car-loan payment made, I offered to turn everything I earned from my bag-packing and caddy jobs over to my parents to help out. But my dad said no, we'd get by somehow. Since the caddies at Lake Forest Country Club were back at school, he wondered whether a 48-year-old striking autoworker might be able to fill in and make a few bucks on the golf course. I introduced him to the caddy master on Saturday morning.

From mid-September until late October's weather put a chill on the golfers, my father and his fellow Ford worker Ted Kasper drove up to Hudson every day, except Monday, when the course was closed, to pull their working-class families through those dismal times. One of them, a World War I German refugee who came to America as a little boy, and the other, who had arrived as an adult from Germany after World War II, carried well-to-do Jewish golfers' 25- to 30-pound bags on either shoulder over 7 to 10 miles of fairways and roughs each day. For that, they brought home $10 or $12 apiece. My dad said the golfers were sympathetic to his situation and that they had friendly conversations.

But there was no sympathy for working stiffs from haughty media executives in a Chicago ivory tower who had no clue about the sacrifices blue-collar workers made for a 90-cent-an-hour pay raise and a little consideration for their seniority.

Vietnam heroes hard to find

Life certainly was tough in the fall of '67 for the families of striking autoworkers, but it was a lot tougher for American warriors on the other side of the world, including U.S. Navy Lt. Cmdr. John S. McCain III, the pilot of a Skyhawk dive bomber that was shot down over North Vietnam on Oct. 26.

Aside from those who had real-life experience in prisoner-of-war camps during the great wars earlier in the 20th century, the vast majority of modern Americans' exposure to that iteration of history came in the comfort of their living rooms with their TV sets on. Rather than factual horror, the POW experience was presented in the form of fictional comedy.

Between September 1965 and April 1971, 168 episodes of the situation comedy "Hogan's Heroes" were aired on the CBS network. They told stories about the imprisonment of U.S. Army Air Forces Col. Robert E. Hogan and fellow Allied World War II captives at Luft Stalag 13 in the German town of Hammelburg as various plots for their escape and precarious covert operations unfolded. The mythical camp was headed by the bungling, tolerable Col. Klink, assisted by the simple-minded, almost likable Sgt. Schultz. Confronted by the prisoners' relentless scheming, Schultz customarily would look the other way and declare, "I know nothing."

We, the amused viewers of this absurdity, truly did know nothing about POW realities. The silly German Nazis we came to know from our American-made televisions were nothing like the inhuman communists in charge of North Vietnamese prisons.

Lt. Cmdr. McCain knew about reality all too well. According to his personal account, as told to U.S. News & World Report in 1973, he was on his 23rd bombing mission when a Russian missile ripped off the right wing of his aircraft and sent it into a vertical spin toward the capital city of Hanoi below. He was able to eject before losing consciousness, which he regained just before his parachute floated him into a lake. Despite broken bones in his leg and arm, he was able to surface by inflating his life preserver. A group of Vietnamese pulled him from the water, stripped off his clothes, smashed his shoulder with a rifle butt and rammed a bayonet through his foot. From there, he was taken to a prison, where he was interrogated, accused of war crimes and repeatedly beaten.

Because of his serious injuries, the North Vietnamese weren't about to waste their time and medical supplies to save McCain's life, he said, which was standard procedure by the ruthless enemy toward American prisoners of war. Regardless of whether their tortured pain and suffering led them to divulge any useful intelligence, they almost certainly died from infection in their filthy, vermin-infested cells.

But McCain was no ordinary POW. He came from a heritage of military brass, including his father, Adm. John S. McCain Jr. Due to such notoriety, his capture and connections were reported by the American media, and that information was considered useful by his captors for propagandistic purposes. So he was hospitalized and survived. For more than two years, he was kept in solitary confinement.

In July 1968, as his father was promoted to commander in chief of U.S. Pacific forces, McCain repeatedly was given the opportunity to go home. He declined, citing the code-of-conduct provision against accepting special favors and his conviction that those who had been imprisoned longer should be released before him. Another year-and-a-half of severe treatment, including regular beatings, stompings and broken bones, followed.

After years of captivity, during which time he refused again and again to confess to war crimes or make favorable statements about his treatment, he had reached the point of suicide, McCain said. He broke down and signed a confession.

In the aftermath of the Paris Peace Accords, signed on Jan. 27, 1973, officially ending U.S. involvement in the Vietnam War, nearly 600 American POWs were released by the Hanoi government. On March 14, 1973, 5 1/2 years after his capture, McCain was among them.

John McCain served on the aircraft carrier USS Enterprise during the Cuban Missile Crisis of 1962. He nearly died inside his burning A-4E Skyhawk on the flight deck of the carrier USS Forrestal in the conflagration that killed 134 sailors and injured 161 others on July 25, 1967, in the Gulf of Tonkin. He had flown nearly two dozen combat missions over North Vietnam, endured untold misery during his captivity and lived with permanent physical limitations afterward. He was awarded the Silver Star, Bronze Star, Purple Heart, Legion of Merit, Distinguished Flying Cross and Navy Commendation Medal.

While employment of the term is debatable and it surely has evolved in its wider application to participants in military engagements subsequent to the Vietnam War, I, for one, consider a man like John McCain to be a hero. But in the minds and discourse of political partisans, regardless of stripe, and those with axes to grind or swords to hone, Vietnam heroes are hard to find.

McCain went on to become a longtime Republican U.S. senator from Arizona and a candidate for U.S. president in 2000 and 2008.

He has been pilloried as part of an alleged government cover-up of missing men left behind in the hands of Vietnamese communists. He has been called a liar and a fraud and a "songbird who spilled his guts" to the enemy by accusers with no torture in their nightmares and no medals on their chests. During his 2000 Republican primary candidacy against then-future President George W. Bush, a dirty whispering campaign by political scum led South Carolina voters to suspect that McCain had fathered an illegitimate black child. His electoral momentum was quashed.

On July 18, 2015, then-future President Donald J. Trump said of John McCain, "He's not a war hero. He was a war hero because he was captured. I like people who weren't captured."

That same Donald Trump, in a 1997 interview by shock jock Howard Stern, speaking of his sexual escapades and the risk of sexually transmitted diseases, boasted, "I've been so lucky in terms of that whole world. It is a dangerous world out there. It's scary, like Vietnam. Sort of like the Vietnam era. It is my personal Vietnam. I feel like a great and very brave soldier."

Such is the inanity of a 50-year-old juvenile.

Heroism has indeed evolved in fanciful conceptualizations.

Chapter 11 | **Kent State**

For Kent State University, the events of May 4, 1970, when members of the Ohio National Guard shot and killed four students, paralyzed one for life and injured eight more, are infamously etched in the annals of American history. That date and that campus are indelibly associated with student unrest and opposition to the Vietnam War.

When I began studies as a freshman architecture student at Kent State in the fall quarter of 1967, anti-war protests were seething in the nation's capital, where some 100,000 people marched on the Pentagon that October, in major cities like New York and San Francisco and on well-known college campuses in places like Ithaca, New York, Madison, Wisconsin, and Berkeley, California. Aside from rowdy beer consumption and blaring rock music in the watering holes on South Water Street and elsewhere downtown, Kent was not known for social disorder.

That certainly was true for the department of architecture, which was established in 1956 and was still headed by Professor Joseph F. Morbito. Mine was the first incoming class to be schooled in the brand, spanking new Taylor Hall, a four-story modernistic structure of the "brutalist" style that was contemporaneously popular on university campuses. Our class of about 20 freshmen, including one female, was assigned to a bank of drafting tables in a long room with a wall of windows overlooking Blanket Hill and the victory bell situated on the university commons.

Taylor Hall, Blanket Hill and the commons all played prominent roles in the tragic chronicles that would put Kent State on the map. When the leaves fell from the trees on Blanket Hill, we could look across the commons and see the rickety old ROTC building, which went up like a tinderbox in the fiery anti-war protest of May 1970 and set the scene for the deadly confrontation between students and weekend warriors.

Overall, my secondary-school grades were good enough to get me into National Honor Society and net me a scholarship, my Scholastic Aptitude Test scores would be high enough to gain admission to most universities, and I had passed an architecture exam. But I was not a good student, and the college atmosphere gave me every opportunity to prove it. I attended classes, but my attention deficit was enduring, and textbooks were too boring to be read. Even my customary mathematics proficiency took a nose dive as calculus instructions competed with mindless distractions.

When I wasn't packing grocery bags at the Click store, I spent most weekday evenings at my drafting table in Taylor Hall, after which I'd visit the downtown bars, often the Loft at the corner of Main and Franklin streets, where I drank beer by the pitcher.

Kent was a hotbed for rock 'n' roll music. The Dome, JBs, the Fifth Quarter, the Kove and other nightclubs were jammed on Friday and Saturday nights. Up close, with pitchers of draft beer on the table, I saw bands like Sonny Geraci's Outsiders, whose hit "Time Won't Let Me" had peaked at No. 5 on the charts a year earlier, the Measles and the James Gang. Guitarist and vocalist Joe Walsh, who was a student at Kent State, left the Measles to join the James Gang in early 1968.

The specifications of my license suspension permitted me to drive to school and work, but I had to be careful about using my car for extracurricular activities. So it was that sticking out my thumb on the side of Kent Road after working at the Click store on a Saturday night ended up having a profound impact on my future life.

Jeff Murphy had been the top diver on the Falls High School swim team, so we knew each other, but not all that well. He thought he recognized the hitchhiker and hit the brakes on his 1960 Chevy Corvair. "Dave, what the hell are you doing? Where's your VW?" he asked when I hopped in the passenger seat.

I explained my situation. We realized that we were both commuter students at the university and that we both were heading to town for some action. "There's a band called the Lemon Pipers playing at the Barn," Jeff said.

I hadn't heard of the band, but I was familiar with the Barn, which actually was a big barn south of Kent that catered to young rock 'n' roll lovers. "Sounds good to me," I said. "Let's go."

Jeff and I agreed that the Lemon Pipers, a so-called psychedelic band from Oxford, Ohio, home of Miami University – which was a university before Florida was a state, by the way – were awesome. They played a tune called "Green Tambourine," which reached No. 1 on the national music charts in 1968.

It didn't take long for Jeff and me to become best friends. He introduced me to Jim Fox, a music student who had been the drummer for the Outsiders and was the founder of the James Gang. Band mate Joe Walsh went on to gain even greater acclaim.

Jeff, who had been the drummer in a garage band himself, also introduced me to Bob Leone, a guitarist in his former band, a fellow Falls High graduate and Kent student. Jeff, Bob, Bob's cousin Jim Cardarelli, also a Falls grad and Kent student, and I began hanging out in the Leones' basement on Monroe Avenue after classes. Bob's parents, who owned Leone's Pizza on State Road, would be working and presume we were studying. Mostly, we were playing pool. The Leones were very kind people who would throw a pizza in the oven for any family friend who paid a visit to the shop, and they made the best pizza in Cuyahoga Falls.

Between classes at the university, my college buddies could be found at a booth in the student union, better known as the Hub, where the needle in the jukebox was intimately familiar with the grooves on Jefferson Airplane's "White Rabbit" and Van Morrison's "Brown Eyed Girl" discs.

When the grades came out for fall quarter, my report card showed one A in physical education and four C's, none of which came as a surprise to me. It was good enough to keep me off of academic probation and to retain my draft deferment.

Since David Miller, of the Catholic Worker Movement, had burned his draft card in New York City and subsequently was prosecuted and imprisoned for that evil deed, its symbolic opposition to the Vietnam War had grown in popularity. Some 1,400 draft cards were burned in protests across the country on Oct. 16, 1967. I never witnessed such a display of civil disobedience at Kent State, and the subject never came up for discussion among my acquaintances.

Although the draft cards in our wallets were constant reminders of the consequences that faced young men without college deferments, some of us – Bob Leone, Jim Cardarelli and myself, in particular – were more interested in beer, pool, girls and rock music than studying. With expert musical interpretations from Bob and Jeff, I became more and more engaged in what we called underground, or psychedelic, music, which was personified by the Jimi Hendrix Experience, Cream, the Yardbirds, Traffic and the Jefferson Airplane.

My new pool-playing and music-loving friends all lived on the west side of Cuyahoga Falls and had attended Bolich Junior High School, but I did not lose touch with the guys I'd grown up with and knew from our east-side neighborhood.

The practically new Chapel Hill Mall was located 1 1/2 miles from my house, just over the municipal border in Akron, where Bailey Road becomes Brittain Road. Built by Cleveland-based Forest City Enterprises, it featured Sears, O'Neil's and JC Penney department stores as anchor tenants among more than 100 retail establishments.

Mike Mooney and I paid the mall a visit. It was similar to Summit Mall just west of Akron in Fairlawn, but it was much more convenient. We checked out the various stores displaying their wares and girls displaying their wearables on the promenade for an hour or so. We didn't make any purchases and walked out empty-handed through the main entrance. Outside, a set of flagpoles displayed the Stars and Stripes at the epicenter, the unique Ohio swallow-tailed burgee on one side and a rectangular banner specially designed as the Chapel Hill signature.

It would have been unpatriotic to steal the American flag and probably disloyal to our state to filch its version of stars and stripes in red, white and blue. But that bright-hued mall flag would make a nice souvenir. So I climbed up on the cement base of the flagpole, unhitched the rope from its metal cleat and lowered the cloth into Mike's arms. All the while, shoppers entering and exiting the mall passed us by and looked our way, maybe assuming that we were a couple of maintenance workers.

Ten minutes later, we knocked on the door of Vicky's house. Lucky for us, her parents weren't home, but her Our Lady of the Elms friend Lisa was there. "We brought you a present," Mike said, unfurling the Chapel Hill Mall flag on the front porch.

Whether they were delighted with the gift or by our visit or by the fact that the cops weren't following us, the girls invited us in. The usual interaction between teenagers of opposite genders transpired in the living room, but no clothing was removed.

"Did you notice that Lisa got her ears pierced?" Vicky inquired of Mike during a break in the action.

"Oh, yeah, those are pretty earrings," he said to Lisa.

"I want to get my ears pierced," Vicky said, looking at me. "I bought a pair of earrings for myself."

She went on to explain that an ice cube from the freezer could be used to numb her earlobes and that I could sterilize a sewing needle with my Zippo cigarette lighter. I followed her instructions with the ice cube until she said she had lost feelings in her left earlobe. I checked the position of the holes in Lisa's ears, lined the needle up, clenched my teeth and gave it a shove. Vicky said she felt no pain. I pushed the needle through to the backside of the lobe and followed it up with the post of the earring. Carefully, I did the same thing with the other ear. I followed Vicky to the upstairs bathroom. She looked in the mirror and smiled from ear to ear. She gave me an appreciative kiss.

Mike and I left before her parents got home. It was the last time I ever saw Vicky. I believe I left her with memories of me.

Movies and rock 'n' roll

There was a pair of movie theaters at the mall, and there were a few memorable movies to be seen that year. Jeff Murphy, Bob Leone and I became regular theatergoers, which piqued our interest in the 40th Academy Awards.

"In the Heat of the Night," starring Sidney Poitier as a black detective from Philadelphia investigating a murder in small-town Mississippi and Rod Steiger as the prejudiced local police chief, won the Oscar for best picture. Steiger also won the Oscar for best actor in that film. Katharine Hepburn won the Oscar for best actress for her portrayal of the mother of a young woman who comes home with her surprise fiance, a black man played by Poitier, in the film "Guess Who's Coming to Dinner."

The performances of Faye Dunaway and Warren Beatty in "Bonnie and Clyde" and Dustin Hoffman and Anne Bancroft in "The Graduate," all of whom received Oscar nominations for best acting but came up empty, were impressive in my amateurish judgment.

It was Poitier, however, who left the deepest and most lasting impression on me, even though the nominators didn't consider him worthy of consideration that year. I hadn't seen "Lilies of the Field," the film for which he won the Academy Award for best actor in 1964, when he became the first African-American to be so honored. His acting ability and the poignant roles he played in "In the Heat of the Night" and "Guess Who's Coming to Dinner" transformed the way that the 18-year-old, callow white boy I was saw people of a different race. Not only were black and white people equal, I came to realize, but this black dude and his movie characters were damn excellent.

Upon further investigation, I learned that Sidney Poitier, who was born in Miami, where his parents were visiting, was raised in the Bahamas before emigrating to the United States as a teenager. By birth, he was an American citizen. When he was 16, he lied about his age to enlist in the U.S. Army in 1943. Unlike my dad, Poitier never left the country during World War II, serving instead as an attendant in a mental hospital. Natural-born actors being good observers, his showmanship merited an insanity discharge from the Army.

If only my interest in movies and rock music would have carried through to the classroom, my life might have turned out differently.

In my Analytical Geometry and Calculus I class, I couldn't keep my eyes on the blackboard, where the professor would chalk up derivatives and such, because I couldn't keep them off a splendrous blond girl seated in the front row.

Through Jeff Murphy's girlfriend, Kay Infield, whom he knew from his church and who was a senior at Kent State University School, a laboratory school with kindergarten through 12th grade located adjacent to the campus, I learned that the splendrous blonde was her classmate, and her name was Darcy Dix. The laboratory school served as a training adjunct for the college of education, and a few of its brightest seniors were afforded the opportunity to earn college credits at the university. Darcy was the daughter of Robert C. Dix, chairman of Kent State's board of trustees and publisher of the daily Record-Courier.

For some reason, Kay conveyed to me that Darcy was interested in making my acquaintance. I was not a particularly shy guy when under the influence of alcohol, which, of course, is an extraordinary remedy to timidity, but, under normal conditions, I was not one to initiate interaction with members of the opposite sex, especially those to whom I was physically attracted. So, rather than walk up to Darcy before or after class or even let her catch my wishful eye, a meeting was arranged at the student center. With welcome support from Jeff and Kay, our meeting went well.

Adding to our circle of friendship, Bob Leone also began dating a senior at Kent State University School. Her name was Molly. The six of us frequently met up at parties with rock 'n' roll playing on the stereo and beer chilling in the refrigerator in and around Kent and Cuyahoga Falls. Sometimes Darcy and I would go to a movie with or without another couple.

Darcy Dix was as nice a person as I could ask for as a girlfriend. She was bubbly, happy and energetic. She brought out the best in me. She was intelligent and a good student, something I had been on and off during my school years. My freshman year of college wasn't good at all. In fact, I was in danger of failing the calculus class, which would have left me scrambling to maintain full-time-student status and, with it, my draft deferment.

On the evening before the final exam, Darcy invited me to her home in Kent, where we would study together. In a matter of a couple hours, she was able to infuse into my brain the lessons of the entire quarter – something our professor had not done, undoubtedly because I had other things on my mind. Both of us aced the final, which earned her an A for the course and miraculously uplifted my grade to a C. If I had only studied with my girlfriend more often, things could have been different.

The most exciting event of the season for me and my group of under-ground-music-loving friends was the Jimi Hendrix Experience concert of March 26, 1968, at Music Hall in downtown Cleveland. It was my first experience of that kind. Eight of us crammed into Bob Leone's car for the trip from Kent to Cleveland. With Darcy pressed close against me in the back seat and then holding hands with me as we walked several blocks to the arena, I couldn't have been happier.

As legendary rock 'n' roll writer Jane Scott described the event the following day in the Cleveland Plain Dealer, "This was Jimi Hendrix, drummer Mitch Mitchell and guitarist Noel Redding of the Jimi Hendrix Experience and it was an experience that many will never forget."

I never did.

"Would you believe a Seattle-born Negro who had to go to England to make it?" Scott asked in her story. "A left-hander who plays a right-hand-ed Fender guitar backwards?"

It was unbelievable to me.

Midway through the show, at about 8:15 p.m., Jimi backed away from the microphone, and Chuck Dunaway, the emcee, stepped up to it. He asked all of us in the audience to check under our seats. Three bomb threats had been received by telephone. Apparently, somebody out there didn't take kindly to 3,000 music-loving young people rocking and rolling to the electric-guitar playing and irreverent vocals of a wild and crazy black man.

Nobody found a bomb. Nobody ran for the doors in horror. Nobody ordered an evacuation. "Nobody but Jimi burns a house down," Hendrix shouted. And the show went on. Imagine that kind of response to bomb threats nowadays.

Several of us returned to Cleveland for other concerts that spring, including a trifecta – the Yardbirds, Traffic and Blue Cheer – at the Allen Theatre on Playhouse Square, Cream and Canned Heat at Music Hall and the Nitty Gritty Dirt Band at La Cave, near University Circle.

The music further diverted my attention from the tedium of college studies and shielded my mind from unhappy world affairs.

Winning battles, losing faith

If I had been better focused, I could have been concerned about what occurred on Jan. 30, the beginning of the Tet holiday, which marks the lunar new year. In what became known as the Tet Offensive, some 70,000 North Vietnamese and Viet Cong forces launched a coordinated assault on dozens of major South Vietnamese targets, including the capital city of Saigon. Even the U.S. Embassy and our military command headquarters were hit by the communists. Some 400 South Vietnamese troops and about 150 U.S. Marines were killed in the Battle of Hue, in the far north of South Vietnam.

Given the intensity of the enemy's attacks, the American public's perception of the war and of our prospects for victory took a heavy hit. That perception was intensified by the American media, which mostly had been hawkish about our anti-communist military engagement but suddenly took a jarring punch to the midsection.

Even during the ongoing offensive that February, when the Boston Globe conducted a survey of the editorial positions taken by 39 leading daily newspapers with a combined circulation of 22 million, not a single one was advocating our withdrawal from the war. A later study of network television coverage by University of California at San Diego history Professor Daniel Hallin found it to be "strongly supportive" of the war. Rather than making moral assessments, the mainstream media were focusing on whether the war was winnable.

Respected "CBS Evening News" anchor Walter Cronkite, previously a strong supporter of the war and an old acquaintance of Gen. Creighten Abrams, then commander of American forces in Vietnam, got an eye-opener when he journeyed across the Pacific to cover the Tet Offensive. Upon witnessing some of the action in Hue, Cronkite reportedly exclaimed, "What the hell is going on? I thought we were winning the war." After returning home, he deviated from his usual objective reporting to surmise, "It seems now more than ever that the bloody experience of Vietnam is to end in a stalemate."

As history shows, he was correct. Admonitions against fighting a land war in Asia were attributed throughout the 20th century to a number of leaders who learned better, including World War II American Gens. Douglas MacArthur and Dwight D. Eisenhower and British Army Field

Marshall Bernard Montgomery. Before the American war, the French had learned that lesson in Vietnam. Simply put, the Asians are in it for the long haul. They're not leaving.

But the media dropped the ball in other ways. Initially, the communists did put on a good show for Tet, but our American fighting men responded with a much better one. An estimated 5,000 North Vietnamese soldiers were killed in the Battle of Hue alone. About 9,000 South Vietnamese and American troops were killed in the Tet Offensive, while the enemy suffered more than 45,000 deaths. The insurgency was routed. We had them on the run.

More poignantly, a key factor in the conduct of the war was underplayed. In the aftermath of the Battle of Hue, U.S. and South Vietnamese forces uncovered mass graves in which 2,800 bodies had been dumped. At least that many more innocent people were missing. It may have been an extraordinary massacre, but there was nothing extraordinary about the cruelty inflicted upon South Vietnam civilians by the ruthless communists.

A different massacre occurred on March 16, 1968, in the hamlet of My Lai, where American intelligence indicated a significant contingent of Viet Cong fighters was holed up. When U.S. Army troops arrived, anticipating a bloody battle, however, they found that the VC no longer were there. There is no excuse for the maniacal slaughter of 347 unarmed civilians, many of them women and children, by American soldiers, even if they had aided and abetted the enemy. When the incident came to light a year later, My Lai became synonymous with the atrocities of Vietnam – rightfully so.

That does not excuse the comparative absence of outrage against the much more prevalent and savage barbarity perpetrated by the communists.

With 536,100 American troops in country and 16,592 of them killed that year, 1968 was the height of the Vietnam War. Contrary to assertions by Gen. William Westmoreland, commander of the U.S. Military Assistance Command in Vietnam, and by the Johnson administration, the end of the war was not in sight.

Just one month after Cronkite's "stalemate" declaration, President Johnson, on March 31, called reporters and TV cameramen to the White

House. He said the Vietnamese communists' efforts to make 1968 the year of decisiveness would fail and that "many men – on both sides of the struggle will take new casualties. And the war will go on." He went on to say that Americans should "guard against divisiveness and all its ugly consequences." In conclusion, citing the political partisanship that was infecting the country, the president dropped his bombshell. "Accordingly, I shall not seek and I will not accept, the nomination of any party for another term as your president." Some other Democrat would have to step up to the impending Republican challenge.

Draft deferments and dodges

Unlike the war without end in sight, the end of my brief experience as a student of architecture was imminent. On the first day of spring quarter, Professor Starr, with his cane tapping the floor, shuffled into the classroom for Analytical Geometry and Calculus II. "I'm only blind in one eye," he joked. "I just can't see out of the other one." A couple students chuckled uneasily. I wasn't amused. Starr stepped to the blackboard, where he scribbled something that remotely resembled an equation. "Don't worry if you can't read this," he said. "I can't either." Not even Darcy Dix could rescue me from that. I was doomed. Within a week, I withdrew from the class. I no longer was a full-time student. The writing was on the wall. It said 1-A, "Available for military service."

My mother knew it. She called the Navy Reserve Center in Akron and set up an interview. Joining the military reserves or the National Guard was a sure way of avoiding the draft and staying far away from Vietnam. It was draft evasion in any rational definition of the term, as was my student deferment, to be quite honest, but being a "draft dodger" was subject to disputatious interpretations. The interviewing naval officer looked over my transcript, which conveniently did not reflect on the current spring quarter. After posing a couple questions to me and my mom, who responded in her German-accented English, he informed us that they had no openings. Furthermore, he doubted that the situation would be any different for the Army or Air Force Reserves, and I shouldn't even bother with the National Guard.

George W. Bush, the man who later would be elected the 43rd president of the United States, was about to lose his student deferment at about the same time I did. In fact, he was 12 days away from that life-altering phenomenon on May 27, 1968, when he walked into the Texas Air National Guard offices near Houston. Seeking to get into pilot training, he took the aptitude test for that slot and scored a dismal 25 percent. His father, George H.W. Bush, who later became the nation's 41st president, happened to be a U.S. congressman. While most other men of his age faced a long waiting list for the National Guard, the younger Bush got right in.

It is not my place to cast judgment upon my contemporaries who found ways to avoid the military draft. All wars are subject to controversy, and, in American history, the Vietnam War probably was second to the Civil War in that regard. There are those who relish war, however, who, with alacrity, send others to fight and die in war, who even invent or cherry-pick premises to justify war but who, when faced with the prospect of serving their country in war themselves, run the other way. Such behavior is accurately referred to as hypocrisy. In the context of such behavior among Vietnam draft avoiders, the term "chicken-hawk" came into popular use. It's an appropriate application.

Lyndon B. Johnson was the president responsible for cherry-picking the premises for the Gulf of Tonkin Resolution in 1964 and for most of the 58,220 American military members who died in Vietnam. Although Johnson was a member of Congress at the time, he served briefly in the U.S. Navy during World War II as an observer for bombing missions in the South Pacific. Whether he actually came under enemy fire, as he claimed, and whether he earned the Silver Star awarded to him by Gen. MacArthur are matters of dispute. Nonetheless, Johnson did go to war. He was a hawk but not necessarily a chicken-hawk.

Clearly, George W. Bush did not go to war. He sought to avoid it, and the evidence is strong that his influential daddy enabled his avoidance. Thirty-five years later, as president, he sent Americans to fight and die in Iraq, substantially based on the falsehood that Iraqi leader Saddam Hussein had connections to the al-Qaeda terrorist attacks of Sept. 11, 2001. Furthermore, the erroneous intelligence regarding Iraq's possession of weapons of mass destruction was cherry-picked from contrary evidence that raised questions about that bewildering conclusion. Bush is a chicken-hawk.

The chief of all chicken-hawks is Dick Cheney, George W. Bush's vice president, who never met a war he didn't like, except that he got four student deferments during the Vietnam War and then impregnated his wife just in time for a paternity deferment to keep his ass safe and sound. In 1989, questioned about Vietnam during his confirmation hearings to serve as the elder President Bush's defense secretary, Cheney responded with the obvious lie that he "would have obviously been happy to serve had I been called." Later that year he told a reporter, "I had other priorities in the '60s than military service."

Of course, many young men of that era had other priorities.

Karl Rove, the second President Bush's leading propagandist for the Iraq War, was one of them. After his high school graduation in 1969, he became a full-time college student with the appropriate draft deferment until 1971, when he reduced his class load to part time. For some un-known reason, he still managed to avoid serving his country in the military. Rove qualifies as a chicken-hawk.

Donald J. Trump, who was sworn in as our nation's 45th president in January 2017, also had his priorities. After turning 18 years old in June 1964, he received 2-S student deferments the following four years. After college graduation in 1968, the athletic Trump was able to obtain a 1-Y medical deferment for bone spurs in his heels, a condition he described as "temporary" and "minor." He said he had gotten a letter from his doctor to certify the medical condition with draft officials but could not identify the doctor.

As reported by BuzzFeed's Nathan McDermott and Andrew Kaczynski, the leader of the free world has equated his professed courage in sexual escapades to that of people going to war. Speaking of the AIDS epidemic on "The Howard Stern Show" in 1993, Trump said, "You know, if you're young, and in this era, and if you have any guilt about not having gone to Vietnam. We have our own Vietnam. It's called the dating game." Reiterating that absurdity, he said, "Dating is like being in Vietnam. You're the equivalent of a soldier going over to Vietnam."

Updating that contention in a 2004 interview with Playboy magazine, Trump said, "I tell my sons just to get a nice girlfriend and be happy, because it's dangerous out there. It's Vietnam. I guess now we can say it's Iraq – same deal, right?"

The documented dishonesty of his claimed early opposition to the Iraq War aside, I wouldn't label Trump a chicken-hawk. In a 2005 recording, he boasted that stars like him "can do anything with women" and that he could just "grab them by the pussy." So he's a pussy-hawk.

Girlfriends come and go

Unlike President Trump's self-congratulatory gropes and sexual conquests, any physical contact I had with members of the opposite sex was by mutual agreement. Being raised by a strong, forceful mother who never took crap from anybody most likely instilled within me a sense for gender equality, even though the world around us didn't look at it that way. Furthermore, as a male in his late teen years, I was passionately attracted to girls my age, but I had not experienced sex.

I did like girls. And some of them did like me.

Buds were sprouting on the elm tree that my father had planted in the backyard and grew shadier every summer, and dandelions were popping up in the grassy devil strip between the sidewalk and curb on Bailey Road. The snow had melted away, and spring was in the air. I wasn't scheduled for work at Click that Saturday, and caddy season hadn't yet arrived at the country club. I sat on the front stoop waiting for Bob Leone to pick me up. "David," I heard my mom call through the screen door. "The telephone's for you. It's a girl."

I hurried into the kitchen and picked up the receiver from the counter. It was Pam Lowe. We hadn't seen each other since the "Itchycoo Park" rendition the previous summer. Her family was moving to California, she told me, and her parents were going to throw a going-away party for her in a big lodge at the park that evening. One of the popular Akron bands would be playing. She wanted to see me there and say goodbye. I said I'd try.

Bob and his cousin Jim pulled into the driveway. I hopped in the backseat and rolled the window down. We headed for Chapel Hill Mall, where we could mosey around, maybe catch a movie, maybe not, maybe buy a new shirt at O'Neil's, maybe not. It was mid-afternoon. "What should we do later tonight?" Jim asked. "We could go to Kent, check out JBs."

"I just got invited to a big party in Akron," I said. "There's going to be a band. Could be fun."

The party started at 7 p.m. We got there around 8:15. The band was playing. People were dancing. It was a pretty good crowd. Two adults stopped us at the door. I recognized Pam's mother, didn't know her father. They didn't recognize me. "Sorry, this is a private party," he told us.

"I'm Dave. Pam invited us," I said.

"Is that right? I'll go get her." Her mom went inside.

"You guys haven't been drinking, have you?" her father asked. "There's no drinking at this party."

"No, we haven't," I replied. It happened to be true.

Pam came to the door with her mom. She smiled when she saw me and gave me an innocent hug. Her blond hair had grown longer. She was just as pretty as I remembered.

"These are my good friends Bob and Jim," I told her. "This is my friend Pam," I said to them. We followed her inside. Unlike me and all my other buddies, Bob was growing his hair long. It covered his ears. He played electric guitar and had been in a band, after all. Quite a few guys in the party had longer hair like that. So did the musicians.

Pam told me she would miss her friends and her hometown, but she was excited about moving to the West Coast. She knew all about the "Summer of Love" in 1967 and was fascinated by the peace movement emanating from California. The band played Scott McKenzie's hit song, "If you're going to San Francisco, be sure to wear some flowers in your hair." Pam and I danced slow and close. Then she went to mingle with the crowd, share memories with the other guests and accept their fond fare-wells. Bob, Jim and I enjoyed the music. It was good.

We stayed until the band quit playing at 11:30 p.m. Other guests were leaving. I went over to Pam and said goodbye. She followed us outside. She held my hand, and we went around the corner of the lodge. It was dark. She wrapped her arms around my neck. I embraced her. We kissed. It lasted. Finally, she let me go. She was going to San Francisco. I wasn't. I didn't know that I'd be passing through.

I worked the early shift the next Saturday at Click. Afterward, I stopped at the A&W for a burger and a root beer then drove to Darcy's house. She wanted to see a movie called "Planet of the Apes," and it was showing at a theater on West Market Street in Akron. Things didn't feel quite right. As we watched actor Charlton Heston get a blood transfusion from two chimpanzees on the big screen, I put my arm around her, but she didn't lean her head on my shoulder. The movie was OK. When we got back to the car, she had something to tell me. We could still be friends, she said, but there was somebody else. I took her home. The ride was quiet. She got out of my car in her driveway. "Goodbye," she said. I watched her go inside. The door closed behind her.

I saw other girls that spring. A couple of them were Kay and Darcy's classmates at Kent State University School. A couple were fellow employees at the Click store. Mike Mooney and I met a couple girls at the dances held at Tallmadge Springs, a local swimming and picnic area with a large pavilion.

Violence in black and white

And then there was the Draught House, a king-size hall with two dance floors and two bandstands so that the music never stopped on Friday and Saturday nights. In addition to Bob Leone and Jim Cardarelli and me, Bob Schoonover, whom I'd known since junior high school, and Rick Morgan, my caddy buddy, would take the drive south of Akron. We'd arrive early to make sure we got a table. The place would be jammed wall to wall with drunk and raucous teenagers once the music started. Everybody at our table would down a pitcher of 3.2 beer by that time.

When the band played Tommy James & the Shondells' "Mony Mony," the dance floor would be jumping. Any guy who wanted a dance partner could find one. Later on, things would slow down with "I Think We're Alone Now." I'd happily put my arms around any one of dozens of attractive young ladies, but I'd be thinking about being alone with somebody else.

After a few dances and with sweat dripping from my forehead, I returned to our table, sat down and replenished my glass from my half-empty pitcher.

"Did you see what happened to Rick?" Jim said to me.

"No, where is he?" I asked, looking around.

"The cops kicked him out," Jim told me. He pointed to the two uniformed, off-duty officers handling security near the main entrance.

"What? What in the hell for?" I looked at the police and scowled. They weren't looking my way.

"I'm not sure. There was some sort of ruckus between Rick and another guy. One cop grabbed Rick, yelled at him and then yanked him outside. The cop came back in without him a minute later. The other cop grabbed the other guy and took him over to the other side. Then he came back. I don't know what happened to the other guy."

"Son of a bitch!" I said. I leapt up from the chair and bounded toward the two officers. They were tall and broad chested. They saw me approaching. One of them stepped forward. I clenched my right fist, raised my arm and took a wild swing. I don't know whether I missed or he dodged the punch. Before I knew it, one of them had me in a half nelson from my left side, and the other one had my right arm in a hammerlock. They bounced all 135 pounds of me across the floor through a doorway marked "Private" and down a narrow hallway. After banging my head against the wall, the first cop pinned both my arms behind me. The other one smacked my face back and forth with his open hand.

When he stopped, he demanded, "What the hell's wrong with you?"

"You threw my buddy out for no good reason," I said.

"He was causing trouble, and now you're in big trouble."

They took my name, and one of them went into an office to make a phone call. A couple minutes later, he returned to the hallway. "Listen," he said. "You're banned from the Draught House for two weeks. If you do come back, we will be watching you. And nothing like this better happen again, because next time we'll be taking you downtown."

I didn't offer any resistance as they escorted me out the main entrance. I stumbled across the parking lot to Bob Schoonover's Ford convertible. I didn't see Rick. I don't know where he went. I sat on the ground, leaned my back against the bumper and closed my eyes. Even in my drunken stupor, I knew I had gotten what I deserved. In 1968, if you got into a physical altercation with the cops, you got roughed up. You didn't file a lawsuit over it.

Dealing with a rowdy white kid was the least of problems for law enforcement across the country.

On April 4, James Earl Ray, a U.S. Army veteran who had served in Germany at the end of World War II and was a confirmed racist, shot and killed Martin Luther King Jr. in Memphis, Tennessee. It was the day after King had delivered his "I've Been to the Mountaintop" address in support of striking sanitation workers.

The assassination precipitated riots in at least 110 American cities. Stores were looted. Buildings were set aflame. Guns were fired. Bottles and rocks were hurled at police. People died. Some commentators called it the Holy Week Uprising. Some 1,200 buildings were burned in Washington, D.C., and some neighborhood blocks were turned to rubble. Eleven people were killed in Chicago, six in Baltimore, five in Kansas City, one in Detroit, two in Cincinnati. Among them, two white men were killed by black mobs, and two black men were killed by police.

It was a violent year, not only in Vietnam but also in America. It also was a presidential election year. President Johnson was sidelined under the weight of Americans bleeding and dying in Vietnam. Even before announcing his candidacy on April 27, Vice President Hubert H. Humphrey was considered the leading contender for the Democratic Party's nomination. But U.S. Sens. Eugene McCarthy, the strong anti-war candidate, and Robert F. Kennedy, who wasn't a big fan of the war either, were campaigning for change. Young people were especially contemptuous toward the candidate who struggled to distance himself from the war-waging administration. "Dump the Hump!" was a popular cry among protesters.

So Humphrey figured he'd reach out to youthful voters with a series of college-campus rallies, and the first one was scheduled for May 3 at Kent State University. As I walked between classes that afternoon, I saw a group of 15 or 20 students gathered outside Memorial Gymnasium, where the vice president was scheduled to speak. Deciding to learn what they were about, I listened in as they planned some sort of coordinated vocal uprising inside the gym. That sounded interesting, so I decided to follow them in. But, as we arrived at the main entrance, which faced the football stadium, I saw a girl I knew. I decided to walk with her to our sociology class instead.

Humphrey probably had some interesting things to say, and he did make an effort to reach out to the college crowd. What received prominent attention in the next day's news accounts, though, was the fact that about 50 members of Students for a Democratic Society and Black United Students, which had organized a Kent State chapter one month earlier, stood up in the middle of the vice president's speech and walked out. According to news reports, the vast majority of students and others in the crowd roundly booed the black and white protesters.

One of the leaders of the protest, James S. Powrie, who had received a football scholarship to KSU, defended the walkout in a letter to the editor in the Kent Stater student newspaper several days later. He reasoned that his action was "to symbolize, publicly, my disassociation with the Johnson-Humphrey administration which has systematically corrupted the highest ideals of democratic government by practicing a policy of deceit that has placed this country into its third bloodiest war without the consent of Congress."

Powrie referred to "platitudes" spoken by Humphrey that "received applause approaching the volume of the boos those of us who refused to listen to such nonsense received as we walked out."

The incident in Memorial Gym on May 3, 1968, probably was the most radical occurrence in the history of Kent State University – until that very date anyway. It wasn't the most apolitical campus in the country, but it wasn't far from it either. Kent was a party school, not a cradle of unrest. It was the thousand boo birds who had their say that day, not the few dozen anti-war and pro-civil-rights protesters who walked out on Hubert Humphrey.

The peace movement that was gaining steam on other college campuses had barely touched a nerve at Kent State. When I had my chance to reach out and touch it, I turned and walked away. And when my freshman year reached its shaky conclusion, I turned and walked away from the college I loved and from the delightful intoxication of juvenility.

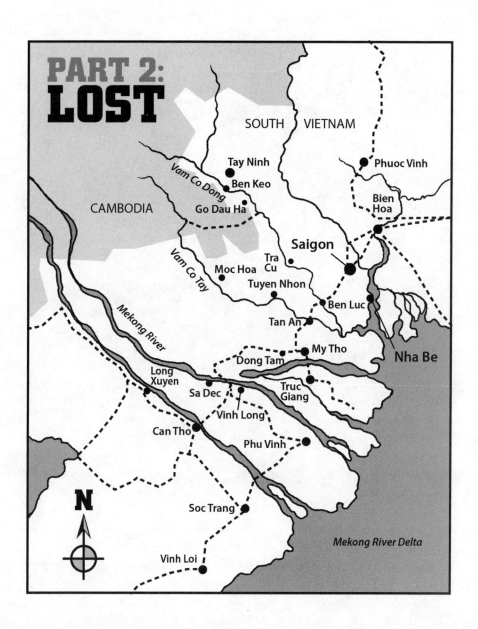

Chapter 12 | **Boot Camp**

The draft notice would be arriving in the mail sometime soon, and I knew it. Like mine, Bill Roach's deferment was lapsing. Mike Mooney was graduating from high school and had no illusions about postsecondary education. We were of like minds. We would beat the Army to the punch. So I drove the three of us into downtown Akron and found a parking lot off High Street. We walked around the block to the Marine Corps recruiting office on Main Street.

There was no waiting line on the sidewalk outside the door. Actually, the place was empty, except for a corporal sitting at a desk and reading a magazine. He was smartly dressed in a khaki, button-up shirt, coordinated necktie and sky-blue trousers. A solitary National Defense ribbon was pinned above his left breast pocket.

His was regulation military attire during the Vietnam War era, as it was in the preceding wars of the 20th century. The olive-drab field uniforms of the world wars and the slightly adapted battle dress of Korea and Vietnam were unacceptable attire for public exposure. It would have been laughable to see an American serviceman dressed for battle while working in a recruiting office or strolling down Main Street. Camouflage uniforms were intended for concealment in prospective conflicts with enemy combatants, not for vainglorious exposition thousands of miles away from battlegrounds.

Times changed in the 21st century. Nowadays, military bureaucrats strut down the halls of the Pentagon in full camo and kids fresh out of basic training sport battle-dress uniforms, or BDUs, while holding hands with their girlfriends to wage the global war on terrorism in suburban lifestyle centers.

The spit-and-polished Marine recruiter closed his magazine, got up from his desk and met us at the counter. "Can I help you?" He didn't seem especially excited by our visit.

"We're here to sign up," Mike said. "We want to get in the buddy plan for a two-year hitch."

"Well, we might be able to get you guys in a buddy plan, but you're going to have to enlist for more than two years," the corporal said.

"I know a couple guys who just got the two-year deal," Bill informed him. "And that's what we want to do."

"You're going to have to talk to the sergeant about a special deal like that," the corporal replied. "And he's not here today. You need to come back tomorrow."

We tried again the next day. Again, we interrupted the corporal from his reading material. Again, the sergeant we needed to see wasn't there.

On the third day, Bill had to work. Mike and I thought we could get the buddy plan rolling with the Marine sergeant and that Bill could follow up later. For the third day running, the sergeant had better things to do than be in the recruiting office when we arrived, and the corporal couldn't be bothered with three buddies wanting to sign up for two-year hitches.

Back outside, we looked at the Navy recruiting office next door. Neither one of us was known for patience. "What do you think?" I said.

"What the hell," Mike replied. "Let's see what they got."

It was late spring. The weather was warm. Aside from two sailors wearing dress-white uniforms and black silk neckerchiefs knotted on their chests, the office was empty. The younger one of the two had a patch with three stripes sewn to his upper left sleeve. He met us at the counter.

"We were wondering if the Navy has a buddy plan," I said to him.

"And also if we can enlist for two years," Mike added.

"Nope, the Navy only has four-year enlistments," the sailor said. "But we can sign you up for a buddy plan. Hey, Stan," he called to the other guy, who had a patch with an eagle and two chevrons on his sleeve and seemed to be in charge. "These guys are interested in the buddy plan."

Stan said he could get us into corpsman training together. After that, we'd both get orders to Vietnam, probably patching up bullet-riddled Marines, but there wouldn't be any guarantees about being in the same unit.

"No, I can't stand blood," Mike said, which was news to me. He didn't care to be a medical corpsman.

"Well, we can make sure that both of you go to boot camp together," Stan said. "Why don't you guys come on back here, and we'll get your information."

I had a seat at Stan's desk, and Mike sat down with the younger guy. Stan took down my name, address, date of birth, place of birth, where I went to school, that kind of stuff. When I told him I had just finished a year of college, he informed me that I could begin my enlistment at the rank of E-3, or seaman, the same as his assistant, two pay grades above E-1, or seaman recruit. Also, the Navy would guarantee me specialized training in Class A School. That sounded like a good deal to me.

Two days later, Mike and I hopped on a bus at the Greyhound station in Akron. Our destination was the New Federal Office Building, located a few blocks west of the Greyhound station in downtown Cleveland. Completed just a year earlier, it was a glistening skyscraper. Topping off at 419 feet and 31 floors, it was the third tallest building in Cleveland at the time. A chilly breeze swept off Lake Erie and ruffled my wavy head of hair as we crossed East 9th Street at Lakeside Avenue. From the lobby, we took an elevator to one of the upper floors, where we were scheduled for pre-induction physical exams.

The window views up there were breathtaking. I had never been so high. To the north, we looked down on Cleveland Municipal Stadium, where I'd witnessed the Indians lose to the Yankees a decade earlier and where I'd watched the Browns win football games on TV. When German boxer Max Schmeling retained his heavyweight championship of the world by technical knockout over Young Stribling in its 1931 dedication, with a seating capacity of 78,189, it was the largest such stadium on Earth.

Just beyond it was Lake Erie, its choppy surface reflecting the crisp blue sky as far as the eye could see, camouflaging the eutrophic, life-choking swill below. To the south and rising above us was the 52-story, 771-foot Terminal Tower, the second-tallest building in the world upon its completion in 1930 and still Ohio's tallest one 38 years later.

The physical exam took a few hours, mostly sitting around and waiting to be called by various examiners, but it was fairly routine. Nobody checked for bone spurs in my heels, and, unlike the pussy-hawk Donald Trump, I didn't have a letter from an anonymous physician to get me a draft deferment. Nobody told me to bend over and spread my cheeks, so, unlike Rush Limbaugh, the immensely popular conservative political commentator and Iraq War cheerleader, no anal cysts were found to disqualify me from military service. Unlike Howard Dean, the onetime presidential candidate and former chairman of the Democratic National Committee, my back passed muster so that I soon would be heading for boot camp instead of 10 months of ski bumming with a physical deferment in Aspen, Colorado.

Not only that, but my urine was good for double duty. Directed to the men's room with a jar in my hand, I encountered a black guy waiting inside.

"Hey, man," he said. "Would you do me a favor and piss in my jar while you're at it?" I looked around and made sure we were alone, just two red-blooded Americans, a skinny white guy and a skinny black guy, in the otherwise quiet restroom, getting ready to serve our country in the military. I figured our urine was pretty much the same, and, if he needed some of mine to pass his physical, who was I to say no? My bladder had plenty.

"OK," I replied. "No problem." I went into the toilet stall and filled both jars halfway to the top. "Here you go," I said as I headed back out to the pee-collection station.

He nodded in appreciation.

I don't know for sure whether the black guy passed the piss test, but Mike and I both got clean bills of health. The Navy recruiter told us it would take a few days to process all our paperwork, and then we'd get instructions for our induction.

Farewell and good luck

I heard from Jeff Murphy a couple days later that the daughter of one of the automobile dealers on the Cuyahoga Falls "Million Dollar Mile" would be hosting a Kent State University School graduation party at her house in Silver Lake that night. He said he'd be going with Kay. One of her classmates, Cathy Hill, who had joined me in the back seat of Jeff's Corvair to watch "Night of the Living Dead" at a drive-in theater the previous weekend, was inviting me to the party. There would be food and beer, Jeff said. I liked Cathy.

The backyard party was nice. Low-powered beer was drunk, mostly by those of the legal age of 18, but drunkenness and disorderliness were successfully deterred by periodic parental observation.

Cathy, Kay and Jeff were talking with a girl they called Wendy the Witch, not because of any ill temperament but because of her enchanting demeanor and penetrating eyes.

Darcy was at the party, effervescent as always. She caught my eye and smiled. I walked across the sandstone patio to say hello. She reached out and held my hand. "I heard that you're enlisting in the Navy," she said with a touch of sadness in her voice.

"College wasn't working out for me," I said. "I was going to lose my student deferment anyway. I'll be going to boot camp in a couple days."

We sat down on a step between the patio and the lush lawn.

"Do you think you'll be going to Vietnam?" she asked.

"Well, I thought so when we tried to sign up for two years in the Marines," I said. "But the guy we needed to talk to at the recruiter was never there, so my buddy Mike and I finally just went next door to the Navy recruiter and ended up enlisting for four years. The Navy's not as dangerous as the Marines, and, if I get stationed on a ship, I should be OK."

Darcy's eyes got watery. "I'm sorry, Dave," she said. "I like you. I wish you wouldn't go."

"I like you too, Darcy," I said. "We had some fun together, didn't we?"

She nodded.

"So what are you going to do now that you're done with high school?" I asked.

She was going away to college at the University of Wisconsin.

"I'll miss you, Darcy," I said. "I'll write to you." She was crying. I was getting choked up, so I looked away. I stood up. "Bye, Darcy," I said. I walked back across the yard to spend the rest of the evening with Cathy.

The following Tuesday, Rick Morgan and I visited a girl we'd met at the Draught House when we weren't busy getting our butts tossed out of the place. We listened to music and drank a few beers in the apartment she was renting above a shop on State Road.

As the clock ticked past midnight, I reluctantly told them I had to go and catch some sleep. I was Rick's ride home. I could tell he was having a good time.

"Aw, come on, Dave, can't we stay another hour or two?" he said.

"Sorry, man, this is it for me. My mom's taking Mike and me to the bus station, and we gotta be there by 7 a.m. for the trip to Cleveland," I said.

"Yeah, I get it," Rick said. "Hey, Laurie, can you drive me home later?"

She said OK.

Rick was a month older than me, but he had another year of high school to go. "Hey, buddy, I wish you the best of luck," he told me. "Next spring, the way things are going, I'll probably be right behind you."

I never saw Rick Morgan again.

After his graduation from Cuyahoga Falls High School, Rick was drafted into the U.S. Army. He arrived in Vietnam on Oct. 18, 1970, attached to the 196th Light Infantry Brigade. About halfway through his combat tour, his armored personnel carrier was hit by an explosive device. According to military records, Cpl. Morgan, 21 years old, was a ground casualty, the result of hostile action, on April 7, 1971, in Quang Tin Province, south of Da Nang. The boy I'd known since we were 10-year-old second basemen, the kid I caddied with and played golf with, the fun-loving beer drinker with whom I met girls at the Draught House was dead and gone. His body was recovered and sent home to grieving parents, a brother and seven sisters. They buried him at Northlawn Memorial Garden.

The harsh reality of Vietnam was still a distant concept for me as I left Rick at Laurie's apartment and got in the driver's seat of my VW. I drove east on Portage Trail, crossed the river and the railroad tracks, turned right at the fire station on High Street and then left for the home stretch on Myrtle Avenue. The whining of a siren caught me by surprise, and I looked to see the flashing light of a cop car in my rearview mirror. "Shit," I mumbled to myself. I couldn't believe I was about to get another speeding ticket. I rolled down my window as the officer approached.

"Do you know what the speed limit is here?" he asked.

"Yes, sir, it's 25 miles an hour," I replied. Of course, I knew. I could practically see the house where I'd been growing up.

"And do you know you were going 47 miles per hour?" he asked.

"Sorry, I did not realize that," I said.

"Well, I have to give you a citation," he said. He took my driver's license back to the squad car.

Ten minutes later he returned with the ticket book in his hand. "I'm gonna schedule you for 10 a.m. in municipal court next Thursday, June 27," the cop said. "Is that going to work for you?"

"No, I'm not going to make it," I said.

"Well, how about Friday then?" he asked.

"Sorry, but I can't make that either," I told him.

"What do mean, you can't make it?" he said with more than a hint of impatience. "If you don't show up in court, we'll have to put out a summons for your arrest."

"Honestly, I'd rather be there than where I'm going," I said. "But I'm getting inducted in the Navy tomorrow, and they're probably not going to let me come home so soon from boot camp."

"Why the hell didn't you tell me that in the first place?" the cop said. "Now I have to void this ticket and then write up a report on why I did that. All right then, get your butt home. And best of luck to you."

At least I was having some luck that night.

Welcome to Great Lakes

Bright and early Wednesday morning, June 19, Mike Mooney and I got back on a Greyhound bus for the 30-mile trip to the Navy induction center high up in the New Federal Office Building. Gathered in a room with a dozen or so other enlistees from Northeast Ohio and Western

Pennsylvania, we raised our right hands and solemnly swore to "defend the Constitution of the United States against all enemies, foreign and domestic."

The petty officer in charge conferred with one of the guys who was familiar with Cleveland. With an envelope full of tickets and chits in hand, the trusted recruit led us several blocks south and west and into the bowels of Terminal Tower, where we boarded a rapid-transit train for the trip to Cleveland Hopkins Airport. Soon we were on a United Airlines flight to Chicago's O'Hare International Airport, the busiest one in the world. Even before reaching boot camp, the Navy was a whole new adventure for me.

From O'Hare, we were herded onto a bus and transported to Great Lakes Recruit Training Command, located about 35 miles north of the "Windy City" and just west of the Lake Michigan shore. Actually, in terms of weather, Cleveland is windier, but Chicago's nickname reportedly is associated with politicians full of hot air.

Darkness was setting in by the time we arrived. We spent the first night in one of the creaky old barracks where our naval predecessors had rested their bones on meager mattresses flopped atop flat-spring bunks during the world wars.

"Reveille, reveille," some guy in a white Navy uniform yelled loud and clear. "Get your raggedy asses out of those racks and put your clothes on."

I rubbed my eyes to catch the glimmer of sunrise through the windows to the east. "Where the fuck am I?" I wondered. Then it hit me. It wasn't my mother dragging me out of bed for swim practice or school. I was a long way from home. I heard groans from left and right and from the bunk below me.

"This ain't your mommy talking to you," the white uniform shouted again. "You're in the Navy now, and your feet best be hitting the deck. Pull your clothes on and line up against this bulkhead over here. And shut your mouths. You will talk when you're told to talk. Do you understand?"

A few "yeahs," "OKs" and "whatevers" came in response.

"That's, 'Yes, sir!'" the white uniform shouted. "When I ask a question, you answer, 'Yes, sir!' or, 'No, sir!' I want to hear it."

"Yes, sir!" most of us replied.

"Louder!" he demanded.

"Yes, sir!"

There were 85 of us. We came in all colors, shapes and sizes – although the military had obesity standards, and there were no Muslims, not even the Cassius Clay-turned-Muhammed Ali variety. And we came from all directions, not just Ohio and Pennsylvania but also Florida, Indiana, Iowa, Georgia and Harlem in New York City, whose favorite sons tended to let you know about it.

Before we knew it, we were lined up at the chow hall. After breakfast of sausage, scrambled eggs and toast with white milk and orange juice, which we gulped down in 10 minutes, or not, we were herded out and lined up at another building. Uniforms were issued. We put on blue bell-bottom dungarees, light-blue, long-sleeved over-shirts and white sailor hats. Civilian clothes were packaged up and addressed for home. Hair was buzzed off of our heads. Service numbers were assigned. Mine was B440308. Unforgettable.

With each "nuts-to-butts" lineup, mooing sounds from the increasingly restive herd of recruits became more pronounced.

"That's enough of that bullshit," came the order from a white uniform. "One more time, and you'll all be doing pushups in that field of weeds and bumblebees over there," he yelled into the reddening face of a kid who had been inducted with us in Cleveland. Mike Mooney had nicknamed him "Chiquita," not because of his small size or his ethnicity but because of a banana sticker he said his girlfriend had affixed to his temple after she kissed him goodbye. That pleasant reminder had stuck with him on the rapid transit, the flight to Chicago and the bus ride to Great Lakes, where it rudely was extracted and flicked into the trash. His tender memories soon were to be similarly expunged.

"Fuck that asshole," came a grumble from ahead of us in the line outside a building where we waited to get our dental exams. "Yeah, that dick ain't shit. He don't scare me none," another voice replied.

I looked at two of the Harlem guys chuckling and prancing around like they were waiting in line outside the Apollo Theater to see Gladys Knight & the Pips. One of them was about 6 feet tall and athletically built. The other one was closer to my size. Two white dudes from Des Moines were backing away, looking for a different place to wait in line.

"You two guys better knock it off," Mike growled and glared at the Harlem pair with the crazy eyes that told me he meant business. "If you get us in trouble, me and him are gonna kick your asses," he said, indicating that I was his trusted accomplice.

I didn't know whether Mike could kick the athletic guy's ass or not, although nothing surprised me about him. As for the smaller troublemaker, well, it would be my first tangle with a black guy, which I was not excited about, but, if Mike Mooney said I'd be kicking his ass, I figured I better.

"Take it easy, man," the athletic guy said to Mike, a toothy grin crossing his face. "Be cool. We're just messing around here. The boss man can't see us now. We won't do you no trouble."

I didn't let on that I was relieved to hear that.

The hurry-up-and-wait was getting interminable as we all sat crosslegged with no room to stretch on the linoleum floor of an assembly area where dental technicians were calling us one by one for oral checkups behind some flimsy curtains. By the time they got from "Anderson" to "Davis" to "Gibbons" to "Jones," an hour had ticked away, and my bladder was ready to burst. I didn't think I could hold it to "Lange," and then what?

I wasn't the only one. "What the hell?" I heard a yelp come from about 10 feet behind me. "God dammit!" somebody else cried out. "He pissed his pants, and it's all over the floor," another one yelled. I turned around to see a half dozen guys standing up, pointing fingers and shaking fists at a recruit who had his head buried between his knees with his hands cupped behind it, forearms covering his ears.

Two white uniforms scurried back into the herd and ordered us all to stand up. The urine-sopped perpetrator and several victims who had been befouled by the smelly liquid waste were rounded up and ushered out of the room. A mop and bucket of soapy water were dispatched to clean up the floor. Apparently alerted to the potential for further urinary expulsions, we all were lined up at the head – a place formerly known to most of us as a restroom.

For my bladder, it was a classic feeling of Schadenfreude, the inimitable German term that applies to the pleasure one garners from the misfortune of others. There must be a reason why no similar term exists in the English language, or most others, for that matter. With German entrenched in my genes, never did a meeting with a urinal feel better, and the seat of my dungarees was satisfactorily dry.

Soon thereafter, my teeth passed muster, at least for the time being.

Humiliation runs wide and deep

On day three, we attempted to march in step to the cadence of our assigned company commander, a first-class petty officer in white uniform, away from the aged side of the training center. We advanced to a three-story, cinder-block barracks surrounded by a multitude of indistinguishable 1950s buildings that housed berthing quarters, mess halls, drill halls and classrooms for thousands of Navy recruits.

Top priority for my company of recruits – some of whom soon would be firing M-16s at Asians and others who would be aboard submarines and destroyers armed with nuclear weapons targeted at Soviet cold warriors – evidently was to fold and stow our military-issue clothing according to arbitrary specifications. Failure to follow explicit instructions for every insignificant detail would result in a demerit.

Or worse. Vince Luchetti, a gregarious guy from Sharon, Pennsylvania, who had been assigned to the rack below mine, found that out in unpleasant fashion.

Upon inspection of his metal storage unit, the company commander, Mr. Jenkins, ripped Vince's entire supply of boxer shorts from a shelf and flung them to the barracks deck. "Luchetti, can't you follow orders?" he growled.

"Yes, sir!" Vince replied.

"Then why didn't you fold your skivvies the way I instructed?"

"I don't know, sir!" Vince said.

"Because you're a scrounge," Jenkins yelled.

"No, sir," Vince said.

"The hell you're not. Pick up that pair of skivvies and put it over your head, scrounge."

"What, sir?"

"You heard the order, Luchetti. Are you gonna follow orders, or do you want to see the inside of the brig?"

"Yes, sir!" Vince said. He bent over, picked up a pair of his boxers and wrapped the elastic waistband around his crewcut, from his forehead to the nape of his neck.

"Now pull those skivvies over your face and get your raggedy ass down to the yard. Then you march around the barracks and announce loud and clear, 'I am a scrounge, I am a scrounge,' repeatedly, until I order you to halt."

"Yes, sir!" Vince followed instructions.

"The company will observe from the windows, but there will be no laughter," Jenkins ordered the rest of us.

"I am a scrounge, I am a scrounge." We heard Vince's refrain as we watched from the second floor. It wasn't funny.

Lined up nuts to butts, we were served three square meals per day, except for one exceptionally skinny Southern boy, who was issued a half-dozen donuts for dessert after dinner. It was a futile attempt to stuff him up to regulation weight. His appetite for the Navy was waning. He passed the sugary alimentation around to some buddies.

Lined up nuts to butts in nothing but our skivvies, we were subjected to various physical inspections and injections, including the notorious bicillin that was rumored to leave an aching, golf-ball-sized lump in your ass cheek. It nearly lived up to its reputation.

We also got daily doses of classroom instruction on everything from the military code of conduct and Navy terminology – no more walls, windows, doors or staircases in our vocabulary – to tying knots and managing masculine hygiene.

The discovery of crab lice in a corner of the barracks resulted in a mass inspection of genitalia amidst whispered threats of serious bodily harm to the guilty party or parties. Homosexuality would be met with a bevy of fists after taps, not with open arms. No crab carriers were identified.

Hours were set aside every day for marching in formation on the steaming concrete grinder. Nobody was talking about global warming, but it was a long, hot summer. Daily highs for Chicago repeatedly eclipsed 90 degrees Fahrenheit, with Aug. 6 peaking at 96 degrees, and the Great Lakes grinder was surely hotter. "Gimme your left ... your left, right, left. Company halt! About-face. Present arms. Shoulder arms." And the beat went on.

Religious observance was required on Sunday morning. Protestant and Catholic chaplains were provided. Lutheran Church-Missouri Synod not being an option, I chose Catholic Mass.

PT, or physical training, was a welcome respite for me but not for everyone.

Inspections in our white dress uniforms were not quite so welcome for me, as the inspectors always seemed to find some deficiency, whether it was a minuscule sprout of fuzz on my chin or an invisible scuff on my spit-shined shoe. Every infraction resulted in a demerit, and my demerits were adding up for additional hours of PT in the evenings. The worst consequence of that, for me, was missing out on cigarette-smoking time during mail call.

The worst horrors of boot camp for a few of my fellow recruits were the swimming tests. A general rule of thumb is, if you can't swim, join the Army, or the Air Force, or even the Marines, but don't enlist in the Navy. That message was missed by those who had tears streaming down their cheeks and helpless pleas bouncing off the walls as they were dragooned by trained muscular goons into the swimming pool and then yanked to the shallow water, gasping, gulping and squalling all the way. Certified as non-swimmers, they were weeded out for the elementary lessons that eventually would get them to survive the tests, or they would be sent packing for their draft boards to sort things out.

As a witness to that pathetic display, I could only hope that the pool was sufficiently chlorinated to account for scared-shitless weenies pissing in their Navy-issue swim trunks.

For me, the swim tests were a piece of cake, which was readily observable to the testers, who designated me as captain of our medley relay for the upcoming command-wide sporting competition. I found a couple other guys in our company who had swum competitively, one a backstroker and the other a breaststroker. Breaststroke also being my specialty, I was confident that I was faster, probably the fastest on the entire base, but we needed a butterflyer, so I decided to fill that slot on the medley relay. I knew Mike Mooney was a decent swimmer and that he could have anchored the relay with the freestyle leg. Dave Lucarelli, a guy from Cleveland, assured me that he was pretty fast, so I went with him. Mike was not happy.

At the pool, our backstroker and breaststroker both held their own, finishing their 50-yard swims in third place among the six competing squads and not far behind the leaders. Butterfly being the toughest stroke, I knew my competitors were likely to be their companies' top swimmers, and the fly wasn't my best stroke. Even so, I was able to take a narrow lead, and Dave Lucarelli was indeed fast enough to bring home the victory. I had made the best choice.

Our success was duly noted by Jenkins, the company commander, that evening, and the entire company was rewarded with extra smoking time during mail call. While puffing on his cigarettes, Mike Mooney pouted from a seat at the opposite end of the room. Dave Lucarelli grabbed a seat next to me.

Evenings were spent swabbing and buffing the barracks deck, scrubbing our work uniforms and skivvies by hand then hanging them in the drying room, shining shoes and the three S's – shit, shower and shave.

When Jenkins was out of the barracks, there was some horseplay. As I stepped out of the shower one evening, John Lance, a lumbering guy from Georgia who had been designated recruit leading petty officer for our company, snapped my bare ass with his scrolled-up towel. I grabbed a mop from the nearby corner and charged him as if I was going to impale his midsection on the wooden handle. We laughed about it. He turned around and picked up his can of shaving cream from the sink top. As he wound up like a baseball pitcher, I backed off. When he followed through, though, the can slipped from his hand and nailed me square in the forehead. Blood gushed out, spewed down my face and splattered on the deck.

Quickly, Dave Lucarelli and Mike Loveland, who was from Fort Wayne, Indiana, sat me on the floor and pressed a towel to my bloody forehead. Another guy ran out to get the officer of the deck, who was posted on the first floor. Somebody handed me my skivvies, and I pulled them on. Lance stood there with his mouth wide open, partly in disbelief over what had occurred and partly in fear that he would suffer some serious disciplinary action. I told him and the several witnesses that we needed to get our stories straight. Somebody, we don't know who, dropped a bar of soap on the floor just outside the shower, I told them. I slipped on it and hit my head on the deck. They all nodded in agreement.

Two corpsmen arrived. They helped me up, walked me out to an ambulance and rushed me to the dispensary. As head wounds often go, the blood that spurts out tends to make them appear worse than they really are. The slice in my forehead was stitched up in no time, and I was transported back to the barracks in time for taps at 10 p.m.

The officer of the deck had duly recorded the witnesses' accounts, which were consistently reported according to my instructions. John Lance owed me big time. It was confirmed later that some people have no loyalty.

Firefighter training is essential for the Navy. If a shipboard fire breaks out, something that is far from unusual, given the amount of flammable and explosive materials and hazardous activities that are necessary for defensive preparedness, there's nowhere to run, nowhere to hide. Either you put the fire out, or the ship goes down. You can go down with it or become floating shark bait.

So we spent a full day at the fire-training facility. Part of it was spent in the classroom, and the remainder was conducted in simulated emergency situations. We learned how to man a fire hose and extinguish a blazing cauldron of oil the size of a large above-ground swimming pool. We crawled and slithered through a smoke-filled maze.

When it was my squad's turn to experience the stifling irritation of a tear-gas-glutted enclosure, for some inexplicable reason, we decided to demonstrate our patriotic dedication to the exercise by singing "The Star-Spangled Banner." Ours might be the "land of the free and the home of the brave," but those weren't ramparts "gallantly streaming" down our cheeks. The instructors were more than willing to wait for us to sing all four verses, even though we stopped after the only one we'd memorized. At least we'd been warned not to rub our eyes, no matter how long it took to get our freedom from that "gloom of the grave."

'Never volunteer for anything'

The Army, Navy and Air Force each have two basic, unwritten rules. Rule one for the Army is, "If in doubt, put down smoke and go left." Rule one for the Navy is, "Don't throw the slops out to windward." Rule one for the Air Force has something to do with cheese tasting the same coming up on a bumpy ride as it does going down beforehand. Rule two for all three is, "Never volunteer for anything." The Marine Corps has only one such rule: "Never volunteer for anything."

I didn't follow the common rule. As my Enlisted Classification Record indicates, early on in boot camp I volunteered for submarine duty. I think I was influenced by the 1958 film "Run Silent, Run Deep," starring Clark Gable and Burt Lancaster. My volunteerism entitled me to take the test for sonar school and required responses to an extensive grid of personal questions, including those that revealed familial connections to Germany, which then was divided into contentious Cold War sectors with intrinsic espionage activities. Not only that, but I was treated to two long, torturous afternoons in a dental chair, where 13 teeth were drilled without anesthetic and packed with high-pressure fillings. It was all for naught. Maybe I flunked the simple sonar test, or perhaps I was a poor candidate for a national-security clearance.

Instead of sonar school, I was recommended for a clerical and administrative rating and subsequently received assignment to the Disbursing Clerk A School in Newport, Rhode Island. In other words, I was doomed to be trained as a keeper of financial records within the Navy Supply Corps, a job that was not high on my list of aspirations and in my mind was as unadventurous as I could possibly imagine.

At about that time, Mike Mooney received a letter from his most recent girlfriend, Mindy, notifying him that he was going to be a father. He told me that he would be getting married. It was too late for him to go the Dick Cheney chicken-hawk route with a paternity deferment, not that Mike was one to shirk duty to country in that fashion anyway.

I had written a couple letters to Darcy but received no reply. I had no girlfriend. Fatherhood and paternity deferments were beyond my imagination. Nor could I picture Mike Mooney as a married man.

About halfway through our two months of recruit training, it was time for "service week," seven days in which we would perform work details at various locations on the base. Our company of partly seasoned "sailors" was dispatched to the older section of Great Lakes, where batches of fresh enlistees arrived every day.

After assisting with barracks cleanup on my first day of service week, during which close supervision by superiors was distinctively absent, I decided to take advantage of the situation with a well-deserved nap. With the success of that enterprise duly noted, the next morning I disregarded reveille to catch up on some of the rest from which I had been rudely deprived over the previous month. I failed to account for roll call, during which no one responded to the petty officer's repeated announcements of my name. I spent the next five days plucking dandelions from the numerous grassy areas surrounding the barracks, mess hall, inspection stations and parade grounds.

Service week being successfully completed, we returned to our barracks in the main section of the base and envisioned light at the end of the boot-camp tunnel of misery.

In celebration of that milestone, Dave Lucarelli, Mike Loveland and I – the three L's, as we called ourselves – figured we'd enjoy an extra smoke not long after taps. The barracks was dark and quiet, except for the two recruits standing fire watch with their unloaded vintage M1 carbines. Neither of them appeared to give much thought to the three of us individually visiting the lighted head, known to civilians as a restroom, where we slipped into the drying room and shut the door behind us.

As we sucked in the nicotine-infiltrated smoke of our filtered Marlboros, the door swung open. It was John Lance – not one of the three L's – who had slammed his shaving-cream can into my forehead three weeks earlier and whose sorry ass we had saved from punitive consequences. He was not there to join us in our covert smoke break. "Here they are," the back-stabbing kiss ass announced with glee, his accusing finger wagging at us like the Wicked Witch of the West or, in his case, the South.

Right behind him was Jenkins, the company commander, who was officer of the deck that night and probably not too happy about that. "Put your butts out and get your asses in your racks," he commanded. "We'll deal with you in the morning."

I took another drag on my cigarette before dousing it in the sink and tossing it in the trash on our way back into the berthing area.

The next morning the three L's were ordered to pack all of our gear in our sea bags and report to the disciplinary officer on the main floor of the next building. Word of our demise had spread through the company. As I emptied my locker, Vince Luchetti whispered in my ear. "That fucking traitor Lance is dead meat," he said. "When we get out of here, we're going to beat the living shit out of him."

"Thanks, Vince," I said. "Have no mercy."

Called into the officer of discipline one by one and standing at attention, we learned that we were being ASMO'd, which stands for assignment memorandum order and supposedly is intended for recruits to receive additional time for improvement. That could mean swimming instruction or fitness training. Our additional two weeks of boot camp were no such thing, as there was no special training for smoking cessation. There was absolutely no doubt that it was punishment for bad behavior, a lesson in subservience to military discipline. The extended time in our boot-camp experience would be barely sufficient to complete the evening hours of PT required to work off the legion of demerits added to our accounts.

Mike Loveland and I were sent back to Company 387, which was commanded by Chief Petty Officer Porter, a short man with an eagle tattoo on his right forearm. Dave Lucarelli was assigned to the brother company in an adjacent barracks.

The setback required a second service week for the three L's. Mike and I were assigned to the deep sink in the main mess hall, which made my previous dandelion-picking duty seem like a picnic. We were up before dawn to be ready for breakfast and still up after dark to finish scrubbing the pots and pans from supper. Downtime between meals was nearly nonexistent. But Mike and I willingly volunteered to clean out a giant dish-washing machine after each meal, because, once we climbed inside, we were hidden from view and could sneak a quick smoke. If we were to hear the likes of a back-stabbing John Lance enter the room, we easily could toss our butts down the drain and avoid another ASMO.

On Aug. 17 and 24, our companies were among those granted Saturday liberties. We could catch trains just outside the naval base and head south to Chicago or north to Milwaukee. Mike Loveland, Dave Lucarelli and I headed north. Both of them being over Wisconsin's legal drinking age of 21, they were able to buy us some beer.

Big showdown in Chicago

On the day after our second liberty, Sunday, Aug. 25, we heard news about a showdown developing for the upcoming Democratic National Convention in Chicago. Thousands of U.S. Army troops were arriving from as far away as Colorado and Oklahoma and setting up quarters at Great Lakes Naval Station in preparation for riot control against war protests in the city. Some of the protesters gathered right outside our main gate, where they bombarded bus loads of soldiers with garbage as they arrived. Rumors circulated about those of us who had completed our training on the shooting range being supplied with live ammunition for our M1 carbines.

The Vietnam War was a major point of contention inside the convention hall. Vice President Humphrey was considered the pro-war candidate and the clear favorite among the contenders. Sen. Robert F. Kennedy's assassination in early June had eliminated Humphrey's leading challenger from the race. There was some unsuccessful maneuvering to draft his brother Sen. Ted Kennedy, of Massachusetts, into the running. That left Sen. George McGovern, of South Dakota, as the peace contingent's last hope.

In announcing his nomination, Sen. Abraham Ribicoff, of Massachusetts, had the gall to say, "With George McGovern as president of the United States, we wouldn't have Gestapo tactics in the streets of Chicago." Mayor Richard J. Daley, the man responsible for maintaining peace in the streets, responded with an unpeaceful, fist-shaking epithet.

However Daley's tactics were characterized, there was no peace in the streets of Chicago. His attempts to keep an estimated 10,000 to 15,000 anti-war protesters miles away from the convention site did not go over well. As they marched toward the hall, they were met by 11,900 Chicago police, 7,500 Army troops, 7,500 Illinois National Guard troops and 1,000 Secret Service agents. The ensuing riots resulted in 589 arrests and injuries to 119 police officers and 100 protesters.

Mayor Daley took umbrage with a subsequent study that found his police department mostly to blame for the violence. Relative to Ohio Gov. James A. Rhodes' response two years later to anti-war protests at Kent State University, where four students were killed by poorly prepared draft dodgers in the Ohio National Guard, Chicago could have been worse.

Thankfully, comparably unprepared Navy recruits in Great Lakes, Illinois, in August 1968 were not dispatched with live ammo to encounter garbage-throwing protesters outside the main gate.

Hubert Humphrey's victorious day at the Democratic National Convention also was a big day for my company and several others at boot camp. My parents made the 425-mile drive, not to congratulate Humphrey on his nomination but to witness my graduation while they sat on the hard benches of sun-drenched bleachers lined up at the parade grounds. It wasn't the hottest day of summer, but sweat drenched the armpits of my dress-white uniform and sopped the rim of my sailor hat. I stood proudly at attention with my eyes front through the hour-long ceremony, even as I heard the bodies of a half dozen fainting fellow graduates thump to the ground in the ranks behind me.

That evening my mom and dad took me to dinner at a nearby sit-down restaurant, a rare treat indeed for members of my family. I never made it easy for them, but they supported me through thick and thin. I told them stories about my winning medley relay, my week in the deep sink, two long days in the dental chair and my collection of 20 bucks in wagers the previous evening from guys who didn't believe my boasting about 100 pushups. After setting a company record for demerits and extra hours of PT, of course I could do that. I didn't share tales about Vince Luchetti circling the barracks yard with skivvies over his head or the three L's getting ASMO'd for smoking in the drying room.

After spending the night at a motel, my dad, who had taken two days of vacation from the Ford plant, drove them home the next morning.

A day later, I packed my sea bag, picked up my orders for Class A School in Rhode Island and caught a bus to O'Hare International Airport. I didn't see the back-stabbing John Lance's beaten and rotting remains on the roadside. Too bad.

Chapter 13 | **Time for Me to Go**

Chrissie Hynde, the Akron-born rock 'n' roller and Firestone High School graduate who studied art at Kent State University, didn't release the hit tune "My City Was Gone" with the Pretenders until 1982. I knew the feeling, though, when I got home from boot camp for a two-week leave. I'd only been gone for 10 weeks when "I went back to Ohio," so downtown Akron was still there. So was Howard Street, where the hookers bared smooth, black thighs at the curb and wise-ass white punks from Cuyahoga Falls taunted them from the rolled-down windows of their lolly-gagging automobiles.

"But my family was gone," as Chrissie Hynde sang it. "My childhood memories slowly swirled past like the wind through the trees."

My family had moved on. The house on East Bailey Road in the neighborhood of my childhood memories had new owners. During my absence, the Langes had picked up their belongings and relocated to a brand new split-level house on a drive called Treeside in a subdivision being developed around the north shore of the 170-acre Wyoga Lake. It wasn't spacious or fancy, but it was roomier and more comfortable than the old place. It was afforded by years of seven-day work weeks, 10-hour workdays and overtime pay won with the blood, sweat and tears of the United Auto Workers, not gifted by the entitled class that governs and molds economic advantage.

The move put my dad about 8 miles closer to work at the Ford plant. The small beach, swimming area and playground were a short jog from their new home for my siblings. There were three bedrooms on the upper level for my parents and four sisters and an extra bed in my brother's basement hideaway to accommodate my visit.

Vonnie, who had completed her junior year at Cuyahoga Falls High School, and Danny, who had attended ninth grade at Kent State University School, transferred to Stow High School. My mom was making headway on that college education she'd been promised when she fled war-torn Germany two decades earlier. She didn't know it yet, but a new school called Cuyahoga Valley Christian Academy was being planned for her future teaching career practically in her own backyard.

With my trusty 1960 VW Beetle having been registered in my father's name, he did me the favor of selling it over the summer. I didn't need a car where I was going next, but I had to rely on my thumb in the meantime. So I stuck it out on Wyoga Lake Road, also designated as state Route 532, and hitched a ride back to Cuyahoga Falls, "A, o, oh, way to go Ohio," as Chrissie Hynde nailed it. "I was stunned and amazed." Like her, I found, "There was nobody home."

John Ferguson and Kenny Chrzanowski, my closest boyhood neighbors, fellow Explorer Scouts and then fellow beer guzzlers, were off to the Army. Kenny had signed up with Ron Chadwell and Tom Quick, who lived halfway up the next block on East Bailey Road. Jim Cardarelli was struggling in Officer Candidate School at some Godforsaken fort. Bob Leone had enlisted in the Air Force. Mike Mooney's two-week leave after boot camp was done and gone. There was a fresh pick of minimum-wage bag packers and shelf stockers at Stutzman's Foodliner. For me, it was like a ghost town. One by one, the military was sucking up the happy-go-lucky lives of my generation.

So I stuck out my thumb and headed across town. A guy who looked to be about 25 years old picked me up in a sedan on Broad Boulevard. "Where you headed, good lookin'?" he said as I climbed into the front passenger seat.

That didn't sound right. I sat close to the door. "Up to State Road," I told him. "Do you know where Leone's Pizza is?"

"Sure, I can take you there."

I planned to say hello to Bob's mom and dad, ask if they heard any recent news from him and how he was doing. I knew they'd be happy to see me and would toss a pepperoni pizza, my favorite, in the oven. Maybe Bob's good-looking younger sister Judy would be there.

We passed the YMCA at the corner of 6th Street. "So what are you planning to do tonight?" the driver asked me.

"I don't know, maybe hook up with a chick later on," I said.

"What type would you like to hook up with?" he wondered.

"I think I'd like a blonde or a brunette," I told him.

"But what if you can't find a blonde or a brunette?" he asked.

His line of questioning was getting suspicious. "You know," I said, "I just got back from boot camp and haven't been with a girl in awhile. Any nice-looking one would be just fine."

"But what if you can't find a girl?" he said. "You know, your dick doesn't care one way or the other who's sucking on it."

"Stop the car!" I screamed, finally certain about what was going on.

"It's all right," he said. "I'll take you to the pizza place."

"Let me out right now!" I yelled, clenching my fist and shaking it at him. "Or I will punch your face in, you fucking queer."

He pulled over. I opened the door and jumped onto the pavement even before the car came to a complete stop. I nearly tumbled over in the boulevard. His tires squealed as he drove away.

You could say I was homophobic, as I sure as hell was scared by what I had just experienced. But it would be presumptuous to say that I hated homosexuals, as I had never knowingly encountered one before. The subject of sexual orientation never came up in my home.

I hadn't even had a clue that Bob Berdella, the kid I knew well in junior high school and who later went to prison as the mass murderer of men that he brought home from gay bars, did not like girls. I knew he was odd.

The word "queer" meant "odd" in a certain sexual context to me, and, yes, I knew from my illicit paperback readings that sex could involve more than the penile penetration of a vagina. Queers were not just odd to kids I grew up with, but we also thought they were extremely rare. So rare, in fact, that we thought slamming each other with the derogation had no relation to reality. Hell, the game "smear the queer," in which a group of boys would toss a football in the air and then chase down and gang tackle whomever it landed nearest to and was compelled to pick it up, was considered normal activity in our neighborhood.

There was a block of green space not far from Akron University known as "queers park," and I'd heard stories about some guys going down there to roll some of the nighttime trysters. It wasn't the kind of action those visitors bargained for.

Not that I was tolerant of unnatural preferences, but I didn't take part in that intolerance. On one occasion, though, Mike Mooney and I, with larcenous intent, did give a shitfaced drunk who'd fallen into a small fountain on Akron's Main Street a lift to his room in a flea-bag hotel. Having cast no judgment on that old man's sexual orientation, it might be said that we were equal-opportunity victimizers. As it turned out, the flea-bag landlord stopped us in the musty lobby. All we got for our trouble was a small wad of sopping-wet singles that we'd rescued from the bottom of the fountain.

My two-week leave from the Navy involved neither romance nor larceny.

On Friday night, I hitched a ride to Kent. I found an empty booth at the Loft and downed a couple pitchers of 3.2-percent Stroh's from the tap. I didn't recognize anybody there. I felt like an outsider but not like a member of the Outsiders, whose "Time Won't Let Me" blared on the jukebox. I had my fill of loneliness in a crowded bar by midnight, so I stepped outside, walked across the bridge, looked at the swirling Cuyahoga River below and held my thumb out again.

A Dodge pulled over to the curb, and the passenger window rolled open. I heard Van Morrison's hit song "Brown Eyed Girl" on the radio and saw one smiling at me. She motioned for me to hop in the rear seat. I opened the door and was pleased to discover three girls already sitting back there, as well as three more in the front seat. They squeezed their slender, young bodies closer together and welcomed me to join them.

As the driver steered the Dodge westbound toward the county line, she blurted out, "Let's have a gang bang!" All six of them squealed in a fit of hilarity. I laughed with them. My imagination kept me smiling. They told me they were beginning their senior year at Kent's Theodore Roosevelt High School and wondered if I was old enough to buy them some beer.

I was 18, I said, so I could get them some at the Bee-Line drive-through in Munroe Falls. We drove along North River Road, past the spot where I'd been ticketed for speeding, which cost me my driver's license a year earlier. I told them I was home on leave and soon would be flying to Rhode Island.

After I bought them three quarts of Falstaff with their money, they drove me out Wyoga Lake Road and dropped me off at the entrance to my family's development, passing the bottles around along the way.

"Thanks for the lift," I said as I stepped out of the car.

"Thanks for the beer," they said.

I heard more laughter as they drove away.

Next stop, Rhode Island

When my United Airlines flight touched down in Providence, actually the city of Warwick along Route 1, south of the capital city, I felt like an experienced flyer. It was my third flight, after all. The T.F. Green Airport terminal was minuscule compared to Chicago's O'Hare and very small compared to Cleveland's Hopkins. Inside, I connected with three other sailors in their dress blues heading for Newport, and we teamed up to pay the fare for a single-engine prop plane to fly us over Narragansett Bay. We landed at a tiny airport not far from the naval base and grabbed a taxi that dropped us off at an administration building.

Like the city of Newport, the naval base there has a rich history. During the Civil War, the Naval Academy relocated from Annapolis, Maryland, to Newport for several years. Naval Station Newport opened in 1881, and the training station began operations in 1887. It was a significant contributor to the victorious World War I and World War II efforts.

When I arrived on Sept. 15, 1968, the North Atlantic Destroyer Squadron was home ported there. It also was home to Officer Candidate School, the U.S. Naval War College on Coaster Harbor Island, just offshore in the bay, and to my temporary assignment, the Navy Supply Corps School.

The next disbursing-clerk class, DK school in Navy jargon, wasn't scheduled to commence until October, so I had a few weeks to kill in the interim. I met a friendly guy in the barracks, Noe Arevalo, from Corpus Christi, Texas, who was waiting to begin supply-clerk school. On a Saturday, he invited me to go with him and two other Hispanic sailors to a dance in Fall River, not far north of Newport and just over the Massachusetts state line.

On the return trip that night, as we sat in the rear bench of the bus, the three of them became engaged in a jovial conversation in Spanish. It was inoffensive to me, as I had heard foreign-language exchanges that I didn't understand between my mom and her German-American friends throughout my life.

Apparently, though, a couple guys sitting several seats forward of us didn't take it the same way. One of them turned around, gave my brown-skinned, dark-haired amigos a teeth-clenched glare and sputtered, "This is America. You people need to speak English."

Noe, Paul and Luis were dumbfounded.

"Kussen mein Arsch, du Scheisse Kopf," I blurted out with my best translation of, "Kiss my ass, you shit head." Yes, I had picked up a few German vulgarities.

The shit head didn't know what the light-haired, blue-eyed white guy just said, but it obviously wasn't Spanish. He gave me a dirty look then turned back around without further objection. My fellow travelers included me in an English conversation, interspersed with a few choice Spanish words that I might care to use in future rebuttals.

During my wait for DK school, I was assigned to the maintenance department, along with Larry Chase, who was built for football and was the sturdiest guy in our class. He was from the city of Springfield, Ohio, located in the flatlands some 40 miles west of Columbus, and had played for Wittenberg University in his hometown. He was justifiably boastful of that experience, as his Lutheran college's Tigers had won the NCAA College Division national football championships in 1962 and 1964 and would do it again in 1969. Larry might have been a decent lineman, but, when we played touch football on the field outside our barracks on Saturday afternoons, I easily outmaneuvered him to catch several touchdown passes.

In mid-October, Larry Chase informed me that he'd run into a guy from back home who was stationed for permanent duty at Newport and that he had a car on the base. They would be driving back to Ohio for the coming weekend, and I was welcome to ride along, if I chipped in for gas. I readily agreed, but there was one small catch. They would drive down the East Coast, head west via the Pennsylvania Turnpike and cross Ohio on Interstate 70, dropping me off at the Interstate 77 interchange, 75 miles south of Cuyahoga Falls.

My solution was to wear my dress blues, instead of civilian clothes. The uniform would get me picked up almost as soon as I could poke my thumb out on the side of the highway. That's what I thought anyway when I stepped out of the car and into the teeth-chattering night air just before dawn, wishing I'd brought my peacoat with me. An hour later, the sun rose over the hills in the east, my bare hands throbbed and my body shuddered with hypothermia as cars and trucks continued to blow by at 70 mph, some of them with contemptuously blaring horns, their tires spewing dewy grime at my bell-bottoms.

That military uniform was no magic touch. Drivers behind the wheels of Lincolns and Cadillacs, station wagons and pickup trucks were not traveling from college dorms in Athens, Ohio, to anti-war demonstrations in Ann Arbor, Michigan, or Rochester, New York. Mostly, they represented the "silent majority" that soon-to-be President Richard M. Nixon would hail as the great body of American patriots who supported the war. They sure as hell didn't support a shivering serviceman in uniform.

A hundred or more passersby later, a mechanic on his way to work gave me a lift to his gas station near Cambridge. I found a pay phone there and called my mom, who came to my rescue.

Peace talks undermined

At the time, I did not know that Vietnam was in my not-too-distant future or that the lame-duck Johnson administration was working feverishly to prevent that from happening. Whether efforts by the outgoing president to bring the North Vietnam government to peace talks in Paris that fall could have resulted in an actual halt to the mayhem is a matter of historical conjecture. Johnson was serious enough about the prospects, however, that he was ready to stop bombing the North as an inducement to negotiate a settlement.

Politically, evidence of any progress whatsoever toward a peace pact could have been a major boost to his vice president and fellow Democrat, Hubert Humphrey, who was trailing former Republican Vice President Nixon in the presidential election polls. Nixon, a certifiable poor loser, was direly aware of that potential turnaround. Given the later exposure of his scatological behavior in connection with the Watergate scandal, it would be no surprise to discover that he was looking for a "monkey wrench" in his hefty toolbox of dirty tricks.

Indeed, there were suspicions at the time that Nixon's campaign cabal was traitorously working behind the scenes to pressure the South Vietnamese government into sabotaging any such peace endeavors. One can only imagine what the reaction would be in 2018, if a presidential campaign were found to have collaborated with Russian autocrats to puncture American democracy.

For nearly half a century, scholars and researchers dug into suspicions about Nixon's treachery, some of them making sturdy but not irrefutable cases. On Dec. 31, 2016, coincidental to contemporary collusions, John A. Farrell, author of the soon-to-be-released "Richard Nixon: The Life," wrote in a New York Times Sunday Review article that he had discovered culpable evidence in the Richard Nixon Presidential Library. The smoking gun came in the form of notes taken by then-future Chief of Staff H.R. Haldeman of a phone conversation he had on Oct. 22, 1968, with Nixon. Based on those notes, Farrell wrote, Nixon "ordered Haldeman to 'monkey wrench' the initiative."

Based on the Nixon team's connections to the South Vietnamese ambassador through influential Republican fundraiser Anna Chennault, there surely was a monkey wrench in the toolbox.

As New York Times writer Peter Baker reported, the revelation supported some long-held suspicions. Evan Thomas, author of "Being Nixon," said Farrell "nailed down what has been talked about for a long time." Ken Hughes, a University of Virginia researcher and writer of "Chasing Shadows," said the Haldeman notes "show that Nixon committed a crime to win the presidential election."

Richard M. Nixon was a criminal, no doubt about it, and he should have been locked up. Whether his belatedly confirmed efforts to derail peace talks in 1968 actually influenced the recalcitrant South Vietnamese President Nguyen Van Thieu to ensure their demise, however, remains conjectural.

By the end of 1968, the deadliest year of the Vietnam War, 37,229 Americans had lost their lives fighting it. Another 11,780 were killed in 1969, my year, the second deadliest one, and 9,477 more died by the official end of the war in 1975. Regardless of whether Nixon and his co-conspirators killed the peace initiative and therefore killed the 21,257 American service members who perished subsequent to that, his intent was clear. His election was more important to him than 21,257 American lives, many of them connected to my own.

Nearly 25,500 of the 58,220 Americans who made the ultimate sacrifice for their country were younger than 21, the legal voting age in November 1968. It wasn't until July 1971 that the government lowered the voting age to 18. Having reached my 19th birthday just three weeks before the election, my country had concluded that I was old enough to be sent to Vietnam but too young to cast my presidential ballot for Nixon. No matter. He defeated Humphrey by more than half a million votes.

Two weeks after the election in which his vice president was rejected by the American voters, President Johnson held a ceremony at the White House in which he presented the Medal of Honor, the military's highest honor, to five heroes of the Vietnam War.

One of them was Capt. Charles J. Liteky, a Roman Catholic priest and Army chaplain with the 199th Infantry Brigade. According to his citation for "exceptional heroism," Liteky's company was on a search-and-destroy mission on Dec. 6, 1967, when it came under intense enemy fire. He shielded two wounded men with his body just 15 meters from an enemy machine gun and then dragged them to the safety of a helicopter landing zone. Despite being wounded in the neck and foot himself in the ongoing fusillade, the chaplain continued to rescue wounded soldiers and administered last rites to those who were dying.

Liteky became known for other activities after returning from the war. He left the priesthood, married a former nun and became committed to social-justice activism, including protests against the School of the Americas, where Central American dictators' militias received training. Among their countless victims, School of the Americas graduates raped, tortured and murdered four Roman Catholic missionaries in El Salvador on Dec. 2, 1980. The victims of that demonic brutality were Ursuline Sister Dorothy Kazel and lay missionary Jean Donovan, both of Cleveland, and Maryknoll Sisters Maura Clarke and Ita Ford, both from New York.

In 1986, Liteky renounced his Medal of Honor and left it in an envelope addressed to then-President Ronald Reagan near the Vietnam Veterans Memorial in Washington, D.C. His fellow veterans did not scurrilously rebuke him for what some could consider a snub, but such stabs generally are directed at the backs of anti-war mongers who aspire for political office.

Mixed bag of trainees

Chaplains were unlikely war heroes, to be sure, and heroism was an even more improbable scenario for those of us training to be disbursing clerks in Newport that fall. Sixteen sailors, a mixture of recent boot-camp graduates and seamen with a year or so under their belts began training for the job that most likely would assign us to offices aboard ships or more securely at stateside naval stations.

One WAVE – the World War II acronym for Women for Volunteer Emergency Service – also began the class. But she dropped out even before forms were passed around that gave us the opportunity to designate preferences for duty assignments. I indicated the Navy Finance Center in Cleveland as a preferred assignment, which no doubt was a long shot, and Great Lakes, which was closer to home than actual seaports. Almost as an afterthought, a simple check in a box at the bottom of the page volunteered me for duty in the Republic of South Vietnam. I often made heady decisions.

One evening in the barracks a classmate from Massachusetts struck up a conversation with me. I'm not sure whether it was the Playboy pinup taped to the inside of one of my open locker doors or the "Hallelujah the Pill!" poster attached to the other one that attracted his interest. Either way, it led to an enduring friendship.

Keith Ball had grown up in Shelburne Falls, Massachusetts, a village of about 1,700 residents located on the Deerfield River in the northwest section of the state, where the Berkshire Hills rise up to the Taconic Mountains of Upstate New York and the Green Mountains of nearby Vermont. The village's claim to fame is the Bridge of Flowers, one of three in the world, a former railway span that brought freight to the mills of nearby Colrain and which was transformed into a garden by the Shelburne Woman's Club in the late 1920s.

Keith was a year and a half my senior, still too young to vote. He had graduated from Arms Academy, a public school in Shelburne, in 1966, one year before it was replaced by Mohawk Trail Regional High School. Mohawk Trail is a scenic byway that follows Route 2 across northwestern Massachusetts and is especially popular when the leaves on the trees fire up the steeps with brilliant fall colors.

Keith was one of the sailors in our class with previous shipboard experience. Both he and John Rowe had come to Newport from the USS Vulcan (AR-5), a repair ship home ported in Norfolk, Virginia. The Vulcan had provided vital assistance to the destroyer USS Kearny (DD-432), which had been torpedoed by a German U-boat in the Battle of the Atlantic off of Iceland in World War II, and also serviced amphibious units in the assault of Okinawa in the Pacific.

John Rowe was nearly 10 years older than me. Before enlisting in the Navy, he had done a stint in the Marine Corps and took part in the ill-fated Bay of Pigs invasion of Cuba in April 1961. He took a bullet to his leg that left him with a slight limp, but it did not diminish his enthusiasm for military service or his lust for life.

After John and I took a bus to Providence one Saturday, he suggested that we visit a drinking establishment. When the barkeep asked for identification, John fumbled with his wallet on his lap and slipped his Pennsylvania driver's license to me before plopping his military ID on the bar. I didn't think I could pass for 28 years old or that my face resembled the photo on John's license, but the barkeep took one glance at it and served me a beer. We put down a few of them before catching a late bus back to Newport.

Cold nights in Massachusetts

Not long before the presidential election, in which we could not vote, Keith, who had a car on the base, a Rambler American two-door sedan, invited me to go home with him for the weekend. It was just a three-hour drive, and he was making the trip regularly to visit his family and his girlfriend, JoAnn Urban, a 17-year-old Mohawk Trail Regional High School senior who lived with her parents and a younger brother, Larry, in Colrain. Keith told me JoAnn had some friends, and she would fix me up with a date. It didn't take long for me to fall in love with Massachusetts.

We took off right after class ended on Friday, Keith at the wheel, me riding shotgun and another classmate, Bud Bullett, who lived in Adams, which is 20 miles west of Shelburne Falls. About 130 miles later, we dropped Bud off on the Mohawk Trail. Drivers in the Berkshire Hills apparently were more sympathetic to a hitchhiker in military uniform than I'd found them to be in the Appalachian foothills of Southeast Ohio. Bud said he never had a problem getting a lift along the winding road past Charlemont, through Mohawk Trail State Forest and to his hometown. On clear days, Mount Greylock, the highest point in Massachusetts at 3,491 feet above sea level, could be seen peaking into the sky 3 miles west of Adams. Bud would get a ride with relatives back to Shelburne Falls on late Sunday afternoon.

Keith's family home, a well-constructed, mature colonial, was situated on Main Street, just north of Route 2 and not far from the center of town. His father, Elwyn, also known as "E.J.," who was president of the local Shelburne Falls Savings Bank, and his mother, Dorothy, or Dot, couldn't have made me feel more welcome. Her home-cooked dinner affirmed that.

On Saturday, Keith took me down the street to meet his older sister, Diane Cosby, his two young nephews and a little niece. We also paid a visit to his sister-in-law, Ann, a cultured Southern lady from Alabama. She was living with her little daughter in Charlemont while her husband, Keith's older brother, Elwyn J. "Jack" Ball, a major in the U.S. Army, was serving one of his tours of duty in Vietnam.

Later in the afternoon, we drove up Route 112 to Colrain, which is situated on the North River, just 4 miles from the Vermont border. The densely wooded Berkshires, which rise up on both sides of every road in that section of the state, may be hills from Vermont's point of view, but they sure looked like mountains to me. Colrain once had a dozen or more covered bridges that transported its people and mill products back and

Following the Nazi surrender in May 1945, U.S. Army Sgt. Charles M. Lange (left) and other infantrymen in the Rainbow Division, who had liberated the Dachau concentration camp, were able to savor their hard-fought victory in Germany.

Helga Lange, who was a 17-year-old war bride, and her first child, David Charles, born 10 months later, lived in a trailer behind her in-laws' house in Natrona Heights, Pennsylvania.

The tiny bungalow where Dave Lange grew up in Cuyahoga Falls didn't have a basement, but it had enough beds for his parents and their six children. The family moved out after he left for boot camp in 1968.

At 8 years old, Lange (kneeling, center) was the smallest member of the Angels baseball team in 1958. The next summer he became the starting second baseman for a team dominated by 11- and 12-year-olds.

Although his third-grade teacher was encouraging to Lange's academic pursuits, his attention tended to be more focused on baseball, swimming and other interests.

Mrs. McKinney's third-grade class at Price Elementary School included Lange (middle row, second from right), his future baseball teammate and later all-district football star Donny Mathew (middle row, third from right) and his future swimming teammate and later state butterfly champ Bobby Heacock (middle row, second from left).

As a freshman, Lange (closest to camera) dove into practice with fellow members of the Archbishop Hoban High School varsity swim team. As a sophomore, he was the team's top competitor in the individual medley.

Lange's senior photo for the 1967 Cuyahoga Falls High School yearbook. "They're clean-cut, nice-looking boys that you would probably like if your daughter brought one home," the truancy officer said of Grandpa's Boys, the gang that welcomed Lange into its fold.

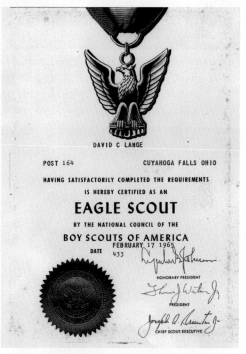

DAVID C LANGE

POST 164   CUYAHOGA FALLS OHIO

HAVING SATISFACTORILY COMPLETED THE REQUIREMENTS

IS HEREBY CERTIFIED AS AN

EAGLE SCOUT

BY THE NATIONAL COUNCIL OF THE

BOY SCOUTS OF AMERICA

FEBRUARY 17 1965

DATE   433

HONORARY PRESIDENT

PRESIDENT

CHIEF SCOUT EXECUTIVE

Always attracted to the woods and the freedom he found there, Lange earned Scouting's highest rank. That experience was useful during his Survival, Evasion, Resistance and Escape training in the Navy.

Lange (top row, second from right) graduated from Class A school in Newport, Rhode Island, in December 1968. Keith Ball (top row, third from left), of Shelburne Falls, Massachusetts, became Lange's lifelong friend. Sherman Lawson (middle row, second from right) became one of his close friends in Vietnam.

Back at their barracks in Little Creek, Virginia, after SERE training, Lange (kneeling, center) and other members of his squad found no reason to smile about the experience that 35 years later was connected to "enhanced interrogation" methods.

With aviation activities for all four U.S. military branches, in addition to commercial airlines operations, Tan Son Nhut, located just outside of Saigon, was the busiest airport in the world at the time.

Enveloped by major rivers and engulfed in wetlands, the residences of Nha Be were interconnected by a maze of raised earthen walking paths.

Small motorcycles and bicycles were the most common mode of personal transportation in the capital city of Saigon.

Lange enjoyed the Navy's two enabled drugs of choice, alcohol and nicotine, during liberty hours in a Nha Be bar.

Seated on the stern of a river patrol boat, or PBR, Lange was transported to one of the Navy's advanced tactical support bases.

Guard towers rose above one of the advanced tactical support bases established along the Vam Co Tay and Vam Co Dong rivers, where naval forces battled an influx of communist infiltrators from the Ho Chi Minh Trail.

Lange traveled by land, air and water to make sure the men fighting Viet Cong forces along the rivers near Cambodia received their pay, which happened to be one of the few pleasures offered to them in a thankless war.

Al Elliott (left) and Lange were ready to hop on board a UH-1 "Huey" helicopter out of Ben Luc, which would deliver them to remote Navy river bases located around the "Parrot's Beak" region of Cambodia.

The one main street of Nha Be was lined with bars and other establishments that catered to the thirsty interests of brown-water sailors on liberty from the nearby Navy base.

The USS Forrestal was anchored in the Mediterranean Sea off the coast of Athens, Greece, in May 1970. Three years earlier, in the Gulf of Tonkin, an explosion and conflagration on the aircraft carrier's flight deck killed 134 sailors.

In his dress blues, Lange was able to visit the Acropolis, among other sights, during a port call in Athens, Greece, while deployed on board the aircraft carrier USS Forrestal.

On July 30, 1971, Lange scrambled to the catwalk with his camera to shoot pictures of crewmen being rescued from a helicopter that somehow missed the flight deck. A Soviet naval vessel surveilled the incident as the helicopter sank below the surface.

A U.S. Navy Helicopter Anti-Submarine Squadron 11 crew tracked a Soviet sub in the North Sea during one of many military encounters between the Cold War enemies.

On the flight deck of the USS Forrestal, Lange flashed the peace sign next to one of Helicopter Anti-Submarine Squadron 11's choppers, with attack aircraft in the background.

Refueling at sea is a dicey exercise even in calm waters, but the Mediterranean was anything but smooth for this connection to the USS Forrestal.

After Adm. Elmo Zumwalt became chief of naval operations in July 1970, Lange took advantage of looser regulations such as growing a beard.

Jeff Murphy (on higher stool) and Dave Lange, who became best friends at Kent State University, enjoyed beers with their wives, Sue Barker-Murphy (left) and Linda Lange (right), who were KSU roommates.

In 1974, Lange bought his own "hippie van" and retraced much of his 1972 hitchhiking excursion across the Rocky Mountains and on to California.

Dave (left) and Danny Lange stopped to sip some beer at Langes Run, a small tributary in what became part of Cuyahoga Valley National Park. For some reason, the park system did not retain the "Langes Run" designation.

After earning his journalism degree, Lange became a newspaper editor and spent most of his 40-year career with the Chagrin Valley Times, the Solon Times and the Geauga Times Courier, based in Chagrin Falls, Ohio.

Swimming has always been part of Lange's life, including some testy river plunges in Vietnam. Continuing to compete in the sport, he won four gold medals and a silver medal in the 2014 Ohio Senior Olympics, followed by five top-10 performances in the 2015 National Senior Games held in Minneapolis.

forth over the river and its tributaries. Most of them were destroyed in the floods of 1936 and 1938.

We crossed the last one remaining, the Arthur Smith Covered Bridge, to reach the road where the Urbans lived. JoAnn's parents, Fred and Louise, were down-to-earth, friendly folks who greeted Keith like a close relative, which he later became, and me like I was no stranger. Blue collar to the core, Fred and Louise both were employed at a local textile mill.

Much to my enjoyment, JoAnn had several attractive and delightful friends who were willing to meet and spend quality time with a charming young sailor from Ohio. That definitely was a good reason for me to fall in love with Massachusetts.

On a subsequent weekend visit, Keith and JoAnn hooked me and his boyhood pal Burt Dubay up with a couple girls and decided that we'd enjoy a visit to the Ball family's summer cottage on Laurel Lake. Theirs is one of about three dozen privately owned cottages surrounding the 100-acre mountain lake at the apex of a narrow, twisting road that ushers summertime swimmers, campers and picnickers into Erving State Forest. But it wasn't summer, and there were no swimmers, campers or picnickers.

It was a cold late autumn night with the star-lit sky casting a shimmer across the still water when we reached the cottage. Keith unlocked the door at the top of an outdoor stairway and led us inside with a flashlight. The electricity and water were shut off for the winter. He stacked several split logs in the fireplace and put a match to some wadded-up newspapers for kindling. Before long, the flickering flames spread some welcome warmth across the main room, where three couples snuggled in the corners.

"We're going to the bedroom," said Keith, whose body heat may have encouraged him to pursue intimacy in cool seclusion. Before leaving us, he grabbed a short rope hanging from the ceiling and lowered a pull-down staircase. "There are some beds up there, Dave," he said with a wily smile. He and JoAnn disappeared behind a folding door. Bert and his date were busy on the sofa.

I looked at Sharon, and her eyes shifted upward. I held her hand and helped her climb the narrow, wooden steps. The attic was pitch black. We felt our way around and located one of the single beds. I slid back the covers. We crawled in and pulled them over our fully clothed bodies. We kissed and shivered and held each other tight. The wind rattled the glass in a window facing the lake. Winter was in the air, and shreds of its early blast whispered through tiny crannies in the clapboard wall. We kissed and shivered and held each other tight. Neither shirts nor pants nor even coats and surely not Sharon's bra were shed on that frigid night.

"Hey, Dave!" The call came from Keith down below after an hour of kissing and shivering and holding each other tight. "We gotta get going. It's snowing outside and coming down hard."

The pavement was clear and dry, and the fallen leaves rustled across the ground on the side of the road when we drove up the mountain two hours earlier. When we stepped out of the cottage, the stairway was coated in fluffy white stuff, and we trudged through a 6-inch-deep snowfall to get to the car. As we brushed off the windshield with bare hands, Keith looked up to the road, where the pavement no longer could be distinguished from its leafy surroundings. "It doesn't look good," he said.

There was no automobile traffic through Erving State Forest during the cold season, and no snowplows were employed to clear the way.

"I'll drive," I said. "I can get us back down."

It was a slow go, but at least gravity was with us. There would be no ascending the mountain in that fast-falling, slip-sliding snowstorm. The headlights ricocheted off the fluttering swarm of flakes like glitter flashing before my blinking eyes. I held my foot softly on the brake and steered clear of the robust trunks of pines and birches that marked the imposing edge of the thick forest. Somehow, some way we made it down to Route 2. From Erving, we followed a snowplow west to the French King Bridge over the Connecticut River and onward to Colrain and Shelburne Falls.

It was on another visit that JoAnn introduced me to a dark-haired girl with sparkling eyes and an infectious smile. Cynthia Call lived with her father, a surly, burly man who liked his liquor, her much-better-humored grandfather and her younger brother, David, in a modest house almost directly across the road from the Urbans. I was drawn to Cindy at first sight. She liked me too. When she and JoAnn planned to have Keith and me spend the entire four-day Thanksgiving weekend at their respective homes, I knew we were in a serious relationship.

Not that kind of serious, which Rolland "Windy" Call made perfectly clear as we played a game of spades in the kitchen on Wednesday evening. With the bottle of bourbon resting near his elbow at the side of the table, conspicuously out of my reach and its contents slipping away, Windy gave me a penetrating glare. "I know what you're up to," he said in a deep, slow snarl.

"Dad!" Cindy protested.

My eyes widened. I could feel my heart bumping my ribs.

"I know what you two are up to," he said, this time glaring at Cindy.

"No, you don't," she said.

"You stay out of my daughter's bedroom," Windy said, shifting his glazed eyes back to me.

"Well, no, I'm sleeping on the couch in the living room," I replied.

"That's right. I'm telling you, keep out of her bedroom, or else."

With that matter being settled, we went back to playing cards. Windy didn't offer nor did he need my assistance in finishing the bottle of bourbon.

Early on Thanksgiving morning, Cindy's brother took me out to the barn, where he introduced me to the turkey he had raised for the holiday dinner. I didn't offer to assist with the preparations. Grandpa Call was an excellent cook, and my appetite appreciated that.

Just an underwater mirage

Word was passed around the Navy training schools in Newport the following week that a unit of SEALs was on the base and would be conducting the physical screening test for UDT training. It was explained that UDT stands for underwater demolition team, and SEAL is for sea, air and land. A short film was shown to give us a visual concept of what that all means. When I saw men leaping from low-hovering choppers into heavy seas on a rescue operation, I knew that was for me. Swimming, either under or above water, was a lot more interesting than hunkering behind a desk with a calculator and pay records in front of me.

I told my buddies that I would be taking the UDT test. John Rowe, the former Marine, said he'd take it too. Keith and Bud decided to go to the base recreation building and give us some moral support.

Another eight guys showed up with their Navy-issue shorts and swim trunks ready for action. The first event, a 1.5-mile run, was, by far, the toughest for me. Heavy smoking over the past 18 months left me huffing and puffing by the first half-mile mark, but I managed to maintain contact with the rear of the pack to finish within the allowable time of 11 minutes and 30 seconds. It was tougher for John, whose bum leg caused him to drop out on the second lap around the indoor track.

After that, doing 42 pushups and 50 sit-ups in less than two minutes each was no problem at all, probably thanks to all the PT those demerits had earned me in boot camp. A couple guys failed that portion of the test. Three others couldn't do the required six pull-ups. I did 20 of them during preseason swim training in high school and still could have done 10 or 12.

Three of us changed into our trunks and were directed to the indoor pool, where the last qualifying event was a 500-yard swim, to be completed in less than 12 minutes and 30 seconds. That would be the easiest part for me, except for one caveat. As we stood at the water's edge ready to dive in, the lead instructor gave us one more directive. "When you finish your swim," he told us, "immediately sink to the bottom of the pool and stay there until you pass out. We will then swim down and pull you out."

My optimism for passing the UDT test evaporated in a hurry as I began my laps and quickly left the other two guys behind. By the time I swam 200 yards or so, I realized that I was alone in the pool. Either they were weak swimmers, or passing out 10 feet below the water surface had scared them off.

As I touched the wall at the end of my swim, I looked up to see the instructors yelling, "Down, down, down," and pointing to the bottom.

I took a deep breath of air and descended. "What the fuck?" I thought to myself as I crouched at the pool bottom. "I can't make myself pass out down here." I didn't want to give up on the opportunity to get out from behind a desk, but I couldn't hold my breath any longer, and I wasn't about to suck a bunch of water into my lungs. Disappointed, I floated to the surface.

There they were again. "Get back down there," they yelled.

So I tried it again. "What the fuck?" I thought to myself again. "I can't do it." I gave up.

To my surprise, the instructors were laughing their asses off when I reached the surface that time. "Congratulations," the lead instructor said. You passed. You'll be getting your orders for UDT training."

The next day in disbursing class, our instructor that week, Petty Officer First Class Will Goodison also congratulated me as he announced my accomplishment. I was the only one on the base to pass the UDT test at that time.

Two weeks later, as graduation day approached, our orders came in. John was returning to the USS Vulcan in Norfolk. Bud received a cushy assignment at the Regional Finance Center in Brooklyn, New York. Keith was going onboard the USS Aoelus (ARC-3), a cable-repair-and-laying ship, which, due to good timing, was completing operations in the Pacific and heading back to port in Portsmouth, New Hampshire. He could still drive home to see JoAnn on weekends. Three guys in our class had volunteered for Vietnam duty, Sherman Lawson, of Mount Pleasant, Michigan, G.V. Medina, a native of the Philippines, and me. And we all got what we'd asked for, orders to Naval Support Activity Saigon.

I was not happy. I thought UDT school was a done deal, and maybe Vietnam after that. I plopped my head down on my desk. Goodison saw it and walked over to me. "Lange," he said, "there's only one thing that supersedes assignment to UDT school for sailors who pass the test. And that is orders to Vietnam. And, you know, about the only way to get orders for Vietnam out of DK school is to volunteer for it."

Once again, I had failed to follow the basic rule of the Army, Navy, Air Force and Marine Corps: "Never volunteer for anything."

Goodbye to New England

During my naval training, I stayed in touch with Chris Schaefer, a guy I'd met in one of my classes at Kent State. Chris was from Akron and had grown up within a couple blocks of St. Vincent High School, where he received his diploma. In those days, St. Vincent was the only coeducational Catholic high school in the city. In 1972, with inner-city enrollment declining, the all-girls St. Mary High School merged with St. Vincent, and a new school was constructed. St. Vincent-St. Mary High School gained national notoriety along with 2003 graduate Lebron James, who went on to become the best basketball player in the world and a loyal supporter of his alma mater and the children in his hometown. St. Vincent was then and remains now the most detested sports rival of Hoban High School, which I attended in ninth and 10th grades.

Nonetheless, Chris and I became friends. In his letters to me, he expressed an interest in the Navy, and, although he maintained his college draft deferment, he was considering an enlistment. When I suggested that he could get a taste of Navy life and that I could even find him a rack in our barracks the night before my graduation from disbursing school, he made the 600-mile drive to Rhode Island. On Dec. 20, 1968, I tossed my sea bag in the trunk of Chris' car, and we headed home in plenty of time for Christmas. I believe we listened to his 8-track tape of Iron Butterfly's 17-minute "In-A-Gadda-Da-Vida" 20 times or more as we drove the length of the Mass Pike and New York Thruway. The Newport visit must have made a good impression on Chris. He soon left college and, I imagine, got a different impression at boot camp.

Christmas with my family in the new home was nice, even though my next duty assignment caused concern for my mom and dad, both of whom were too well acquainted with the up-close-and-personal experiences of war.

Despite Vietnam being clearly designated as my destination on the Permanent Change of Station orders attached to my personnel-records packet, it was a distant figment in the recesses of my mind. My heart was in Massachusetts. So I caught a flight to Bradley International Airport, just north of Hartford, Connecticut, where Cindy Call and her grandpa were waiting in the terminal. Cindy was just a junior then at Mohawk Trail Regional High School, but she would be nearly 18 years old and approaching her graduation day when I hoped to return from Vietnam four months after my 20th birthday. That was some serious thinking about a relationship, but I knew I'd be sleeping on the couch while spending New Year's week in her father's house.

New Year's Eve was a bodacious series of celebrations for me, my new lifelong friend, Keith, with whom many good times and some sad ones lie in the years ahead, his soon-to-be wife, JoAnn, and the vivacious girl who was lighting up my life because of their friendship.

I don't know if it was the bar just over the New York state line, where hard liquor was served to 18-year-olds. Maybe it was the abundant exchange of lip-sucking smooches that circulated through the party hall in Vermont when the clock struck midnight. Or perhaps it was the reality of life moving ahead for a sweet 16-year-old Massachusetts schoolgirl without a boyfriend who would be growing up to a different reality 7,500 miles away.

As the Brothers Gibb, or Bee Gees, sang it in their 1967 hit, "And the lights all went out in Massachusetts." Whatever it was on New Year's Eve was gone on New Year's morning. My warm and cuddly girlfriend had become cool and distant.

Seriously, it was time for me to go.

Chapter 14 | # Vietnam Training in Winter

The sprawling Little Creek Naval Amphibious Base was built on the south shore of the Chesapeake Bay at the eastern edge of Norfolk, Virginia, in the early 1940s as a training center to prepare U.S. troops for the anticipated amphibious assault on Europe in World War II. With its mission of amphibious operations continuing today on some 2,000 acres within sight of the Chesapeake Bay Bridge Tunnel, it is the largest such base anywhere.

On Jan. 12, 1969, I was transported to one of those aging World War II barracks where long johns beneath olive-drab issues mitigated the intrusive winter chill. A potbelly stove exuded toasty heat in the adjacent compartment, where showers and toilets were accessed, but only filtered a whiff of warmth where I curled up in my top bunk under my gray wool blanket.

A few dozen Vietnam-bound sailors were assigned to Barracks No. 3311 for a three-week amphibious school called Counterinsurgency Training, the final, dreaded week of which was known as SERE training – Survival, Evasion, Resistance and Escape.

The CI classroom lectures were informative. They provided an introduction to the very different culture with which we soon would be enmeshed, including the Buddhist religion, which, before the communist heathens conquered the South, was predominant. There were tips on how not to offend its practitioners. We were treated to slide photos of Ao Dai dresses and other common Southeast Asian apparel. We learned about Nuoc Mam, the odorous fish sauce that fermented in fields and paddies everywhere, among other Vietnamese delicacies.

Insight was provided on the prostitution enterprises that thrived in the vicinities of most major American military posts. Unfortunately, we were told, gonorrhea had spread like wildfire through the whorehouses of Saigon, Da Nang and Vung Tau and scorched unprotected urethras. Even more debilitating venereal diseases could be contracted. But don't blame the Asian hookers, our instructor made clear, because it was the French colonialists who imported those odious afflictions and bolstered the world's oldest profession. And we Americans, with our "rest-and-re-cuperation," or R&R, sabbaticals to wayward destinations like Sydney, Australia, were augmenting the contagion.

Based on the enlightening categorization by draft-dodging celebrity philanderer Donald J. Trump in his 1993 radio interview, the path to her-oism could be found in the seamy back rooms of Vietnamese bars. But then, the path to the American presidency for real Vietnam War heroes would be betrayed by spiteful slanderers whom they once called brothers.

More frightening was the class in which the wide variety of tactics be-ing used by the enemy to kill and maim Americans was lucidly examined.

Avoid group gatherings in public places, we were advised, as they were open invitations to Viet Cong suicide bombings. Beware of little children, we were told, as they could be unknowing deliverers of makeshift bombs attached to their bosoms sent to blow themselves up amidst groups of Americans on the streets of Saigon. During the 1968 Tet Offensive one year earlier, a 19-man VC suicide squad blew a hole in the wall of our embassy in the capital of South Vietnam.

No place would be secure from enemy attacks, we learned. My orders said Saigon. Although the naval support activity actually was located in Nha Be, 7 miles south of the capital, which I learned upon my arrival, my missions would take me through the city regularly and include several overnight stays there each month. Even without the Tet Offensive of early 1968, the year was rife with enemy terrorist attacks in Saigon.

On May 3, a taxi loaded with explosives killed three civilians and injured 30 people, including five Americans, outside the Armed Forces Radio Television Station. On June 6, an estimated 200 pounds of explosive destroyed a Chinese newspaper building and killed five Vietnamese civilians. On July 21, nine civilians were killed and 96 were injured in separate VC terrorist bombings of a theater and restaurant. On Aug. 9, a terrorist tossed a grenade into a Military Police Jeep in downtown Saigon, killing one American and wounding another.

On Sept. 3, terrorists set off a grenade at the U.S. Agency for International Development headquarters. On Sept. 9, they set off a 75-pound charge and destroyed the Government of Vietnam Information Office. On Sept. 25, a TNT charge was set off outside the Army Post Exchange in the Cholon district. Those attacks resulted in nine dead and 70 wounded.

History being eminently oblivious to American consciousness, terrorist attacks in the Middle Eastern military incursions of post-9/11 have been widely interpreted as some sort of novel, panic-inducing and unsporting strategy. Of course, Vietnam wasn't unprecedented in that respect either.

The more customary wages of war did not overlook Saigon either. Rocket attacks from outside the city, small-arms battles with VC infiltrators and sniper fire within it were regular occurrences in 1968. Heavy fighting resulted in a 24-hour curfew for Cholon on May 7. About 150 houses were destroyed by rockets near the Central Market on May 19. Nineteen Vietnamese were killed and 67 wounded in a June 11 rocket attack. Seventeen were killed and 69 wounded by rocket attacks on Aug. 22.

Tan Son Nhut Air Base, on the outskirts of Saigon, where many of the sailors in my CI class soon would be touching down, also was in the enemy's sights for rockets and mortars. Two American and four Vietnamese civilians were killed and 24 were wounded by 122-millimeter rockets on June 12. Twelve more Vietnamese were killed and 28 wounded there on June 20 and 21.

During my training in Little Creek, on Jan. 23, 1969, in what was described as a "night of terror" in Saigon, numerous targets were hit by enemy shelling, including the bachelor officer quarters at the Annapolis Hotel. The Annapolis also served as the Navy's temporary barracks for new arrivals, myself included, and contained small personnel and disbursing offices.

Nonetheless, Saigon was a relatively safe haven within the war zone.

There were reasons why the soldiers who spent their days trudging through rice paddies, Marines crawling through jungles, sailors patrolling rivers and canals and airmen dodging anti-aircraft fire referred to those stationed in places like Saigon as REMFs – rear-echelon motherfuckers.

Counterinsurgency classroom training devoted a good portion of a day exploring the numerous ways that ground pounders could be killed or maimed without even encountering the actual enemy. Booby traps would be waiting on the beaten tracks, off the beaten tracks and maybe even in commode flushers, we learned.

Punji sticks, actually sharpened bamboo stakes smeared with bodily wastes and other vile goop, were one of the Viet Cong's most versatile traps. They would be jabbing up through the weeds alongside the path or in a shallow pit cannily covered with sticks and grass on the trail. The unsuspecting GI who slipped into the weeds or stumbled into the pit would be subjected to multiple punctures, often suffering fatal wounds to vital organs and otherwise contracting debilitating infections.

Trip wires would unleash the tiger trap, which consisted of a heavy, spike-studded cylinder strung to a tree branch above; the swinging gate, an arced bamboo pole, would fling open and jab a spike into a man's chest; or a hand grenade would eject from a can mounted on a tree trunk and turn human limbs into mincemeat.

Deadly bamboo pit vipers would be hidden in the VC's complex underground network, waiting for the American "tunnel rats" who were sent into those holes in search of weapons and information. Or they would be left inside backpacks amidst weapons caches to be opened by American search-and-destroy exercises. Or they would be tied by their tails and hung from trees at eye height. Or one of those vipers might just snap its fangs into the fleshy calf of a soldier and inject him with a lethal dose of venom of its own accord.

We received cursory instructions on vipers that slithered in the jungles, cobras that coiled in the ditches, kraits that lurked in the rice paddies and pythons that swam in the rivers of Vietnam but could hardly identify the 30-some poisonous species there. The rivers also were home to crocodiles and other predators that discouraged human bathers.

There are few verifiable accounts of deadly wildlife attacks on American warriors in Vietnam. Memories of those who served in country, however, recall a number of bestial tiger encounters, including two instances in November 1968, when an infantryman was dragged away from his nighttime perimeter watch and partially eaten and a Marine was killed while on patrol.

As for the flushers that often were connected to tanks on the walls above commodes in Vietnam's more civilized locales, the enemy's ingenuity with hand grenades and booby traps was not lost on the REMFs. After all, there were no flush toilets in the villages and hamlets where real combatants might have occasion to move their bowels.

For good measure, the booby-trap instructor left us students with a cautionary piece of insight. The whores in Saigon have been known to attach razor blades inside their vaginas, he said.

Even to me, that seemed like a stretch. Overall, though, the classroom indoctrination gave me second thoughts about my knee-jerk volunteerism.

According to general statistics compiled on the Vietnam War, 11 percent of the American deaths there were attributed to booby traps and mines. That amounts to about 6,400 men killed by those devious means alone. As a matter of comparison, after 16 years, fewer U.S. service members' lives had been lost as the result of all hostile action in the Afghanistan and Iraq wars. Improvised explosive devices became indelibly associated with the horrors of the post-9/11 wars, surely for good reason. Yet, so many Vietnam horrors are buried bygones, for no good reason.

Moderately trained killers

Counterinsurgency school also involved some physical training and a day on the shooting range, where we got a feel for some of the weapons used in combat, especially the M16 assault rifle. We fired the .50-caliber machine guns, which were used on the Navy's river patrol boats. We were introduced to an assortment of other weapons, such as the M79 grenade launcher, but did not get to try them out. Back in the classroom, we learned how to disassemble, clean and reassemble some of them.

The majority of us who were not expected to engage in combat operations became moderately trained killers. For those with occupational ratings such as gunner's mate and others who would be helicopter door gunners and PBR machine gunners, they already were trained to kill.

On the morning after we went to the shooting range, Jermaine Roberts, the black man who was the designated leader of my otherwise all-white squad, asked me if my ears were ringing. They did ring for a couple hours after the ear-piercing .50 calibers were fired, I told him, but I thought I'd get over it. I was the youngest, least-experienced guy in his squad, and Jermaine, a second-class petty officer who was on his second four-year enlistment, befriended me like a big brother. He said his ears were still ringing and that we should go to sick bay to get checked out. It was an opportunity to skip a lecture on mosquitoes and malaria, so I agreed.

When I told a corpsman about the ear-ringing symptom brought on by the firing range, he said, "Well, duh! It'll go away in a day or two. If it isn't gone by the time your SERE week is completed, come back and let us know." He jotted down a brief synopsis of my ailment in my health records, which apparently was to my advantage when I filed an application with the Veterans Administration many years later.

Jermaine, who spent his nights in a rooming house off base, decided to host a send-off party there for our seven-member squad the evening before we were to begin SERE week. He arranged for a cab to deliver us to the house in a section of Norfolk where not many white people resided. He provided us with a good supply of beer and gin and soda and had his hearty landlady prepare the most delicious dinner of fried chicken I'd ever tasted. Motown music was playing on the radio. A couple of young female renters soon joined us to share the chicken, beverages and revelry. Jermaine and I danced with them. The other white guys were disinterested in dancing with black girls, but I was enchanted.

After a while, I asked about the bathroom and went upstairs to relieve myself. The door to one of the bedrooms was wide open. Inside, two black guys were fiddling with a couple of handguns, and I saw a half dozen more weapons spread out on the bed. They didn't invite me to join them. By the looks on their faces, they were not at all receptive to my presence. Did they think the six white guys drinking beer and gin downstairs had capacious bladders? The bedroom door was closed when I got finished in the bathroom. The race riots that had rocked our country the previous spring were not far behind us. Unlike Jermaine Roberts, some black people did not welcome white people into their homes with open arms. I returned to the kitchen, opened another beer and enjoyed another dance to Motown music with a friendly black girl.

Survival and evasion

My head was throbbing, and my stomach was churning when I boarded one of the two buses waiting outside the barracks the next morning. It transported my squad and several others about 120 miles north to U.S. Army Fort A.P. Hill, which consists of some 76,000 acres west of the Rappahannock River. Dressed in jungle greens, we were dropped off in a thick forest, although it was mostly devoid of foliage in the first week of February. It didn't seem like an ideal setting for jungle training. And the weather didn't seem quite right for acclimating us to a tropical environment.

The squads were dispersed to widespread locations in the forest. Evidence of previous occupation by SERE participants was apparent. Logs cut to reusable lengths had been strewn about the area, which enabled us to reconstruct shelters anchored in low-hanging tree limbs. Less bulky logs were used to fashion a floor and roof. Dried leaves helped cushion our fitful slumbers. Live, needled pine branches were layered over the log roof to diffuse rain and sleet into squirts and dribbles. We started a campfire with a limited supply of matches and found plenty of dead wood to keep it burning. Jermaine assigned an overnight fire-watch schedule.

Aside from weathering the northern Virginia winter chills and drizzles, our greatest discomforts were growling bellies. A key to the survival sector of SERE training is food deprivation. Someone in another squad somehow managed to catch a fish in a nearby lake. If bait had been procurable from the cold, hard earth, we may have been tempted to fry up some worms. Edible wildlife was nowhere to be found. There were no berries to be picked in February, but we were able to make some soup with wild onions.

Despite the rigors imposed on us, the experience was not entirely dissimilar to my Boy Scout adventures. Winter camping was much colder in Northern Ohio, and I wasn't skinny through gluttony anyway. Although I heard some grumbling from others in my squad, no one was whining about it.

On the fourth or fifth day, the special operatives running the program mercifully delivered a live chicken to each squad. If we were to get shot down over a Vietnamese rain forest, it's unlikely that we'd run into Colonel Sanders. One of our guys, having been raised on a Kentucky farm, skillfully wrung the chicken's neck. We plucked its feathers, chopped it up and tossed the meat, innards and all, in a pot of boiling water with onions. Our cooking was no match for that of Jermaine's landlady, but it was satisfactory.

Early the next morning we were transported to a distant section of Fort A.P. Hill, where the evasion sector of SERE training was conducted. We were issued a compass and coordinates but no bacon and eggs. The operatives in camouflage fatigues warned us that, if we were captured before reaching the end point, there would be hell to pay. The squads were separated and sent into the woods.

Jermaine, our squad leader, took charge of the compass and led the way. The terrain was hilly and rugged. It was traversed by small streams that we could leap over in a single bound or balance our way across via horizontal trunks of fallen trees. Even without the luxuriant foliage that would sprout in the coming months, our concealment was ample. It wasn't a far cry from the Scouting hikes I'd experienced in Carroll County and Mohican State Park. Despite the relevance, there were no choruses of "We're the Fockowwee."

After a couple hours of over the streams and through the woods, we estimated that we must be closing in on the designated terminus. We came upon a clearing and cautiously stepped out from the trees. Suddenly, three armed men in camouflage jumped out from a clump of bramble and cornered us. We were captured. After some rough jostling and vulgarity-laced commands, we were shoved to the ground and compelled to do 50 push-ups, which required several rest stops for a couple guys. "Next time it won't be so easy," one of our captors snarled as they released us to complete our evasion trial, which we had just flunked.

As we learned at the meeting point, other squads also had been "captured" and subjected to similar punishment on their straight-line hikes. We also learned that it was just the beginning of the evasion course. A new direction and new distance were issued.

Not being enthusiastic about another capture and not-so-easy consequences lying ahead, I approached Jermaine with an alternate plan. I had some experience with compass navigation as an Eagle Scout, I told him, conveniently omitting the overnight "Fockowwee" episode, and I could take us on an alternative route to our destination. He willingly delegated the compass operation to me.

As soon as we were sufficiently inside the tree line to be unseen by our adversaries, I took a 90-degree right turn to the north-northwest for 200 yards. At that point, I took a right-angle left turn to the west-southwest so that we followed the designated direction out of range of the would-be captors. By carefully counting my strides, I determined when we had sufficiently passed the destination. At that point, I made a 45-degree left turn so that we arrived at a slight angle from the rear instead of the anticipated head-on arrival. Mission accomplished.

As similar scenarios played out several more times during the course of the long day, I patted myself on the back for being the most evasive son of a bitch in our squad, if not the entire SERE class. I was in my Scouting element.

Unfortunately, that all changed at dusk, when the squads arrived at the point of inevitable captivity. Our evasion was over. Our previous encounters with instructors, despite their unfriendliness, left us with the impression that they were on our side and they were there to provide invaluable training that just might save our lives. The ones who met us here were different. They were not in American military uniforms, at least not in anything recognizable as such. Some of them had black-and-green-painted faces. They held weapons at the ready. They looked un-American.

These guards ordered us to march. Trudge was more like it, as solid ground became soggy and then mushy and then muddy and then marshy. The cold water gradually rose above our boots and up to our knees. No talking. Keep trudging. The Virginia February night became darker and colder, exhausting and tiring. Into the night, we trudged on. Squish, squish, squish.

Finally, we reached solid ground and saw lantern lights amidst the trees ahead. The guards herded us into a "prisoner-of-war camp" with several makeshift huts encompassed by barbed-wire fencing. We were led inside a gate, which slammed shut behind us, and were ordered to sit cross-legged, shivering in the dirt. No talking. No moving. No shut-eye.

As the sun rose and its rays shimmered through the bare trees, our captors lit a pile of logs in a large fire pit at the center of the compound. They directed our attention to the "People's Pool," a burial-sized pit where anyone who failed to follow instructions or resisted their commands in any way would be treated to a frigid dunking in muddy water. We were ordered to remain on our hands and knees at all times and to keep the dirt tidy by picking up any and all twigs and other bits of clutter then feeding it to the campfire.

'How could that be torture?'

At the time when I completed my SERE training and for decades thereafter, it was shrouded in secrecy from the public and even from fellow members of the military. Matthew Downer, a former employee of the U.S. Department of Defense, Marine Corps veteran and 2009 graduate of the Navy training, responded to the question, "What is it like to go through SERE school?" a few years later. "We could tell you, but then we'd ... be in violation of a non-disclosure agreement," he wrote. Without crossing the line of confidentiality, he concluded that it's "an excellent and important training program that substantially depends upon those in training not knowing what to expect."

In addition to classroom strategies to be used in potential interrogation situations, Downer explained that the field experience was "heightened by continual food and sleep deprivation" and that it "included increasing degrees of exertion, stress, disorientation, and pain."

Based on my recollections, the training didn't change one hell of a lot in 40 years.

The secrecy shit hit the fan, though, when the "enhanced-interrogation" practices of the George W. Bush administration in connection with the Iraq and Afghanistan wars was subjected to intense scrutiny. In the lead of an April 21, 2009, New York Times report, Scott Shane and Mark Mazzetti wrote, "The program began with Central Intelligence Agency leaders in the grip of an alluring idea: They could get tough in terrorist interrogations without risking legal trouble by adopting a set of methods used on Americans during military training. How could that be torture?"

An examination by the Times found that none of the officials pushing for those methods, including senior aides to the president and leaders of the congressional intelligence committees, had "investigated the gruesome origins of the techniques they were approving with little debate." According to top officials involved in the 2002 discussions, "they did not know that the military training program, called SERE ... used ... methods that had wrung false confessions from Americans," the Times reported.

The Times reporters revealed that, despite CIA Director George J. Tenet's insistence to the contrary, he and other officials "did not examine the history of the most shocking method, the near-drowning technique known as waterboarding." Furthermore, they reported that those officials "did not know that some veteran trainers from the SERE program itself had warned in internal memorandums that, morality aside, the methods were ineffective."

Following up on those revelations, Ben Sherwood, of the Huffington Post, reported that the SERE programs taught "soldiers, sailors and aviators how to survive in hostile environments, evade and resist the enemy and, if necessary, escape. Resist, in military shorthand, means to withstand the punishment of captivity, including torture, and to find ways to fight back."

Sherwood's report continued, "Only in harsh and realistic conditions, the military believes, can trainees begin to understand what it's like to be shot down, captured or brutalized by the enemy. The more miserable and uncomfortable, the better. Every single one of the ex-POWs I've interviewed believes this training was invaluable in surviving their ordeals."

I can vouch for the misery and discomfort, which were being exacerbated by my bony knees. They were resistant to crawling around in the dirt and picking up twigs, which the guards periodically replenished from a pile in a corner of the perimeter. With some distress, I looked up as several higher-ranking captives were knocked around, forcibly undressed and thrust into the "People's Pool" after taking their turns in the interrogation chamber.

When one of the guards planted the sole of his boot in my side and told me to stand up for my visit to interrogation, my aching knees were relieved. My psychological anguish was momentarily unburdened as well when I was met inside a tiny hut by a non-threatening man who invited me to have a seat. He told me he was with the International Red Cross and was there to ensure that we prisoners were treated in accordance with the

Geneva Conventions. He asked me where I was from.

Having paid some attention to the lessons of Counterinsurgency Training, I wasn't about to fall for that kind of trickery. "America," I said, even though that bit of information was more than the "name, rank and serial number" required by the conventions.

"Well," he said with a reassuring smile, "I'm not here to cause you any harm. I'm here to help you. I can arrange for you to contact your mother so that you can let her know you're OK."

"No, thanks," I replied. "I don't like my mother." That was easy, I thought, being a hard ass, at least in my own mind.

"Guard!" the supposed Red Cross guy yelled, his friendly demeanor taking a sudden turn. "Get this prisoner out of my sight before I rip his face off."

Two guards grabbed me by the armpits, rustled me to another small wooden chamber and thrust me into a chair. "Now you're going to talk to us," one of them snarled.

"David C. Lange," I said. "Seaman. B440308."

"What is seaman?" he demanded to know.

"E-3," I replied.

The other guard rapped me on the side of the head. It could have been harder.

"What is E-3?" the first guard said.

"Enlisted man," I acknowledged, assuming that was part of my rank.

"What is your job?" he asked.

"Seaman," I reiterated.

The other guard lifted my 140-pound body out of the chair like I was a loaf of Wonder bread and smashed my skinny ass back down.

"Where is your base?" he asked.

"I don't know," I replied.

"How many men are on your base?" he demanded.

"I have no idea. I'm a simple seaman," I told him.

I was bracing myself for a dip in the "People's Pool" as they dragged me out to the compound. But they shoved me back to the ground and ordered me to resume picking up twigs.

My knees were not pleased. I may have been a good evader, but I wasn't much of a resister. There wasn't any resistance of any consequence going on among my fellow prisoners of war, all of whom were obediently crawling around on their hands and knees. And there was no escape in sight. I couldn't speak for the rest of them, but, after another hour of that, my knees couldn't take it anymore.

Reverting to my evader talents, whenever the guards' attention was diverted in other directions, I stood up, in clear noncompliance with their commands. When I saw their attention redirected toward me, I quickly scooted back down to all fours. This behavior did not go unnoticed. The repeated blows to my midsection, I noticed, could have been inflicted with greater force. Maybe they were more for show than for actual injury. It became a conflict between my throbbing knees and their less-painful reprisals, and my knees were prevailing. I simply could not crawl any longer.

So I was yanked to the edge of the "People's Pool," where one of the guards said, "This is your last warning. You either stay down on your hands and knees, or we will hold your head under the water."

"I can't do it," I whispered, almost begging for mercy. "My knees are killing me."

They whisked me past the crawling twig pickers and outside the gate. "All right," the guard told me. "We're putting you in charge of the fire pit. You'll feed it with the logs. Don't make the fire get too high and do not let it burn out." They took me to the wood pile, loaded as many split logs in my arms as I could carry and led me back into the compound.

The afternoon wore on, the sun moved westward, and two dozen tormented prisoners kept crawling. With each guarded trip to the wood pile, I pondered my escape. Even if I could outrun the guards, though, there was nowhere to go, no civilization within miles, no restaurant or grocer to feed my empty belly, no soft bed on which to lay my weary head and no money to pay for any of that anyway. If I did make a run for it but failed to make a clean getaway, the consequences of gasping for air between dunks in the "People's Pool" and then being knocked back to my aching knees were foreboding.

With the light of day waning and another night of misery on the horizon, restless whispers circulated among the prisoners. Then it happened. The solitary officer in our ranks, Lt. Kline, who had an earlier dip in the

"People's Pool," stood up and ordered the others to do the same.

"Get back down on your knees," the head guard bellowed.

"Stay on your feet, men," Lt. Kline said.

"Order the prisoners to get back down now," the guard yelled.

"Stay on your feet, men," Lt. Kline repeated.

"You imperialist pig, get over here and stand at attention," the guard said, pointing at me.

I complied.

"Hold out your arms," he told me.

I did so.

He had another guard load two fire logs onto my outstretched arms.

"Lieutenant," the lead guard commanded. "Order the prisoners back down, or this pig will pay."

"Stay on your feet, men," Lt. Kline said.

Another log was loaded onto my arms. "If any of these logs fall to the ground," the guard said, "you will perish in the 'People's Pool.'" He turned to Lt. Kline. "Now, will you order your men back down?"

No response.

Another log. The showdown continued. Another log. No response. My arms began to tremble. I looked toward the "People's Pool" with dread. Another log. The stack was chin high, and it wobbled. One more log, and the stack was bound to topple. I leaned back and strained to steady the load. The top log tumbled over and crunched me square in the nose. Blood spurted out. I closed my eyes and held on tight.

Instead of being led to the "People's Pool," two guards quickly unloaded the stack, grasped me by my nearly numb arms and ushered me out the gate. They took me down a short path to a wider trail, where, to my surprise, a van with medical supplies and a nurse was parked out of sight of the POW camp. After she stopped the bleeding, determined that my nose was unbroken and applied a gauzy bandage, I could hear a loud cheer arise from the compound.

Upon my return, I learned that the day-long-awaited resistance had finally been accomplished through the leadership of Lt. Kline and that our rescuers had arrived. Amidst tempered joviality, superficial self-congratulation and unspoken rumination, we were treated to a decent dinner.

Matthew Downer, the Marine veteran who later wrote about his 2009 SERE experience, said it was followed by a briefing about its physical and emotional ramifications. "They told us that nightmares and hallucinations were likely the first night or two but that, if they or the physical pain continued, that we should let them know," Downer said. "I didn't think I had any hallucinations, but my wife begged to differ."

I don't recall any such concerns being expressed in our post-SERE briefing back at the Little Creek Naval Amphibious Base. We were subjected to some minor criticism over the time it took for us to rally sufficient resistance. With transparent satisfaction, the instructors went through a short list of supposedly valuable information they had extracted from us captives through their various coercive techniques, none of which they classified as torture.

At the top of the list, the briefing leader noted that one of us "broke down and confessed to the interrogator that he did not like his mother." I almost blasted snot out of my bruised nose as I choked back my astonishment. As the New York Times revealed in its 2009 report on the origins of tough terrorist interrogations, the SERE program used "methods that had wrung false confessions from Americans." I loved my mom.

Chapter 15 | **Cherry Boy No More**

The direct flight out of Cleveland landed in San Francisco five hours later. I rode with several other uniformed men in a van that crossed the bay and took us 50 miles northeast to Travis Air Force Base. In a few more hours, I was on another westbound commercial airliner, oddly, I thought, after expecting a military flight. Even stranger, in my estimation, it wasn't even an American airline. The flight attendants, known as stewardesses in those days, spoke in broken English, but they didn't say much.

Most seats on the plane were occupied by young men with a common destination, Tan Son Nhut Air Base, South Vietnam. We were the only passengers. The long flight was broken up with landings and takeoffs in Honolulu, Midway Island and Guam, where I had enough time to buy a fresh pack of Marlboros in the terminal.

The last stop, Clark Air Force Base on Luzon Island in the Philippines, was a four-hour layover. It was a welcome opportunity to visit the enlisted men's club. By and large, EM clubs welcomed female clientele from surrounding communities. Their companionship was seen as a morale boost for the men stationed on military bases. I was hypnotized by the unfamiliar beauty of the blossoming Filipino women who shared drinks and snacks with the regulars at their tables and joined them on the dance floor. The more I drank, the more stunning they appeared to my widening eyes.

There were no Asian women in Cuyahoga Falls. I might have seen one once at a bus stop in Akron.

Evidently, I was not among the heaviest drinkers who re-embarked for the final leg of our journey across the South China Sea. Barf bags came in handy during the turbulent flight.

It was dark when our plane touched down at Tan Son Nhut Air Base just outside of Saigon. The head stewardess had one word for us as we disembarked. "Goodbye," she said. There was no, "Welcome to Vietnam. Have a nice stay. We hope you enjoyed your flight. It's been a pleasure to serve you." Granted, she was not well versed in English pleasantries – or any pleasantries, as far as I could tell. Even so, that guttural "Goodbye" landed with a thud.

With aviation operations for all four U.S. military branches based there, plus commercial airlines delivering and removing civilians, not to mention tons upon tons of human cannon fodder, by the mid-1960s, Tan Son Nhut reportedly was the busiest airport in the world.

It was quiet when I arrived. My senses were on high alert. It was Feb. 15, the middle of Tet 1969. One year earlier, the massive Tet Offensive had shaken American military and political leaders to the core. It had rattled the confidence of the media and even the "silent majority." It wasn't just the newcomers. Our forces also were on high alert, and rightfully so. Communist insurgents again were attacking U.S. bases, including nearby Long Binh on Feb. 22. Although the attacks were less intense than the previous year and were successfully repelled, they reinforced the communists' ability to inflict damages and casualties.

After collecting our baggage, we were separated by branch of service. The Navy guys piled into a gray bus with sturdy wire mesh covering the open windows. The bus lurched forward, and we soon were chugging along the ghostly streets of Saigon. Sandbags and water barrels fortified many building fronts, most notably the Annapolis Hotel on Plantation Road, where we were delivered after a few miles. At some point in the past, it was a hotel. The wages of war had transformed it into a Navy transfer facility for in-country arrivals and those who had done their time and were going back to "the world."

I turned my records packet over to the duty man and was shown to a bunk on the second floor. I'm a heavy sleeper. The unfamiliar, dubious surroundings quickly were lost in dreamland. Reveille over the loudspeaker the next morning introduced me to a much different Saigon. Plantation Road was bustling with traffic – military vehicles, compact blue-and-white taxis, cyclos carrying pairs of passengers in open seats connected to motorbikes in the rear, pedal-driven bicycles and horse-drawn-carriages. More than anything, Honda 50 motorcycles sped past, many of them carrying families of five or six, little children hanging onto each other for dear life. Odors of exhausts and especially diesel fuel permeated the heavy air.

After a visit to the head and showers, I pulled on my dungarees and followed directions to the Army's Montana bachelor enlisted quarters a few blocks away, where breakfast was served in the chow hall.

Processing in the Annapolis offices took some time. U.S. currency was exchanged for MPC, military pay certificates. Possession of greenbacks, being a prized international exchange mechanism for black-market weaponry, was forbidden. Olive-drab work uniforms, jungle fatigues and boots were issued.

I spent most of my first day in Vietnam sitting alone, like in a cocoon, peering down from the second floor at a new world that, one day earlier, had been beyond my comprehension. Normalcy, to those whose existence flashed past my eyes on Plantation Road, was nothing of the kind to me. The "night of terror" just three weeks earlier, when the Annapolis itself was a target of enemy shelling, may have been just another night among many in what was widely considered the safe haven of Saigon. By July 10, five months later, when those sandbags piled up on the street level below would be blown to smithereens in a bombing attack, it would be just another night for me somewhere else not quite so safe in Vietnam.

On the morning of my second day in country, I took my seat on a bus outside the Annapolis Hotel and was on my way to Naval Support Activity Saigon. It actually was located in the village of Nha Be, about 7 miles south of the capital. It was accessed via a two-lane paved road slightly elevated above watery rice paddies on either side. We passed several tiny hamlets that exuded the rotting-fish pungency of Nuoc Mam.

The people who existed in the village of Nha Be mostly did so in tiny, wooden-walled hooches under roofs fashioned from scrap metal scavenged from canneries. They were connected to the main road by raised earthen walking paths that traversed the river overflow like a giant maze. Outhouses dropped human waste directly into the stagnancy, which raised quite a stench, but it conveniently washed downstream toward the sea with the changing tide. The main road itself was cluttered with street-level bars, second-floor sleeping quarters and sultry greeters at the doors.

Robert H. Stoner, a gunner's mate second class who served on the Mekong River during his 1970 tour of duty, authored "The Brown Water Navy in Vietnam," which provides basic histories of operations there. Based on his research, the naval operation at Nha Be was established in 1966 "as a major combat and logistic base" and "was strategically placed at the junction of the Long Tau and Soi Rap, the main rivers between the port of Saigon and the South China Sea. In addition, Nha Be lay astride waterways traversing the Viet Cong-infiltrated Run Sat special zone and the eastern Mekong Delta region."

I knew the wide waterway that wrapped around the base as the Saigon River. Some modern-day maps identify it as the Nha Be River. A major tributary flows into the wider river from the distant shore. However those rivers are identified, there was water everywhere.

According to Stoner's account, "20 acres of nearby swampland were filled with dredged soil, and, by December 1966, work was begun on permanent base facilities, which included depot-level repair, administrative, communications, storage, maintenance, quartering and messing buildings, four 1,000-barrel fuel-storage tanks and a boat pier."

Nha Be was a key contributor to Operation Game Warden, one of the most successful naval actions of the war. The base supported 40 river patrol boats, commonly known as PBRs; Helicopter Attack (Light) Squadron 3, or HAL-3; Mine Squadron 11, whose minesweepers ensured safe passage of commercial and military ships upriver to Saigon; and SEAL Team 2.

Thankfully, swampland had been turned to sand and dust before the bus dropped me off just inside the main gate. Unlike the ramshackle structures we had passed on the way through town and even the aging Annapolis Hotel in Saigon, the array of bright white buildings inside the base were a sight for my wandering eyes. The military construction battalions that had completed their work only months before my arrival did good work.

I was directed to the personnel office in a building not far from the gate and then to the disbursing office, my duty station. Like most of the other buildings on base, it was well ventilated through wall-to-wall screens shielded from the broiling sun and driving monsoons by a louvered exterior. I approached a guy in dungarees seated inside a cage near the entrance to the office. I told him I was a disbursing clerk reporting for duty. He was the cashier, he said, and I should go over to the counter.

A guy in olive drab got up from one of about 15 desks in the spacious office. After I introduced myself, he turned around and announced, "Hey, everybody. The new DK has arrived." Following a quick introduction to my coworkers, Mike Loomis, a third-class petty officer, led the way to our barracks in the next building over and pointed me to an open rack and locker. "Don't mind my face," he said, motioning to his right cheek and temple, which were heavily pocked with scabbing blisters. "I guess I shouldn't have been messing around with a smoke grenade," he said with a laugh. "Anyway, I'm outta here in two weeks, goin' back to the world. My face will be all healed by then, so Jody can kiss my ass."

"Jody," as I learned, was the guy who avoided going to war and was messing with your girlfriend back home. "Ain't no use in goin' home," the cadence goes. "Jody's got your girl and gone."

The barracks had flush toilets and showers with running water. It was cloudy but not as brown as the river. You wouldn't want to drink it. If you used either a toilet or a shower during the day, you shouldn't be surprised if a Vietnamese cleaning lady happened to be scrubbing the one next door.

A couple DKs showed me the way to the mess hall for breakfast the next morning. Then we went to the office, where Petty Officer 1st Class "Guzzy" DeGuzman, one of the supervisors, showed me to my desk and turned over a stack of pay records for my keeping.

Guzzy was one of tens of thousands of Filipinos to serve in the U.S. Navy since the Spanish-American War. Apparently, it was one of the benefits of their country's colonization. Compared to the economic opportunities found in the Philippines, Navy life offered a steady job and decent wages. Most of those who enlisted were either college graduates or had at least attended some college. The common rating for Filipinos enlisting in the Navy was steward, basically serving as servants to officers. Prior to the influx of Philippine nationals, African-Americans tended to fill those slots.

Those Filipinos who managed to move into other job ratings generally remained within the Supply Corps, which included disbursing. A few Filipino disbursing clerks volunteered for Vietnam duty, including G.V. Medina from my class in Newport. They did so knowing it would entitle them to the week-long vacation known as R&R, including free air transportation to Manila. They saved their money, minded their own business and avoided trouble. I got to know many Filipinos during my enlistment. They were remarkably intelligent people.

My initial record-keeping assignments included river divisions and support personnel based in Dong Tam and My Tho, both along the My Tho branch of the Mekong River; Sa Dec, on the Mekong; and aboard YRBM-17, a yard repair messing berthing vessel anchored in the middle of the river.

Eye-opener on the perimeter

I also was issued my own M16 rifle, which I knew how to use, thanks to a day on the range in Counterinsurgency Training. It would be necessary for perimeter watches scheduled every third night. Military duty comes first. So, that night I was awakened by the officer of the deck at 11:45 p.m. for my four-hour shift at the Three Alpha watch station. I pulled on my olive drabs, grabbed the loaded M16 from my locker and arrived for duty, along with a more experienced perimeter watcher, to relieve two guys on the 8 p.m.-to-midnight shift.

Three Alpha was situated on the river at the northeast corner of the base. To the north was the outskirts of the village. A few dark and silent little houses were within view. To the south was a series of dry docks, where PBRs and other watercraft were brought in for repairs. The experienced guard elected to hold his position in the guardhouse, where he would keep his watchful eye out for any activity beyond the concertina wire. He directed me to pace the riverfront, where I would conduct security checks on the boats and be alert for possible underwater-demolition attacks or floating mines.

Beneath the star-lit sky, I stepped along oversized railroad ties that topped the sea wall at the edge of a paved roadway. I looked at the water lapping against the dry docks that were afloat about 6 feet below. It was high tide. Underwater assaults across that wide river teeming with who knows what kind of slithery reptiles seemed like a stretch to me. I checked out a 31-foot-long PBR with bullet holes in its fiberglass hull. It looked like it would be a fun ride on Lake Erie but not so much fun for a slow cruise along a narrow canal with AK-47s waiting in the bush around the next bend.

How fortunate I was to be stationed in a safe place like Nha Be, I thought, as I completed my round and returned to the sandbag-ensconced guardhouse. Maybe there was no actual "rear" in this war of insurgency, but our pillowed beds, showers, often with hot water, even, and hot breakfasts in the morning were just 100 yards or so away. Somewhere out there in the distance, where tracers slashed through the darkness and rocket bursts flashed above the tree line, other 19-year-old kids were knee deep in muck with leeches sucking blood from their calves, never knowing whose arms or legs would be blown off that night.

Suddenly, before my wide-open eyes, one of those flashes lit up the entire riverfront. Debris was flung into the air, a thunderous boom blasted my eardrums, and the ground shuddered beneath my feet. A small structure near where I had just made my perimeter round was gone, blown apart. "Holy shit!" I yelped.

"Put your helmet on," the other guard yelled. "It looks like we're under attack. Keep your eyes on the water for any sign of movement. Grab a couple percussion grenades. I'm watching the hooches outside the wire."

We held our M16s at the ready. Sirens sounded across the base. Orders were shouted to our rear. Men hustled from their barracks to the bunkers, some of them in skivvies and bare feet, carrying their uniforms and boots with them. Less than one week into my 12-month tour, I was getting a taste of the Vietnam War. Not a big gulp, though.

Then all was quiet. After intensive security checks around the base, the all clear eventually was given. Word circulated the next day that the ammunition dump had exploded. A single enemy mortar attack with such precision was deemed highly unlikely. Were some of the Vietnamese day workers VC partisans? Probably. Could one of them have booby-trapped the ammo building? Possibly. Did it just blow up on its own? Who knows?

What I did know was, if the explosion had occurred 10 minutes sooner, I could have been the victim of collateral damage. Would I have been listed as KIA, killed in action, or WIA, wounded in action? Did an exploding ammo depot qualify as action? Would I have been awarded a Purple Heart? How about a Combat Action Ribbon? I had a gun in my hands. Would anybody in the Vietnam era have suggested that being in the wrong place at the wrong time was heroic? Application of the term may have been substantively altered in the era of memorial signs along interstate highways, but most people, myself included, would rather be alive and in one piece than be thus rewarded.

Swift-boat back stabbers

And I'd rather be on perimeter watch in Nha Be than aboard the 50-foot-long PCF-94, a patrol craft fast, also known as swift boat, on the narrow Dong Cung River in the VC-infested jungly southernmost tip of South Vietnam. That's where 25-year-old Navy Lt.j.g. John F. Kerry was officer in charge on Feb. 28, 1969, and where actual heroism was confirmed.

Based on well-documented accounts, all three boats on that mission came under intense enemy fire. Kerry ordered a counterattack that routed the entrenched superior enemy force and resulted in the capture of many weapons. Responding to the request of Army advisers on shore, Kerry ordered PCF-94 and PCF-23 farther up the river, where they again encountered enemy fire, including a rocket attack close to his boat. He and his men again charged numerically superior enemy forces, beached their boat, launched a ground pursuit and destroyed a supply area.

Two weeks later, on March 13, on a five-boat operation on the Bay Hap River, the swift-boat sailors encountered another VC aggression. Amidst small-arms and automatic-weapons fire, mines detonated in the river, damaging one of the boats and wounding Kerry in the right arm. One man was knocked overboard and was under sniper fire. Kerry sent his boat to the rescue and pulled the man out of the water. He and his crew followed that up by escorting the disabled boat to safety.

For his service in Vietnam, among his other medals and ribbons, John

Kerry was awarded a Silver Star and Bronze Star for valor and three Purple Hearts for injuries.

After his short, 4 1/2-month stint in Vietnam, Kerry returned to the United States, served in the U.S. Senate from 1985 to 2013 and was the Democratic nominee for president in 2004. His first mistake upon his return was membership in Vietnam Veterans Against the War and joining with other veterans to demonstrate against the war by throwing their medals and ribbons over a fence onto the Capitol steps. His second mistake was becoming a member of the Democratic Party.

The first mistake angered many fellow Nam vets who cannot fathom any suggestions that their war was unjust, that any atrocities occurred there, not even the My Lai massacre, or that the end result was anything but the fault of liberal politicians, media and protesters.

I wonder how angry they were about President Donald Trump's 2017 appointment of Lt.Gen. H.R. McMaster as his national security adviser. In his 1997 book, "Dereliction of Duty," McMaster, a decorated tank commander in the 1991 Gulf War, wrote, "The war in Vietnam was not lost in the field nor was it lost on the front page of the New York Times or the college campuses. It was lost in Washington," even before "the first American units were deployed."

Kerry's second big mistake incurred the wrath of Karl Rove, the underhanded Republican operative whose dirty trickery extended from President Richard Nixon's 1972 re-election campaign, to the racial smears against GOP presidential candidate John McCain in South Carolina in 2000, to the traitorous outing of covert CIA officer Valerie Plame in 2003.

Thus, in 2004, with the filthy financial support of fellow Republican horror mongers, Rove, the draft-dodging traitor to his country, coalesced with a group of traitors to their fellow Vietnam veteran and formed what they called Swift Boat Veterans for Truth. Their anything-but-truthful objective was to twist Kerry's honorable military service into a figment in the gullible minds of voting citizens. Their dishonorable betrayal helped re-elect the draft-dodging chicken-hawk President George W. Bush.

Solid reporting by Stephen Koff, of Cleveland's Plain Dealer, Kate Zernike and Jim Rutenberg, of the New York Times, and other members of the Fourth Estate exposed the lies.

A leading betrayer was George Elliott, the former Navy captain who recommended Kerry for the Silver Star. "In a combat environment often requiring independent decisive action, Lt.j.g. Kerry was unsurpassed," he wrote in 1969. Even during a 1996 news conference, Elliott said what Kerry did "was an act of courage." In 2004, though, he changed his story, saying, "John Kerry has not been honest about what happened in Vietnam."

During a 1996 news conference, Vietnam veteran Adrian L. Lonsdale told about the "bravado and courage of the young officers that ran the swift boats." Furthermore, "Sen. Kerry was no exception," he said. "He was among the finest of those swift boat drivers." With the Swift Boat Veterans revisionism of 2004, that same Lonsdale said Kerry "lacks the capacity to lead."

Van O'Dell, another swift boat veteran, claimed in 2004 that Kerry encountered no enemy fire when he rescued a man from the Bay Hap River. Jim Rassman, the Army Special Forces lieutenant who was pulled out of the water that day, a longtime Republican, to boot, countered that he was indeed under fire from both banks of the river and that Kerry risked his life "to save mine."

The shameful skulduggery in the Swift Boat Veterans' advertising was scrupulously refuted, but big money and big lies besmirch democracy. It was bad enough that so many civilians turned their backs on Vietnam veterans. But it was so much lower when Vietnam veterans back-stabbed fellow veterans.

Low-flying money baggers

Perimeter watches along the wide river that flowed around two sides of the triangular Nha Be naval base were about as close to the action as most disbursing clerks and other support personnel would get. As payday approached in late February, though, I learned that a few of our guys participated in what was called the mobile pay team. The team was headed by Chief Petty Officer Price, the senior enlisted man in the office, whose small stature reputedly gave him a "Napoleon complex."

Chief Price informed me that, since I had taken over the pay records of naval forces based in Dong Tam and My Tho, I would be joining him and "Guppy" Guptile on the pay trip there. As a member of the pay team, I was issued a .45-caliber semi-automatic pistol to holster on my side, in addition to carrying my M16. My role on the team would be to double check the chief's counts of cash being paid to our men and to retain their pay chits for record keeping. Guppy would be at the head of the line to tell the men how much they had due and answer any questions they might have regarding their records.

Pointing to a hefty, black leather lock box, Chief Price said, "I'll be loading this up with $150,000 in MPC tomorrow, and we will guard it with our lives."

With the chief behind the wheel and Guppy riding shotgun, we drove out the gate in the disbursing office's gray Ford Bronco the next morning and followed the road past paddies, through hamlets and into Saigon proper. After a quick stop at the Annapolis, we continued to the air base at Tan Son Nhut. For some reason beyond my knowledge, we caught a prop plane bound to an airstrip in Long Xuyen, more than 100 miles southwest of Saigon, even though Dong Tam was less than half that distance.

We were picked up in Long Xuyen by a bulky transport helicopter they called a "Jolly Green Giant," the same nickname that was applied to its much larger relatives manufactured by the Sikorsky Aircraft Corp. I was told it was vintage World War II and that it took highly skilled pilots to handle it. The ride was loud and choppy, but it was an adventure for me, and, with both doors wide open, the ventilation and views were extraordinary. Far below, bomb craters pockmarked sections of the lush landscape like acne on an adolescent's face.

Our arrival in Dong Tam was met hospitably. Payday, unsurprisingly, offered a pleasant distraction from the tension on the rivers, and those who delivered the goods were most welcome. I realized that being a member of the mobile pay team was one of the most rewarding jobs in the war and certainly a lot less hazardous than the ones being performed by the mobile riverine forces who cheerfully waited in line with their pay chits. Chief Price tended to be a by-the-book military man, but even his domineering personality lightened up some when we were treated to free beer by our hosts.

Robert Stoner's "The Brown Water Navy" documents development of Naval Support Activity Dong Tam as beginning in August 1966 with dredging sand from the river to fill in an abandoned rice paddy and excavating a boat-turning basin. That labor was still underway during my pay-team visits. "The work was dangerous; three of the five dredges used at Dong Tam from 1966 to 1969 were damaged or sunk by Viet Cong swimmers," Stoner recounted. "Another vessel was sunk when it dredged up live ordnance that exploded."

That was good reason for me to be on high alert during my riverfront perimeter watch at Nha Be's Three Alpha.

The Dong Tam detachment played a critical role a year earlier when it "enabled the Mobile Riverine Force to surprise and destroy widely sep-arated enemy units," according to Stoner's research. "During the Tet Of-fensive of 1968, the MRF saved My Tho, Can Tho, and Vinh Long from complete enemy destruction."

After completing the Dong Tam pay line, which took a couple hours, we traveled by land to the much smaller naval detachment within the city of My Tho, which was just a few miles downriver. The narrow dirt road took us through a heavily wooded area, so we were transported by a small but well-armed convoy.

Our return trip to Dong Tam about an hour later was the same. We were picked up there by the Jolly Green and flown directly to our Bronco parked at Tan Son Nhut. It was a long day, but we were back at Nha Be in time for dinner.

I came to look forward to our semimonthly pay trips, because they broke up the relative boredom of office work. Without any more struc-tures disintegrating before my very eyes, even those four-hour perimeter watches in the middle of the night at Three Alpha became routine.

I damn near slept through the next explosion at Nha Be, even though it shook our barracks and rattled our racks. As sirens blared and every-body else hustled out to the bunkers, Terry "Matt" Mattive, a clean-living, muscular guy from Pennsylvania, had to yank me out of my dreamland. According to the March 16 Associated Press account, two 100-pound pro-jectiles "crashed into an oil-storage area at Nha Be. ... A small fire start-ed at the fuel depot was quickly extinguished. Allied artillery batteries opened up on the so-called rocket belt in swamplands south of" Saigon.

Unit patches were displayed on the right shoulders of uniforms worn by members of many combat squadrons in Vietnam, and some noncom-batants as well. Those worn by members of our mobile pay team displayed a pink elephant, the significance being that we were hard-drinking characters prone to alcoholic hallucinosis and that our monetary deliveries could be contagious.

After sewing a pink-elephant patch on the sleeve of my jungle greens the previous night, I joined Chief Price and Guppy on the tarmac of the airfield on the south side of the Nha Be base. Evidently, someone had pulled some strings to get the Jolly Green to pick us up there, which spared us the drive into Tan Son Nhut. "You can wear that patch with pride," Guppy told me, looking more serious than usual. "We don't go up the rivers in the PBRs looking for VC, but a helo with one of our pay teams on board got shot down last year, you know. Shit happens in this fuckin' hell hole."

With that enlightenment, I clutched my M16, ducked my head, followed him and the chief under the swirling blades and hopped into the Jolly Green. The pilots nodded as we took our seats, and we lifted off. About 30 feet up, I heard a pop, and the helicopter plunged straight down to the tarmac, where it bounced up a couple feet and dropped back down. One pilot turned around with a smile, gave us a thumbs up, and we took off for the Mekong Delta. I looked at Guppy. He rolled his eyes.

Landing that Jolly Green on the tiny helicopter pad aboard YRBM-17 anchored in the middle of the river seemed to me like a skillful maneuver, but our pilots didn't flinch. It was all in a day's work for them, even though that plunge back at Nha Be was fresh on my mind. They shut her down and settled in for a little relaxation on the deck as we went inside the ship to pay the crew and attached PBR sailors.

An hour and a half later, we got back into our seats, the pilots fired the engines back up, and the copter blades gathered steam. We lifted off, hovered over the pad for a couple seconds and lurched forward. As we cleared the fantail, the Jolly Green dove toward the greenish-brown water like it was the Big Dipper roller coaster at Geauga Lake Park. My heart jumped up to my throat, and I thought sure we were going to take a swim. Maybe it was all in good fun for our pilots, as the helo picked up speed, almost skimming across the surface of the river, and then banked upward to clear the treetops. I looked at Guppy. He rolled his eyes.

'We Gotta Get Out of This Place'

Every evening after regular working hours, the streets and bars in the village of Nha Be would be teeming with sailors looking for a good time. We would pick up our liberty cards at the main gate and drop them off on our way back two or three hours later. The cards were intended to ensure that everybody who left the base for liberty returned before darkness set in and the town became off limits. The shore patrol maintained some semblance of order during liberty hours, but the village was any man's land at night.

Vendors along the road offered such delicacies as smoked squid and hard-boiled eggs, whose yolks, I discovered, were matured to the point where little chick figures and even tiny beaks were discernible. Shoe-shine boys and girls selling trinkets solicited our attention and our piasters.

Then there were beggars. One woman who reached out with a quivering hand sat in the dirt with an infant whose eyeballs were blank, all white, no irises, no pupils. I pulled a 100-piaster bill, less than a dollar, from my wallet and handed it to her. In their hopelessness, Vietnamese women would take desperate measures to reach out for sympathy, Matt told me. "They stick a needle in their babies' eyes," he said.

Matt didn't smoke. He didn't drink alcohol. And he didn't partake in any of the other illicit activities that occurred in the bars of Nha Be. He was going to be a professional wrestler when he got back to the world. In an effort to steer me on the straight and narrow, he accompanied me into town on my first few liberties. He took me to several bars where he knew the female owners or managers – mama-sans, they were called. He ordered soda pop and encouraged me to do the same.

When a pretty Asian girl sat on my lap and asked me to buy her a "Saigon tea," Matt explained that many of the "tea girls" were bused into town each evening from Saigon and would return home at night. Most of them were paid to entertain us Americans in the barrooms and to sell Saigon tea, he said. When I decided against buying her a second 100-piaster tea, my tea girl moved on to a different lap.

Soon another pretty Asian girl paid me a visit. "Hey, cherry boy," she whispered in my ear. "You want go boom-boom?" No, I did not want to do that, Matt informed both of us. She moved along. There was a difference between the tea girls from Saigon and the bar girls of Nha Be, he said. Terry Mattive was a good influence, to be sure.

I was a 19-year-old cherry boy, all right, but I was not a 19-year-old teetotaler. So I began going into town with other guys from the office, guys who introduced me to Ba Muoi Ba, the Vietnamese beer with "33" on the label that sold for less in the bars than American beers like Pabst Blue Ribbon, also known as PBR. With their encouragement and exemplification, I began to get tired of being called "cherry boy" by the bar girls.

The Navy knew that the bars in town and the Vietnamese girls waiting there were good for troop morale. Likewise for cigarettes sold in the small Navy Exchange on base for 20 cents a pack and for the enlisted men's club, where cans of American beer and mixed drinks were offered for a quarter or 35 cents.

On Sunday afternoons, the EM club featured live music with rock 'n' roll bands brought in from the Philippines by the USO. We didn't get Bob Hope or Raquel Welch, like some of the big bases did, but dancing Filipino girls in skimpy dresses and Eric Burdon and the Animals tunes like "The House of the Rising Sun" and especially "We Gotta Get Out of This Place" got the club rocking. If you didn't get too shitfaced by the time the band wrapped up its performance, you could still catch dinner at the chow hall and make it into town for liberty. That wouldn't be a good idea if you had perimeter watch at midnight, although you could sleep it off by the 4 a.m. shift.

Napalm up close and personal

The Pulitzer Prize-winning picture taken by Associated Press photographer Huynh Cong "Nick" Ut in Trang Bang, not far from the Cambodian border northeast of Saigon, on June 8, 1972, captured one of the most striking images of the war. It shows five Vietnamese children, one of them naked 9-year-old Phan Thi Kim Phuc, running down a road in horror after a Vietnamese Air Force napalm attack. "She was screaming, 'Too hot! Too hot!'" Ut told Time magazine in a 2013 interview. The photo, which was printed in newspapers around the nation, raised public awareness about the use of the incendiary chemical in warfare.

Napalm, a mixture of naphthenic and palmitic acids with gasoline, was first used in the bombing of Berlin by the United States in March 1944. A year later, 330 American bombers dropped 690,000 pounds of napalm on Tokyo in one hour, killing an estimated 100,000-plus people. Also used for flamethrowers, napalm was considered "the most outstanding weapon" of the Korean War.

It was considered one of the most useful weapons of the Vietnam War, where 388,000 tons – not pounds – of napalm were dropped between 1963 and 1973. It was especially useful in flushing out enemy forces from bunkers and jungle positions. Napalm generates temperatures as high as 2,200 degrees Fahrenheit. The sticky substance adheres to surfaces, including human bodies, and burns for up to 10 minutes. More often than not, the liquid fire melts flesh through to the bone. Few of its victims survive.

Kim Phuc was one of the lucky ones. Taken by Nick Ut for medical treatment in Saigon, she underwent 17 surgeries, including skin grafts, during her 14-month hospital stay. She lived but never really healed.

The brutality of napalm was covered up by the government in the previous wars. But "Napalm Girl," as Kim Phuc became known due to the notoriety attached to her by Ut's photograph, plus courageous coverage by other Vietnam War correspondents focused intensifying attention upon the incendiary chemical's contributions to the savagery.

The use of napalm against military targets is not prohibited under international law, but the United Nations Convention on Certain Conventional Weapons banned its use against civilian populations in 1980. Some chemical weapons, it seems, are somewhat conventional.

Thanks to a teenage bar girl called "Napalm Baby" by GIs who took liberties in Nha Be, I became intimately and unforgettably familiar with its unconventional consequences on the human body.

"Chao anh," she said, greeting me as I took a seat at a table with two other guys from the disbursing office. "What you drink today?"

"Chao co," I replied. "Ba Muoi Ba for me." My buddies asked for PBRs.

A minute later she return with our beers. She sat on my lap. "Buy me tea, numbah-one GI," she said.

"OK, just one," I told her.

Mama-san brought the nonalcoholic Saigon tea to the table.

It was near the end of my first month in country. I'd been to three or four bars, downed four or five beers already, and this was one of my regular stops. Napalm Baby, the only name we knew her by, was familiar with me by now. She said she was 17, but all Vietnamese mark their birthdays in conjunction with the Tet new-year celebration. By Western counts, she more likely was 16. The scars that crept three inches above the neckline of her Au Dai had spared her unblemished, dark-skinned face. The long sleeves and skirt cloaked most of her slender body, only revealing the red, blistery, lumpy skin on the back of her right hand. Her straight black hair floated gently against her back. Her eyelashes fluttered, and her glistening lips widened into a smile. "Hey, Lange," she said. "You still cherry boy?"

"Yep, he's still a cherry boy," Joe Bazel said. "How long are you gonna stay virgin, Lange?"

"Yes, Lange, how long you stay virgin?" Napalm Baby said. "Pay me 500 P, and you no be cherry boy now. You be numbah one, huh?"

So I followed her to a backroom. Watching her undress, I trembled at the sight. Deeply scarred skin covered much of the right side of her body, from her neck to her hips and from her spine to the edge of her small breast. All Vietnamese women had small breasts. I had never seen breasts in the flesh before. Even so, my eyes were diverted by the charred and wrinkled skin that encroached upon the intrigue of her quarter-sized nipples just inches away.

"Come on, Lange," she said. "Take off clothes. Don't be afraid. I show you how."

So she did. Napalm Baby showed cherry boy how. I was cherry boy no more.

Chapter 16 | # The Parrot's Beak

The high tide was receding much more rapidly and more forcefully than I imagined before I plunged from the pier at the tip of the peninsula that was the Nha Be naval base. The river was no swimming hole. Despite what I'd heard in Counterinsurgency Training about creatures that could be lurking in the murky waters of Vietnam, two senior members of SEAL Team 2 said it was what I had to do if I was serious about joining their outfit. So that's what I did.

I had taken charge of the team's pay records. The SEALs were the toughest fighting men in the Navy, if not the entire military. I already was responsible for some 600 pay records, more than any other man in our office. My load included the PBR divisions engaged in what was called Operation Giant Slingshot. Another dozen records for the SEAL platoon were icing on my cake.

I told the SEALs about the physical test back in Newport and how my orders to Nam had superseded my hopes of going to UDT school. They offered to retest me and get the results into my service record this time. I'd be able to get into training when I returned to the States – although it probably would require an extension of my enlistment.

The first half of the 500-yard swim test was quick and easy, as the current swept me away from the pier and into the surging river. The second half, swimming back to the pier, was the opposite. Unlike the leisurely swim in the pool for my previous UDT test, this one was a rigorous challenge to my strength and endurance. A lesser swimmer would have been swept away. If there were stronger swimmers in Nha Be, I didn't know them. The SEALs weren't about to pull my unconscious body up from the bottom of the river. I won my battle against the current, but it was a tough fight. I nearly crawled to the finish of the 1.5-mile run.

According to research summarized in "War in the Shallows: U.S. Navy Coastal and Riverine Warfare in Vietnam, 1965-1968," by historian John Darrell Sherwood, published in 2015 by the Naval History and Heritage Command, "Overall, 49 U.S. Navy SEALs lost their lives in Vietnam. None was captured. SEAL intelligence proved instrumental for Game Warden operations, resulted in many significant ambushes, and thwarted river crossings. SEALs also achieved one of the highest kill ratios of any combat unit during the war and were successful in helping to destroy Viet Cong leaders in the Mekong Delta, especially during 1968-1970. From June 1969-April 1970, SEALs in the delta conducted 1,192 missions resulting in 581 Viet Cong killed and 193 captured."

Because of their jungle camouflage, the VC called the SEALs "men with green faces." Because of their efficiency in jungle warfare, they often had bounties on their heads. Three Navy SEALs were awarded the Medal of Honor during the Vietnam War.

One of those Medal of Honor recipients, Lt. Bob Kerrey, who lost part of a leg in combat on March 14, 1969, later became governor of Nebraska for four years and then served in the U.S. Senate from 1989 to 2001. A Democrat, he ran for president of the United States in 1992, when then-Arkansas Gov. Bill Clinton won the party's nomination. We don't know which back-stabbers would have slithered out of their snake holes if Kerrey had become the nominee.

On Feb. 25, 1969, about the time that I got my first glimpse of war, Kerrey led his SEAL team on a raid of a peasant village called Thanh Phong. "The thing that I will remember until the day I die is walking in and finding, I don't know, 14 or so, I don't even know what the number was, women and children who were dead," he recalled three decades later.

"I was expecting to find Viet Cong soldiers with weapons, dead. Instead I found women and children."

One member of his team, Gerhard Klann, remembered things differently, claiming it was the SEALs who decided to "kill them and get out of there," because, otherwise the civilians would betray them to the enemy. That version was firmly refuted by other team members.

There is no denying the horrors of war. "You can never, can never get away from it," Kerrey said. "It darkens your day. I thought dying for your country was the worst thing that could happen to you, and I don't think it is. I think killing for your country can be a lot worse."

One of the SEALs on my payroll, a hulking black man whose massive upper body and bulging biceps strained the seams on his camouflage uniform, stepped to the counter in the disbursing office to check on the new pay rate associated with his advancement to E-5. I called him Rock. I was fascinated by the looping gold ring hanging from his pierced left ear, something I'd never seen on men, aside from a couple movies about 17th-century buccaneers. He told me that men wearing earrings was not uncommon in Africa, where it was a symbol of strength and machismo. "It means I don't take shit from nobody," Rock said. That was a fact.

So, after several hours of contemplating that fashion statement while downing my usual five or six Ba Muoi Bas in town and then a couple PBRs in the EM club, I returned to the office and pulled the sewing kit out of my bottom desk drawer. Feeling no pain, I poked a needle into my left earlobe. Unfortunately, my contemplation had fallen short of how to proceed from there. "Hey, Ronnie," I called to the only DK still working in the office at that late hour. "Could you come here and give me a hand with this?"

Ronnie Calloway got up from his desk and walked over to mine.

I pointed to the needle in my ear.

"What the hell, Dave?"

"I'm piercing my ear, Ronnie. I just need you to thread the needle so I can finish pulling it through and keep the hole from closing up before I can get me an earring."

"Oh, jeez," he said. "You gotta be kidding me." Anyway, he did what I asked.

The next day I bought myself a gold loop from one of the tea girls in town. Maybe I became the first American white guy and the second American guy of any color to sport an earring in the modern era. I didn't see any others. Men have worn earrings at various times and places throughout history, including American Indians, Egyptians, Bronze Age Grecians and even Sir Walter Raleigh and William Shakespeare, of the Elizabethan era, but they were out of style for centuries. You might say I was fashionably ahead of my time. Only in the Navy and only in Vietnam could a member of the military be so stylish.

Giant Slingshot to Cambodia

In late 1968, Vice Adm. Elmo R. Zumwalt, commander of naval operations in Vietnam, decided that a new strategy was needed to stem the tide of enemy infiltration into the South from neighboring Cambodia. Operation Giant Slingshot was a fixation from the map of two rivers, the Vam Co Dong to the north and Vam Co Tay to the south, which flowed eastward from opposite sides of a region known as the Parrot's Beak. The beak-shaped section of Cambodia jutting into South Vietnam was giving the VC and North Vietnamese convenient access from the Ho Chi Minh Trail to a point just 50 miles from Saigon. In addition to feeding fighters and weaponry into our backyard, the enemy was disrupting commerce along the rivers.

Under the leadership of Navy Capt. Arthur W. Price Jr., the operation officially got underway on Dec. 5, 1968, with the arrival of YRBM-16 at Tan An on the Vam Co Tay, just west of where the two branches meet to form the Vam Co River. While the YRBM could support just two 10-boat river divisions, reinforcements were only 20 miles away up the Nha Be River.

In his 2002 historical novel, "Slingshot," Edward Vick, a naval officer who led more than 100 combat missions during his two tours of duty in Vietnam, put things in perspective this way: "Thirty yards wide at its widest point, the Vam Co Dong was a vicious little river. It bent and twisted unpredictably. Few straight-aways mean short sight lines. Surprise was round the next turn. There always seemed to be too much cover for the enemy and not enough cover for the good guys. Overgrown vegetation mixed with the defoliated product of Agent Orange. No part of this river could be trusted. It was crawling with Viet Cong guerrillas and soldiers of the regular North Vietnamese Army or NVA."

The two Vam Co river branches were mirror images of each other, and the Navy reflected that with coordinate outposts known as advanced tactical support bases, or ATSBs: Ben Luc and Tan An near the eastern mouths of the Vam Co Dong and Vam Co Tay; Tra Cu and Tuyen Nhon about halfway up the slingshot; and Go Dau Ha and Moc Hoa to the west, almost on the Cambodian border. Also, Ben Keo is a little farther northwest, near the larger city of Tay Ninh.

From the get-go, Operation Giant Slingshot was successful, in that encounters with the enemy were intense and frequent. In his 1988 book, "Brown Water, Black Berets," Navy Lt. Cmdr. Thomas J. Cutler, who served in Vietnam in 1972 and later taught history at the U.S. Naval Academy, pointed out that they gave rise to the term ENIFF, meaning enemy-initiated firefight. "ENIFFs on the Vam Co Dong between Tra Cu and Go Dau Ha were so frequent that this stretch of the river became known as 'Blood Alley,'" he wrote. "Some of the heaviest fighting and consequently the highest casualty rates of the war for the Navy occurred during Giant Slingshot. The total number of ENIFFs and FRIFFs (friendly initiated firefights) for this one operation was more than double that of all the other operations combined. Over a thousand firefights occurred during the 515 days of the operation, an average of two per day."

Having earned a promotion to petty officer third class and, after the departure of "Guppy" Guptile and "Matt" Mattive, being one of the longer-serving in-country members of the disbursing staff by early summer, I was able to finagle nearly every pay record of the Navy's Slingshot forces into my custodianship.

I had multiple motives for that. For one, as a key member of the pay team, it got me out of the boring office for two full days and three nights every other week, two of those nights being in Saigon. On one of the three nights, I was excused from being dragged out of my rack at 11:45 p.m. or 3:45 a.m. for a four-hour watch on the perimeter. That was especially advantageous in the height of the monsoon season, between June and August, when afternoon and middle-of-the-night downpours dropped from the sky like a million Brandywine Falls. Pay-team schedules submitted to the head of security were marked "confidential." We were transporting a hundred thousand bucks or more in cash by land through Saigon to Ben Luc and Tan An one day and then a reduced amount around and across the Parrot's Beak by air the next.

More than anything, I was honored to deliver the small delight of paydays to the courageous men whose lives were much less joyful during day and night patrols on those enemy-infested waters.

In October 2017, the American media hyperventilated themselves into a protracted frenzy after four U.S. soldiers were killed by an Islamic State-affiliated ambush during a secret operation in Niger. Our Navy river rats in Vietnam routinely were ambushed by Viet Cong infiltrators lurking in the overgrown banks of the Vam Co Dong and Vam Co Tay. That's what PBR sailors did. It was their job to draw the enemy into firefights. Good men die in firefights.

As I pulled their pay records from my files, slipped them into my manual typewriter and keyed the capital letters K-I-A next to their names and service numbers, I could see faraway looks in the eyes of stolen youth lined up for their military pay certificates at Go Dau Ha. I could hear their voices as they pointed to AK-47 punctures in flak jackets while we downed beers and relaxed on sandbags in Ben Luc. I could feel their longing for home when they shared letters from girlfriends. Thank God I didn't have to deliver the news to their loved ones.

The political furor of October 2017 called upon President Donald J. Trump to personally express his condolences to the families of those four dead American soldiers. And, after he did so, the furor further intensified over his alleged clumsiness in speaking with a grieving widow.

In the summer of 1969, during the height of the Vietnam War, an average of 18 American men were killed in action every day. Every single day. Did their loved ones expect consolatory phone calls from then-President Richard M. Nixon? I don't think so.

Encounter with Agent Orange

Early on, Chief Price headed up our pay teams for Operation Giant Slingshot. He'd drive the Bronco into Saigon a day ahead of time and meet me and usually either Sherman Lawson or Al Elliott at the Annapolis Hotel early the next morning. We could take the bus but preferred to hitch rides on our own terms. We could get picked up by the main gate of our naval base, at the Marine Corps post adjacent to it or near an Army installation less than a mile down the road. Sometimes an ARVN Jeep would give us a lift or even an occasional civilian vehicle would pick us up.

I knew Sherman from A School in Newport. He was from Mount Pleasant, Michigan. We were good buddies. With sidearms holstered to our waists and M16s in tow, we walked off the base in mid-afternoon. It was several hours before liberty call, so the town was quiet. A couple incoming military vehicles passed us by, but there was no traffic heading our way. We walked past the northern edge of town and reached the turn-off to the Army installation. A flatbed truck loaded with barrels approached. We stuck out our thumbs.

"Where you headed?" a sergeant in the passenger seat asked.

"Annapolis Hotel in Saigon," I said.

"Hop on the back and hang on for the ride," he said.

The cargo was well secured. We plopped our butts down, leaned back against a couple barrels, let our feet dangle over the edge of the truck bed, closed our eyes, soaked up the sunshine and enjoyed the bumpy ride. When the truck stopped in front of the Annapolis and I sat up, I felt something moist sticking to the back of my head, just above the hairline. I wiped it off with my hand and then onto my pant leg. Something was dribbling down the side of the barrel that I'd used as a backrest. I didn't think much of it.

We knew that herbicides were being sprayed to defoliate forests and rural areas of Vietnam in a strategy to deprive our enemies of concealment and food sources. Herbicides also were used to clear vegetation around our own military bases. The ones at Nha Be and Ben Luc were like deserts surrounded by tropics. Incidentally, the Tropic of Cancer circles the Earth 975 miles north of Saigon. I didn't think much about that either.

When the itchy rash that periodically broke out on the back of my head was diagnosed as a nervous problem in 1973, I didn't think much about that. Nor did I worry much about my elevated blood pressure at the age of 24.

Between 1962 and 1971, in a program known as Operation Ranch Hand, our military sprayed about 20 million gallons of herbicides and defoliants in Vietnam. Some 5 million acres of forest were destroyed, and 12 percent of the total land area of South Vietnam was sprayed in that campaign. One of those noxious mixes, known as Agent Orange, later was found to have been contaminated with dioxin, the toxic chemical associated with the infamous environmental disaster that resulted in the 1978 evacuation of the Love Canal community in northwestern New York.

The Agent Orange Act of 1991 established a number of health ailments associated with exposure to the herbicide for which Vietnam veterans are entitled to benefits, among them chloracne. My persistent and recurring rash has received a variety of diagnoses over the years, but not chloracne. I'm lucky. I'd much rather scratch my head than waste away with one of the cancers or have a son or daughter with birth defects connected to Agent Orange.

After my exposure to whatever was in that barrel, I took a good shower at the Annapolis that night.

Wild rides with door gunner

Chief Price was waiting in the disbursing office the next morning, MPC stashed in his black leather box. We loaded the money box, my satchel with pay records, our weapons and ourselves in the Bronco. The chief drove through the city and then about 35 klicks southwest on Route 4 to Ben Luc, the Navy's main support base for Operation Giant Slingshot.

Traffic close to Saigon was steady, but it became sparse as we passed broad tropical wetlands, scattered clumps of foreboding woodland and a few tiny hamlets.

Robert Stoner's "The Brown Water Navy in Vietnam" points out that the Ben Luc base was constructed on the Vam Co Dong bank closest to Saigon, "in case the Viet Cong destroyed the bridge" and cut off supplies. It was commissioned in July 1969 and provided working and berthing spaces for more than 800 men plus docking and anchoring facilities for 70 boats.

Payroll lines were long and steady from mid-morning until well into the afternoon. The men kept us supplied with beer and brought us sandwiches from the mess hall.

After completing the Ben Luc payroll, it was back in the Bronco to continue down Route 4, crossing the Vam Co Dong, where the road got lonelier for three lightly armed men transporting a box of cash. On the southern bank of the Vam Co Tay, within sight of the bridge, the mobile support base at Tan An consisted mostly of pontoons. The pay line there was shorter and quicker. We'd shoot the breeze with a couple Navy river rats or an Army Green Beret for a while before taking the short drive back to Ben Luc in time for dinner.

Nights at Ben Luc were different from those at Nha Be. There was no liberty, no bars in sight for such frivolity, no Saigon tea girls sitting on our laps. The latrine, with multiple side-by-side seats, could be located in the dark by sense of smell. Of course, there was plenty of beer and more convenient places to dispose of it. The river rats didn't mind taking a couple disbursing clerks on a PBR cruise up the Vam Co Dong – before dark and before things would get serious out there. Nighttime mortar rounds and small-arms harassment were more routine at Ben Luc than at Nha Be. I usually found an empty rack in the barracks but sometimes crashed in the back seat of the Bronco and a couple times on the dusty ground next to it. At either base, the heavy artillery zinging overhead and booming explosions where it cratered into the earth had little bearing on my sleep.

Hangover or not, I'd be waiting for the Slingshot Swingship at the helicopter pad in the morning with the other two men on the pay team plus a postal clerk for what would be a whirlwind day. Giant Slingshot was a coordinated operation involving the Army and Navy. The Army provided the Bell UH-1 "Huey" helicopter that transported our mobile pay team to the four ATSBs on the second day of our trip.

The Huey crew included a pilot and copilot, mostly Army warrant officers, who were younger and lower ranking than the Navy pilots on the Jolly Greens, and a door gunner on each side, daring enlisted men, some of them still teenagers like myself. The door gunners sat on benches positioned on the outside flank of the aircraft. Their trigger fingers were at the ready on their mounted M-60 machine guns. In the heat of a firefight, they could step out onto the helicopter skids to widen the angle of their sights. There was a saying that the lifespan of a Huey door gunner in Vietnam was about five minutes, which, like many sayings, embellishes a point, this one being that they were wide-open targets. Helicopter crews accounted for 10 percent of American combat deaths in the war.

Fortunately for our pay team, the objective of the Slingshot Swingship was not to engage the enemy; it was to deliver us and our cash cargo safely and efficiently to our destinations. Efficiency and safety are not always congruent. The Hueys were not designed for passenger service, and seating accommodations were not commodious.

That was apparent when our four-man team boarded the chopper at Ben Luc for our first swing up to the Cambodian border. When it appeared that I'd have to sit my skinny ass on the deck, one of the door gunners, a young black guy with a slender physique like mine, motioned me to have a seat on the bench next to him.

It was the biggest thrill of my young life. There was nothing more adventuresome for me than soaring over the treetops at 100 knots, angling around a river bend like a Porsche 911 burning rubber on Turn 8 at Nelson Ledges Road Course, diving and climbing like the Wild Mouse at Chippewa Lake Park, all of it with the cool wind whipping away the sweat of the day. Marcus, the door gunner, and I were tight, seated side by side on the Slingshot Swingship.

The regular flights out of Ben Luc to Tuyen Nhon, Tra Cu, Moc Hoa and Go Dau Ha were analogous to the proverbial having my cake and eating it too. On occasions when we heard the crack of enemy fire above the clatter of the whirling blades, Marcus, with me jammed in next to him, would lean into his M-60 and scour the bush for signs of belligerence, but the pilots would abruptly take evasive action. On one return trip out of Go Dau Ha, we swooped down for a quick medevac, after an ambush had been repelled. The ARVN's bloody but minor leg wound was stitched up in Ben Luc.

Our pilots flew so low over a long Army convoy lumbering up the road out of Tay Ninh one afternoon that we could see eye to eye with the troops being trucked to battle and riding high on their armored personnel carriers. Two-fingered salutes were raised skyward. Marcus and I responded in kind. It's not oxymoronic for the signs of victory and peace to be one and the same. Euphoria could be experienced both ways.

At one of our Slingshot destinations, the helicopter pad was situated downstream and on the opposite side of the river from the ATSB. A PBR was dispatched to pick up the pay team. The Huey crew would keep weapons trained on the thicket that stretched across the rugged plain and be prepared for a quick takeoff, if need be.

When the PBR guys shuttled us back after the hour-long pay line, a grinning boy, about 10 years old, paddled his sampan over to the helicopter pad, perhaps hoping for a handout or maybe just being friendly. One of the pilots grabbed a smoke grenade from the chopper, pulled the pin and dropped it in the kid's little boat, which he gave a shove back into the river. Laughter erupted as the boy frantically scooped water into his sampan in a futile effort to extinguish the sizzling joke. It was a harmless prank to those who knew the Asian enemy much better than I and to whom communist supporters and sympathizers came in all ages. I just saw a kid with tears in his eyes and fear in his heart and nobody to blame but us Americans. The billowing green smoke, generally used as a landing-zone marker, faded out of sight as we flew northwest toward the Cambodian border.

Moc Hoa on the Vam Co Tay and Go Dau Ha on the Vam Co Dong are located at opposite sides of the Parrot's Beak. As the bird flies, they are just 18 miles apart, but that would require flying over the section of Cambodia that juts deepest into Vietnam and where heavy concentrations of NVA found sanctuary. It was where the infamous Ho Chi Minh Trail most conveniently fed communist incursions into the South. Until April 29, 1970, when President Nixon's Cambodian Incursion incited mass student protests around the country, including the deadly one at Kent State University, American forces respected the border of the supposedly neutral neighbor – officially anyway.

The distance between Moc Hoa and Go Dau Ha by rounding the Parrot's Beak and remaining in Vietnamese airspace is about 35 miles, nearly twice as far as an expedient bird would fly. I cannot speak for the propitiousness of our Slingshot Swingship pilots, but they did tend to fly the Huey at higher altitudes for that leg of our pay trip. And, to my inexpert observations, it seemed to be a pretty quick and straight flight.

On Feb. 5, 1970, a five-man PBR crew was captured on the Mekong River 6 miles inside Cambodia after "accidentally" crossing the border on a night mission. The crew members were held as prisoners of war until negotiations with the Cambodian government headed by Prince Norodom Sihanouk resulted in their release on Feb. 28.

Just 18 days after that, Sihanouk, the country's monarchical head of state since 1954, was removed from power in a coup spurred by anti-Vietnamese riots. His "semi-toleration" of NVA and VC activities within Cambodia was a major reason for growing opposition to his rule.

Sometimes the Slingshot Swingship waited patiently on the Moc Hoa and Go Dau Ha helicopter pads as we paid our men. Other times the Huey crew would fly off for more pressing activities. The pilots and door gunners were much more than escorts. They were combatants, true warriors.

Their detours would give us some extra time to connect with the Navy combatants who manned the PBRs and the watchtowers where interdiction of enemy infiltration was the rule of the day.

After Sherman Lawson and I took a short hike with a couple river rats along the Vam Co Dong for some extracurricular firing of our M16s at logs and other debris floating downstream, Chief Price admonished us upon our return to the helicopter pad. "That's pretty stupid," he told us. "If you hit a Claymore mine in the river, you could blow us all up."

The PBR guys scoffed and walked away.

Claymores were posted around perimeter wires, where they could be detonated to hurl hundreds of steel balls apiece at a wide radius, riddling the bodies of enemy attackers. Stealthy VC infiltrators had been known to creep up on some of our perimeters and reverse the placement of the Claymores, turning the tables with repulsive consequences. But those mines wouldn't be floating down the river.

Shortly after we became engaged in the Giant Slingshot operation, Chief Price's tour of duty in Vietnam was up. We heard that his leadership of the mobile pay team was recognized by the Navy with a Bronze Star Medal. The Bronze Star is awarded for "heroic or meritorious achievement or service."

Sure, there was merit to the chief's service. But service in itself is not a matter of heroism. Serving your country is not heroic. Serving in Vietnam at a time of war or in a different combat zone at a different time is not heroic. Performing your military duty is not heroic. Yes, my life was in danger every time I performed my perimeter duty. Yes, my life was in danger every time we drove along Route 4 with a box of cash and every time we flew to the bases on the Parrot's Beak. But I knew of no heroes on our mobile pay team.

Going above and beyond the call of duty and deliberately putting your life in extraordinary peril – now that's heroism. By any measure, heroic acts were common among the courageous combatants I was privileged to serve and proud to know during my 12 months in Vietnam.

On the road to Ben Luc

After Chief Price went back to the world, I obtained a military driver's license so that I could get behind the wheel of our Bronco. Driving on the cluttered streets of Saigon could be interesting. One day on my way to the Annapolis, I slammed on the brakes in a gaggle of traffic, felt a heavy plunk at my rear and watched a young man tumble along the pavement next to me. He stumbled back onto his feet and began screaming at me in Vietnamese.

I wasn't about to pay him off for his own bad driving, as some Americans were coerced into doing. So I pulled my pistol from its holster, leveled the barrel toward the guy's head and said loud and clear, "Di di mau before I blow your fucking brains out." He got the message. I kept the gun on him as he limped back to pick up his crippled motorbike and wheeled it away on the sidewalk.

Generally, I found the Vietnamese to be courteous drivers, more so than Americans. On the two-lane road to Ben Luc, you didn't have to wait for a quarter mile of clearance to pass a slower driver. Travelers in both directions would squeeze against the berms to make space for you. I figured I'd give that maneuver a try when I got back to the world.

Another courtesy was extended to me one afternoon when the Bronco suddenly stalled out and refused to restart in the middle of one of Saigon's busiest traffic circles. Just when I thought I'd have to hitch a ride to the Annapolis Hotel, arrange for a tow and hope our vehicle would still be there an hour or two later, a Vietnamese man pulled over and asked if I needed some help. He ended up pushing the Bronco with his sedan several miles to the Annapolis and declined to accept my offer of 1,000 piasters for his trouble.

Not wishing to take any blame for the mechanical breakdown, I decided to wait until the following morning, when Lt. J.F. Jacot, Al Elliott and I would get in the Bronco for our trip to Ben Luc and all together learn that the damn thing wouldn't start. To my surprise and also to my concern, it fired right up.

And it ran just fine until we got about halfway out Route 4, where the traffic got sparse and the foliated surroundings became more shadowy. Three guys with three M16s and three side arms were sitting ducks on a box of cash that could enrich friend or foe. The situation did not put the lieutenant at ease, and I wasn't about to confess my previous knowledge of the Bronco's aberrant conduct.

Fortunately, an APC with room for one more passenger rolled alongside us a half hour later and whisked Lt. Jacot with his money box away toward Ben Luc. "I'll send someone out to tow you guys to the base," he promised.

"Let's see if we can jump start this baby," Al said, pointing out a slight incline in the road ahead. So we struggled to push the Bronco a couple hundred yards up the gradual slope, hopped in, and it gathered some momentum on the downside. My experience told me that there was plenty of juice in the battery, so the jump-start failure came as no surprise, but we did roll far enough down the road to park next to a tiny hamlet nestled in a shady cluster of palms. To our good fortune, we found a Vietnamese woman who was willing to sell us a few bottles of Ba Moui Ba. It was warm beer, but beggars can't be choosers.

The rescue tow dispatched by Lt. Jacot, which arrived an hour later, located the sidelined Bronco, but its feeling-fine driver and passenger were nowhere in sight. It took several blasts from the horn to roust us from the edge of a lagoon, where we were admiring a serpent with a squirming rat in its jaws.

I kept in touch by letters with my hometown friends who also were in the military, including Kenny Chrzanowski and Jim Cardarelli in the Army and Bob Leone in the Air Force. When I learned that Jim was with part of a maintenance battalion in a small compound just outside of Ben Luc, I decided to pay him a visit after finishing our pay line at the Navy outposts there and in Tan An. Bob Webb, a pot-smoking surfer boy from California who was the third man on the pay team that day, went along for the ride. We followed a narrow dirt road for a mile or two through the bush and pulled up just outside the Army compound not long before dusk.

Apparently, the men on perimeter watch were unaccustomed to visitors and were caught off guard by our arrival. It appeared as though we raised a high alert for the company of about 50 men holed up in the makeshift base where metal shipping containers covered with sandbags served as berthing compartments. Even our guys up in Go Da Hau and Moc Hoa had better living conditions. Anyway, after an officer with armed security came out to meet us, I learned that my buddy Jim Cardarelli had moved out a few days earlier. Too bad. Even with its rugged circumscription, I heard that the compound had a small "Boom Boom Room," complete with a bar, TV set and some games. Lurid insinuation aside, no women could be found anywhere near that hell hole.

'Vietnamization' on the run

In March 1969, flags were flown at half-staff over American military bases in honor of Dwight D. Eisenhower, the great general who had led the Allies to victory in Europe in World War II and who had warned the country about the abuses of the "military-industrial complex" during his presidency in 1961. Eisenhower was my favorite president. Still is.

Three months later, his presumed but sidetracked successor, President Nixon, in a meeting with South Vietnamese President Nguyen Van Thieu on Midway Island, announced a program called "Vietnamization," meaning a gradual transition of military operations. After 19 years of American involvement in the war between two Vietnams, our president said South Vietnamese forces finally were ready to fight for themselves, and we could begin winding down.

Not according to some of the stories I heard. One night at Nha Be, Al Elliott and I joined a couple river rats for a few beers in their barracks. As part of the so-called Vietnamization program, they told us, they would transport a platoon of ARVNs – Army of the Republic of Vietnam – upriver on PBRs and insert them onshore for nighttime search-and-destroy missions against suspected VC hideouts. The boats would return a couple hours later to extract them. After a few of these operations resulted in reports of successful raids but no signs whatsoever of ARVN casualties, not even superficial wounds, the river rats got suspicious. "Those little fuckers would jump off the boat, hide there in the bush and just wait for us to come back and get them," Jerry, the guy who manned twin 50s, said.

The next ARVN insertion came with instructions to reconnect with the PBRs on the bank of a different narrow tributary about a mile away and on the opposite side of the suspected enemy location. The results were similar.

"So we got wise to them," Jerry said. "We put a two-man crew in hiding at the designated extraction point ahead of time to see what was up, and, wouldn't you know, them chickenshit ARVNs arrived there in about 15 minutes. They jumped off the insert PBR, ran like hell and hoped no VC shot them before they got to the other side. I'll tell you what, when we're outta here, the commies will march right down Highway 1 from Hanoi and take over in no time."

Most of us who served our country in the Vietnam War bought into the perennial tale about fighting for freedom. We were fighting for freedom from communism. After a series of military dictatorships, the American manipulation of Ngo Dinh Diem's takeover in 1954, his assassination in 1963, also with American backing, and the quasi-democracy under President Thieu, the Vietnamese people, including their military, may have been less enthused by our notion of freedom. Many of them threw down their weapons and ran after our troop withdrawal in 1973.

Many thousands of ARVNs did die for their country, though. Too many Americans died for the illusion of freedom in Vietnam.

According to Thomas J. Cutler's research for his book "Brown Water, Black Berets," the U.S. Navy's presence in the Vietnam War was very small. Our river forces represented less than 0.5 percent of the American manpower in country during Operation Game Warden, for example. "One out of every three PBR sailors was wounded during his tour in Vietnam, many of those more than once," he wrote.

During the comparatively short Operation Giant Slingshot, Cutler reported, "38 American Navy men had been killed in action and 518 had been wounded. Considering the low number of participants, this casualty rate was extraordinarily high. The total number of wounds received was greater than the number of personnel involved."

In the preface to his book "Slingshot," Edward Vick wrote, "Finally I should note, with melancholy pride, that the River Divisions that took part in Operation Giant Slingshot were later awarded the Presidential Unit Citation, to this day the highest honor that an American military unit can receive for its actions in combat." My peripheral participation did not apply.

In concluding his final chapter of "Slingshot," Vick recounted the ambush of a PBR on a canal off the Vam Co Dong, with three KIA and two WIA. Directed to write Bronze Star recommendations for the casualties, a yeoman shook his head and said, "They're all heroes when they're fucking dead."

Chapter 17 | **Near-death Experiences**

Summer evening monsoons showered freshwater from the heavens that beckoned naked sailors with bars of Dial or Lifebuoy outside the barracks. The gushing rains made us shiver, but they sure provided a cleaner feel than the cloudy river water being delivered through the pipes.

Impetuous torrents during midnight-to-4 a.m. Nha Be perimeter patrols were less refreshing. The guardhouse at Three Alpha and watchtower at Four Bravo provided some shelter, at least from vertical downpours, or I could crawl for cover onto a minesweeper tied up at the pier. But, if the monsoon let loose when I paced the far end of the seawall or the southern waterfront, where rodents pranced on the stony shore, there was no escaping the drenching blitz.

By late August, dry weather returned. It was dark and still as I paced the edge of the familiar seawall. Across the river to the east, flashes from firefights cast silhouettes of distant trees. Shells whistled across the night sky.

The tide was out. I missed something. An unnoticed gap caught the heel of my left jungle boot. My right knee buckled. Gravity yanked the rest of me 12 feet straight down. I slammed against the water horizontally and sank below the surface. I was stunned, not sure what happened. I gripped my M16 and kicked myself upward. My shoulder thumped against the hulking steel hull of a dry dock. Better my shoulder on the way up than my skull on the way down. I had missed a bone-cracking, conscious-ness-bashing collision by 6 inches, maybe less.

Once again, I might have cheated myself out of a Purple Heart, this time by mere inches instead of the 10 minutes that had separated my pres-ence from the exploding ammo dump on my watch six months earlier.

I looked around. The deck of the dry dock was out of reach, even with the forceful frog kick that had propelled me to breaststroke victories in my youth. The slimy, sheer flank of the seawall wasn't about to be climbed, not without a harness and crampons anyway. I listened. Nothing but dis-tant booms. I was out of earshot of the Three Alpha watchman. I called for help anyway. No answer. I yelled again. Nothing.

I held onto my weapon with one hand, kicked off the wall and did a one-armed swim 20 yards downstream to the next dry dock. I couldn't reach up there either. Still no sign of activity. My boots were heavy, and my uniform was wearing me down. I found a crease where I could set my gun and cling to the seawall. If I stashed the M16 there and ditched my boots and fatigues, I could swim to the pier and climb out of the river. But I didn't know what I might encounter along the way or what I might be mistaken for as I rippled across the swarthy water on a moonless night.

Finally, I heard the motor of an approaching Jeep on the roadway above the seawall. "Help!" I yelled at the top of my lungs.

The engine stopped. I heard footsteps.

"Help!" I yelled again. "I'm in the river."

The head of security peered over the edge. "What in the hell are you doing down there?"

"I was walking my perimeter watch, and I must have stepped in a hole at the top of the wall," I said. "Then, all of a sudden, I'm down here."

"All right, hang on," he said. "We'll get you out."

Fifteen minutes later, two men arrived in a PBR and pulled me aboard. "Hey, aren't you the guy who comes up to pay us when we're in Moc Hoa?" one of them asked.

"Yeah, I'm on the Slingshot pay team," I said. "Thanks for coming to my rescue."

"So, what happened, did you fall over when you went to toss your empty beer can in the river?" he said. They thought that was hilarious.

I loved those river rats.

Different kind of action

A couple days in Nha Be was the next-best thing to a weekend in Saigon, which was the next-best thing to R&R in Singapore, for the brown-water sailors who spent most of their time on the rivers and canals around the Parrot's Beak. Rest and recuperation wasn't exactly what they had in mind when they went into town for liberty, though.

Most of them were eager to pound down a few whiskeys and beers and do some "boom-boom" with the resident bar girls in the backrooms or upstairs. But others couldn't shake visions in the recesses of their minds of savage Vietnamese killers lurking in the bush and loathsome glares of Vietnamese peasant women shot their way from a river hamlet a half mile before last week's ambush.

I don't know what uncontrollable impulse it was that jerked a husky PBR sailor named Stinson out of his chair two tables away from us in a Nha Be bar. I don't know what compelled him to grab a Saigon tea girl and shake her like a Raggedy Ann Doll. I don't know what provoked him to thrash her scanty body every which way but loose.

What I knew is that someone had to intervene. That someone was me. I leapt across the barroom, hopped onto the back of the larger and stronger man, locked my right arm around his neck and held on tight as he crashed against the wall and knocked over tables in a futile attempt to extract me, the mediator. Other men in the bar moved out of the way or shifted in their spectator positions. Screaming women ran onto the street to summon the shore patrol. Three SPs arrived with whistles blaring to break up the fracas. Stinson was subdued and escorted away.

I sat back down at my table with fellow DKs Sherman Lawson and Smitty. It all happened so fast, they said, that they didn't even realize it was me who had put himself in the thick of things. Mama-san and the tea girl who had been attacked thanked me for my intervention.

I ordered another beer. I sang along as the Armed Forces Vietnam radio station played the 1966 hit tune "Wild Thing," by the Troggs. After a while, Lan, one of the regular tea girls who rode the bus from Saigon to Nha Be on most afternoons and returned home at nightfall, came over to our table. "You like trouble, huh, Lange," she whispered in my ear and smiled. "You wild thing." Lan was a sweet 18-year-old with looks that made my heart sing, as the English rock band sang it. She was a girl, and she had become my closest Vietnamese friend. You could have called her my girlfriend.

She made the trip to Nha Be to earn some money, and I wasn't about to buy her Saigon tea after Saigon tea, so it was understood that she would spend time with other men at the bar. She was not one of the resident bar girls who invited them for boom-boom in the backroom. When I made my regular overnight visits to Saigon, I liked to spend them with Lan. She sometimes kidded me about becoming Lan Lange. "Wild thing, I think I love you, but I wanna know for sure ..." I knew for sure that I liked the Troggs' song.

Saigon had been commonly referred to as the Pearl of the Orient or Paris of the East, probably an association with its former longtime occupation by the French. It was a cosmopolitan place during the American War.

It definitely had its wild side. Tu Do Street, meaning freedom or liberty, would be teeming with Americans in military uniforms. It flourished with drinking holes where bar girls invited us in for a "bukku good time," their pronunciation of the French "beaucoups," meaning a lot.

The Cholon district offered a variety of retail establishments, many of them owned by members of the Chinese minority that historically had taken refuge there from racial persecution inflicted by the natives. The Chinese generally could be distinguished from the Vietnamese by their fleshier facial features and stoutish bodies.

There were places within the capital city where you could get away from the hustle and bustle and maybe even forget that you were in a war zone for awhile. There were few military uniforms at the Saigon Yacht Club, where American businessmen and media types could join their Vietnamese counterparts for cocktails.

The Tonkin Gulf Yacht Club, on the other hand, had no docking slips or cocktail bars. It was a tongue-in-cheek nickname for the attack carriers and battleships of the U.S. Navy's Seventh Fleet that ceaselessly pummeled our enemy from the Gulf of Tonkin.

My first visit to the capital, under the tutelage of Terry Mattive, a veteran of the 1968 Tet Offensive, included a peaceful afternoon at the Saigon Zoo, where well-dressed Vietnamese families pretended we weren't there. Viet Cong, who were holed up in the zoo for several weeks as their offensive fizzled, ate monkey meat and zebra chops after being cut off from food supplies, Matt told me. Some of the wildlife exhibits were empty.

A couple high-rise hotels towered over sections of the city, including one with a swimming pool on the roof, where our annual disbursing office party was held. The Navy, ever cognizant of boosting morale, provided an ample supply of booze, steak dinners and music, and there were plenty of pretty Vietnamese girls at the hotel for dancing. But you were on your own for the room and overnight companionship, if that was your pleasure.

Al Elliott was a well-traveled man, having spent his growing-up years in places as diverse as Louisiana and Alaska. He was married to a young Mormon woman from Idaho, where he might settle down after his enlistment. He also was a fun-loving man with a streak of adventure. He called me "Doo-Lang," a takeoff from the Chiffons' 1962 top doo-wop hit, "He's So Fine," with its "doo-lang, doo-lang, doo-lang" backup vocal.

Al managed to get both of us sets of camouflage greens through a friend of his with the Marine detachment at Nha Be. Camouflage uniforms were fitting attire for our pay trips on Giant Slingshot but absurd for office personnel, although official military dress got turned on its head in the 21st century. Al also talked me into exchanging my .45-caliber semi-automatic pistol for a .38-caliber revolver, because it was more "cool," he said.

Weapons were prohibited during liberties in Nha Be – except for the shore patrol, of course – but our pistols were easily concealed under our jungle jackets, so we often carried them in Saigon, even off duty.

Some of the bars on Tu Do Street didn't mind if you brought your own liquor in with you, as long as you paid top price for the cola to mix with it. When I stopped at the large Army Post Exchange in Saigon to pick up a fifth of rum and checked my weapon with the guard at the gate, he told me that the .38-caliber was unauthorized and that he'd have to confiscate it unless I could produce a written authorization.

Adding insult to injury, when I went to pay for my booze, the American woman at the register demanded my identification. "Sorry, but you're only 19 years old," she said. "You have to be 21 to purchase liquor here."

"You gotta be shitting me," I grumbled. "The damn government says I'm old enough for them to send me up to the Parrot's Beak, where I can get my ass shot off, but you tell me I'm too young to drink."

"That's the policy," she said with a scowl. She pulled my bottle of rum off the belt and stashed it underneath.

"Fucking bullshit!" I yelled as I stomped out the door.

I had to hail a cyclo ride back to the Annapolis Hotel, get the personnel office to write me up an authorization to carry my .38-caliber pistol and then get another ride across town to retrieve it from the assholes at the Army PX.

Any Vietnamese bar would be happy to sell me as many rum-and-Cokes as I wanted, and they didn't care what I had holstered under my jacket.

It was late afternoon the day before our scheduled trip to Ben Luc. Seated on two stools in a Saigon bar off the beaten path, Al and I were slugging down a few drinks when a man in a Philippines Army uniform decided to join us. The Vietnamese called it the American War, which it certainly was, but we weren't alone. We had some allied support, including forces from Australia, South Korea, New Zealand and the Philippines.

The Filipino soldier struck up a conversation and persuaded us to buy him a drink. Aware that his pay rate was substantially lower than ours, we indulged his freeloading and meaningless chatter for a while. Then Al stood up to visit the bathroom and motioned me to follow him. When we got back there, he said, "This guy is a pain in the ass. We gotta ditch him."

"Yeah," I said, as we pissed from opposite sides of the single toilet. "Let's walk back out there and keep going right out the front door."

"Nah," Al said. "He'll just follow us. Let's go out the back door, and we'll find our way around to the street." We stepped outside, and the door shut behind us. We found ourselves hemmed in by buildings and had no escape route. Al pointed out that we could latch onto some pipes and pull ourselves up to the roof, which we proceeded to do, even though our strategy was getting foggier by the second.

We tiptoed across the quivering metal-on-board roof, trying our best not to make noise that would draw attention in the bar below us. But our weight was too much for the flimsy building overhead to bear. A 6-foot section gave way. We both crashed through and landed with a thud amidst splintered boards and dust in the middle of the bar. Clearly, it was not a mortar shell that blew a hole in the roof. The manager, bartender, tea girls and customers, including the Filipino, were shell-shocked just the same. Young, agile and surprisingly uninjured, Al and I picked ourselves up and ran like hell out the front door, which probably is what we should have done in the first place. We got halfway down the street before the manager ran outside and yelled a series of Vietnamese epithets at our backs. We didn't look back. It was the last time we patronized that establishment.

Pay trips were a good excuse to visit Saigon, but there were others. Deciding that we weren't seeing things as well as we used to, Al Elliott and I received permission to travel into the city to get our eyes tested at the big Army hospital. They gave us each a pair of ugly glasses that we never wore, but we had an opportunity to see the insides of a couple bars on Tu Do Street before heading back to Nha Be.

We paid a cyclo driver to take us to the edge of Saigon, where we hitched a ride with a couple Vietnamese civilians who were taking a chicken home for dinner. The chicken hopped in the back seat between us, and Al took a liking to it, so he bought it for 200 piasters, which was enough for our delighted transporters to buy themselves several dinners. They dropped us off at the north edge of Nha Be just in time for liberty, so the chicken joined us. The proprietors thought nothing of a couple drunk GIs bringing a chicken with them into the bars. They even brought us an extra glass so that we could share some beer with our feathered friend. At the end of the day, sadly, we gave him away for somebody else's dinner.

Picked off by Saigon sniper

"Whitey" White, a yeoman with one of the Giant Slingshot river divisions, frequently paid visits to the disbursing office in Nha Be to coordinate the paperwork for a KIA or settle some confusion over one of the men's pay status. He and I decided that one particular issue had to be addressed by the higher-ups at Military Assistance Command, Vietnam, headquarters in Saigon. Due to the mid-afternoon hour, we wouldn't be able to get back to Nha Be until the following day.

After clearing the matter up much more readily than was presumptively conveyed, Whitey and I were the earliest customers for a couple happy hours on Tu Do Street. Three or four drinks into our happy circumstances, a white woman strode into the bar and plopped her plump rear end on the stool next to mine. Aside from the cashier who had checked my ID at the PX and the friendly hostesses at the Saigon USO, she was the first American woman I had encountered in Vietnam. Being old, at least 30, overweight and unattractive, she was no sight for my sore eyes, but Whitey's blurry blues lit up.

Probably noticing that our jungle greens were unpressed and overdue for the laundry, the woman asked, "So what brings you boys to the big city?"

"We just had to take care of some business at MACV today," Whitey replied. "We'll be back upriver tomorrow."

"So where did you come in from?" she wondered.

"We're working up on Slingshot by the Parrot's Beak," he said.

"What are you boys drinking?" she asked as she got up from the stool next to me and took the one close to Whitey.

Mama-san behind the bar mixed three rum-and-Cokes.

The woman told us she was a reporter for one of the weekly news magazines, that she had been in country for a month, and she had a suite in a hotel on the next block. Before long, she invited us to join her for some more drinks at her place. Free booze was a good enough incentive to get me up to her room, but it soon became apparent that we weren't up there to talk about our war experiences for a magazine story. She was white and American, but she wasn't my type. I excused myself and left Whitey alone with the writer.

A half hour later, he returned to the bar with a shit-eating grin on his face. Aside from a few bar girls, one of whom was socializing with me, the place was still empty. When another one of the girls approached Whitey, asking, "Buy me Saigon tea?" he shoved her away, knocking her on the floor.

"Hey, you no treat my girls like that," the mama-san yelled at him.

"Fuck you, gook!" he yelled back. "Just keep that slant-eyed bitch away from me."

"You numbah-10 American," she said. "You go out of bar now, and you no come back."

Whitey vaulted across the bar, growling like an angry bear at the mama-san, who jumped away from his would-be grasp, banged against a counter and knocked over several bottles of booze. Glass smashed, and liquid flushed across the floor.

I don't know what got into Whitey, didn't know that he harbored such disdain for Vietnamese people, even in his alcohol-induced state of mind. I knew the kid in his river division whose life had been snuffed out in a VC ambush the previous week, because I was the custodian of his pay record and handed him his cash in the pay lines. But I didn't really know him. I didn't have to write the letter of condolence for the commanding officer to sign and send home to the kid's mom and dad. No, that was Whitey's job. Whitey saw that kid every day. He knew him by name. He knew where he was from. He knew what kind of music he liked. He played poker with the kid.

I couldn't feel Whitey's pain. My head couldn't connect the brain waves that oscillated seamlessly within his discombobulated mind between the image of ferocious communist infiltrators in Tay Ninh Province and defenseless Vietnamese women struggling for their own survival in the war-ravaged country.

Something in my own mind snapped. I jumped to my feet, grabbed Whitey around his waist, pulled his wrenching body off the bar and slammed him on the floor. I plunged my knee atop his chest and thrust my fist into his face. His body went still. His glassy eyes glared into mine. There was no amity in that look, no hostility, no fear, no emotion whatsoever. Just haunting blankness.

I got off of him. He stood up, brushed himself and walked out the door. I ordered a Ba Muoi Ba.

That evening, before the sun sank over the western horizon, I caught a cyclo ride to the other side of town and waited for Lan to return home on the bus from Nha Be. "Hello, wild thing," she said when she saw me.

When I got back to the disbursing office in Nha Be the next morning, I received some disturbing news. "Did you hear what happened to Whitey in Saigon last night?" Sherman Lawson asked me.

"No, what?" I responded, not sure if it had something to do with me.

"He was walking down Plantation Road, probably going to the Annapolis to crash after hitting the bars," Sherman said, "and he got shot in the face."

"What?!" I said. "Who in the hell did that?"

"They don't know. It must have been a sniper holed up in one of the buildings across the road," he said. "Probably VC. Whoever did it, he got away."

"So, is Whitey OK?" I asked.

"It doesn't look good. I think they medevaced him to Japan."

That didn't seem right. Whitey was a guy who spent most of his time on a stretch of river known as "Blood Alley," an area crawling with VC and NVA, and then, when he gets a little R&R with us REMFs in Saigon, he gets picked off by a damn sniper. It blew my mind.

Viet Cong tax collectors

Al Elliott's Marine friends, whose small detachment was outside the Nha Be Navy base gate, were not bound by our liberty constrictions. One of those constrictions was bearing down on us as we finished our beer in a bar at the far end of town.

Looking at the watch my dad had given me at the Cleveland airport, I said, "We better get going, Al. We gotta get back to the base in 10 minutes."

"Hold on there, Doo-Lang," Al said. "Let's go find Smitty or Newberry, give them our liberty cards, and they can drop them in the slot at the gate. Nobody will know we didn't go back. The Marines sometimes party the whole night long here in town. I know where they'll be tonight. We can join their party."

I didn't think that was such a good idea. There must be good reasons why we were supposed to be back on base before dark.

"Don't be such a wuss, Doo-Lang," Al said. "Nobody's gonna mess with the Marines."

So we joined six or seven assorted after-hours party animals, drinking, smoking cigarettes, joking and telling tales of woe in one of the seamier bars. Around 4 a.m. a couple guys went upstairs with well-worn hostesses, one of them affectionately known as "Hungry Helen." The rest of us eventually crashed in the barroom. Early the next morning, we hailed the bus transporting Vietnamese workers and new arrivals to the base. We were back in time for work.

Emboldened by the experience, I suggested to Lan soon thereafter that we might spend a night together at Nha Be and that she could catch the bus back to Saigon the next morning. Having gone to the rescue of the tea girl who was being assaulted at her bar a month earlier, I was in good graces with the mama-san there. Lan and I were welcome to stay in one of the upstairs rooms. After I sent my liberty card back to base with Jose Newberry and having another drink, Lan and I decided to retire for the night.

It wasn't long after midnight when Lan shook me awake. I heard knuckles tapping on the main door downstairs. "Be very quiet," she whispered in my ear. It was dark in our room, but we could see a light flicker on through the loose-fitting floorboards, and we heard the door open below. A low, imperious tone of male voices received conciliatory-sounding responses from mama-san. I couldn't understand any of it.

"It's VC," Lan said, her hushed voice quivering, her warm breath brushing my cheek.

I had heard tales about the village being anybody's territory at night. Anybody could be hunkering in the hooches. Anybody could be slinking along the maze of narrow dikes. With the heavily armed Navy base on the riverside of town, the small-but-battle-ready cadre of feisty Marines between the base and the village plus the Army installation not far away, the enemy would be foolish to initiate daring hostilities in Nha Be. But the wages of war come with a price, and the enterprises that thrived on Americans' MPCs during the day could be fair game for AK-47 gun toters in the quiet heat of the night.

How many of those gun toters were in the bar below was hard to tell, maybe three or four. If I had been with Lan in Saigon, chances are that my loaded .38-caliber pistol would be in its holster next to the bed. I could have pulled it out, unlocked the safety, hunched down behind the bed, trained the barrel at the door and braced for a dreaded intrusion. If I were a hero – which I wasn't – I even could have crept down the stairs and plugged the intruding enemy tax collectors with five rounds from my cylinder. But this was Nha Be. I was unarmed. I was a cooped-up duck lying in bed, ready to be plucked.

Quiet and motionless in that bed, we listened to the sound of clinking glasses. Mama-san had poured the tax collectors drinks. Their low voices became more cordial, less demanding. I might have heard some chuckles.

Surely, mama-san wouldn't betray me, I thought. I hoped. I prayed. After all, what price would she pay for harboring an American trespasser who was listening in on the VC tax collection? What would be Lan's fate for sharing a bed with that colonial occupier?

And, if the American's bullet-riddled body was found in the upstairs bedroom of that off-limits bar the next day, what would be the consequences? Would I be listed as KIA – killed in action? Would I posthumously be awarded a Purple Heart? Would such an engagement with the enemy merit a Combat Action Ribbon? By the grace of God, because I have no other explanation, such questions have no answers.

After what seemed like an eternity, I heard the front door open, then it closed, and then the latch slid shut. Downstairs fell silent. The visitors vanished into the night. My breath came more easily. The pounding of my heart gave my ribs a break. Lan held my hand tight. "VC go away, Lange," she said softly. "We go to sleep now."

There were very good reasons why liberty hours were limited and why we were supposed to return to the base before sunset. I learned.

Body bag for Benny

Sometimes my mother's letters arrived within a week after she put them in the mail. Other times they took longer. There were no phone booths in Vietnam, no long-distance service anywhere that I knew about. We had no iPhones, no iPads, no email, no Facebook, no FaceTime, never heard about or even imagined such communications devices. Letters and occasional packages from home were all we got. We were grateful for that.

A letter from Mom arrived in late November. It was bad news. Ben was dead. Benedict J. Linnen III was known as Benny to those he grew up with in Cuyahoga Falls. I knew him casually as Ben, the carhop who delivered burgers and fries to teenagers hanging out at the Hungry I. If his family hadn't moved to Wyoga Lake in Stow, he would have graduated from high school with me. Because they did, my mom and his mom, Pauline, were neighbors. Because their sons were in Vietnam, they became close. They shared the letters their boys wrote home from the war. They shared their joys of motherhood from the past and their hopes for their sons' return. And they shared their fears.

Pauline and Benedict J. Linnen Jr.'s fears were horribly realized with news that Benny's life had been snuffed out in Thua Thien, a province squeezed between the South China Sea and the Laotian border in the northern section of South Vietnam. He died on Nov. 15, 1969. He was 21 years old. Spc.4 Linnen, trained as a combat surveillance and target acquisition crewman, was attached to XXIV Corps, 1st Battalion, 44th Artillery, B Battery. Twenty-four other Americans perished in Vietnam on that date.

Based on military records, Ben's death was attributed to "non-hostile action ... reported as suicide or self-inflicted injury." I don't know how or when that demoralizing determination was shared with his loved ones. A Purple Heart was not listed among the awards for his Army service.

Ben had been in country for 10 months, meaning he was a "short-timer." His return to the world was getting nearer. I can't imagine why a young man who had put in most of his wartime and who could see the light at the end of a daunting and dreary tunnel would turn his weapon on himself.

According to military records in the National Archives, among the 58,220 Americans who died in Vietnam, 382 are listed as the result of self-inflicted injuries. Accidents accounted for 9,107 American deaths.

Another 236 deaths are listed as homicides. "Fragging," a term associated with the accessibility of fragmentation grenades and their demolition of evidentiary culpability, was an all-too-familiar modus operandi during the Vietnam War. Racial tensions and disillusionment with military leadership are among the pretexts for these soldier-on-soldier murders. Some 156 fragging incidents resulting in 46 deaths were documented for 1969, and the numbers escalated as the war began to wind down in 1970 and 1971.

The arrival of Ben Linnen's casket home and his burial at Northlawn Memorial Gardens in Cuyahoga Falls did everything to heighten his family's agony and my mother's commiseration. Don't do anything careless or risky or foolish, she told me in the letter. Be vigilant, she said. Avoid any and all perilous situations, she urged.

Great escape to Bangkok

R&R officially was a matter of rest and recuperation, but it also carried politically incorrect connotations that reflected the bawdry and bawdiness that was most conspicuously proffered by the host destinations. Either way, R&R was the great escape. Five days in Bangkok, Thailand, made a freshly turned 20-year-old feel like the proverbial kid in a candy store.

During my R&R, I persuaded a cab driver to find me a tattoo artist, which involved a search-and-inquire mission far removed from the city's thriving boulevards and glitzy nightspots. Although tattoos have been around practically forever, in 1969, they were displayed only by a small minority of sailors, prison inmates and motorcycle gangsters, which is why I wanted one. Aside from major naval port cities, the needle-wielding artists who applied them were few and far between, which is why I ended up in a shop off a narrow back alley in a shabby section of Bangkok.

There was no electrically powered machinery there to pneumatically or electromagnetically insert ink with precision one eighth of an inch deep into the epidermis at a rate of 100 or more injections per second. There were no sterilized needles to be sanitarily disposed of after each individual use. There were no certifications or accreditations hanging from the dingy walls. There was just a dark-skinned little Siamese man with missing front teeth ready to work on the left biceps of a fair-skinned Caucasian, the likes of whom had rarely, if ever, ventured into his shop, or even his neighborhood, before.

The creation of a 5-by-2-inch, snarling black panther, accented with a green-tinted spine and clawed red scratches, was inked with a clasped needle one imprecise jab at a time in about three hours. The price was 50 baht, the equivalent of $8.75. The result is no work of art, certainly not by modern-parlor standards, but it is unique.

If the tattooist had spoken any English, he might have cautioned me to keep my freshly tattooed arm out of untreated water for several days. If he had, I might have skipped the bus trip to the beach on the Gulf of Siam the next day, or at least contented myself with a sunny afternoon of building a castle in the sand. But I couldn't pass up the opportunity to collect memories of water-skiing in the Indian Ocean. Anyway, the infection was readily treatable by a corpsman back at Nha Be.

If the AIDS epidemic had revealed itself to the so-called civilized world and if the ravages of the deadly disease had overrun Bangkok 15 years earlier, I surely would have thought twice about having those un-sterilized needles poked into my arm thousands of times.

If I had foreseen the love affair with so-called body art germinate from the few bicepses and pecs of sailors and bikers to myriad ankles, buttocks and necks of athletes, entertainers, punks and women in the decades ahead, I would have second-guessed my rebellious conceptualization.

Of course, if I had listened to my mom, I would have paid attention in my college calculus classes.

Chapter 18 | # Welcome Home, Baby Killer

Whoops, cheers and vigorous applause resounded through the fuselage of the jet plane on Feb. 3, 1970, as the wheels left the pavement. The runways and hangars of Tan Son Nhut Air Base shrank below our glazing eyes. We were going back to the world.

More than 11,000 of my fellow Americans went home in body bags during the year I spent in Vietnam. That was about eight times the number of Americans killed during the deadliest years of the 21st-century wars in Iraq and Afghanistan, combined. Mine was the second-deadliest year of the Vietnam War. Nearly 16,600 Americans died there in 1968. Yet, in 2010, I found myself countering false information spread by the federal government and regurgitated in public addresses on patriotic holidays that those latter-day conflicts were far more hazardous than mine.

During the deadliest year in Iraq, 2007, 965 Americans lost their lives there, 5.7 per each 1,000 troops in country. During my year in Vietnam, 1969, 24.4 of my brothers were killed per each 1,000 troops in country, more than four times the death rate at the height of the Iraq War. The Vietnam death rate was even higher at 31 per each 1,000 troops in 1968.

These facts do not diminish the sacrifices of those who served in Iraq and Afghanistan. But, after four long decades, the government's continuing effort to sweep Vietnam veterans under the rug really does get tiring.

For the final time, I looked over the bomb-pocked earth of South Vietnam stretching as far as the eye could see toward the Central Highlands. In North Vietnam, where our pilots and bombardiers put their lives, limbs and tortured captures on the line, more tons of bombs were dropped during our war than the totals dropped on Japan, Germany and Italy in World War II.

Yet, nearly a half century later, with the self-imposed encumbrance of 20/200 vision, revisionists insist that victory was in sight, if only we had continued our bombardment. Sure, we could have kept bombing Hanoi, even though 600,000 of the city's 800,000 civilians had been resiliently evacuated to the surrounding countryside and mountains. Hell, we had only dropped $6 billion worth of bombs on North Vietnam.

Prior to his election as leader of the free world, Richard M. Nixon was convinced after the 1968 Tet Offensive that the killing was futile. As revealed in John A. Farrell's enlightening 2017 book, "Richard Nixon: The Life," he said so in no uncertain terms to speechwriter Richard Whalen. "I've come to the conclusion there's no way to win the war," Nixon said. "We can't say that, of course. In fact, we have to seem to say the opposite, just to keep some degree of bargaining leverage. But the war can't be brought to a successful military conclusion."

So the killing continued for seven more years. One-and-a-half years after Nixon reached his conclusion, Ben Linnen, the son of my parents' neighbors, became one of his dead bargaining chips. Two-and-a-half years after Nixon reached his conclusion, my buddy Rick Morgan perished with no successful conclusion in sight. More than 21,000 Americans died in Vietnam during Nixon's presidency. What a bargain!

In addition to 58,220 American military losses during the Vietnam War, our allies suffered about 224,000 deaths, mostly South Vietnamese fighting men. An estimated 390,000 South Vietnamese civilian lives were snuffed. For our part, we killed about 444,000 North Vietnamese Army and Viet Cong combatants, plus an estimated 618,000 North Vietnamese civilians died. Yet, the war hawks continue to argue that we just didn't kill enough.

The point often has been made that we won every major battle of the Vietnam War. Then-President Barack Obama reiterated that contention in a 2011 speech to the American Legion. Noting that Vietnam veterans did not receive the respect they deserved, he said, "But let it be remembered that you won every major battle of that war. Every single one."

What constituted a major battle in Vietnam probably defies specifications from earlier wars, certainly the ones that engulfed the world earlier in the 20th century. Among the personal accounts relayed to me by the riverine men I knew, it was smaller hit-and-run battles that dominated our war. Based on body counts and who most often ran for their lives, we won those battles too.

Detractors might point out debatable results of a couple "major" battles, including Landing Zone Albany in November 1965 and Fire Support Base Ripcord in July 1970. During my tour, the battle for Hamburger Hill in May 1969 resulted in 46 dead and 400 wounded Americans, with enemy dead estimated at 673. Just a few days later, however, our courageous men were ordered to walk away from the hill they had seized at great cost. That's the kick-in-the-ass kind of war it was.

When all was said and done on April 30, 1975, with South Vietnamese President Duong Van Minh's announced unconditional surrender to the communists, more than 20 months after U.S. military involvement had ended, it cannot be denied that our side lost. The decision by the United States Congress to cut military aid to South Vietnam from $2.8 billion in fiscal 1973 to $1 billion in fiscal 1974 and then to a meager $300 million in 1975 practically left our allies defenseless.

By any means, ours was not "The Great War," the volumetric title bestowed on World War I. We did not become known as the "Greatest Generation," the accolade associated with World War II. Nor did we fight "The Forgotten War," the term so often mentioned with the Korean War, which could be re-engaged at any unforgettable moment.

For most of us, forgotten would have been better than "losers." As for body counts, our side, including the South Vietnamese military and civilians, suffered about 672,000 losses in the war, while we inflicted about 1.06 million losses upon our communist enemies. Somehow, though, we were the "losers," according to many who distinguished themselves as winners.

As our commercial plane full of relieved Vietnam veterans jetted northeast across the South China Sea toward Okinawa, there were no losers among us.

We didn't just face off against the communists of North Vietnam and their surrogate Viet Cong in the South. Mostly forgotten about our mercilessly unforgotten war is the fact that we persevered against the largest and most powerful communist collaborators in the world, Red China and the Soviet Union.

Where did the moviemakers and baby-killer accusers think all those state-of-the-art AK-47s came from? What about the thousands of surface-to-air missiles that were used to blast our bombers and helicopters out of the sky? And hundreds of North Vietnamese tanks, aircraft and naval vessels?

According to Rakesh Krishnan Simha's April 2015 piece in Russia & India Report, "By the late 1960s, more than three-quarters of the military and technical equipment received by North Vietnam was coming from Moscow." That supply line "completely transformed the nature of the war," he wrote, and the Vietnamese "hit the Americans with firepower on a staggering scale. Their arsenal included 2,000 tanks, 7,000 artillery guns, over 5,000 anti-aircraft guns and 158 surface-to-air rocket launchers."

Weapons supplied by the USSR "were more advanced than the American ones," Simha reported. "Entire waves of American aircraft were blasted out of the skies because the Vietnamese fired ceaseless barrages of SAMs, knowing more Russian supplies were on their way."

Unlike doomed-to-repeat-history politicians and their amnesic worshipers, Vietnam veterans know about the autocratic enemies in the Kremlin who conspired to annihilate us then and would do the same now. Conveniently ensconced in the rewards of self-enrichment above duty to country, Vietnam War evaders and Moscow connivers became chosen ones in the political campaign and administration of pussy-hawk-in-chief Donald J. Trump.

Officers and just plain men

I leaned back in my cushioned airline seat, breathed easy and patted the inside breast pocket of the stylish sport jacket that I acquired from a tailor in Bangkok. The contents of the unopened pack labeled Lucky Strike were safely stashed. I pulled the opened pack of Marlboros from a flap pocket at my side, put one in my mouth and flicked my Zippo. I reread the engraving on its side: "Yea, though I walk through the valley of the shadow of death, I will fear no evil; for I am the evilest son of a bitch in the valley."

I took a deep puff on my cigarette, closed my eyes and smiled. I thought about events of the past month.

Shortly after midnight on Jan. 1, I had led a small party of hardy celebrators out of the EM club to wish "Happy New Year" to our uppity leaders in the officers club at Nha Be. Instead of sharing a toast with us lowlifes or even reciprocal good cheer, a lieutenant junior grade from the communications staff snarled at us, "What do think you're doing in here? Our club is off limits to you enlisted men."

"What an arrogant asshole," I thought of the junior officer whose acts of courage were daily treks from the BOQ to the comm office, from there to the officers dining hall for lunch and back, then back to the dining hall for dinner and on to the officers club before hitting his rack back in the BOQ.

My naval performance evaluation noted my "ability to accomplish, with dispatch, whatever task is assigned him." But my evaluator also emphasized that I "could well be a top notch DK were it not for a few 'chinks in his armor,' i.e. occasional fits of rage and behavioral inconsistencies."

"Fuck that asshole," I thought of the lifer who never ventured out of the office to deliver paydays to our fighting men or even walk a perimeter watch. On second thought, I should have smashed my desk chair over his head instead of against the wall. Don't give me your shit.

Just because I took a joy ride to Saigon without his consent, Lt. Jacot got pissed at me and postponed my rotation out of country from Feb. 15 to Feb. 28. It wasn't like I ditched the damn Bronco in a rice paddy.

"Dear Mom," I wrote after being summarily penalized. "I'm afraid I won't be getting home in time for Vonnie's wedding ..." Obviously, Lt. Jacot didn't know whose mom he was messing with. Two weeks later, he received a directive from the commanding officer that David Charles Lange's transfer date was rescheduled to Feb. 3. I don't know how my mother pulled that one off.

"Fuck the lieutenant," I thought.

More than 9 million Americans served in uniform during the Vietnam War era – about one third of the draft-age men at that time. Fewer than 2.6 million of us actually served within the borders of Vietnam, about 8 percent of the men of my generation. An estimated 520,000 of the in-country service members regularly engaged the enemy on the ground.

The vast majority of those combatants were enlisted men, who account for more than 50,000 of the names engraved on the Wall in Washington, D.C. The names of about 7,900 officers and warrant officers are listed on the Wall. According to information compiled by Doug Sterner, curator of the Military Times Hall of Fame, and provided to the Veterans of Foreign Wars in 2014, "Vietnam's Most Highly Decorated Servicemen" include 43 officers and just six enlisted men. So, while 13.6 percent of the Americans who died in Vietnam were officers, they accounted for 87.8 percent of the ones recognized as the most courageous heroes. There's an inverse relationship between officers and just plain men.

Introduction to evil weed

A Congressional Quarterly article about a U.S. Senate Juvenile Delinquency Subcommittee hearing in March 1970 indicated growing concerns about the wide use of drugs in Vietnam. Subcommittee chairman Thomas J. Dodd, a Democrat from Connecticut, said, "In Vietnam, dangerous drugs and even heroin are almost as available as candy bars. Estimates of drug abuse among Vietnam troops run as high as 80 percent, compared to 50 percent among youth in the United States. Furthermore, Vietnamese marijuana is usually more potent than that available in the United States."

Charles West, a former Army sergeant who had participated in the 1968 infamy, told the subcommittee, "At least 60 percent of the soldiers in Charlie Company, the unit involved in the My Lai incident, had smoked marijuana at least once. Some soldiers smoked marijuana the night before they went to My Lai on the day of the alleged massacre."

James W. Teague, a former Army psychiatrist in Vietnam, reported, "One survey of enlisted men at the end of their duty tour there revealed that 31.7 percent admitted – and I stress the word admitted – using marijuana while serving in Vietnam. Three-quarters of those said they used it experimentally, while the others admitted to being 'heavy' users. Of course, troops leaving Vietnam may be the most apprehensive in admitting any drug use."

I can't say whether 80 percent of the troops were drug abusers or 60 percent of the soldiers in Charlie Company tried marijuana or 31.7 percent of those leaving country had been toking. Again, I patted the inside breast pocket of my stylish sport coat. I was pretty sure those tenderly rolled doobies of Vietnamese ganja inside the recycled Lucky Strike pack were pretty potent, though.

Yep, my introduction to the evil weed came courtesy of the Vietnam War. I didn't realize it at first, when, upon hearing Cream's "Sunshine of Your Love" blaring on a record player, I paid a surprise visit to a neighboring barracks at Nha Be. A strange odor hung in the smoky air of the head-banging river rats' compartment.

Surfer Boy Webb familiarized me with the odor, taste and euphoric impact of smoking pot on a back alley in Saigon six months later. For some reason, I never experienced the "psychotic episodes," "violent criminal acts," "feelings of persecution," "general psychic disequilibrium" and various other adverse reactions cited in Rep. Dodd's subcommittee hearing. It just made me feel relaxed and happy, for the wrong reason, I guess.

So I decided to take a sample home and share it with some friends. I would have packed my .38-caliber inside my sea bag to take home as well, except for the jerk at the Saigon PX who caused me to create a paper trail for the gun at the Annapolis. There were no metal detectors and intrusive pat-downs at the airports in those days.

Happy homecoming nonetheless

There were no hordes of hocker-hurling hippies waiting for returning Vietnam veterans at the San Francisco Airport either – not when I arrived.

The spitting image of veterans being splattered with spittle upon their homecoming was crystallized by actor Sylvester Stallone's character, John Rambo, in the 1982 film "First Blood." "It wasn't my war," the vengeful veteran Rambo said. "You asked me. I didn't ask you. And I did what I had to do to win. But somebody wouldn't let us win. Then I come back to the world and I see all those maggots at the airport. Protesting me. Spitting. Calling me baby killer."

After skeptical Chicago Tribune syndicated columnist Bob Greene asked veterans in 1987 about what he suspected was the spitting myth, he received so many gut-wrenching accounts that he compiled a collection of them in a 1989 book, "Homecoming: When the Soldiers Returned from Vietnam." Of more than 1,000 responses he received, a total of 234 were reprinted in the book. Eighty-one of those letters detailed spitting incidents. The victims included a wide variety of veterans, from combatants to a surgeon, a dentist and even a Catholic priest – their Vietnam service verified through the Veterans Administration. All types of perpetrators were described, from "sweet little old lady" and "rude couple" to "college types" and "flower children."

Contrarily, "The Spitting Image: Myth, Memory, and the Legacy of Vietnam," a 2000 book by Jerry Lembcke, an associate professor of sociology at Holy Cross College and a Vietnam veteran, conducted thorough, objective research into the issue. He reported that not one incident of an anti-war protester spitting on a returning veteran has been verifiably documented. The fact that Lembcke was a member of Vietnam Veterans Against the War, as pointed out by his detractors, does not debunk his research.

Even so, a shortage of documentation does not mean it didn't happen.

The common refrain involves returning warriors in uniform encountering hateful groups of anti-war protesters when they debarked at San Francisco International Airport. First of all, I didn't debark at a civilian airport. Few of us did. My flight landed at Travis Air Force Base, and we traveled by bus from there to San Francisco. Secondly, most of those on my flight from Tan Son Nhut, via Okinawa, were wearing civilian clothes when we landed on the West Coast. Thirdly, if a big guy like Stinson were to spit on me, a violent clash would be sure to follow, regardless of the results. And I guarantee, if the spitter were a pissant little hippy, he or she would be well bloodied – which most likely would result in some verifiable documentation.

I suppose there are those whose response would be different. A dose of slimy saliva in the face might hurt the feelings of some Vietnam veterans and cause them to sulk away. I just don't know them.

There were no slobbery excretions on the pungent lips of the young woman seated next to me on the flight to Cleveland, but her asinine attitude left a bad taste in my mouth. Plus it was a rude awakening. Two years earlier, I had seen pretty young things at the Hullabaloo swoon over a uniformed guy fresh out of basic training, which gave me the unenlightened idea that a genuine war veteran like me might get a modicum of courtesy. Wrong!

"Hi, my name's Dave," I said with my friendly smile. "Are you going to Cleveland?"

"Yes," she said. No smile.

"Been on vacation in San Francisco?" I asked.

"Yes," she said.

"Well, I just got back from Vietnam," I said, "and I can't tell you how happy I am to be going home."

"So, how many babies did you kill?" she said with a stabbing glare.

"Babies? I didn't kill any babies," I stammered.

"Of course you did. All you guys who go to Vietnam participate in killing babies one way or another," the bitch asserted.

"The fuck we did!" I concluded.

That was the end of that conversation. My good humor was spoiled. While I cannot corroborate stories about hippies spitting at returning veterans, I, for one, was called a baby killer by a well-dressed woman on an uncomfortably quiet flight to Cleveland. I didn't mind exhaling tobacco smoke in her direction.

News of the My Lai Massacre of March 1968, when the scapegoat 2nd Lt. William Calley Jr.'s platoon murdered as many as 500 unarmed civilians, including women, children and infants, had just broken three months earlier. Explicit images of dead villagers were fresh in the minds of American newspaper and magazine readers and TV viewers, but I had been far away from the world, and the military media didn't bother me with such distractions.

Talk about baby killers went wild in the aftermath of the war, with Ayn Rand "objectivists," for example, claiming that the communist regime was responsible for killing as many as 7.5 million South Vietnamese and anti-war pacifists insisting that the bloodbath was an imperialist fiction.

R.J. Rummel, a Cleveland native and professor emeritus of political science at the University of Hawaii, painstakingly extrapolated deadly measures from actual analyses, body counts, refugee reports, written records and other data in his 1997 book, "Statistics of Democide: Genocide and Mass Murder Since 1900." "Democide," as redefined by Rummel, involves "indiscriminate killing resulting from or consistent with higher commands."

From 1965 to '72, the height of our involvement in the war, he determined that American-directed "democides" ranged from 400 to 5,000 and most likely totaled some 800. His post-Vietnam War "democide" calculations ranged from 346,000 to 2,438,000, with the most probable total being about 1,040,000.

So, according to Rummel's scientific analysis, the communists killed 1,300 times as many Vietnamese people, including their babies, as we Americans did. But the bitch seated next to me on the plane called me a baby killer.

The limousine shuttle from Cleveland Hopkins Airport to Kent, where most of the other half-dozen young passengers probably had college classes the next morning, was no more conversational. My quip to the guy seated next to me that I hadn't encountered any "round-eyed women for the past year" probably had something to do with that, although it didn't seem racist or misogynistic to me. Hell, I liked, respected and defended Asian women.

Finally, after the limo driver dropped me off in the center of Stow and I stuck my thumb out on Darrow Road, a compassionate young woman picked me up. Not only did she welcome me back and tell me about her brother in the Marines, but she drove 5 miles out of her way to deliver me to my family's front door on Treeside Drive.

It was a happy homecoming after all. My dad welcomed me home with a cold beer from the refrigerator. He had one with dinner every evening and then another one or two on some nights. His was the only "welcome home" I ever received from a World War II veteran. Ever.

Yet another icy reception

With the sun peeking through stratus clouds on the crisp early-February morning that followed, I found my old hockey skates in the basement. I put on a heavy coat and gloves for the first time in a year, slung the skates over my shoulder and took a leisurely walk over to the lake. A thin coat of fresh snow covered the ice. All alone, I sat on a bench by the beach, pulled off my shoes, squeezed my feet into the skates and laced them up.

It was time to embrace the winter's chill, time to put the perpetual tropical sweat in my past, time to revisit the joy of youth, time to put the insanity that we call war out of my head.

Across the frozen beach I trudged. The blades beneath my feet slid onto the ice. The skates glided forward. I gathered speed and approached the dock island where a springboard vaults divers for refreshing plunges into cool water on hot summer days. Suddenly, I felt a fracture under my left foot. My right knee buckled. The ice ripped apart in a crackling commotion. Gravity yanked me into the frigid lake. I grabbed for my M16. It wasn't there. This was Wyoga Lake, not the river at Nha Be. I kicked myself to the surface, grabbed the jagged edge of inch-thick ice. I looked around. Nobody in sight. Nobody to call for help. No PBR coming to my rescue. Clinging to the busted ice with my gloved hands, I pushed myself back below the surface. The blades of my skates hit the sandy bottom. I bent my knees, sank farther down and then sprang upward with all my might. I hoisted my torso onto the ice and slithered back to the beach. It was a cold walk back to the house.

My sister Vonnie's wedding to Albert LaRue, a 1968 Cuyahoga Falls High School graduate and an engineering student at the University of Akron, was a joyful occasion. I was a member of the wedding party. A short reception after the ceremony at Redeemer Lutheran Church included finger food but no alcoholic beverages. A small party with beer and mixed drinks followed at my parents' house. It was all they could afford.

My mom took me across the street to meet Ben Linnen's parents the next day. They were very nice people, but it was awkward. I didn't know what to say. What does a guy who came back from Vietnam in one piece say to the still-grieving mom and dad of a kid who returned home in a body bag less than three months earlier?

I called my friend Jeff Murphy, then a junior at Kent State. He picked me up and took me to a party in Kent. I knew his girlfriend, Kay Infield, and a few other students there. I shared a few of the joints that I sneaked out of Saigon. They liked my ganja. They shared their pot with me. I liked it. Nobody in Kent spit at me. Nobody there called me a baby killer.

Eastward, onward and upward

With my next duty assignment being Helicopter Anti-Submarine Squadron 11 based at Naval Air Station Quonset Point, Rhode Island, I figured I could use some transportation. My dad took me car shopping. With most of the savings in my account at the First National Bank of Akron, I bought a 1966 yellow Chevrolet Impala convertible for $1,300 at a dealership in Kent. I was so delighted with my new wheels that I put the top down. I didn't care that it was still winter in Northeast Ohio. I turned up the heat.

Sherman Lawson, who had graduated from disbursing school with me in December 1968 and arrived for duty in Nha Be around the same time as me, became one of my closest friends during our time there. We both had requested Rhode Island for our next duty stations, and he also received orders to a helicopter squadron out of Quonset Point. We decided to make the trip east together, so I picked him up at Cleveland Hopkins Airport early on Friday, and we reported for duty at the naval station on Feb. 28, 1970.

When we arrived at the large disbursing office on base Monday morning, I learned that my squadron, HS-11, had shipped out in early December aboard the USS Forrestal, CVA-59, an attack aircraft carrier home ported in Norfolk, Virginia. It was operating somewhere in the Mediterranean Sea and wasn't scheduled to return stateside until July. As soon as the Navy brass could find its bearings, I was told, arrangements would be made for me to fly to Europe and meet up with my squadron. In the meantime, they would find some work to keep me busy in the Quonset Point office.

Faced with the prospect that the freedom of owning a car would be short-lived, I suggested to Sherman that we make the 140-mile drive to New York City for the weekend. Despite heavy traffic on Interstate 95, we arrived in plenty of time to enjoy New York's liberal drinking laws and the friendly college-age crowd at a lively bar in the Bronx. At closing time, our high hopes of being invited to spend the night with a couple young ladies in a nearby apartment had not come to pass.

There didn't appear to be any cheap motels in the neighborhood, so our final option was to sleep in my convertible double parked on a Bronx street. New York temperatures at night in early March tend to be 60 or 70 degrees lower than those we were accustomed to in Nha Be and Ben Luc, which caused me to periodically start up my car and run the heater for 15-minute intervals.

Those were not ideal sleeping conditions to begin with, and a hard rap on the window was even worse. I blinked my eyes at a shining flashlight pointed at me by a man in blue and rolled my window down. "You can't park here overnight," he growled. "Somebody's gonna walk by here with a blade, slash through your convertible top and slit your throat all in one motion."

"Yeah, well, we were in Vietnam last month, so you're not scaring us none," I told the cop.

"Whatever," he said. "You still can't park here."

I started the car up, pulled around the block and found a new parking spot on the street.

During the 1970s, an average of 1,905 murders were committed each year in New York City, more than five per day. In 2016, when certain political fictioneers claimed the country's big cities were experiencing an unprecedented crime wave, there were 334 murders in New York City, fewer than one per day.

I was used to sleeping through gunfire, rockets whistling across the sky and bombs exploding in the distance. But I could have slept better if it wasn't so damn cold in New York.

Chapter 19 | # Life at Sea;
Death at Home

"Permission to come aboard, sir," I requested with a crisp salute to the officer on duty as I joined a line of other sailors climbing the ladder from the liberty boat.

Space conservation being essential – at least for enlisted men – shipboard stairways are narrow and steep, which is why they're called ladders in naval parlance.

"Granted," the officer replied.

Observing the sea bag on my shoulder, a dead giveaway that I was a new arrival on the USS Forrestal, a petty officer checked my orders and directed me toward my workstation. The disbursing office was located just below the flight deck at the stern of the 990-foot-long aircraft carrier with more than 5,000 men on board. I found my way to the aft end of the hangar bay and then obtained further directions through passageways and up a ladder to the compartment where pay records were maintained, checks were written and cash was disbursed.

My arrival had followed a flurry of travels. Unhappily, because I had no idea when I'd be back in my driver's seat, I made the 600-mile trip from Rhode Island back home to leave my Impala in limbo. Then I caught a flight from Cleveland to Newark, New Jersey, where I hopped on a bus to McGuire Air Force Base. After spending the better part of two days amidst boredom and body odor in the concourse there, I was put on a military flight to Torrejon Air Base near Madrid, Spain, which, based on my sketchy orders to a helicopter squadron, I imagined was my destination. My dad had suggested that I might even meet a sweet, young Spanish lady there. Fat chance! My stay at Torrejon lasted a day and a half. From there, I was flown to Barcelona, where the Forrestal was anchored offshore.

"You're in the Navy now," I told myself. Named in honor of James Forrestal, the first secretary of defense, upon its commissioning in 1955, my ship was the first complete "supercarrier." I was assigned to the top of a three-rack stack in a cramped berthing compartment on a lower deck, where I would be sleeping during the day, because I was working the night shift.

As we sailed in the Tyrrhenian Sea between Sardinia and Sicily and the Ionian Sea between the sole of the Italian boot and the west coast of Greece, I quickly became accustomed to slamming touchdowns of fighter jets and rumbling cables snatching tailhooks overhead. It did not put me at ease, though, to be told by my new shipmates that everyone in our work compartment on July 29, 1967, less than three years earlier, had been incinerated.

The worst tragedy on a U.S. Navy ship since World War II occurred on that date in the Gulf of Tonkin as the Forrestal prepared planes for a major attack on North Vietnam.

Much has been written and argued about the incident, partly because soon-to-be prisoner of war and future U.S. Sen. John McCain was in the thick of it. As so often has been the case with Vietnam veterans who later got involved in national politics, facts and fiction became twisted. Based on the ship's logs, this is what actually occurred:

"The tragic fire began with the accidental launching of a Zuni rocket from a F-4B Phantom aircraft. This rocket launch was not the result of error on the part of the crew. The rocket streaked across the flight deck and struck the external fuel tank of an A-4E Skyhawk aircraft, spilling volatile aviation fuel across the flight deck. Within five seconds the fuel ignited, spreading under other aircraft loaded with ordnance and fueled for the second launch of the morning. Huge clouds of black smoke billowed three hundred feet into the air. Scores of flight deck personnel rushed to contain the spread of the flames from reaching thirteen adjoining aircraft all loaded with ordnance. In one minute and thirty-four seconds after the fire started, the first 1000 lb. bomb exploded. Flying shrapnel tore into other aircraft, ruptured more fuel tanks, and spread lakes of flaming aviation fuel over the deck. In a period of four minutes, seven major high order explosions shook the entire ship ripping seven huge holes through the thick armored steel flight deck with some reaching through the ship to the water line ..."

With 1,000-pound bombs exploding and tens of thousands of gallons of jet fuel igniting, the scorching result was 134 dead sailors and 161 wounded, 64 of them severely. Many of the dead perished while fighting the fires. If it hadn't been for the heroics of sailors battling the blazes and dumping bombs overboard, the losses would have been worse. The ship may have been lost. As it was, damages exceeded $72 million, which, adjusted for inflation, is the equivalent of more than half a billion dollars today.

As for fighter pilot Lt. Cmdr. McCain, his plane was one of the first ones destroyed in the incident, but he managed to jump out of his cockpit and escape with his life. According to rational accounts, he was not among the heroes that day, and, contrary to irrational, politically motivated accusations, he neither started the conflagration, nor did he aggravate the situation through irresponsible action. Three months later, after volunteering for fighter-pilot duty on the USS Oriskany, McCain was shot down over North Vietnam and taken prisoner by the communists.

Heartbreaker at Kent State

Following repairs, the Forrestal was back in service, this time on the other side of the world facing the Soviet menace. I became one of its Cold War sailors.

From a distance, Soviet naval vessels frequently accompanied the Forrestal and other ships of the Sixth Fleet during our exercises in the Mediterranean Sea. Often visible from our fantail, they would collect whatever plastic garbage bags floated on the surface after evening rubbish call, presumably in futile efforts to obtain classified information.

In mid-April, we anchored for a few days in Argostoli Bay, Greece, where there was no liberty call. Then we dropped anchor off Valletta, Malta, a small island nation between Sicily and the north African coast that was still a British commonwealth at the time. I was impressed by ancient fortresses built into the seaside cliffs of Valletta and also visited a few taverns during my two days of liberty there.

After that visit, the Forrestal steamed in the Ionian Sea before making a port call in Athens in mid-May. I joined a couple shipmates in a visit to the Acropolis and other historic sights of the Greek capital. Being attached to my helicopter squadron and also working in the ship's disbursing office, I was treated to two company parties. HS-11's party was a raucous affair of drunkenness and gluttony in a park outside the city. A wild game of "Buck, Buck," popularized by entertainer Bill Cosby's "Fat Albert and the Cosby Kids," was my first opportunity to fit in with the "airedales" and other crewmen of the squadron.

The smaller disbursing office party included an ample supply of alcoholic beverages and fine food as well, but it was served aboard a yacht cruising the picturesque Greek islands. Unfortunately, my joyful humor was spoiled by a conversation one of my shipmates initiated with a couple of American tourists.

After the tall, bespectacled, balding Rob Herdman told the married couple from Chicago about his plans to finish college in Illinois and become a schoolteacher after his Navy discharge, they asked me if I was thinking about my future.

"I went to a year of architecture school before I lost my draft deferment," I said. "I always thought I'd be an architect someday, but now I realize that's not gonna happen. I might go back to college, but I don't know what I'd major in this time."

"Oh, where did you go to architecture school?" the woman asked.

"Kent State University," I said.

She and her husband looked at me in shock. I wondered what that was about.

"You didn't hear the news, did you?" the man said.

"What news?" I asked.

"A couple weeks ago, the National Guard shot and killed four students during an anti-war protest at Kent State," he said.

I didn't know what to say. I was dumbfounded. Kent was such a fun place. The kids at Kent State went to classes during the day and drank beer at the bars in town at night. I couldn't believe something so crazy could happen there. The yacht was a few hundred meters from the pier at an island with the steeple of an old church spiring above the trees high up on a hill. I walked over to a quiet corner of the deck, stripped off my dress-white uniform and spit-shined shoes and left them in a heap. With just my boxer shorts on, I dove over the gunwale and into the sea.

After returning to Athens that evening, I found a copy of the May 18, 1970, Newsweek magazine on a newsstand. Kent State photojournalism student John Filo's Pulitzer Prize-winning picture of 14-year-old runaway Mary Ann Vecchio bawling over the lifeless body of 20-year-old Jeffrey Miller cried out to me from the cover. I took it back to the ship, laid in my rack and nearly cried myself.

Jeff Miller, one of the war protesters, was 20 years old, the same age as me, when he was gunned down in Kent. He was 285 feet away from the skirmish line, the closest of the four dead students, when he was shot through the mouth. Allison Krause, barely 19 years old, an honor student, was 330 feet away from the Guardsman who fired the deadly bullet into her chest. William Schroeder, also 19, who ranked second in his ROTC class, had books in his arms and was not a protest participant when he was shot in the back from 382 feet away. Sandy Scheuer, another 19-year-old, an honor student who was walking to class, died after a bullet hit her in the neck from 390 feet away.

Over the next few weeks, my mom mailed me numerous Akron Beacon Journal clippings of news stories about the Kent State shootings and letters to the editor in response to them. The prevailing attitude among letter writers was that draft-dodging weekend warriors were heroes for killing four kids who were well out of stone-throwing range and that more of them should have been massacred – just for being college students.

That's when it hit me. I thought I'd gone to Vietnam for freedom. I thought I was on the front lines of the Cold War for liberty. I was proud to serve my country. But my country was infested with leeches sucking the lifeblood from freedom and maggots swarming over liberties like a pile of reeking garbage.

After Athens, the Forrestal again cruised the Ionian Sea, again laid anchor at Argostoli Bay, again without liberty call, and then arrived at the mountainous Greek island of Corfu on May 28.

When two of my shipmates and I boarded a bus out of the port for a trip along the eastern shore, they took the last unoccupied seat. I was left standing in the aisle. That didn't last long, as an elderly man gave a teenage girl seated near me a command. She immediately stood up, and the man pointed for me to sit down. After I shook my head to decline his gesture, he became more animated about what I presumed was Corfuian etiquette. I took the seat.

The bus dropped us off near a wide, sandy beach. We walked inland. An hours-long hike up a narrow, winding road to a tiny village near the top of a mountain gave us a view across the narrow strait to the distant shore of Albania. Fortunately, a small tavern populated by card-playing men enabled us to quench our thirst before we made our way back down the mountain. As we left, we encountered a procession of women, old, young and in between, returning from the fields with bales of grain strapped to their hunched backs.

Evidently, feminism was foreign to Corfu.

Back in the Ionian Sea, we participated in a joint NATO exercise called Operation Dawn Patrol, preparing for a potential naval confrontation with the Soviet Bloc. We anchored for several days in Souda Bay, Crete, another location where liberty was infeasible, or perhaps where American sailors were unwelcome.

After more than a week at sea without the pleasure of alcoholic beverages or even the sight of young women, we sailors were itching for our scheduled visit to Naples, Italy, but those plans took a sudden detour when bloody battles broke out in Jordan. Some 1,000 people were killed or wounded during the week of June 9 to 16, when Yasser Arafat's PLO forces confronted King Hussein's Jordanian army. Arriving in the eastern Mediterranean off the coast of Israel, the Forrestal's squadrons were poised to provide air coverage for the evacuation of Americans. Fortunately, the violence in Jordan eased up, at least temporarily, and we were able to make an abbreviated port call in Naples.

The Forrestal ended its Mediterranean exercises on June 29 and arrived back in Norfolk on July 13. Members of HS-11, in particular, earned special recognition for being the first helicopter antisubmarine squadron to deploy aboard an attack aircraft carrier.

Given a few days of leave, I flew home to pick up my car.

A visit to the Kent State campus with my friend Jeff Murphy just two months after the day of infamy imposed upon it by the reckless Gov. James A. Rhodes and his haplessly dispatched National Guard troops gave me an eerie sensation. Summer quarter typically was quiet, compared to the regular school year, but this one was dead silent. It was like a ghost town. No students walking to class. No classes. No lights in the dorms. No Frisbees on the commons. No blankets on Blanket Hill.

Security was high. In more ways than one. While dorm students were at home in Cleveland or Pittsburgh or Rochester for the summer, Jeff was among a small cadre of commuters who were hired for nighttime security in the classroom buildings. I accompanied him for his shift in Bowman Hall. In a dark classroom, we smoked a joint and caught up with recent events. Jeff had been right there when the skittery guardsmen squeezed their triggers and let loose with the volley of live ammunition that riddled the bodies of his fellow students and tore the soul out of our beloved university. He told me about that near-death experience. I kept mine to myself.

When his relief arrived a couple hours later, the three of us smoked another joint. Then Jeff and I went downtown for a few beers. The bars were uncannily lifeless.

Helicopter squadron connections

The naval base at Quonset Point, on the other hand, was full of life. While at sea, I was berthed with the ship's company disbursing personnel, which gave me limited exposure to the men in my squadron. In port, I worked with the land-based and squadron-attached disbursing clerks during the day and was barracked with HS-11 at night. It was an eclectic mix.

"Hey, Lange, give us a hand over here," an airman with a Tennessee drawl called me from the next cubicle in our second-floor barracks.

"What are you doing?" I asked when I saw two guys yanking one of the mattresses off of a rack.

"Open that window," Steve Powell said. "That fucking Grayson never takes a shower, and he smells like shit. Now his mattress is stinking up the whole place. So it's going out the window."

I opened the window, helped fold the mattress in two, and we squeezed it through the frame. We watched it plop onto the grass below. I wasn't around when "Stinky" Grayson returned to find his rack with nothing but bare springs. I do not know if he took a shower that night.

Commissioned in 1941, Quonset Point Naval Air Station is located on the western shore of Narragansett Bay. It played a major role in training pilots for World War II. As a deep-water port, it provided docking for several aircraft carriers over the years.

For those of us stationed there, Quonset Point met a variety of needs and desires, from a mechanic shop where we could do our own auto maintenance, to a fully stocked Navy exchange, to a bowling alley and an enlisted men's club, where local women were more than welcome to share cheap drinks with sailors in the evenings. There also was a Marine Corps club on the base, where pitchers of beer were poured at lunchtime, and the adjacent Davisville Naval Construction Battalion Center's EM club was even more accessible to female visitors. The Marines, Seabees, "airedales" and regular sailors mostly got along just fine.

As I enjoyed a few beers with a half dozen HS-11 crew mates at the Quonset Point EM club on a noisy Friday night, a comment from a group of black sailors at a nearby table caught me by surprise. "What's the brother doing hanging around a bunch of honkies over there?" one of them grumbled, his voice plenty loud enough to be heard over the jukebox.

Ed Holmes, probably the roughest customer in our squadron, black or white, lifted his 6-foot-2, athletically composed frame from his chair. Directing his index finger straight at the table of brothers, his reply was firm and steady. "I will choose my buddies any way I damn well please," he said. "If you got a problem with that, stand up, and we'll settle it right now."

None of them stood up, and none of them spoke another word in our direction.

Ed Holmes was the kind of man I would want as a friend. To my good fortune, I was the kind of man he chose as a friend as well. It was 1970, and race relations were not the best in our country. It would be naive to believe that men in the military were color blind. Even among those who fought together against a common enemy in Vietnam and those who worked side by side under mutually hazardous conditions at sea, many white men distrusted and avoided off-duty interaction with their black counterparts. For many black men, the feeling was mutual. There also were those among us who got to know each other as people with thoughtful minds and feeling hearts and soulful souls beneath skin that is the same, except for its many shades.

One day after returning to the barracks from work, I heard that an airedale who had just arrived for duty with our squadron was from near Akron. When he lugged his sea bag into the barracks an hour later, I recognized Gary Sheppard. Not only had we graduated from high school together, but we were in the same class in fourth through sixth grades at Price Elementary School. We knew each other well.

That Friday, Mitch Yudin, a guy in my cubicle, told me about a movie playing that night at the Quonset Drive-In Theater, which was in North Kingstown, not far from the naval bases. He told me it was about a rock festival that had been held at a dairy farm in upstate New York the previous summer. When I learned from Mitch that some of my favorite performers, including Jimi Hendrix, Jefferson Airplane, Canned Heat and Ten Years After, were there, I was raring to go. Gary seemed less enthused by the music but was ready for a night out, and he was 21 years old, so we were able to buy a case of beer on the way to the drive-in.

"Woodstock," the documentary movie, has been preserved in the U.S. National Film Registry by the Library of Congress, recognizing its cultural, historical or aesthetic significance. Witnessing not just the music but also the "freaky" activities among the 400,000-some peace-loving, long-haired hippies in attendance – all of it through the windshield of my 1966 Impala – was a startling cultural adventure for me. It made me wish that I'd been in rural Sullivan County, New York, in August 1969 instead of the hinterlands of Kien Phong Province, South Vietnam.

As my speedometer hit the 70 mph mark driving on Davisville Road back to the base, my eyes popped wide open when the flashers lit up on a Navy patrol vehicle parked off the berm. "Quick, throw those empty beer bottles out the window," I yelled to Mitch in the back seat. By the time I pulled over and the patrol car caught up to us, the remnants of our inebriating resource were safely in the weeds well behind us. Fortunately for me, there was no Breathalyzer, but the speeding violation resulted in my car being banished to the parking lot outside the main gate for 60 days.

Even so, the Impala convertible got a lot of use.

Overnight drives took Gary Sheppard and me back to Cuyahoga Falls on several weekends. His wife and their infant son were living with his parents on Munroe Falls Avenue, and they were especially appreciative of the visits. Their precious little boy had arrived in this world with health complications, and his dad's absence for military duty wasn't making life easy for any of them. Gary applied for a hardship discharge, which was granted several months later. Our close friendship was brief, but I appreciated it.

On one three-day, sunny summer weekend, the Impala, with the top down, took me and Mitch Yudin to Long Beach Island in New Jersey, where his high school sweetheart and several other Jersey girls had rented a cottage. I thoroughly enjoyed the wild surf, smoking weed on the beach all afternoon and rocking to a band in one of the dance clubs at night.

In October, Victor Perez, a career man from Guam who was one of the supervisors in the disbursing office and who also worked as a part-time cook in a local restaurant, treated me to my first lobster dinner for my 21st birthday. Two-and-a-half years after I enlisted in the Navy and eight months after I finished my year in Vietnam, I was old enough to vote. Absentee ballots not being readily available and 1970 not being a presidential election year, I did not exercise my democratic duty that November. In March 1971, the 26th Amendment to the U.S. Constitution was passed, lowering the voting age to 18 for all American citizens.

Many evenings were spent smoking weed, drinking beer and listening to John Lennon's "Imagine" LP with a couple guys from the disbursing office who rented a small house in Bonnet Shores, just north of Narragansett. Sometimes we'd patronize a bar near Scarborough Beach, south of Narragansett.

Other times I'd drive up to Providence with Ed Holmes and a couple other men from the squadron. We'd toke on a couple joints along the way. Guys of my complexion were in a distinct minority when we visited certain legal drinking establishments and also a couple places running under the radar after hours. Not once did anyone mention that distinction or make me feel unwelcome. People didn't tend to mess with "Coffin Ed" and "Gravedigger Jones," as two of my companions called each other in tribute to the legendary "Harlem Detective" series characters. Legal establishment or not, I arrived with the "mens."

'You are one crazy fucker'

When he wasn't working on helicopters, Max Winslow was an easy-going, slow-talking, hard-drinking, chain-smoking man. In the middle of his second four-year enlistment, he was in no hurry to get out of the Navy, but he wasn't committed to a life at sea either. The tattoo on his forearm pictured a rooster facing a cocktail glass, both of them above the slogan, "The cock that watched the cherry fall."

Max, who hailed from Midwestern farm country, had a hearty laugh and a philosophical bent. "David," he would say, using my proper name like my mom always did. "If you'd drink more gin and less beer, you wouldn't have to piss so much."

"You know, Max," I'd say. "If you smoked Viceroys, like I do, instead of Marlboros, people wouldn't bum as many cigarettes from you."

On a late Saturday morning, I accompanied Max to help a woman he knew move her furniture from one apartment to another one in a suburb south of Providence. Nancy treated us to free beer and lunch, although there's no such thing as a free lunch. After we finished by early evening, the three of us went to a different apartment complex, where one of her friends was hosting a party. Some guys from our squadron whom I normally didn't hang around with were there, and the alcohol was flowing freely.

Max and I were inside the flat talking to several of the young ladies when a loud ruckus developed outside. A girl named Betsy stormed in the door with tears on her cheeks and said her boyfriend, Jerry Mason, a sizable airedale, had given her a rough shove when she told him he had too much to drink. Shouting among the men in the yard continued, so Max went out to try to calm things down. Betsy stood by the open door. Suddenly, she backed away and screamed, "He's coming. Somebody stop him."

Being the only male still inside, I thought that somebody must be me. So I set my cigarette down in an ashtray, plopped my half-empty bottle of beer on an end table, got up from the comfortable easy chair and hurried over to the door in time to see Jerry stomping up the outdoor staircase.

Just as he reached the stoop, my 158 pounds hit him full force in the chest. It was enough to knock him off his feet and through the air, seven steps down, where he hit the sidewalk flat on his back with me on top of him. His bulky body cushioned my fall, and I wasn't feeling any pain anyway, so I went back up to finish my beer. When poor Jerry finally was able to recover his breath and pick himself up off the ground, Max informed him that he wasn't going back in the apartment, even if he wanted to.

As we drove down Route 1 after dropping Nancy off at her new apartment, Max looked over at me and broke out laughing. "David, you are one crazy fucker," he said.

"Well, Max," I said, "you must be rubbing off on me."

He laughed even harder.

If Jerry Mason remembered why his entire body was aching the next morning, he didn't say anything to me about it. We weren't that chummy anyway.

Chapter 20 | **Soviet Menace**

On Sept. 17, 1970, as the USS Intrepid (CVS-11), "The Fighting I," conducted exercises in the western Atlantic, civil war broke out in Jordan. Once again, Palestinian guerrillas, this time assisted by Soviet ally Syria, were battling the Jordanian military. For the second time in just three months, the warring Yasser Arafat and King Hussein were about to draw my ship into their Middle Eastern embroilment.

Hasty plans were made for the Intrepid to head east. Our short deployment was about to turn into an extended one. Petty Officer 1st Class John Opdyke, the disbursing supervisor assigned to Carrier Anti-Submarine Air Group 56, and I were on a mission. We were to transport the squadron pay records back to Quonset Point, prepare the upcoming payroll, pick up a supply of cash and get it back to the ship a couple days later.

So we climbed aboard a prop plane on the flight deck. We took our seats about halfway back in the compact fuselage, me on the aisle and John by the porthole. We were the only passengers. I had watched takeoffs and landings from the island, or superstructure, numerous times. I knew how the catapults jettison aircraft off the bow of the ship, much like biblical David's slingshot blasted a rock into Goliath's noggin. But watching isn't experiencing.

I sat on pins and needles as the deck crew positioned the tow bar to the shuttle and set the holdback behind the wheel. I saw the pilot in the cockpit signal the crew. The propellers roared at full throttle. I planted my spine and skull firmly against the seat back and held tight to the armrests. Wham! The aircraft shot forward with a force that quivered my lips and flapped my eyelids. Whoosh! Something flashed past my head like a cannonball. Slam! I heard it crash against the aft bulkhead. The plane dropped down from the flight deck. My stomach lurched against my ribs. Then we gained altitude and soared over the deep, blue sea. What a rush.

I looked back and saw what had been a half-gallon Thermos crushed on the deck. Smoking-hot coffee spurted through its ruptured encasement. At least cerebrospinal fluid wasn't oozing out of my skull. The pilot had neglected to secure his mid-flight energizer. He turned around to see the messy consequences of his oversight and apologetically held his palm out toward me. I gave him a thumbs up. No harm, no foul.

Five days into the uprising, Jordan's air force took the upper hand. By Sept. 24, a cease-fire was called. The "Fighting I" did another about-face and returned to port almost on schedule. I missed my chance to land on an aircraft carrier, a pinpoint-touchdown, tailhook-grabbing, stop-dead execution that I imagined would be even more breathtaking than the catapulted takeoff.

Of course, I could only imagine the skill and bravery possessed by pilots who landed fueled and armed bombers and other fighting aircraft on unforgiving flight decks as a matter of their regular duty. I could only imagine the courage of crew members on those aircraft and the sailors who loyally attended to their takeoffs and landings on those minuscule, undulating runways at sea. And I could only imagine the gallantry of men like John McCain, who not only performed that hazardous duty but also engaged in combat in the skies over North Vietnam, where he and others crashed to the earth and endured untold misery as captives of ruthless communists.

With the exception of our unprecedented deployment aboard the attack-carrier Forrestal, HS-11, proudly known as "Double One First," was part of Carrier Anti-Submarine Air Group 56. Our regular deployments were aboard the anti-submarine carrier Intrepid. In addition to HS-11, CVSG-56 included: HS-3, a sister helicopter squadron; Air Anti-Submarine Squadrons 24, 27 and 31, with Grumman S-2E Tracker fixed-wing prop planes; Attack Squadron 45, with Douglas A-4E Skyhawk jets; and Carrier Airborne Early Warning Squadron 121, with Grumman E-1B Tracer radar-equipped aircraft.

The Intrepid, an 872-foot-long carrier, was more than 100 feet shorter than the more modern Forrestal but nearly big enough for three football fields. She had an impressive history in the Pacific during World War II, when she survived a Japanese torpedo attack plus four separate kamikaze strikes. After WWII, she was converted from an attack carrier (CVA-11) to anti-submarine warfare and made three Vietnam deployments. In 1969, the Intrepid was home ported at NAS Quonset Point, where she was docked alongside the USS Wasp (CVS-18).

While the squadrons spent most of our time on station between the 1970 Mediterranean cruise and the next major deployment in April 1971, we set to sea for several shorter exercises in the interim. The one that was nearly diverted to the Middle East had included a port call in Halifax, Nova Scotia.

Gobsmacked in Bermuda Triangle

Then there was the Bermuda Triangle. Also known as the Devil's Triangle, the oceanic region has been associated with mysterious disappearances of ships and aircraft attributed to paranormal and extraterrestrial superstitions. The Bermuda Triangle is loosely delineated by Miami, Florida, Puerto Rico and Bermuda, which lies about 665 miles east of Cape Hatteras, North Carolina. Tales of the devilish triangle appear to have originated with the Dec. 5, 1945, disappearance of U.S. Navy Flight 19, with five Grumman TBM Avenger torpedo bombers and all 14 of their airmen never heard from again. A Martin PBM Mariner flying-boat aircraft with 13 crew members dispatched to search for the missing Flight 19 also disappeared.

On Oct. 12, 1970, a subtropical depression developed northeast of the Bahamas and intensified as it moved northeastward. As it skirted Bermuda on Oct. 16, it was classified as a Category 1 hurricane, which blasted the islands with 100 mph gusts and shut down transportation, schools and businesses. Continuing northeast on Oct. 17, it transitioned into an extratropical cyclone and then was upgraded to a Category 2 hurricane.

Somewhere in the Bermuda Triangle, the USS Intrepid was conducting training exercises, and the sailors had visions of sandy beaches and tropical drinks dancing in our heads.

The seas were high on a stormy evening when I joined about a dozen fellow enlisted men in the HS-11 ready room after dinner on the Intrepid's mess deck. Tony Pagano threaded film through the reels in the projector. I hoped to see some familiar scenery in "Malta Story," a British World War II film.

The 27,000-ton Intrepid listed back and forth more precipitously than a vessel of that immensity should. The angry sea sent powerful waves crashing over catwalks. Aircraft strained against tie-down cables on the flight deck and inside drenched hangar bays. The 2,500 officers and men on board hung onto racks and chairs or braced themselves against bulkheads as they lurched along passageways below decks.

A massive thud jolted the ship like a 3,000-pound torpedo. We rolled to starboard like an inverted pendulum on a gigantic cuckoo clock. Our chairs began to slide. I hopped up onto my seat and from there jumped high enough to latch onto a beam on the overhead. Several other men did the same. Clinging tight, my body swung back and forth. Gymnastically, I jackknifed at my hips and watched furniture and sailors below me crash from one bulkhead to the other. Stumbling and rumbling they went, some of them yelping in pain, all of them wide-eyed in their helplessness.

Finally, the Intrepid somehow righted itself – not likely through the intrepidity of the exalted brass at the helm who had steered us broadside into a humongous wave. The ship went back to bouncing and rolling, but at least the deck was mostly down and the overhead was mostly up. I looked around the ready room. We all looked around the ready room. I dropped down from the beam. Disheveled sailors plucked themselves from the strew of tables and chairs. Three of them limped out through the hatch under their own power and headed to sick bay, where mostly minor injuries kept corpsmen stitching cuts, icing contusions and repairing crunched bones deep into the night.

We had not encountered a storm like Typhoon Cobra, which ravaged the Navy's Pacific Fleet with 60-foot waves and sustained winds of 145 mph in December 1944. That one sent three destroyers and nearly 800 men to the bottom of the sea. The carrier USS Cowpens nearly capsized as well, and eight of its aircraft, Jeeps, tractors, crane, whaleboat and gun sponson were swept overboard.

Nevertheless, rumors ran wild on board the Intrepid. According to scuttlebutt among the enlisted men, when the big wave hit our ship broadside, we rolled within 1 degree of capsizing.

But there was no official accounting of the incident to the crew. Straight answers were not forthcoming from the Navy. We never heard what degree it was that the carrier tilted. We never knew how close we came to disappearing in the depths of the Bermuda Triangle. We never knew whose brass asses were being covered and why. It was all a big mystery.

In a mystery that haunts his family in Michigan and buddies from the Intrepid to this day, somewhere between Bermuda and our return to home port in Quonset Point, Michael E. Haley, an airman with VS-27, disappeared. No one knows where he went. As the Detroit Free Press reported in a Jan. 23, 1972, story, rumors circulated about murder, suicide and the consequences of drug use. Some anonymous sailors told the newspaper that Haley had been depressed, he hated the Navy, and he thought he saw God on an LSD trip but then concluded that it was the devil.

Thirty days after his disappearance, the Navy declared Haley a deserter. It wouldn't be that difficult to track down a 22-year-old white guy on the Main Island of Bermuda, which is a mere 14 miles long and less than a mile wide and where most of the inhabitants are of African descent. The family never could get straight answers from the Navy or the FBI about their investigations into the matter. "If he's dead or missing at sea, it's a little different than being a deserter," his mother, Mary Ann Haley, told the Free Press.

Deliberate poke in the eye

On April 16, 1971, the Intrepid and the squadrons of CVSG-56 set sail from Quonset Point for a six-month NATO deployment.

My immediate supervisor, John Opdyke, our two Filipino disbursing trainees, aka strikers, Jaime "Jimmy" Padilla and Eutiquio "B.J." Biaggio, and I made the transition from shore to sea. At about 6-foot-7 and 280 pounds, John was the largest man on board. He ducked his head every time he made his way through a door or hatch. In fact, life at sea had encouraged big John to slump his shoulders much of the time, as though he had to apologize for his size. He was a gentle giant. He and I played cribbage during most evenings at sea.

The four of us attached to the air group fit in genially with the eight-man ship's company crew in the disbursing office. Their supervisor, Petty Officer 1st Class "Rosie" Rosenbaum, a paunchy, gregarious man of mixed-race parentage, was comfortable in his African genes.

Aside from the ensign in charge, whose superior rank was well established but who maintained the usual hands-off distance from daily business, I was next in seniority behind John and Rosie. I had been a 3rd class petty officer for nearly two years and recently had passed the exam for advancement to 2nd class. I was scheduled for that promotion in August, but there was a catch. Navy regulations required a year remaining on your enlistment at the time of the advancement, and I would have just 10 months to go. There were general expectations that I would sign a short, two-month extension in order to receive the increase in salary and respect associated with the Navy rank that is equal to sergeant in other branches of the military. In my own mind, however, the sooner I became a civilian again the better, and I never did have a superiority complex.

During our comparatively brief ocean exercises between the summer of 1970 and spring of 1971, I was berthed with members of my squadron. For the next six months, though, I was assigned to a maze of four-rack units below deck in a ship's company berthing compartment. Mine was one of the top racks, which I accessed by carefully stepping on the frames of each of the three racks below. Inches above my head were several pipes of various diameters delivering heat, water, chemicals and who knows what to different sections of the ship. Those pipes were insulated with a deteriorating material that sprinkled minute specks of fiber through cracking and splitting encasements.

Prior to the mid-1970s, according to Military.com, asbestos "was considered a wondrous mineral that was used in thousands of products due to its insulation properties and the fact that it is impervious to flame: it absolutely will not burn." Prior to that time, the Navy had no concern about its potential deadly consequences for breathing human beings. I had no concerns about asbestos and knew nothing about asbestosis, asbestos cancer or malignant mesothelioma, whose latency can be as long as 20 to 50 years. Because of such consequences, asbestos essentially has been banned from use in the United States. Based on Military.com's reporting, "While veterans represent 8 percent of the nation's population, they comprise an astonishing 30 percent of all known mesothelioma deaths that have occurred in this country." I count my blessings.

A chronology of the USS Intrepid's 1971 exploits has been compiled by Steven R. Butler, who holds a Ph.D. from the University of Texas at Arlington, is an adjunct professor and prolific chronicler of history and personally experienced that deployment. As a fellow participant in "NATO antisubmarine warfare exercises in the North Atlantic Ocean, Mediterranean Sea, North Sea, Baltic Sea, and Arctic Ocean," Butler reported, our purpose was "to prevent a surprise nuclear attack upon the United States and its allies by the Soviet Union."

As history shows, our mission was accomplished. Most of us who participated in that mission had grown up with the threat of nuclear war hanging over our heads. As young men, we were on the front lines of the Cold War, not hiding under classroom desks or crouching in school hallways. On clear days, we could practically look our enemy in the eye. If we failed to stand up to the Soviet menace, we would be among the first to go down.

A few days into the Intrepid's journey across the Atlantic, we connected with a task group that included five destroyers, an oil tanker for refueling and a submarine. It wasn't long before we came under relentless Soviet surveillance.

Shortly before HS-11 returned from our previous Mediterranean deployment, Admiral Elmo R. Zumwalt Jr., at the age of 49, became the youngest chief of naval operations, effective July 1, 1970. He previously served as commander naval forces, Vietnam, where he was awarded two Navy Distinguished Service Medals for meritorious service. The significance of Zumwalt's appointment by President Nixon – as far as us lowly enlisted men were concerned, anyway – was his liberalization of Navy regulations. Among them were the authorization of beard growing and installation of beer-dispensing machines in land-based barracks, both of which I took to heart. More broadly appreciated by sailors was the sanction of civilian clothes for liberty calls. Uniformed military men during the Vietnam era were not uniformly treated with respect and appreciation by civilians at home or abroad.

We reached our first port of call, Lisbon, Portugal, on April 28. After 12 days at sea, where the vast majority of the crew abided by the Navy prohibition against shipboard alcohol consumption and, of course, where no members of the female gender could be found, the bars of Lisbon were in our cross hairs.

On our first day in port, Max Winslow, Steve Powell and I obtained three bottles of Portuguese wine and sampled them before hopping on a train to visit the picturesque coastal city of Cascais. By the time we chartered a horse-and-buggy ride into the hills overlooking the bay, we were thoroughly juiced. We were happy to share our frivolity with the buggy driver, and he was happy to help us drink our wine. Along the winding road above Cascais, we encountered a crew of linemen working on utility poles. At our direction, the driver stopped the buggy at successive poles, and we three drunken sailors took turns climbing the iron foot posts to deliver samples of "vino" to the linemen, who happily accepted our friendly gestures. What I do remember about Portugal is that the people were very welcoming.

Back at sea, the Intrepid and its squadrons participated in a NATO exercise, "Rusty Razor," along with several of our allies. Steven Butler's "Cruise Chronology" includes a report from VS-27 that our "Squadron flight crews localized opposing submarines and conducted simulated attacks." "Opposing submarines," of course, referred to the Soviets, and "simulated attacks" occurred on a two-way street.

After a brief port call in Plymouth, near the far southwest corner of England, where the English Channel meets the Atlantic, the Intrepid proceeded to engage in one of the most daring operations of the Cold War. After cruising across the North Sea and through the Skagerrak strait and Kattegat Sea off the coasts of Norway and Sweden, we entered the Baltic Sea. Word from the HS-11 administrative office was that the Intrepid was the first U.S. carrier in the Baltic since World War II. Other reports, according to Butler's research, indicated that ours was the first "warship" of any kind to do so or that we were the "first carrier to conduct flight operations in the eastern Baltic." At one point, we were within 20 miles of the Soviet coast.

It was a deliberate poke in the eye to our hated communist enemy. Soviet naval vessels were on our tail throughout the Baltic operation. On one occasion, a Soviet helicopter buzzed across our flight deck. Some of us who happened to be topside at the moment gave it a middle-finger salute. After one of our HS-11 copters flew to the island of Bornholm to pick up the U.S. ambassador to Denmark for a visit aboard the Intrepid, the Soviet Union protested that it violated some sort of treaty against military activity there.

Back to my German roots

On May 21, we pulled into the West German port of Kiel, on the southwestern shore of the Baltic. It was the first time for me to set foot in the country of my heritage. Coincidentally, my mother had planned a visit to her mother, sister, brother-in-law and two young nephews in Frankfurt at that time, so I arranged to take a leave and meet up with all of them there. I found the train station in Kiel. Several hours and about 300 miles later, I arrived at my destination, the spacious and well-accommodated home of Heinz and Gisela Friedrichs on the tree-lined Kennedyallee, just a few blocks from the Main River. That's right, the West Germans were proud to name a prominent residential street in honor of America's 35th president.

My Aunt Gisela, who had been an actress in her younger days, and Uncle Heinz, who had been a successful grand-prix driver and became an even more successful businessman, were known for their art collection and philanthropy. Gracious hosts, they happily stocked a refrigerator in my guest room with fine German bier. They treated my mom, Oma and me to dinners at exquisite restaurants, the likes of which were beyond my American family's means. They even flew the three of us to West Berlin for a three-day visit so that I could get a feel for the city where they once lived happily – before Allied bombers turned it to rubble and turned them into World War II refugees.

I also got a chance to meet Ewald Hingst, my grandfather and my mom's estranged father, who arrived by train from Hannover. He wore a toupee to cover his scarred scalp, the result of a motorcycle crash, and did his best to match my drinking expertise at a Frankfurt biergarten.

During my leave, the Intrepid set sail for the Mediterranean, passing through the English Channel and Straits of Gibraltar. There were reports that our fearless leaders nearly steered the carrier into the hazardous waters of a shipping graveyard in the channel but were warned back on course in the nick of time by rocket flares from a British ship. Official response from the Navy was that the command was "in full control of the situation," probably just as it had been several months earlier in the Bermuda Triangle.

I took a flight on the Italian airline Alitalia from Frankfurt to Naples, Italy, with a short stopover in Venice, and arrived in the port not long after the Intrepid laid anchor a few miles off the coast.

Assault with deadly weapon

As a petty officer, my military duties included a fire-control squad, which was activated for preparedness drills during general quarters while at sea but, fortunately, never was called upon to battle an actual fire. Shore-patrol assignments, on the other hand, commonly were called upon to deal with drunken sailors. Upon my arrival to the ship via an early-afternoon liberty boat, I learned that I was scheduled for shore patrol that evening. I much would have preferred a smooth transition from leave in Germany to liberty in Italy.

The boat ride back to shore was rockier than the one that had delivered me to the ship a few hours earlier. The seas were getting heavier amidst intensifying winds. The lieutenant in charge of shore patrol assigned me to duty on the pier, which I assumed would be less stressful than patrolling the drinking and whoring establishments where rowdy sailors were more apt to let loose in rectification of pent-up demands. That turned out to be a mistaken assumption. As the day turned to evening, saltwater swells thrashed against the sea wall with increasing intensity, so much so that, even before dark, the liberty-boat shuttles had to be shut down.

Some of the returning sailors, most of them in civvies, took the situation in stride and returned to nearby bars. Others, having had their fill, grumbled as they sought out spots upon which to plop their rears and rest their chins on their chests. Still others stumbled about the pier, relieved their bladders in the shadows and spewed pointless vulgarities at the shore patrol – the guys in uniform with "SP" bands on our sleeves and billy clubs on our belts – as if we were at fault for the agitating weather.

The blurred sun moved out of sight to the west, passing by Sardinia and Catalonia toward its journey across the Atlantic. Gray sky turned to black. The moon flickered in and out. Stars were hidden. A light rain was falling.

An Italian paddy wagon pulled up to the pier. Two guards opened the rear doors and ushered a cuffed but resistant man across the pavement, where they presented their prisoner to the lieutenant. The sailor had become shitfaced drunk, belligerent and abusive, according to the broken English I overheard. The local police were washing their hands of him. He was our problem now.

"Lange, get over here," the lieutenant commanded.

"Oh, great," I muttered under my breath.

"You're in charge of this man," he told me. "Keep him under control."

The Italian officers removed the cuffs and returned to their vehicle.

"How ya doin'?" I said to the guy in a feeble attempt to be reasonable. "Pretty shitty night, huh?"

"Fuck you, you little puke," he said.

I grabbed his arm gently and walked him away from the lieutenant, who was guarding the sea wall and not much else. My wobbly prisoner was 10 years my senior, a slight man, about my height but lighter by a few pounds. Holding his arm, I steadied his tottering traipse. "I got no problem with you," I said as we moved out of the expanding jam of soggy, impatient sailors. "Let's just hang out over here and be cool."

"Fuck you, you little puke," he reiterated.

A trio of tipsy sailors made their way over to us. "Hey, Ralph, you OK?" one of them asked my charge.

"Fuckin' aye I am, except for this asshole," he replied, pointing at me as he struggled to maintain his balance.

"Do you know this guy?" I asked.

"Yeah, he's supervisor of our division, a boatswain's mate first class," one of them told me.

So the damn lieutenant had put me in charge of a drunken sailor who was two ranks my senior. Under different circumstances, I could be taking orders from him or facing the consequences.

"Listen, you little pussy," Ralph, the first-class drunk, sputtered at me.

"I ain't taking any more shit from you." He reached into his trousers pocket and pulled out a single-edged razor blade. His three deck hands backed away in a hurry. He lunged at me and thrust the blade toward my torso.

I dodged the clumsy assault so nimbly that I surprised myself. I grabbed his blade-wielding right wrist with my left hand and his throat with my right hand and flung him to the pavement flat on his back. I plucked the razor blade from his grasp and tucked it away in my breast pocket. With my knee on his chest and my right hand still at his throat, I pointed my finger in his face. "Now, you listen to me, shit for brains!" I yelled. "If you give me any more trouble, I will fuck you up."

"Yes, sir!" he answered.

I let him get up. He stood at attention, as if I were a superior officer with the authority to throw his ass in the brig.

I looked over at his three wide-eyed deck hands. "You guys best move back over with the rest of the men," I said.

They did.

About an hour later, the winds and waves subsided sufficiently for the liberty boats to start running again. Accompanied by two SPs whose shifts had been extended by the weather, Petty Officer 1st Class Ralph Shitfaced took a seat on the first boat and promptly dozed off.

I told the lieutenant what had transpired and said I was willing to assist him in filing any paperwork necessary for disciplinary action. Apparently, assaulting a peace officer with a deadly weapon was not considered serious enough for the Navy to pursue such action – at least not against a lily lifer, more civilly referred to as a white career man.

Naked truths about race relations

My Navy enlistment gave me the opportunity to get to know men of various cultural and racial backgrounds. The better I got to know them, the more I realized that we have more in common as human beings than we have divisive differences.

Junius T. "Butch" Caldwell, a black guy my age from Boston who was a member of the ship's company disbursing crew, happened to be on a liberty boat with me heading for shore on our second day in Naples. He shook his head in disbelief as I recounted my experience on shore patrol the previous night. Not far from the pier, we stopped at the USO, where we discovered a common affinity for Ping-Pong. He gave me a few pointers. After that, we took a cab to the NATO base and cooled off in the outdoor swimming pool. I gave him a few pointers. Later in the day, we visited a couple bars, then bought a bottle of wine, some cheese and bread and watched shooting stars from the grassy lawn of a cathedral. We also agreed that we enjoyed smoking marijuana from time to time and would try to find some on our next liberty call.

Butch and I became fast friends, both at work and at play. We generally sat together for mess call, watched movies together in the HS-11 ready room after work and smoked cigarettes together on the fantail late in the evening. I introduced him to some of the black guys in HS-11, including Ed Holmes, who was our age, and Aaron Dean, who was a few years older and was making a career of the Navy. Butch introduced me to some of his black buddies in ship's company.

After we reached our next port stop, Cannes, home of the world-famous film festival on the French Riviera, Butch, Aaron and I headed toward the lively Boulevard de la Croisette. Rounding a corner, we encountered a couple black sailors whom I knew and a couple others that I did not know at a sidewalk cafe. They invited us to join them for a beer.

Being the only white guy in the group dawned on me when two other blacks came by and greeted their "homeys." One lifted his camera and pointed it at the group. "Ahhh," I said, beginning to stand up from my chair. "Do you want me to step aside for a minute?"

"No way, homey," Cleve Jones said. "Sit your ass down."

It seems that I was uncomfortable in the color of my skin, at least at that point in time, but my black brothers wanted me in the photo.

I got a lot more comfortable as the day wore on – probably a bit too comfortable – after consuming plenty of beer and deciding to take a walk along the beach. "Hey, you guys want to go for a swim?" I asked Butch and Aaron after we removed our shoes and felt the sand between our toes.

"Well, maybe I would, but we don't have our swimsuits with us," Aaron said.

"But this is the French Riviera. You don't need swimsuits here," I informed them, even though there had been no evidence of nude swimming in our observation of the sunbathers.

"I don't think that's a good idea," Butch said. "And there's a French cop keeping an eye on things down there."

"Aw, he don't care. I'm gonna take a dip," I said as I stripped my clothes off and began traipsing buck naked toward the gentle surf.

They both laughed, but I failed to appreciate the hilarity.

Then I heard the shrill tweet of a whistle and saw the gendarme running toward me with a beach towel. "Non, non, arreter, arreter," he yelled. "Nudite prohiber," he hollered, or something to that effect.

Butch and Aaron laughed harder and harder.

I ran toward the water, but swiftness was not inherent to my inebriety, and my zig-zagging evasion was no match for the gendarme and his beach towel, which he wrapped around my nude midsection and steered me toward my clump of clothes and a nearby dressing facility.

Butch and Aaron were nearly falling over in convulsive laughter.

I didn't spew any vulgar invectives toward the gendarme. I didn't threaten him in any way. I didn't even have a razor blade in my pocket. Well, I didn't even have any pockets with me at that point. I just followed his directive and put my clothes back on. He didn't feel a need to put me in cuffs and call for a paddy wagon.

So I joined my two friends and headed for another bar that catered to drunken sailors. They were still laughing.

My desire for a dip in the Mediterranean was answered three days out of Naples somewhere in the middle of the sea, where an announcement came over the intercom for a "swim call." Swim calls at sea are rare for any naval vessel and even more unusual for aircraft carriers, on which flight decks are nearly 60 feet above water level and hangar bays are about half that far up. Broken necks or even cracked ribs being inadvisable, diving and jumping into the sea were prohibited. So an expansive mesh rope ladder was extended down from the aircraft elevator opening in the hangar. A couple dozen members of the 2,500-man crew made the climb down and took a swim as armed Marines in a liberty boat kept watch for sharks. The climb back up was tougher than the descent, but it was worth the effort.

After anchoring off the coast of Barcelona, Spain, where I had met the USS Forrestal 16 months earlier, Butch, Aaron, Ed Holmes and I took a liberty boat into the city. According to legend, Barcelona was founded by the mythological Hercules thousands of years before the birth of Christ. The city's rich history includes Hannibal's Carthaginian invasion in the Second Punic War around 200 B.C. and conquests by the Romans around 15 B.C., the Visigoths around 500 A.D. and Charlemagne's Carolingian Empire around 800 A.D.

We intended to find some entertainment and a hotel room to spend the night amidst Barcelona's iconic architecture. Even better, we met up with two charming summer tourists – one of them an African-American coed at Stanford University, the other an African lady who spoke some English. The female companionship greatly enhanced our evening enjoyment at a dance hall with a live rock 'n' roll band, after which the six of us retired to the hotel suite with two bedrooms – a separate one for the ladies. To my knowledge, both Butch and Aaron, who was the father of two young children, were faithful to their wives back in Boston and San Diego. Ed and I did not get lucky.

Around midnight, Felicia, the Stanford student, said she was hungry and asked if anyone wanted to go out with her to find a restaurant. I did. Presumptuously perhaps, I noticed a few sailors looking our way as the fine-looking woman and I waited for a cab in the heart of the entertainment district. I enjoyed our ride in the back seat and the chicken dinners we shared at a cozy table in a late-night restaurant. We were friendly but not romantic.

Aaron and Ed headed back to the ship for their work shifts the next morning, and the African lady went her separate way. Butch and I had a second day off. Felicia joined us for a bus ride to the Plaza de Toros Monumental and an afternoon of bullfighting. It was quite the bloody spectacle. The cheering crowds that regularly filled the arena were silenced after bullfighting was banned by the Parliament of Catalonia, effective in 2012.

Back at sea, the Intrepid sailed southwest toward the Straits of Gibraltar, where we would end the Mediterranean portion of our journey. In the ready room that evening, Tony Pagano gave me a big smile. "Fine-looking lady I saw you hop in a cab with the other night. Good goin', Dave," he said.

I nodded, didn't say anything in response. I was happy to let Tony think whatever he wanted. And if he were to spread a rumor about me hitting it off with a beautiful black woman, I wouldn't mind one bit.

Carrying my tray with two fried eggs, over easy, three strips of bacon, a slice of toast and an orange across the mess deck the next morning, my eyes were opened to a different light. "Nigger lover," the words came from behind me in a deep, throaty voice slightly above a whisper. I spun around. My eyes surveyed the tables between me and the chow line. I saw a number of white guys dispersed among those tables, some sitting silently alone, others eating breakfast with shipmates. I couldn't have been the only one to hear it, but nobody looked my way. I glared from table to table. Still, no one looked my way. Slowly, I turned away. At a table in the far corner, I sat down across from Butch, the man who had become my closest friend on the Intrepid, a man who happened to be black.

My head was spinning, shaking a good night's sleep out of my groggy cerebrum. I grew up in a blue-collar, lily-white suburb. I knew the N-word. It was slurred aimlessly like spittle from the mouths of tough-talking kids and adolescents in my neighborhood of cheap tract houses. We didn't know any black people and didn't care what they thought of the word. But childhood ignorance was behind me. It was just one man among 2,500 who uttered that racist term for me to hear, but there surely were others who shared his hateful sentiment. It didn't hurt me. I had progressed to appreciate and enjoy the friendship of people because of who they were, not because of their pigmentation.

I took offense to the slur, not because it was directed at me but because it was directed at people I cared about, people who cared about me. I stewed about it. I clenched my teeth even as I nibbled the soft egg whites and the yolk-soaked toast. But I didn't speak a word of it to Butch. Nothing good would have come from that.

Evil eyes from both sides

Naval exercises in the North Atlantic and North Sea during July were rewarded with weeklong port calls in Hamburg, Germany, and Copenhagen, Denmark, both of which were highlighted by generous supplies of marijuana and hashish, some of it opiated for even greater highs. An early itinerary had included a visit to Amsterdam, Holland, where such pleasures were said to be even more prolific, but it was canceled, we were told, for our own protection.

Little known to the crew, our Copenhagen visit caused a bit of a stink due to Denmark's adoption of a policy three years earlier that prohibited nuclear weapons in its ports. Although we were in clear violation of that treaty, the Danish government, no doubt aware of the Soviet menace the free world was up against, pretended that all the bombs we carried were of the conventional variety.

Inspections aboard ship were few and far between and more for show in foreign ports than to effectuate uniform protocol. Nonetheless, my shoes were shined, my dress whites were pressed, and my three medals were in order above my heart. I was one of the few members of my squadron – actually one of the few sailors on the entire ship – to display the Vietnam Service Medal and Republic of Vietnam Campaign Medal on my chest.

So it did not concern me when a lieutenant commander with a chest full of medals but none of them indicating service in a combat zone stopped and gave mine a long, hard look. Officers of such rank and longevity, for whatever reason, routinely are rewarded with much greater medallic distinction than their enlisted counterparts, but maybe, I surmised, there was some envy over my Vietnam service. Then he glowered at my untrimmed, full beard, so maybe, I suspected, he saw the rebel in me. Vietnam veteran plus long beard equals pot smoker, right? He looked straight in my eyes. He wouldn't forget my face. Finally, he moved on to the next man in the inspection lineup and then the next and the next in rapid succession.

Somewhere in the North Sea en route to Greenock, Scotland, in the light of day on July 30, one of our SH-3D helicopters, returning from routine submarine surveillance, missed the flight deck and plunged into the sea. I grabbed my 35 mm Canon camera and hurried up to a starboard catwalk. I pressed the shutter button as one of the liberty boats was dropped to the water and rescued the crew just before the chopper sank below the surface. One of the Soviet ships was taking in the action from the distance. I flipped the communists the bird, hoping I was in focus of a telescopic lens.

I pictured the enemies of liberty, the chokers of democracy reveling over our despair, probably wishing that the helicopter had slammed into the flight deck instead, craving a repeat of the 1967 USS Forrestal conflagration.

More than 45 years later, they are called Russians instead of Soviets.

But the Kremlin remains emboweled with authoritarians who poison the roots of our democracy from afar and assassinate freedom fighters up close and personal on the streets of Moscow. Meanwhile, autocratic connivers who call themselves Americans embrace that oligarchic calumny, label facts as fakery, drift in their hallucinatory swamp of mendacity and relentlessly excoriate the Fourth Estate's search for truth.

Dazzling psychedelic side trip

In early August, the Intrepid pulled into port at Greenock, Scotland, where Butch Caldwell, Aaron Dean and I took a bus to Glasgow, the country's largest city. Wandering along downtown streets, we encountered a group of other guys from the ship. One of them, Joel Randall, a hippy type from California, had received a packet of treats from home. He pulled a sheet of blotter paper from his signature leather handbag and told us the little imprints on its surface were tabs of Orange Sunshine.

Of course, I had heard plenty about LSD, or lysergic acid diethylamide, and had read accounts of psychedelic experiences. Its use had been advocated by the likes of academic Timothy Leary, "Brave New World" author Aldous Huxley and "One Flew Over the Cuckoo's Nest" author Ken Kesey and through the music of the Grateful Dead and Jefferson Airplane, among others. I knew Orange Sunshine was a close relative of LSD. It was known as the highest-quality form of acid. But I had not yet taken an acid trip.

As a few of my shipmates eagerly accepted the Californian's invitation, I figured, what the hell. It was just a blot on a slip of paper. I decided to give it a try. It melted in my mouth.

Writer Michael Barron, in a November 2015 article for Vice Media, publisher of a "politically incorrect" pop-culture magazine in Montreal, covering the documentary film "The Sunshine Makers" and "The Long, Strange Trip of the Chemists Behind the Legendary LSD 'Orange Sunshine,'" had this to say: "Everyone who has taken LSD remembers their first time. It's as pivotal as losing your virginity – the walls of the mind are broken open, Humpty Dumpty-style, and cannot be put back together again."

At the peak of his first LSD trip, taken on his 21st birthday, Barron recounted, "I began to feel the menacing gaze of objects as they oozed and dripped around me. I glimpsed into a mirror and saw a lost soul: my own. 'I need to be reborn,' I kept saying over and over, like a mantra." Acid, he said, prompted him to go back to college and "made me want to devote myself to my life."

On the other hand, Nicholas Sand and Tim Scully, the chemists who developed Orange Sunshine, devoted their lives to LSD. "We thought LSD was going to change the world," Sand said in "The Sunshine Makers." "By opening people's minds, everyone would experience such a sense of love as to bring about world peace."

I can't vouch for either point of view. My first encounter with LSD was memorable, for sure, but it didn't change my life, and any sense of love and peace I got from it was fleeting.

After separating from the other group of sailors, each of us heading for trips into our own minds or souls or whatever, Aaron, Butch and I continued our Glasgow wandering until we came upon a brick building with Marvin Gaye's "Heard it Through the Grapevine" blasting through the front door. It was a private dance-and-drinking club, a muscular black bouncer with a Scottish brogue informed us, but we could purchase one-day memberships for a couple pounds.

Inside, I was somewhat surprised to see such a racially mixed crowd in the heart of Scotland. The three of us were pleased to find three empty chairs at a table occupied by three young black women, even more so when they welcomed us to join them. I soon discovered, perhaps through insight instilled by the LSD, that I was a fantastic dancer with incomparable energy. I was convinced by the smiles and moves of one of those three young black women that she recognized that talent within me.

It took a visit to a urinal in the men's room for me to realize my insight truly had become extraordinary. For a while, it seemed that my bladder had been filled to capacity with Scottish ale, even though my consumption of the beverage was unremarkable. After the second or third man had come and gone from the urinal next to mine, I looked down and was dazzled by the sight of a technicolored geyser, the origin of which was way more impressive than the Neapolitan Fountain of Neptune. After the fourth or fifth man had come and gone from the urinal next to mine, I began to wonder whether my amazing fountain would ever end. So I reached down to touch it. My geyser vanished. My fingers were dry. LSD had given me an exotic mirage.

The band was playing "Smiling Faces Sometimes," a new Temptations tune, when I returned to the dance floor. My body was ready to shake, rattle and roll all night long. But eventually, Butch pointed out that the last bus back to Greenock wouldn't be burning the midnight oil. So we returned to the streets of Glasgow in search of the bus station.

As we turned the corner, I saw a police car with its lights flashing at the curb a block ahead. "Uh, maybe we should go the other way," I said.

"Don't be paranoid," Aaron told me. "We got nothing to worry about."

We kept walking. When we passed the police car with its lights still flashing, I looked in the open window and saw two uniformed officers giving me the eye. We turned another corner. Up ahead, sitting at the curb was another police car with its lights flashing. "I don't like this," I said.

"Don't worry, we'll be past him in a minute," Butch said. "We aren't doing anything wrong."

Again, we walked past the police car with flashing lights. Again, two uniformed officers sitting inside looked at me. We turned the corner. There it was again, a police car waiting for us with its lights flashing. "Something's going on here," I said. "There's too many of them."

"What are you talking about, too many what?" Aaron said.

"Too many cops all over the place," I answered. "They're out to get us."

"Get a grip, Dave, you're freaking out on the acid," Butch said. "There's just one cop, and he's writing a ticket for the guy that he pulled over. Don't stare at him. We're passing him now. He doesn't care about us."

We found the bus station and made it back to the ship.

We met Hal Preston on the gangplank. Hal, who had been with the other group of sailors to share in Joel Randall's Orange Sunshine distribution, invited us down to the office where he edited the Intrepid's monthly publication, the Achiever. Hal, a well-educated and thought-provoking black man, engaged us in conversation about our psychedelic experiences of that night and the insight it had given us about peace and war, militancy and civility, love and hate, equality and inequity and other matters.

He told us he was planning a section on poetry for the upcoming September edition of the Achiever and suggested that we might want to contribute to it. I was no poet, didn't even care to read poetry, but the creation of a poem swept across my sensory-heightened mind. It was about brass, the deadly brass that sends leaden projectiles into bloody foreheads, the brass that commands men to pull their triggers and looks down upon them with privileged contempt. Yes, I would put my thoughts on paper.

The brass had other notions

Fresh out of port in Scotland on Aug. 12, the Intrepid was invaded by two Soviet bombers roaring dangerously close to our flight deck. A pair of our Skyhawk jets were hot on their asses. It was a brassy message from our bitter enemy in the ongoing Cold War. Cruising north, we headed for NATO exercises above the Arctic Circle in the Norwegian Sea and Arctic Ocean. It was a reminder that we were not alone in that war and that our allies – including the navies of the United Kingdom, the Netherlands, Portugal, France, Belgium and West Germany – had our backs. It takes astounding ignorance by 21st-century American leadership to twist history around, turning allegiance into rivalry and responding to antagonism with genuflection.

Our voyage into the "Realm of the Arctic Circle" was ceremoniously recognized with "Bluenose" certification by the "Order of the Polar Bear," a naval tradition that dates back to the early 19th century. "I, Boreas Rex, Ruler of the North Wind and Sovereign of all the Frozen Reaches it touches, do hereby declare this warm blooded Neophyte to my Royal Domain to be a True and Trusty Brine Encrusted Bluenose," the certificate states. "Be it known: That by virtue of the power invested in me I do hereby command all my subjects to show due honor and respect to him wherever he may be."

A port call in Portsmouth, England, in early September, enabled me to join Max Winslow and Steve Powell for a two-day visit to London, where we pretended to be tourists.

A couple weeks later, the Intrepid pulled into port at Bergen, Norway, directly east of the Shetland Islands. The city's local swim team challenged the ship to a competition. A junior officer who had swum somewhere at the collegiate level and was called upon to organize a squad asked me to take part. I agreed to swim the 100-meter breaststroke. We got in the pool for one practice the day before the meet. Although the Bergen team had a few good swimmers, including one guy who was hyped as a likely Olympian, my old high school Black Tigers would have won the contest going away. As it turned out, a ragtag bunch of hard-drinking, tobacco-puffing, out-of-shape sailors was no match for the Norwegians, who took first and second place in every event – except for one. In a close race, I placed second in the breast, which gave my team at least something to cheer about.

Another NATO exercise in the Norwegian Sea preceded our return journey across the North Atlantic toward our home port in Rhode Island.

My poem, entitled "Brass," was published in the Achiever:

> *The bright brass reflected the rays of the sun unnaturally.*
> *Sending the golden streams of light in multitudinous directions.*
> *Some being caused to intersect by imperfections in the form.*
> *Now slowly becoming smothered by the surrounding dust.*
> *The brass shell had performed its murderous duties well.*
> *And its leaden projectile was buried deep within the bloody*
> > *forehead of my dead friend.*

Close friendships with my shipmates. "Bluenose" award. Lone "star" on the Intrepid swim team. Published poet. Sailing home to the USA. I had a lot to be cheerful about. But the brass had other notions.

Chapter 21 | **Busted**

Alone at my desk in the Intrepid's disbursing compartment, I was wearing my work dungarees. It was late morning, Oct. 15, 1971, one day after my 22nd birthday. The ship was afloat near the mouth of Narragansett Bay, waiting for clearance under the Newport Bridge.

I held the world's two deadliest drugs in my hands.

I took a drag on a Viceroy cigarette. Based on analyses by the World Health Organization, the Centers for Disease Control and Prevention and other objective resources, some 6 million people on Earth die annually from tobacco use and exposure to its smoke. I loosened the cap on a fifth of Ronrico 151-proof Puerto Rican rum, lifted the bottle to my lips and took a swig. Alcohol is responsible for nearly 88,000 deaths annually in the United States.

Those were the drugs of choice in the United States Navy, which provided them in ample supplies at below-market prices for its members. Most of us were hooked on one or the other or both.

Tobacco consumption occurred just about everywhere on the ship. Sailors smoked on the mess decks, in berthing compartments, on the fantail, in ready rooms and in toilet stalls. The flight deck and hangar bays were exceptions. A spark from a flung cigarette butt and a dribble of air-craft fuel could be an explosive combination.

Alcohol was forbidden at sea but encouraged just about everywhere else in the Navy. It was cheap in the enlisted men's clubs and cheaper in the Navy Exchange. Beer was distributed from vending machines in our HS-11 barracks in Quonset Point. It flowed freely for my pay team at advanced tactical support bases around the Parrot's Beak in Vietnam. Drunkenness was abetted with free liquor at naval company parties, from Saigon to Athens and probably the mythical base in Bumfuhk, Egypt, too.

Sitting in front of me on my desk were four bottles of booze I had just purchased duty free through the Navy for my happy return to the continental United States. Hell, that return was running a little late, and I deserved a little belated birthday celebration, didn't I?

When I stepped out of the office to visit the head, I was in for a rude awakening. Authoritatively stomping toward me down the passageway, attired smartly in his dress blues with a copious display of ribbons on his chest was the lieutenant commander who had given me a lingering evil eye during inspection a couple months earlier. I stood at attention along the bulkhead.

"What are you doing in your dungarees, sailor?" he demanded of me. "Dress blues are the order of the day as we head into port."

"Aye, aye, sir," I replied. "I'm going down right now to get changed." I turned to walk toward my berthing compartment.

"Hold it right there, sailor," he said. "You're not going anywhere."

He flagged down a couple noncommissioned officers and ordered them to hold me at bay while he summoned security. The lieutenant commander returned with two men who accompanied me to retrieve the packed sea bag from my rack. I was commanded to unlock it, and they proceeded to inspect my personal belongings, piece by piece.

The Fourth Amendment does not apply to certain citizens, members of the military, who supposedly fight for fellow Americans' rights, such as the one about being "secure in their persons, houses, papers, and effects, against unreasonable searches and seizures."

The searching and seizing proceeded through carefully folded uni-forms, civilian clothes, socks, skivvies, caps, belts, jackets and various other personal effects until the seekers reached the bottom of my sea bag. Lo and behold, one of them declared, "Aha!" In front of my face, he dangled the little hash pipe I had acquired for a few deutsche marks in Hamburg, Germany. I was escorted down to sick bay, where blood was extracted from my arm, again without benefit of the Fourth Amendment.

The pipe had been used once or twice. The flexible plastic stem was untarnished. The bowl was clean as a whistle. The only drugs I had in my possession were nicotine-laced tobacco and high-alcohol-content rum. Nevertheless, the shabby treatment being inflicted on me at the order of a spiteful senior officer for reasons beyond my comprehension led me to believe I soon would be slammed in the brig like a common thief or savage rapist.

During the unreasonable search and seizure and my prolonged detention, the ship made its way up the bay to Quonset Point and was tied to the pier. Members of the crew and squadrons were reconnecting with loved ones and connecting with extracurricular activities in the land of the free.

A duty officer arrived at sick bay with some welcome news. My mother and father and two youngest sisters were waiting for me topside. The commander had sent down instructions for my release.

I had written home with information about our scheduled return to port and an invitation for families to meet the ship. I hadn't received a reply and didn't know whether they were coming. I could have been happier to see them. They must have sensed something was amiss, but a fathomable explanation of my unfathomable situation would have to wait for another day. They had left home before sunrise. My dad had driven 11 hours in my Chevy Impala across Pennsylvania, over the lower Hudson Valley of New York and up the Connecticut coast to reach Rhode Island.

Under normal circumstances, I could have treated them to a personal tour of the aircraft carrier – up to the bridge, across the flight deck, along the catwalks, down the ladders, inside my workstation. "There's my rack, the fourth one up, right below those crumbly pipes," I could have told them as we visited the berthing compartment. But I just wanted to get the hell out of there. We stopped for some fast food along Route 1, then I hopped in the driver's seat for the return trip to Ohio.

Along Interstate 95, past Westerly, Rhode Island, and Mystic, Connecticut, I considered never going back and plotted my escape from it all. Along Route 34 following the Housatonic River, I wondered why that son of a bitch lieutenant commander was out to fuck up my life. Down Route 209 through the Poconos, my mind concluded that the evil conspiracy against me should not go unpunished. On the long ride westward on Interstate 80, I envisioned a scenario by which I would acquire a Saturday night special in Lower Akron, take it back to Quonset Point, follow my contemptuous antagonist from the ship to his fancy officer quarters somewhere off base, fire a couple rounds into his cranium and calmly watch his bloody brains flop onto the pavement. If only I could get away with it, I thought.

My dad was sitting in the front passenger seat. The man who fought for his adopted country against the country of his birth in World War II and who suffered painful consequences for the rest of his life. The man who spent so many of his waking hours on the clattering, fuming, sweltering factory floor to pay the mortgage and grocery bills. The man who coached my baseball team and cheered me on at swim meets. The man who took us to church on Sunday. He was 52 years old. I saw sadness in his eyes. I glanced in the mirror. I saw cute little Wendy, the girl who loved it when I pulled her sled up the frozen creek behind the house on Treeside Drive, and blond-haired Tammy, who giggled when I let her touch my beard. They were huddled with our loving mother in the back seat. They had traveled 600 miles to meet my ship. There I was, letting my parents down again. How much more disappointment could I heap upon them?

So I didn't take off for Canada or Mexico, I didn't buy a gun, and I didn't blow the lieutenant commander's fucking brains out, although he surely deserved it. Two days later I drove my Impala back to Quonset Point and faced the music.

I was directed to an office in the administration building, where uniformed bureaucrats issue life-altering verdicts against peons like me. There was no reading of Miranda rights, as affirmed by the U.S. Supreme Court's 1966 interpretation of the Fifth Amendment, no provision for "the assistance of counsel" supposedly guaranteed by the Sixth Amendment. Just a hostile interrogation by two officers who were bound and determined to establish my guilt in the heinous criminal activity of smoking a little marijuana and hashish. They had undeniable proof, they told me, a hash pipe seized from the bottom of my personal belongings and blood seized from my veins, both without my consent.

They knew I was guilty, they said, and things would go better for me if I just fessed up. If so, I would receive a discharge under honorable conditions. But, if I denied the undeniable, things could get pretty nasty. If my use of those wicked drugs was just "experimental" and if I'd pledge to quit smoking them, they said – an acknowledgement that the government's incessant preaching about the addiction of marijuana was a damn lie – they might even let me complete the final eight months of my four-year enlistment.

The whole thing was beyond my belief. My introduction to the evil weed came in Vietnam when I was 19 years old. The reason I was in Vietnam was that I volunteered to go to Vietnam. The reason I volunteered for Vietnam was that I believed it was the honorable thing to do for my country. The reason I believed that was that the political leaders of my country were feeding us a crock of shit. They lied about fighting for freedom and democracy for the Vietnamese people. They lied about winning the war. They lied about marijuana.

And now these military bureaucrats who had never collected one red cent of combat pay or even sea-duty pay were lying straight to my face. There wasn't any evidence in that hash pipe. I hadn't smoked any weed in at least a week, so any remnants of tetrahydrocannabinol were long gone from my bloodstream. But what did I know?

To hell with it, I decided. Sure, I smoke a little grass and a little hash, I told them. It makes me feel good. It calms my nerves. It gives me a sense of humor about the petty bullshit excreted down the chain of command. I could quit toking anytime I felt like it, I said, but I wasn't inclined to do so. I'll take that Honorable Discharge and be on my way, thank you very much.

Well, after I agreed to their conditions, I realized that wasn't exactly what they intended. I was being recommended for a General Discharge under honorable conditions, which is a whole different thing from an Honorable Discharge. My 22-year-old brain was bedazzled by duplicity swirling around me. I signed the agreement. The ultimate blame lay with my own naivete.

According to the agreement, "I understand a general discharge may deprive me of certain Veterans' benefits based upon my current period of active service and I may expect to encounter prejudice in civilian life ..." I might have read it before I signed it, but, in my state of mind, I didn't fully digest it. In the final analysis, it probably didn't matter. The powers that be decided that, after nearly 3 1/2 years of performing my military duties in an exceptional manner, sometimes under hazardous conditions, I was being discharged "by reason of unfitness involving drug abuse."

I was deemed unfit for military service because I smoked a little pot, which never interfered with my military duties and never caused me to initiate acts of violence. But good old Petty Officer 1st Class Ralph Shit-faced, who had attempted to slice me up with a razor blade while I was on shore patrol back in Naples, well, he was perfectly fit for a Navy career.

Furthermore, the agreement, which I signed, falsely stated that "My military lawyer counsel has fully advised me of the meaning and effect of this agreement ..." If any legal advice had been provided to me, it was not done by anyone representing my interests.

In fact, when I did meet with Lt. Stephen T. Refsell, of the Judge Advocate General's Corps, he expressed shock over my treatment and told me he believed an appeal to the chief of naval personnel would get me the Honorable Discharge that I deserved. "I was very surprised that DK3 Lange received a general discharge. His service record is the best I have ever seen," he wrote, noting that he had been involved in some 40 administrative discharge proceedings.

"I found DK3 Lange to be a very honest person," Refsell said of his meetings with me. "Even though he knew he could lie about the possibility of future use of drugs and fall squarely within the 'experimenter' classification, he simply could not bring himself to falsify a sworn statement. With so much dishonesty around today, I find it difficult to accept the fact that an honest but self-injuring person cannot be treated with more discretion."

As a matter of fact, my most recent performance evaluation, signed by Cmdr. R.J. Switzer, HS-11 executive officer, stated, "Lange has shown superior knowledge in his work and much concern for the upkeep of his roll. ... Nothing can be said against Lange's military behavior. His moral character is impeccable ... He promotes a fine example of the highest Navy traditions."

Hell, yes, I'm a "very honest person." Of course, my "moral character is impeccable." I'm an Eagle Scout, damn it! "Once an Eagle Scout, always an Eagle Scout." I had taken the Boy Scout Oath to "do my best ... to do my duty to God and my country ..."

Of course, I also had taken an oath of military enlistment, and I did indeed "solemnly swear that I will support and defend the Constitution of the United States against all enemies, foreign and domestic," which I did do. But, by smoking weed, maybe I failed to "obey the orders of the President of the United States ..." That president happened to be Richard M. Nixon – you know, the one who had concluded in 1968 that "there's no way to win the war" but sent 21,000 more Americans to die in Vietnam anyway.

Lt. Refsell went on to list several previous cases in which other sailors in similar situations were either granted Honorable Discharges or even retained in the Navy.

For some reason, I was special. For some reason, my superior knowledge and impeccable moral character didn't mean crap. Somebody was out to screw with my life, and his influence overrode Refsell's appeal.

Processing of my discharge would take several weeks.

Things could be worse

Butch Caldwell, my buddy from the Intrepid, invited me to join him for the weekend in Mattapan, a largely African-American section of Boston where he and his wife rented a high-rise apartment. As we shared a joint on the drive up Interstate 95, I told him about my situation. He was sorry to hear that I'd be leaving the Navy under those circumstances and said he hoped we could stay in touch.

Butch had some worse news. "Cleve Jones is dead," he said.

That hit like a ton of bricks. "How could that be?" I said. "We just saw him a couple days before we got back. He was fine."

"He OD'd on smack the same night that the ship got into port," Butch said. "I couldn't believe it either. Heroin is a killer. I thought we all knew that."

I was feeling sorry for myself. But Cleve was dead.

Based on the Drug Enforcement Administration's listing of Schedule I drugs, the federal government couldn't tell the difference between marijuana and heroin then – and it still couldn't in 2018. Based on annual reports by the CDC, the number of Americans dying from marijuana overdoses has been consistent. That number is zero. None. Zilch. The CDC reported nearly 13,000 heroin overdose deaths in 2015.

Even in the 1960s, we had been propagandized through drug "education" that smoking marijuana could cause insanity, criminality and addiction. Those of us who tried it knew that was a lie, so what other falsehoods about drugs were being promulgated by the same government that was officially subjecting me to prejudicial treatment in my civilian life? Did Cleve Jones figure the hazards of heroin use were just another lie?

When my generation began laughing at the 1939 propaganda film "Reefer Madness," an absurd story about manslaughter, suicide, attempted rape and hallucinations, the government altered its mind-blowing story. Well, maybe marijuana didn't cause insanity and maybe it wasn't physically addictive, the fear mongers begrudgingly acknowledged, but they insisted it was a gateway drug or stepping stone to cocaine, peyote and heroin.

You know, like sucking on nipples is a gateway to sucking on nicotine sticks and sipping caffeinated cola is a stepping stone to alcoholism.

Butch and I stopped at a corner store to stock up on beer and smokes.

During the Intrepid cruise, two of my pals in HS-11, Mitch Yudin and Steve Sowell, and I were planning to live off base when we returned to Rhode Island. We found the perfect place, a small, three-bedroom house just a couple blocks from the sound near Scarborough Beach. But, when they heard I'd been busted, they asked me to move out. I couldn't blame them. Living with a known pot smoker like me could cast suspicions upon my cronies.

Ed Holmes, Aaron Dean and a new kid in the squadron whom they dubbed "Poop Butt" welcomed me to take an empty rack in their cubicle.

Ed and Aaron suggested that a first class petty officer in HS-11's personnel office had some legal knowledge and that he might be able to help me out. So, on a Saturday afternoon, we visited Roy Cummings at his off-base Navy apartment.

Roy looked over the paperwork I had foolishly signed and asked me a few questions. "Essentially, you have waived your right to a review by the Administrative Discharge Board," he told me, "and, frankly, I wouldn't be too optimistic about the JAG officer's request for reconsideration by the chief of naval personnel."

"So, I'm SOL, huh?" I said.

"Well, as you know, smoking weed is no big deal, but it's still against the law, and the government is determined to punish people who get caught," Roy said. "A lot of our brothers are sitting in prison for it."

I was still feeling sorry for myself. But, as I sat in the apartment with five black friends, I knew things could be worse. I knew that the pure luck of my birth to white parents had endowed me with certain privileges that they had never known in a society where people are judged by the color of their skin. I also knew how lucky I was to have friends who cared.

"What I can do," Roy said, "is I'll write up an argument about your civil rights being denied. They didn't have probable cause to search your sea bag. They lied to you about evidence that didn't exist. You should have had legal counsel advising you against self-incrimination. The Navy might be able to pull that kind of crap, but there are laws in the civilian world.

"After you get discharged, you'll need to take all your paperwork and what I'm gonna write for you to the American Civil Liberties Union. They have lawyers who specialize in fighting for people's rights."

As Roy pounded the keys on his typewriter at the kitchen table, I joined my friends in front of the TV in the living room. We sipped on gin-and-tonics, smoked cigarettes and watched a movie called "Brian's Song." It's a true story about the friendship that developed between two running backs with the Chicago Bears, of the National Football League. One of them, Gayle Sayers, a black man, went on to stardom and enshrinement in the Pro Football Hall of Fame in Canton, Ohio. His good friend Brian Piccolo, a white man, had flashes of brilliance on the gridiron before terminal cancer began to sap his strength.

The movie won accolades for its depiction of the first interracial roommates in the NFL and the affection that grew between them. In accepting the 1970 George S. Halas Most Courageous Player Award, Sayers told the crowd that it was going to the wrong person. "I love Brian Piccolo, and I'd like all of you to love him, too," he said. "And tonight, when you hit your knees, please ask God to love him."

It was a real tear-jerker. I stopped feeling sorry for myself. I had real friends, and that meant everything to me.

My most loyal friend

My most loyal friend of all had earned his Honorable Discharge from the Navy in July, just a few months before my General Discharge under honorable conditions was in process. I had kept in touch with Keith Ball, the guy from Massachusetts who befriended me in disbursing school nearly three years earlier. He and his wife, JoAnn, were back in Shelburne Falls, renting an upstairs apartment not far down the street from his parents' house.

"You should come up for the weekend," Keith said when I reached him by phone.

My discharge was going to take a few weeks, so I continued to work in the disbursing office as if nothing was out of the ordinary. I'd go to lunch each day with a couple friends from the office, Jim Tompkins, from Newburg, New York, on the west bank of the Hudson River, and Bruce Crenshaw, from Bangor, Maine, on the west bank of the Penobscot River. Sometimes we'd stop in the Marine Corps EM club for a pitcher of beer. We'd frequent the Navy EM club and local bars or take a drive over to Newport on some evenings.

After work on Friday, I hopped in my Chevy Impala, planted my foot on the accelerator and drove north through Providence, up Route 146 into Worcester, Massachusetts, and then on the curving, two-lane Route 122 to the Mohawk Trail. Arriving in Shelburne Falls after the three-hour drive, I carried my weekend suitcase and a bottle of 151 rum up the outside staircase to Keith's apartment.

We had only known each other for a few months back in A school, but we were like old buddies. We reminisced on the good times we had then and caught up with our current lives. Keith had gotten a job in sales with a local company. I still had my job in the Navy, but it wouldn't be for much longer, I said, because I was getting the boot for smoking pot. "No shit," he said. "You might be able to find a job up here then."

JoAnn's older brother, Bill, and his wife, Ruth, stopped over. We all had a couple rum-and-Cokes before we went out for more drinks, music on the jukebox and hardy partying at the Charlemont Inn.

As I prepared for my return trip to Rhode Island Sunday afternoon, Keith and JoAnn told me I had an open invitation to visit and stay in their extra bedroom anytime.

Back in the office Monday morning, John Opdyke, my immediate supervisor, who remained unaware of my disciplinary circumstances, agreed to my request for some extra time off that coming Thursday afternoon and all day Friday.

When I arrived in the driveway at Keith's apartment Thursday and grabbed my suitcase from the backseat, I was confronted by Mr. Harris, the elderly landlord who lived with his wife on the lower floor. "You are not welcome here," he said, jabbing his finger at me. "You need to leave."

"What do you mean?" I asked. "What did I do?"

"You know what you did," Harris said.

I had no idea. Harris went back inside. I planted my rear on the hood of my car and considered my options: either drive back to Rhode Island or find somewhere else to stay.

JoAnn came down from their apartment. "I just called Keith at work and told him that Harris won't let you come up to our apartment," she said. "He'll be home in a few minutes."

When Keith pulled in the driveway and jumped out of his car, he said, "What the hell's going on?"

As I began to explain that I had no idea what the hell was going on, Harris came back outside. "He's not welcome here," he said, wagging his finger at me again as if I were some little snot throwing stones at his bedroom window.

"Well, maybe I could stay at Bill and Ruth's place for the weekend," I said to Keith.

"No, Dave," he said. "You'll stay with JoAnn and me. We'll find us another place to live."

"You can't do that, Keith," I told him. "Where would you go? You'd have to move all your stuff out of here. I'm OK. I'll go over to Bill and Ruth's. We'll get together in Charlemont tonight."

"Nope," he said. "You're my friend. We don't have to put up with Harris' crap."

So we got in my car and drove down the street to his parents' house. "I'm sorry, Keith," I said. "I don't know what I did. I don't want to cause you all this hassle."

"Hey, we're buddies, man," Keith said. "That old fart Harris is getting to be a pain in the ass. He probably saw your long beard and just figured you're some kind of hippie."

Keith made a few phone calls and learned that an upstairs apartment was available in Colrain. We took the drive a few miles up Route 112, near the Vermont state line, to check the place out. The owners, a young couple, lived downstairs. My beard didn't bother them a bit. The rent was about the same as Harris' apartment. "We'll take it," Keith said.

With a borrowed pickup truck, Keith's dad, Elwin, and his father-in-law, Fred Urban, arrived to assist with the move. Old man Harris wouldn't even let me inside to help lug the furniture downstairs.

"What in the heck is wrong with you?" Elwin asked of the old neighbor he had known for years. "You can't let him help us load up?"

"He's not welcome here," Harris reiterated.

"Why not? He's Keith's friend from the Navy. What did he do?" Elwin persisted.

"He knows what he did," Harris insisted.

Elwin looked at me.

I shrugged and held my hands up. I had no clue.

"Unbelievable!" Elwin said, looking at Harris.

The crotchety old landlord turned around and went back into his house.

I helped load and unload the truck and hoist the furniture upstairs in Colrain.

I made the drive from Quonset Point to Colrain each Friday in November. Along with Keith and JoAnn and Bill and Ruth, I became a regular at the Charlemont Inn.

On a Saturday, Keith was relaxing in my passenger seat as I drove to pick up some supplies in Greenfield. The car in front of us was slowly chugging uphill on Route 2, which is a two-lane highway with limited sight distance along the Pocumtuck Ridge. I stomped the pedal to the metal, and the Chevy roared across the double yellow lines.

"What the hell are you doing, Dave?" Keith hollered as he grabbed ahold of the dashboard. "Holy shit!"

A van approached us from around the bend. The driver laid on his horn.

I scooted my Chevy to the right, closing in on the vehicle driven by the slowpoke who was causing the whole thing.

The van driver swerved to his right as well. His tires rolled smoothly along the edge of the berm. All the while, he held his hand on his horn.

I chuckled as my speedometer hit the 80 mph mark before I swerved back into my lane and let up on the gas.

"Are you trying to get us killed, man?" Keith yelped.

"That slow fucker in the Ford should have moved over and made more room for me to pass," I said.

"But it's a no-passing zone," he insisted.

"That's the way we drove in Nam," I said. "People are polite over there. Slow drivers don't hog up the road. They move over for you, and oncoming traffic makes some space for you to get past."

"Well, that ain't gonna happen in this country," Keith said. "You damn near gave me a heart attack."

This time joke wasn't on me

Back in the office at Quonset Point the next week, John Opdyke, my supervisor and good-natured cribbage adversary, walked over to my desk with a serious look on his face and some paperwork in his hand. "I've got some news for you, Lange," he said.

I figured it was my discharge papers and felt sorry that John, a gentle giant of a man, had to learn about my pot bust and the consequences of it.

"Your orders just came through for duty on a tin can out of Norfolk," he said. "You'll be shipping out on a six-month Med cruise in a couple weeks. It's a one-man disbursing operation, and they need an NCO. The Navy knows you passed the E-5 test, even though you turned down the promotion. They expect you down in Norfolk next Monday, so you have time to take your car back home first."

Man, that was some cruel joke. But this time the joke wasn't on me. It was on the Navy. "Nah, I won't be going on no destroyer," I told John.

He laughed. "You have to go, Lange. Here's your orders."

"Nope," I said. "Not happening."

That night I drove over to a nightclub on the Newport waterfront with

Jim and Bruce. We had plenty to drink as we admired some of the Salve Regina College coeds dancing with their boyfriends from nearby institutions of higher learning. We probably didn't look like college students.

Well after midnight, as my Impala reached the apex of the Newport Bridge, 400 feet above the waters of Narragansett Bay, the longest suspension bridge in New England, I slammed on the gas pedal. Assisted by gravity, my car picked up speed in a hurry. The needle on the speedometer passed 60 mph, 70 mph and 80 mph.

"Hey, that's fast enough, Dave," Jim yelled. "Oh, man, oh, man, slow it down."

The needle hit 90 mph. Bruce crawled onto the floor in the back seat. "Dave, you're scaring the shit out of me," he shrieked.

Jim lowered his head between his knees.

The needle passed 100 mph. I wanted to feel the thrill of 120 mph, but I saw the lights of the toll booth as my speed hit 110 mph. At 115 mph, I could see the toll collector through the window of the booth. I let up on the gas and pumped the brake. I couldn't stop. We sped past the booth in a flash. Fortunately, there was no gate to crash through.

Jim and Bruce sat back up to watch us zip across Conanicut Island and then over the shorter bridge at Plum Point. I took a left at Route 1A and delivered them safe and sound to their rental cottage at Bonnet Shores. It was the last time they asked me to drive.

My General Discharge came through on Dec. 2, a Thursday. I packed my bags, tossed them in the trunk of my Chevy and went back to Massachusetts.

Bill Urban was building a house for himself and Ruth in Buckland, which actually shares the downtown Shelburne Falls business district that straddles the Bridge of Flowers. He could use a hand, he said, and would actually pay me 10 bucks a day for my help. Over the next couple weeks, we installed the floor on top of the basement foundation and made progress on the exterior and interior framing. It was a learning experience for me, and the money came in handy. I needed cash for our evenings at the Charlemont Inn and a couple trips east to a dance hall called Walt's in the town of Orange.

The Balls connected me with some lady friends, including Renee, a tall, slender, curly haired girl who was a healing nurse during the day at the hospital in Athol and liked to dance the night away at Walt's.

Renee sat between me and JoAnn in the back seat of Bill's car on the way back toward Colrain, when Ruth, who was sitting between her husband and Keith in the front, let out a gurgling belch. "Bill, stop the car!" she yelled. "I'm gonna throw up."

Fortunately, Bill found a spot to pull over on the side of the Mohawk Trail, where a heavily treed slope drops steeply to the rushing Millers River, which empties into the Connecticut River a few miles to the west. Ruth disappeared into the trees, and we three men decided it was a good opportunity to relieve our bladders. As I splattered the wide trunk of a healthy oak in the darkness, I heard a shriek. It was Ruth. "Damn it, Bill!" she screeched. "You're pissing on my head!" Ruth was the only one who didn't think that was hilarious.

Back in the car, she was out cold. I don't know if she woke up and washed her hair when they got home.

A few nights later, when Keith and JoAnn took me over for some card playing and hard drinking at the home of his friends Bob and Connie Bassett, who had a small farm near Shelburne Falls, I was the one who missed out on the hilarity. Keith was still chuckling about it when I woke up with a hangover the next morning.

"How you feeling, Dave?" he asked. "Are you ready for breakfast?"

"Ugh," I said. "Not so great. I could use a cup of coffee."

"Your hands were a little bloody, and you were a little banged up last night," Keith said.

I looked at my hands and wrists. I saw a few scratches but nothing serious. My knees were stiff. "What happened?" I asked warily.

"You got so excited after you won a game of shit on your neighbor that you jumped up from the table, danced around the kitchen like an idiot and then ran out in the snow without your shoes," Keith said. "By the time we all stopped laughing and Bob and I went out to find you, we couldn't see where you went. We heard you yelping out by the pasture, so we walked around back and found you snagged in the electric fence. The way you were wriggling on the ground with your pants falling off, we couldn't help but laugh our asses off some more. Bob called me a little while ago and said he had to repair his fence this morning."

As much fun as I was having with my friends in Massachusetts, Christmas was approaching, so I decided I should go back to Ohio and spend the holidays with my family.

Dad wouldn't give up on me

With the narrative that Roy Cummings had written up for me, I drove up to Cleveland in early January and found the local ACLU office on the second floor of a downtown building. After reading over Roy's report for about five minutes, the solitary man in the office looked up at me and said, "I really don't think you have a case to appeal this. There doesn't appear to be any constitutional issues on which we could initiate a challenge to your discharge. I wish I could be more helpful. I'm sorry."

I was sorry that Roy's time and effort had been wasted on my behalf, thinking that the ACLU was some sort of emancipator for the injustice that had been imposed on me. As my discharge agreement made clear, I could "expect to encounter prejudice in civilian life." I stopped to buy an eight-pack of Rolling Rock beer before gunning the engine of my Chevy and weaving through traffic on my way south on Route 21. I downed the last two cans of beer as I sat in my car back in my parents' driveway on Treeside Drive.

I was resigned to living my life with the stigma of that General Discharge hanging over me. But my dad wasn't.

We can look back at our past lives and surmise how things could have gone differently.

I don't know many details about my father's past. But I know he was stationed with the U.S. Army in the Canal Zone prior to joining the 42nd Rainbow Combat Infantry Division in defeating the nationalistic fascism of Germany's Nazis and liberating thousands of starving Jewish prisoners from the Dachau concentration camp in 1945. I know from recorded history that marijuana smoking was common among American soldiers stationed in Panama during World War I. But I have no idea how its availability there during World War II might have influenced my dad's perspective on my experience.

I do know that my life would have been different if I had been a draft dodger like Dick Cheney or Donald J. Trump and avoided military service altogether. I'm quite sure that, if I had an influential father like George H.W. Bush, who successfully volunteered his son for a cushy assignment with the Air National Guard, I wouldn't have volunteered for duty in Vietnam. I know that Vietnam is where I was exposed to the supposed evils of marijuana. I know that my friendship with some fellow members of the U.S. Navy included our mutual enjoyment of pot and hash smoking. If I hadn't been in the Navy, I know I wouldn't have been subjected to the illegal search and seizure and denial of bona-fide legal representation that resulted in the General Discharge that was intended for me to "encounter prejudice in civilian life."

Of course, being part of the generation associated with Ian Dury's 1977 tune "Sex and Drugs and Rock and Roll," as opposed to the "wine, women and song" of previous generations, I can't say what I would have done if I hadn't served in the military. Well, actually, I can. Just about everybody I knew smoked marijuana in the 1970s. Many of us will still be getting buzzed now and then into our 70s – a half century later.

It was my father, more than me, who knew that something had to be done about my mistreatment by the Navy. It was my father who prevailed upon me to appeal my discharge, repeatedly.

He advised me to seek the assistance of my congressman, James V. Stanton, a Democrat from Cleveland. A graduate of Cleveland's Holy Name High School and an Air Force veteran of the Korean War, Stanton was a member of Cleveland City Council for 11 years before winning election to Congress in 1970. Despite his support and his contacts inside the Pentagon, my first appeal was denied in August 1976.

Through a culture of criminality in which Spiro Agnew, a corrupt vice president, and Richard Nixon, a treasonous president, were forced out of office, Gerald R. Ford had become president of the United States in August 1974. Ford, a U.S. Navy veteran who saw combat onboard the light aircraft carrier USS Montgomery (CVL-26) in the Pacific during World War II, somehow saw fit to pardon the felonious Nixon on Sept. 8, 1974. But his administration saw no reason to upgrade the Navy discharge of a lowly Vietnam veteran pot smoker like me.

Neither my dad nor Rep. Stanton gave up. They encouraged me to keep fighting.

My salvation came with the election of President Jimmy Carter in November 1976 – in no small part due to Ford's coddling of Nixon. Carter, a U.S. Navy veteran who saw sea duty on a nuclear submarine during the Korean War, issued a directive to the secretary of defense in early 1977, encouraging discharge upgrades for veterans who met certain criteria. Several of those criteria were applicable to my situation, including service in Southeast Asia, two years of satisfactory military service prior to discharge, extenuating circumstances contributing to my drug use and a record of good citizenship since discharge.

On Sept. 19, 1977, a five-member discharge review board unanimously voted to issue me an Honorable Discharge. Shortly thereafter, the certificate arrived in the mail.

Chapter 22 **Spring Break**

The mercury in Northeast Ohio thermometers dipped through single digits. In the wee hours of a late-January Saturday, biting winds out of Manitoba whipped across frozen Lake Erie and rattled no-parking signs 35 miles inland along North Water Street in Kent.

Jeff Murphy and I had closed our favorite watering hole, the Depot, at 1 a.m. and were downing a couple nightcaps at the Rendezvous, whose liquor license kept it open till 2:30 a.m. Jeff, whose long, dark head of hair lapped against his upper spine, left the bar to visit the men's room. Hearing a ruckus in that vicinity, I swiveled around in my bar stool to see him surrounded by a half-dozen fraternity types – frat rats, as we called them – so I walked over to investigate.

Standing just outside the perimeter of antagonists, I overheard some comments about the sterling silver loop dangling from Jeff's left earlobe. The matching one from the pair we had purchased from the Montgomery Ward store two days earlier was hanging from my ear, but the post-military length of my hair apparently had escaped the frat rats' contempt.

"Why don't you go to a gay bar in Akron, you fucking faggot?" one of them barked at Jeff. "You don't belong in this place, little bitch."

"You need to get a life, man," Jeff said, keeping his calm. "I'm not bothering anybody, just having a good time and drinking some beer, just like everybody else."

As more epithets were hurled at him, he tried to walk away, but they blocked his retreat.

One of the frat cheerleaders stepped into the clucking ring of chicken-shits, cocked his fist and let loose with a sucker punch to Jeff's face.

Recoiling quickly from the minor whiplash, Jeff sputtered, "What did you do that for?"

Before he could get an answer, I planted my fist squarely on the jaw of the sucker puncher, and he stumbled against the wall. All hell broke loose as the frat rats attempted to retaliate. My elbows were flying, and my knees were jabbing every which way.

The frat rats never got a chance to lay their hands on me, as the Rendezvous owner and two burly regulars at the bar ran over to break things up. They grabbed me by both arms, yanked me to the front door and shoved me out into the cold.

"Hey, I didn't start it," I yelped. "I'm not the one you should be kicking out of here. Come on, at least let me get my coat."

The door slammed shut. Fortunately, Jeff came out with my coat before my shivers gave way to hypothermia and my reddening bare hands turned blue with frostbite.

Living in my parents' basement, I was back in class for winter quarter at Kent State. I was considering a major in sociology. Academically, things were going much better for me than they had four years earlier. Maybe my naval experience had matured me. Maybe not. Maybe marijuana, which subsequently has been demonstrated to be beneficial for people suffering from a variety of ailments – from childhood seizures to multiple sclerosis and Parkinson's disease – had requited my attention deficit. Maybe not. But it didn't hurt my grades. I made the dean's list with a 3.82 GPA.

Jeff had earned his bachelor's degree in broadcasting and was working on a master's degree. On weekends and occasionally during the week, he and I would step outside the Depot to take a few tokes between the railroad tracks and Cuyahoga River. Sometimes we'd share a joint with some young ladies at a booth inside the bar. We weren't the only ones.

Often, my old friend from the neighborhood Ken Chrzanowski, who had received his Honorable Discharge from the Army after defending West Germany from the Soviet menace and was working at an Akron rubber plant, would join us. Ken and I also would visit the Veterans of Foreign Wars post on Front Street in the Falls. He said I should join, but, except for Ken and a bartender named Red, nobody made me feel welcome there.

John Musgrave, a U.S. Marine Corps veteran who spent two years in military hospitals after being severely wounded in action, probably hit the nail on the head during one of his interviews for the epic 2017 Public Broadcasting Service series "The Vietnam War."

"They treated us disgracefully when we came home," Musgrave said. "There were people accusing us on the right of losing the war – mostly the World War II veterans that we joined to emulate were calling us losers." I didn't hear it, but I felt it in the VFW hall. They didn't talk to me. They didn't invite me to join their veterans organization. If they looked at me at all, it was with a contemptuous glower. How dare the men of my generation intrude upon their sense of unparalleled heroism. They were the "Greatest Generation." They won the big war. We couldn't win a little one. "They more than anybody else we wanted to make proud," Musgrave said. Good luck with that.

The intent was indubitable in 1978, when the new organization Vietnam Veterans of America adopted as its founding principle: "Never again will one generation of veterans abandon another." I became one of VVA's earliest members.

In all fairness, Musgrave pointed out that contempt for Vietnam veterans came from divergent directions. "And on the left, we were war criminals, baby killers," he said. I knew that to be true. The bitch on the flight out of San Francisco made that perfectly clear to me. But nobody at Kent State – not my instructors, not my classmates, not the juicers in the downtown bars, not the potheads in the off-campus party houses – ever made me feel like a loser or a baby killer.

Serious legal consequences

During my years away from home, my little brother, Danny, grew up. He no longer was little. He was 18 years old, had graduated from Stow

High School the previous spring, was working at his first full-time job and had his own car. Like most people his age and mine, he enjoyed smoking a little grass.

"Check this out, Big D," he said, inviting me into his bedroom in our parents' house. He closed the door and pulled a big copper bong out from a dark corner of his closet. It must have weighed 10 pounds. "I made this on the job at Highway Products," he said of the bus-manufacturing plant where he was employed in Kent. "I got some good weed. You want to take a ride and give it a try?"

Of course, I did. We went out to the driveway, hopped in my Chevy Impala, and I drove us out of the Wyoga Lake development. Danny loaded the bowl when we reached Wyoga Lake Road, which was old Route 532, and fired it up as we headed north to Route 8. By the time we cruised through Akron's Virginia Kendall Park, which became a major section of the new Cuyahoga Valley National Recreation Area in 1974, we were thoroughly buzzed. "Good stuff," I said. We stopped along Akron-Peninsula Road at the bottom of the forested valley to reload the bowl and admire a sign designating a rippling tributary then known as "Langes Run," although it bore no familial relationship to us.

My driving under the heightened perceptivity influenced by cannabis was flawless, naturally, but the uncanny, coincidental presence of three police cars waiting at three corners for the traffic light to change at Route 8 and Steels Corners Road popped my eyes wide open. After I negotiated a precision left turn back toward Route 532, two of the cops flipped on their sirens and pulled me over, one behind my car, the other in front of it.

Gov. James A. Rhodes' signing of Ohio's marijuana decriminalization bill, making possession of 100 grams or less a "minor misdemeanor," didn't occur until 1975, so Danny and I were facing potential serious legal consequences. On top of my General Discharge "by reason of unfitness involving drug abuse," that wouldn't look good on my future resume.

Danny shoved his bong under the front seat, and we rolled down the windows as fast as we could. Even so, I can't imagine the ambrosial aroma of our enchantment being undetectable to anyone taking a whiff outside my car. Quickly, there were two professional law enforcers sniffing next to us, one outside each open window.

"Let me see your driver's license and registration," the one next to mine commanded.

After fumbling through my wallet, I handed him my BankAmericard and the motor-pool operator's identification I had been issued back in Saigon.

"Nope, this military license is not valid here, and a credit card is not a vehicle registration," he said, handing them back to me. "I need to see your current Ohio license and registration."

I fumbled again and somehow produced the correct items.

"OK, we need to do a safety check on your vehicle. Follow my instructions," the officer said as he stepped toward the rear and his partner went to the front. "First, step on your brake pedal."

I was good with that.

"Release the brake and turn on your headlights," he said.

Easy enough.

"Now, the left turn signal," he instructed. "No, your other left."

They both worked.

The cop returned to the driver's side window. "All right, you're free to go," he said. "Be careful."

I was. Plus I kept glancing in my rearview mirror as I drove back to Treeside Drive.

I don't recommend driving with a marijuana buzz-on. Nor do I recommend driving while on an LSD trip. And I sure as hell do not recommend driving while under the influence of alcohol.

Actually, I don't recommend using marijuana at all – except for people who may be suffering from multiple sclerosis, epilepsy, Alzheimer's disease, fibromyalgia, glaucoma, cancer, sickle cell anemia, Parkinson's disease, Tourette's syndrome, post-traumatic stress disorder or a host of other afflictions for which it has been found to be beneficial. It's quite possible that heavy smoking of marijuana, which remains illegal in most states, can be stressful to human lungs, although nothing compared to the highly addictive nicotine-laced cigarettes that are perfectly legal in every state of the union.

Of course, I don't recommend smoking "cancer sticks." Also, I don't recommend breathing the air anywhere near a major highway or within 100 miles or so of a coal-fired power plant. According to the Centers for Disease Control and Prevention, cigarette smoking is responsible for more than 480,000 deaths per year in the United States. According to a 2013 Massachusetts Institute of Technology Laboratory for Aviation and the Environment study, air pollution causes about 200,000 premature deaths each year in the U.S. Emissions from road transportation and power generation are the most deadly.

Unlike the pharmaceutical corporations, the duped doctors who abet their addiction to huge profits and the politicians who suck up their polluted campaign donations, I do not recommend opioid prescriptions for every little physical discomfort. Researchers with the Boston University School of Medicine and Brown University School of Public Health found by way of a 29-month review published in August 2017 that the pharmaceutical industry had paid more than $46 million to some 68,000 physicians to promote its opioid products.

According to the Ohio Automated Rx Reporting System, 631 million opioid doses were dispensed in 2016, about 54 for every man, woman and child in the country's seventh-largest state. Fortunately, that was down from 785 million doses in 2011. Unfortunately, Ohio, with 5,232 drug-overdose deaths in the 12 months ending June 30, 2017, trailed only Florida and Pennsylvania.

My friend Cleve Jones' fatal heroin overdose on Oct. 15, 1971, cannot be blamed on the subsequent proliferation of Vicodin, Percocet and other opioid painkillers, but the connections were unmistakable 45 years later. "Most of the heroin users now, their first opioid exposures are the prescription drugs," Dr. Wilson Compton, deputy director of the National Institute on Drug Abuse, said in February 2016. "That's true for at least 80 percent of today's heroin addicts."

The CDC reported 66,972 overdose deaths nationwide in 2016. Prescription pain pills and heroin cut short most of those human lives, while sedatives, cocaine and methamphetamines contributed their share. As always, marijuana overdoses caused zero overdose deaths.

It's the pharmaceutical pushers and their enablers who should be rotting in prison cells, as so many African-Americans do – or at least "expect to encounter prejudice in civilian life," the adjudication conferred upon me because I smoked a little weed in the Navy.

Destined to fall in love

Spring break has been a wild and crazy tradition for college students since the 1930s. In late March 1972, many of our classmates at Kent State were planning visits to popular destinations like Florida's Fort Lauderdale, Daytona Beach and Panama City Beach, where booze was sure to be chugged with abandon and bikini tops were sure to be abandoned in the sand.

Jeff Murphy, Ken Chrzanowski and I had returned to our booth in the Depot after stepping outside to smoke a joint. "We need to go somewhere cheap for spring break," Jeff said, "because I don't have any money."

"I can't go anywhere, because I have to work, and I got no vacation time coming," Ken said.

"Jeff, I think we need to go somewhere for free, not just cheap, because I'm broke too," I said.

When World War II veterans returned home in 1945 and 1946, the GI Bill of Rights covered their entire college tuitions and all of their book costs plus $75 per month to live on. Re-enforcing the country's attitude that Vietnam veterans were worth so much less, the GI Bill paid us a total of $175 per month to cover everything. Even at a comparatively low-cost public institution like Kent State, it didn't come close. At least the General Discharge didn't deprive me of the GI Bill, but I was broke nonetheless.

"We could go to Denver for spring break," I said.

"Why the hell would we go to Denver?" Jeff said. "There aren't any beaches there. There aren't any bikinis there in April. It's cold out."

"Well, one of my Vietnam buddies lives in Denver now. He's invited me to visit him," I said. "He said it's beautiful country. It might be sunny in springtime."

"I do hear that a lot of young people are moving to Colorado," Jeff said. "I wouldn't mind checking out the grad school at the university in Boulder. We don't have money for gas, so we'd have to hitchhike out there. We could sell some blood for 20 bucks at the Red Cross," he said.

"Hey, wait a minute, I see a girl coming in the door that I talked to a couple weeks ago. I'm going to say hi. I'll be back in a while."

Jeff got up and walked over to the table where two coeds had just sat down. The one with long, light brown hair smiled at him, and he sat down next to her. I looked at her friend, a petite brunette with sparkling eyes and a soft Mediterranean tint to her skin. She was stunning. I thought I'd like to meet her.

I did. Jeff motioned to our booth, and the three of them walked over. He sat on one side with the coed named Sue. I stood up and welcomed the brunette to sit between Ken and me. Her name was Linda. They were sophomores, old enough for 3.2 beer but not the high-powered stuff. They were roommates living in an eight-story dormitory called Beall Hall in a complex known as Twin Towers. Sue was from Rochester, New York. Linda was from a suburb of Cleveland.

At 1 a.m., closing time for the Depot, the five of us walked to the lot where Jeff had parked the 1971 Ford Maverick his parents bought him for his graduation. Sue sat next to Jeff in the front. Linda sat between Ken and me in the backseat.

Jeff pulled into a short-term parking spot at Tri Towers and turned off the ignition. Without saying a word, he leaned over and kissed Sue. She kissed him back. They didn't stop. I looked at Linda. She scooted her slender body closer to mine. I put my arm around her shoulders and pulled her tight. I didn't know then whether I'd ever see her again. I didn't know then that we were destined to fall in love. I didn't know then that Linda would become the most important person in my life.

Poor Ken. He sat there silently, motionless, alone in his thoughts amidst two impassioned couples who someday would become husbands and wives and fathers and mothers and grandfathers and grandmothers.

Circuitous road to Denver

Two weeks later, soon after sunrise on a crisp Saturday morning, Ken drove Jeff and me out West Market Street to the Interstate 71 interchange. He dropped us off with our Boy Scout backpacks and sleeping bags in tow. We did not have any marijuana, and I had decided to kick my addiction to nicotine, the world's deadliest drug, for the 11th or 12th time. The contraband switchblade I had acquired on the back streets of Naples,

Italy, and managed to conceal from the illegal search of my personal possessions upon arrival back in the States was stashed in an outer pocket of my backpack. It might come in handy for an encounter with rattlesnakes or rapscallions.

Two uneventful rides and seven hours later, we were sticking our thumbs out along Interstate 70 in Indianapolis. I was wishing I'd worn a coat and maybe a hat and gloves to boot.

Two hours after that, as the sun slid toward the western horizon at our backs and a Midwestern chill sent shivers down my spine, a Volkswagen Microbus, also known as a hippie van, pulled over to the berm. "Where you heading?" shouted a long-haired dude from the passenger-side window.

"Denver," Jeff yelled as we trotted up to the ride.

"Hop in the back," he said. "We can get you as far as St. Louis."

Another passenger, one of two guys in the back, popped open the side door, and we hopped in. The floor, ceiling and interior walls of the van were covered with plush shag carpet. Cushions and pillows were strewn about the compartment, and the heat from the air-cooled engine in the rear made it comfortably warm. The fragrance of a gently smoking incense stick mounted in a holder between the two front seats and redolence of marijuana vapor suspended in the air made us feel welcome.

The four travelers were on their way to Mexico, they said, where they intended to enjoy sunny weather and certain other advantages that could be found south of the border. Thanks to our obliging hosts, the journey across Illinois was relaxing and infused with good humor.

A reintroduction to the crisp outdoors during a refueling stop just east of the Mississippi River led Jeff and me to rethink our planned departure from the toasty van at a dark highway interchange for our continuing westward journey on Interstate 70. We were welcome to ride along through the night and onward to the Texas panhandle, the driver said, where we could hitchhike our way back north to Colorado. We decided that was a good idea.

After snoozing through the Show Me State and most of the Sooner State, I woke up to bright rays of the sun shimmering through the rear-door windows of the van somewhere west of Oklahoma City. By the time Jeff and I parted ways with the Mexico-bound hippies, the sky-high afternoon sunshine made early spring in Amarillo, Texas, feel like late June in Northeast Ohio.

It didn't take long for our thumbs to catch the attention of two young women heading north on U.S. Highway 87 with the windows rolled down in a four-door Dodge sedan. They were on their way home to Clayton, New Mexico, after visiting the Corpus Christi sound, they told us. Tammy Wynette's "Stand by Your Man" was playing on the AM radio.

Both women puffed on cigarettes as the Dodge sped past Lake Meredith and across the prairie. Being in the company of fellow nicotine addicts isn't easy for someone who's trying to quit smoking, but I resisted the urge to bum a cigarette. I wasn't partial to candy-like menthol flavoring anyway.

A stinging singe against my pelvic area prompted me to look down at my long-sleeved flannel shirt, the heaviest piece of upper-body attire I had with me. It was smoldering. Apparently, an ash flicked out the window from the driver's cigarette had blown back inside the car and set fire to the material. I was able to pat it out with my fist inside the cuff of my sleeve but not before a sizable section of my shirt was scorched. With just 20 bucks in my jeans pocket, I wouldn't be buying a new one. But maybe I could afford a pack of smokes in Clayton.

That wasn't going to happen. Highway 87 delivered us to the south end of town, and our driver was kind enough to transport us about a mile up the main road to drop us off at the northern edge. It was something more than a one-horse town, but the hardscrabble history of its establishment not far from the Cimarron Route of the Santa Fe Trail could not be lost on outsiders, certainly not those of the long-haired variety. Nobody in Clayton would mistake Jeff and me for cattle-ranch hands.

To the northwest, where we hoped the highway would lead us into southern Colorado, we saw miles of desolate flatlands jutted by several buttes on the distant horizon. To our chagrin, we saw virtually no traffic heading in that direction. To the south, we looked back at the straight-as-an-arrow and level-as-the-plain 1st Street passing through Clayton. Shortly after dinnertime, the second one our empty bellies were sorely missing, in what appeared to be a popular pastime, townsfolks began cruising in vehicles up and down the main drag, greeting friends and neighbors with waves and honks along the way.

Curiously, we watched the cruisers, some of them with shotguns racked inside the rear windows of pickup trucks, make U-turns at the edge of town and proceed along their long, narrow loops. Curiously, they glared out their windows at the two stalled hitchhikers, who were wishing and hoping for deliverance from that bizarrerie before nightfall.

"Get out of town," one of the cruisers yelled at us from a passenger window as the driver made his U-turn.

"Start walking," someone yelled from another vehicle.

We picked up our gear and moved 100 feet farther up the road into the dusty, deserted, barren outskirts.

"Get out of town," the command came again and again as certain vehicles became forebodingly recognizable. "Keep walking."

Not a good idea, we figured. We had no good ideas, only the hope that someone, anyone would be driving through Clayton, not just up and down the main road, and give us a lift out of that nightmare.

The warming sun dipped behind one of the distant buttes, and a chill scooted down my spine. A sedan and a pickup truck, their seats occupied by young men with cowpoke blood running through their veins, rumbled past Jeff and me and pulled to the side of the road. One by one, they scrambled from their vehicles. One of them slung what appeared to be a Louisville Slugger over his shoulder. If only I had smuggled my trusty .38-caliber home from Vietnam, I thought, I could pitch a couple slugs his way. Another guy twirled a thick wooden shaft like a baton. I reached into the outer pocket of my backpack and grabbed my switchblade. Hopefully, I could slash one or two wrists or throats before I got my head bashed in.

There was nowhere to run, nowhere to hide. Visions of VC tax collectors storming up the stairs of a Nha Be bar flashed in my brain. I thumbed the button on my knife handle, and the blade sprang open. As another life-wrenching story unfolded before my eyes, the roar of a diesel engine reverberated behind us. Screeching brakes brought a tractor-trailer to a halt. We looked around and saw the driver motioning us to climb in. Jeff grabbed his gear, bounded up the steps to the cab and swung open the door. He slid in next to the driver. Lugging my gear, I jumped in next to Jeff and yanked the door closed. The driver shifted his rig into gear and stepped on the gas. We looked out the window to see baffled looks on the faces of seven wrathful men from Clayton. Stealthily, I closed the blade and put it away.

"I saw what was happening there," the truck driver said. "I couldn't leave you two hanging in that situation."

Who knows whether that posse had nooses in the car trunk.

"Thanks a lot, man, we sure are lucky you came along when you did," I said. "Things were not looking good."

"Where are you guys going anyway?" the man who had just rescued us from a terrible beating and maybe worse asked.

Denver, we said.

"Well, I can get you up to Colorado at least," he said.

Twinkling stars and a sliver of the moon cast a glimmer through our vaporized breath when the driver exited Interstate 25 at a lonely interchange and dropped us off into the frigid night. We watched the truck lights disappear over a rise and listened as the engine's roar faded into silence. The highway was empty. We had been solitary travelers for miles. It was dark, no lights in sight. We walked away from the pavement and trudged across the flat, hard ground. We rolled out our sleeping bags and burrowed ourselves inside them. It was too cold to worry about rattlesnakes and rapscallions. I closed my eyes, clasped my numbing hands between my thighs and thought about the warm companionship I had experienced on the cushioned backseat of Jeff's Ford Maverick on a recent night back in Kent.

We were awake at the crack of dawn and had been semiconscious off and on with shivers and unrest in the dead-silent darkness. We heard the whoosh of a car fly by on the nearby highway. "Let's hit the road," I said with a yawn as I slithered out of my sleeping bag.

"Hey, look out there, Dave," Jeff said, pointing to the northwest.

"Wow!" I said. Purple mountains could be seen rising up from the unblemished plain on the distant, bright blue horizon. I had looked down at the snowy-peaked Rockies and the Alps from high above them in the sky, but this was my first sight at such wonders from ground level.

"Yep, we're in Colorado, all right," Jeff said. "I wonder what that huge mountain is that's towering over the other ones."

The rising sun soon soothed the chill from my bones, and we soaked it up almost like spring breakers on Florida beaches – except there were no bikinis to engage our wandering eyes. Traffic was sparse, but two men in an aging Cadillac on their way to a job in Pueblo picked us up within an hour.

They informed us that the outstanding mountain in our sights was Pikes Peak. Formerly known as "Heey-otoyoo," meaning "Long Mountain," by the Arapaho people, it was renamed in honor of explorer Zebulon Pike, who tried but failed to climb it in 1806. The peak is famous for its inspiration of the song "America the Beautiful" and the annual Race to the Clouds up the switchback-embedded Pikes Peak Highway. Officially, at 14,110 feet above sea level, Pikes Peak ranks only 20th on the list of Colorado's highest mountains, but it is second behind Mount Elbert in terms of its prominence at 5,530 feet from foot to summit. It's no wonder that it inspired our awe.

Unlike former President William McKinley, whose legacy was disengaged from America's highest mountain by the Barack Obama administration in 2015 in favor of the abstract Denali, Zebulon Pike's dominion remains secured over the native Heey-otoyoo.

Out of Pueblo, a traveling man transported us to Colorado Springs. He treated us to a touristy side trip through the Garden of the Gods, a public park with fantastical red rock formations, ancient petroglyphs and prehistoric connections to Native American visitations. It was designated as a National Natural Landmark the previous year.

Finally arriving in Denver in late afternoon on the third day of our journey, Jeff and I were deposited in the heart of the city with growling stomachs and too little cash for a sit-down restaurant or even a Taco Bell. I dropped a dime in a pay phone and dialed up my Nam buddy Al Elliott but got no answer. Nobody I ever knew owned an answering machine in the 1970s. I'd never heard of them. But we did run into some fellow visitors and learned about a church close to downtown where free dinners were served to street people, a category we decided was applicable.

Vietnam veterans reconnect

Afterward, I gave Al another call. He answered his phone this time, said he was glad to hear from me and he'd pick us right up. Within 15 minutes, he was downtown, where Jeff and I were waiting on a corner. "Doo-

Lang," Al shouted when he hopped out of his white Ford sedan, which had seen better days. We hadn't seen each other in more than two years, but he looked the same, except his red hair was growing over his ears and he had a matching beard on his face.

After I introduced Al and Jeff to each other, we loaded up our gear. Al drove out East Colfax Avenue to the first-floor apartment that he and his new wife, Allana, shared on Gaylord Street. The marriage to the Mormon girl in Idaho didn't work out, but Al was happily married now, he said, gainfully employed as a drywall finisher and managing a local rock 'n' roll band on the side. With Allana's blessing, we three guys visited several Denver nightspots, where Al splurged for more than our fill of beer. I slept soundly on the living-room couch that night.

On Tuesday morning, Al was long gone to work by the time Jeff and I caught up with our sleep. Allana told us about the nearby Cheesman Park, where we joined other young people enjoying the sunshine and tossing Frisbees. We also visited the adjacent Denver Botanic Gardens, which include a tropical greenhouse indoors and several outdoor exhibits. On Wednesday, Jeff and I hitchhiked to Boulder and toured the University of Colorado, where he picked up an application for grad school. I don't know if he ever submitted it.

Al was working as a drywall finisher for a company called Pacemaker Corp., not to be confused with the electronic devices that are inserted in human chests to help maintain steady heartbeats. Inside a warehouse-type structure on the south end of the city, Pacemaker employees assembled living units, complete with electricity, plumbing, wallcoverings and flooring, which were delivered on flatbed trucks to be hoisted with cranes into Denver's burgeoning apartment complexes. They were working 10-hour days, four days a week.

So, when Al got home from work on Thursday, he was ready for his three-day weekend. He had arranged for his four-member band, which had recently regrouped, to entertain a farewell party at the home of a young co-worker who was leaving for the Air Force. The kid's parents did not seem too pleased when we arrived with the musicians and a host of party animals to take over their basement with an ample supply of alcoholic beverages and more than a few joints. Al and Allana were not pot smokers, but Jeff and I got along quite well with the band members.

At the end of a wild weekend, Jeff and I were planning our return trip to Ohio. But Al had other ideas. We stepped outside his apartment to smoke cigarettes, which I didn't give up after all, and he said, "Doo-Lang, you gotta stay here in Denver."

"But I don't have any money," I said.

"Listen, it's all set," Al said. "Tomorrow morning, you come into work with me. I got it arranged for an interview with the manager. I told him you did some finishing work with your dad, so you got some experience."

"But I don't," I said.

"Trust me. He won't know any better," Al said. "We need another finisher. He'll hire you on the spot. Then I'll teach you what to do."

"But I got no place to live, and my car's in Ohio," I said.

"No sweat," Al assured me. "You can sleep on the couch and stay here with Allana and me as long as it takes. We'll go get your car sometime after you get settled."

The next morning I got the job, just like Al said. Thanks to union membership, it paid more than $2 an hour. That was better than the federal minimum of $1.60 but less than members of the International Brotherhood of Painters and Allied Trades were earning out on the construction sites.

Jeff left for home on his own that Wednesday, and I settled in for my job as a construction worker. I bought myself a set of drywall tools with my first paycheck, began paying Al and Allana $20 per week for room and board, which was a real bargain, and covered my share of the beer. Usually, Al and I went out for a pitcher at lunch and stopped for a drink or two after work. In addition to becoming reasonably adept at finishing, I got some experience with drywall hanging.

It took about six weeks for me to conclude that it was not the life for me. Even though Denver was a lively city for young people and there were plenty of parties to attend, I wasn't having much luck in connecting with young women. So, when the manager of Pacemaker decided it was time for me to switch to the night shift, while Al remained on day shift, I told him, "No thanks."

Chapter 23 | **Reunion Tour**

I heard that California was a fine place to be in the spring. I rolled up my sleeping bag, loaded my backpack with my gear, including the switchblade in an outer pocket. I thanked Al and Allana for their friendship, bid them farewell and hit the road. I walked along 17th Avenue into Denver's downtown area, where I hitched a ride up to the I-70 interchange.

It didn't take long before a big guy with long hair and a scraggly beard driving a small box truck pulled over and picked me up. Mark was going to Salt Lake City. He wasn't Mormon, although, coincidentally, he conformed with the Latter Day Saints' abstention from alcohol, tobacco and caffeine, he informed me. Marijuana was a different story entirely, and, happily, he was well supplied. He praised weed for its enhancement of sociability, whereas fences, including those separating the public highway from private pastureland, were detrimental to peace and harmony.

We soon departed the interstate in favor of the two-lane U.S. Highway 40, a more direct, albeit sinuous, route to Salt Lake City and more scenic and less traveled route over the Rockies. Singer-songwriter Henry John Deutschendorf Jr. wouldn't record his hit "Rocky Mountain High" until later that year, but I got the feeling in more ways than one.

With apologies to John Denver, somewhere in a place I'd "never been before," Mark pulled his truck off the road and parked "in quiet solitude the forest and the streams." I can't say, "I've seen it rainin' fire in the sky," but, "The shadow from the starlight is softer than a lullabye." Sitting on rocks by our campfire, Mark and I shared another joint and stories about places we'd been and girls we'd known and our Rocky Mountain high. Long after the sun set in the west, I believe I did "talk to God and listen to the casual reply." We tossed our sleeping bags into the back of the truck and listened to the mountain stream gurgling with snowmelt as we slipped into a deep, dreamy sleep.

Early the next afternoon, Mark drove me through Salt Lake City and dropped me off on the western edge of town, where he said it would be more convenient to hitch my next ride. In no time at all, a beater sedan stopped, a rear door swung open, and I squeezed in with a jovial carload of young American Indians, three men and two women.

"Do you want a beer?" the guy next to me asked, offering me a cold can of Hamm's from a loaded grocery bag on the floor.

Of course, I did. I was no party pooper. "Where are you all heading?" I asked.

"Stockton," the driver said as he took a chug from his can.

"Great!" I replied, associating the name "Stockton" with a city of some size somewhere in California. Hell, I figured, I could chip in for the next sack of beer. It could be a fun ride.

So it was a bit of a surprise when they turned left onto a dusty road barely 25 miles west of Salt Lake City and dropped me off next to a sign with an arrow pointing south to Stockton, Utah, population 469. I looked both ways before crossing the road, toward where sunshine shimmered against the ripples of the Great Salt Lake. Back toward the city, I saw no traffic. To the west, a haze wafted above a flat line of pavement that vanished into the desert. Again, I saw no traffic.

But I was not alone. A solitary figure stood at the side of the road not 50 yards past the turn-off to Stockton. It was a one-armed man. He didn't wave. Neither did I. I didn't know how he got there, in the middle of nowhere, in Utah. He was there first, but he had ventured past the turn-off. I was there second, but I was first in line of sight for westbound travelers. Would a westbound traveler stop to pick up a hitchhiker in the middle of nowhere, in Utah? Would a westbound traveler stop twice to pick up two hitchhikers in the middle of nowhere? Would there be any westbound travelers? I wondered. And I waited. So did the one-armed man.

Westbound travelers toward the Desert Peak Wilderness, the Cedar Mountain Wilderness and the Great Salt Lake Desert were few and far between. They sped right on past the Stockton turn-off, past the Vietnam veteran with light brown hair curling over his ears and a new beard sprouting from his cheeks and chin, past the middle-aged man with close-cropped hair, a clean-shaven face and one long sleeve tucked inside his black, button-up shirt. I counted them: five cars in the first hour, seven in the second hour.

Then, a station wagon towing a small trailer stopped. The driver told me to hop in the back. Two brothers in their late 20s, Gary and Greg, were up front with the driver's wife seated between them. The couple's little boy, 4 years old, was alone in the backseat. "Hi," I said to him with a smile. He climbed over the seat to join a German shepherd riding in the rear compartment. The wagon lurched forward, stopped to pick up the one-armed man. I made space for him in the backseat, and we all were off into the desert.

I was going to San Francisco, I told them, and was hoping to look up a childhood friend whose family had moved from Ohio when we were 10. The one-armed man was going to Reno, Nevada, where a job was waiting for him in a casino. The driver, his wife, their son, the brother and the dog all were from Wisconsin. The brothers had purchased a vacuum-cleaner franchise and were moving to California to set up their business in Yuba City, north of Sacramento.

I had heard of Yuba City. Everybody who paid attention to anything had heard of Yuba City. It made big news in 1971, when the bodies of 25 migrant farmworkers who had been stabbed and hacked to death were found buried in shallow graves in fruit orchards along the Feather River just outside of Yuba City. Juan Vellejo Corona, a schizophrenic immigrant from Mexico, was arrested in May 1971 and convicted two years later in one of the country's most notorious serial murders. I shuddered to think about it.

After a long, hot day through the Great Salt Lake Desert and across the similarly deserted ranges of Nevada, the one-armed man was deposited at the front entrance to his casino in Reno.

The two brothers, the wife, the little boy, the big dog and I continued over the state line and up the steep climb toward the Donner Pass. The heat of the desert sun quickly succumbed to the Sierra Nevada freeze, where Truckee, California, temperatures plummet below 32 degrees an average of 228 nights per year, including this one in mid-May.

It wasn't the best location for one of the bearings on the trailer to start smoking. We pulled into a truck stop, yanked the wheel and removed the faulty bearing. Greg, the younger brother, and I left the rest of the family to catch some shut-eye and hitched a ride with an eastbound trucker for the 30-mile jaunt back down the mountain to Reno. It may not be "The City That Never Sleeps," but "The Biggest Little City in the World" did have at least one auto-parts store that was open after midnight, and we found it. Plus, we hitched a ride back to the Truckee truck stop, replaced the wheel bearing and were ready to roll.

Fatigue had set in for the entire family during the long, weary day, but I was wide awake, so I took the wheel of the wagon as they slept through the night. At a refueling stop after sunup, Gary returned to the driver's seat. After following Route 20 past places called Nevada City, Grass Valley and Smartville, we arrived in Yuba City, where I got out on a rural road leading to Sacramento, the state capital. Juan Corona, the mass murderer of Yuba City, was behind bars, but I kept a wary eye on the eerie orchards anyway.

It was late morning when my fourth ride of the day crossed the San Francisco-Oakland Bay Bridge and delivered me to the heart of the city where I'd been labeled a baby killer while waiting for takeoff from the airport two years earlier. I found a bench in a downtown park and took a well-deserved snooze. A couple hours later I wandered around town until I found the corner of Haight and Ashbury streets. The 1967 "Summer of Love" had come and gone by then. I saw no evidence of the Grateful Dead or the Jefferson Airplane on the streets. None of the hippies I saw walking around with "Smiling Faces Sometimes" pretended to be my friend, as the Undisputed Truth and the Temptations had it in the 1971 tune. I might have encountered the Beatles' "girl with kaleidoscope eyes," but she had no "Cellophane flowers of yellow and green" to share and no living-room sofa to spare.

That being the case, I hitched a ride down to Palo Alto in the southern San Francisco Bay area, which soon would be better known as the Silicon Valley. My hope was to connect with the family of my old elementary-school friend Kevin Golub and maybe visit them in nearby Mountain View for a couple days. I found a listing for his father, Morton Golub, in the telephone directory and dialed it up in a phone booth, but there was no answer. Downtown Palo Alto didn't look like a good place to sleep overnight on a park bench, and I didn't see any free public showers, so I decided to splurge for a hotel room.

The next morning I got through to the Golub residence, and Joanna Golub picked me up an hour later. Unfortunately, she informed me, I missed Kevin by just a few days. He and his wife had moved to Eugene, Oregon, but I might be able to pay them a visit after they got settled there. Mort, a research chemist at the Ames Research Center, their younger son, Eric, a high school student, and especially Joanna were accommodating hosts. She treated me to an in-depth tour of San Francisco and Golden Gate Park. She drove Eric and me to the coast for a Saturday afternoon on the beach at Half Moon Bay. They invited a couple young acquaintants over for interesting dinner conversation. Best of all, I slept in a comfortable bed for several nights.

Visit to Imperial Avenue

The big news in Santa Clara County on June 4, 1972, was the not-guilty verdict handed down in favor of Communist Party USA leader and Black Panther Party associate Angela Davis. She had been listed on the FBI's Ten Most Wanted Fugitive List for charges of aggravated kidnapping and first-degree murder in connection with a Marin County courtroom melee that took the life of a judge, two black convicts and the 17-year-old black youth who attempted to free them. Davis had purchased the firearms used in the crime. Her flight from the law, subsequent capture as a "dangerous terrorist" and 16-month incarceration made for sensational national news. So did her exoneration by a psychologically sifted jury on the premise that her ownership of the guns did not establish responsibility for their deadly utilization.

As the National Rifle Association points out, "Guns don't kill people; people kill people." Therefore, people who buy guns for people to kill people don't kill people either.

After reading the Angela Davis report in the San Jose Mercury News the next day, I decided to pay a visit to my black Navy friend Aaron Dean, who was not a member of the Black Panther Party, in San Diego. Joanna Golub dropped me off at U.S. Highway 101, and I was on the road again.

Hitchhiking has a rich history in the United States, popularized by World War I soldiers on furlough, extended by college students in the 1920s and then out of necessity during the Great Depression. "On the Road," Jack Kerouak's 1957 novel celebrating cross-country hitchhiking journeys and his Beat Generation, brought the countercultural mode of transportation to a heightened consciousness. Vanity Fare's 1969 hit single "Hitchin' a Ride" followed a new generation's shifting gears along the hippie folkway. "A thumb goes up, a car goes by; it's nearly 1 a.m. and here am I," the British band sang it for the whole world to hear.

It was more like 1 p.m. under the Southern California sun when my thumb went up where my third ride of the day dropped me off on the main drag through the coastal city of Santa Barbara. Again, I was not alone. This time it wasn't a solitary one-armed man 50 yards away. This time there were dozens of young men all around, each of them with one arm reaching out to display a thumb. This time plenty of cars were going by. Trouble was they all kept going by. It was hitchhike heyday. Nowhere was that more evident than Santa Barbara.

Fortunately for me, most of the hitchhikers there were in pairs or threesomes. A young driver pulled his Corvette convertible over to the curb, got out and opened his trunk for my gear. I hopped in the passenger seat, and he peeled out past my fellow hikers. I was the last one there and the first one out. I was treated to a breezy ride along a smooth, sandy beach somewhere between Santa Barbara and Los Angeles, which was the Corvette driver's destination.

A Mexican man with two small children, a girl strapped in the front passenger seat and a boy in the back, picked me up on the edge of an LA freeway ramp. I understood that they were heading south of the border but not much else. "I'm going to San Diego," I told him. "Si," he replied.

I began to see San Diego signs along the highway within a couple hours but had no idea which exit would take me to Aaron's apartment, so I kept on riding. That was until we stopped behind a line of vehicles at the

Mexican border. I decided to stay in the United States. "Adios," I said to the Mexican man. "Gracias." That was the extent of Spanish I'd picked up from the 1950s TV series "The Cisco Kid."

A guy on a motorcycle returning from Tijuana stopped for me nearly as soon as I got to the side of the highway. He said he could take me into San Diego, so, with my pack and sleeping bag strapped to my back, I hopped on. When he dropped me off in the city, he handed me a joint and said, "This is dynamite stuff. Enjoy." Then he sped away.

Aaron's wife, Bessie, and their two kids had remained in San Diego, which is home to the Navy's fourth-largest base, during his duty assignment with HS-11 out of Quonset Point. He was a lot happier to receive his orders back to San Diego at the same time that I received my orders to get the hell out of the Navy, so he gave me his home address and told me I was welcome to visit anytime.

I had that address with me, but its location was a mystery to me, and it was getting dark on the streets of San Diego. I stuck out my thumb and hoped for the best. Soon enough, a man picked me up and asked where I wanted to go. I told him I was going to visit a friend and gave him the address.

"Is your friend black?" he asked.

"Yes," I replied with an apparent tone of curiosity. Of course, having grown up in Cuyahoga Falls, Ohio, sometimes referred to as Caucasian Falls, and having experienced both side of Sumner Hill in Akron, I was totally familiar with segregation. The question should have been no surprise.

He was a taxi driver during the day and was going home after his shift to a much different neighborhood than my destination, the man who picked me up explained. Cab drivers were not fond of taking fares into the area of Imperial Avenue and 30th Street, he said, but he would get me there.

"According to police crime statistics," the Los Angeles Times reported in a 1988 story, "there is no other location more notorious than 30th and Imperial for killings, shootings, stabbings, assaults, rapes, robberies, burglaries and a litany of other crimes and assorted mayhem. Police crime analysts say more blood is shed on that corner than anywhere else in San Diego."

"I'll wait here to make sure your buddy's home and you get into the apartment all right," the driver told me when we arrived at Aaron's address.

I knocked on the door. Aaron opened it and greeted me with a big smile. We gave each other a big bear hug, and he pulled me inside. He introduced me to Bessie, a pleasant, welcoming woman, and their cute kids, 7-year-old Jerome and 5-year-old Cherise. They called their dad, Aaron, and their mom, Bessie, and were happy to meet a white man named Dave.

"At night, particularly weekend nights, large numbers of young men and women, black, brown and many of them gang members, gather to talk and drink and hang out," the Times article said of the Imperial Avenue locale.

It was Monday night. Aaron and I walked over to a bustling bar on Imperial Avenue to talk and drink and hang out. I was the only white person there, but none of the black people in the bar were averse to talking and drinking and hanging out with me in their midst.

Aaron was not a pot smoker, so, after a few games of pool, I invited one of my new acquaintances outside to sample the weed which I had been gifted by the biker returning from Tijuana. I don't know what it was laced with, but the joint knocked both of us out cold. We were sitting on the sidewalk, leaning our shoulders against each other, with our backs against the building wall when Aaron came out an hour or so later and nudged us awake. The pool player went back inside. Aaron took me back to the apartment, and I rolled out my sleeping bag for a peaceful night on the living-room sofa.

I spent four days and five nights with the Dean family. When Aaron was at work on the naval base, I visited Bessie's friends with her and the kids. Jerome and Cherise held my hands and skipped along the sidewalk when their mom sent us down to a neighborhood store for some groceries. In the evenings, Aaron and I would visit the bar and play pool or join other men on the street corner to share swigs of gin from a bottle with its neck sticking out of a paper sack. I didn't see any white people during my visit. The black people didn't seem to care about that.

"It's been called The Set for years, because it didn't matter if you went back there in one year, five years or 10 years," police Sgt. Anne O'Dell told the Times reporter. "It was always the same, the same scene, the same stage, the same players. It was The Set."

I can't say. I never went back.

I hit the road to hitchhike back up the coast to the San Francisco Bay and maybe to Eugene, Oregon.

It was lunchtime when a young woman picked me up in LA. She asked me if I was hungry, and I was. She took me to her low-rent apartment at Venice Beach, which, at that time, was an enclave of beach bums, artists and other denizens of the multi-colored counterculture.

"Wow, this place is beautiful," I said as I looked out the window to see waves splashing on the wide beach.

"It is now," she said as she made us sandwiches. "But it's changing. The owners want to raise the rent. They're going to tear down some of the apartments and build new, fancy places for rich people. They don't want people like me to be living here anymore. It's called gentrification."

I told her I was going back to San Francisco, and she said I should visit a place along the way called Big Sur. "You'll never see anything else like it," she said. Later that afternoon, she drove me to Route 1, the Pacific Coast Highway.

A Santa Monica cop pulled over and issued me a warning citation, because I had slipped my right foot off the curb and planted it on the edge of the road. He did not conduct an illegal search of my backpack and sei-zure of any illicit contents. I thanked him with a one-finger salute after his squad car disappeared around a bend.

That night I made it to Ventura on the Pacific Coast Highway, not the Ventura Highway. Actually, there is no Ventura Highway, although the American soft-rock group America made it famous with a song of that name later in 1972. If "The nights are stronger than moonshine" there, I was too tired to notice. I found a quiet spot concealed amidst some thick bushes and fell fast asleep. No rattlesnakes snuggled up next to me.

Awakened by early-morning traffic, I hitched a ride with a young cou-ple who were as excited about the coastal venture as I was. They said they'd be happy to drop me off in the place called Big Sur. The drive up Route 1 out of San Luis Obispo, past Morro Bay, past San Simeon was breathtak-ing, and it got even better along the stretch north of there known as Big Sur. What I didn't know is that the village identified as Big Sur on my map isn't big at all. It's tiny. Evidently, I wasn't the only one to be misdirected by that misperception. Hitchhike heyday was every bit as evident in the village of Big Sur as it was in the city of Santa Barbara.

"Are you sure you want us to let you out here?" the young man behind the wheel asked me. His young wife surveyed the hitchhikers lined up along the road and giggled.

"I think I'd like to keep on riding with you guys," I said.

I arrived back at the Golub residence in Mountain View for a couple more days of rest and relaxation. Kevin was still getting settled in Eugene, the Golubs informed me, and he wasn't ready for a visitor.

Time to go back to Ohio

It was time for me to go back to Ohio. So Joanna delivered me and my gear out to the highway, and I spent the day hitching rides back up to San Francisco, across the bay, through Oakland, Sacramento and Truckee, which was much warmer during the day than it was at night.

After I got dropped off on the east side of Reno, past the casino where the one-armed man had a job offer, a cop stopped by to inform me that hitchhiking was prohibited within city limits. "Start walking," he said, but not with the threatening imposition that had been thrust at Jeff and me in Clayton, New Mexico.

Eventually, a man was kind enough to drive me to a deserted rest area in the middle of what sure looked like the desert to me. I rolled out my sleeping bag on a picnic table, figuring rattlesnakes would be less likely to join me up there than on the equally hard ground. I had a "Peaceful Easy Feeling" as I slept in the desert that night "with a billion stars all around," even though Glenn Frey and the Eagles didn't release the soft-rock tune with that title and those lyrics until the following December.

My sweet dreams were let down the next morning, when I caught a short ride to the U.S. Highway 95 turn-off and found myself standing on the ground back in hitchhike heyday. Well, it was a far cry from Santa Barbara and Big Sur, but eight hitchhikers stranded in the middle of nowhere, where one or two vehicles passed by every 10 or 15 minutes, was not an ideal situation.

Six hours later a man in his 30s on his way to Minneapolis stopped for me and also picked up two long-haired, bearded California hippies who were going to New York City to catch a flight to Europe. Our driver, Hank, made excellent time across Nevada and into Salt Lake City, where he parked at Temple Square. He insisted on taking a photo there of his three passengers, whom he claimed bore modern-day likenesses to historic church figures like Joseph Smith, Brigham Young and Wilford Woodruff. We humored him. I took a shift behind the wheel across Wyoming overnight, and Hank dropped us off early the next day somewhere in Nebraska.

Traffic entering the highway was sparse, so Duane and Norm, the two longhairs, and I ventured down the ramp, where we figured our thumbs would draw more attention. It wasn't the attention we bargained for, when a police cruiser pulled down the ramp and the officer told us to get in the rear seat. "It's against the law to hitchhike on the highway," he said as he made a U-turn and drove to a small town hall. "Follow me," the officer said, leading us into the building. "Sit here." He pointed us to a short row of chairs in a meeting room.

I set my gear on the floor, clasping my backpack between my ankles. The illicit concealed weapon was in the outer pocket.

A man wearing pressed slacks and a polka-dot necktie strapped around the collar of his striped shirt came into the room. "I need to see your identifications," he said. We produced three driver's licenses, two issued by the State of California, one by Ohio. He jotted down some information and handed them back to us. "It is a misdemeanor offense to hitchhike on the highway," he told us. "The fine is $20 each."

Duane and Norm reached into their wallets and pulled out the cash.

I didn't have it. My cash reserve was pretty much depleted in the bar on Imperial Avenue in San Diego. "Can I get a check cashed?" I asked the magistrate as I retrieved my final week's pay from Pacemaker Corp.

"Nope. Cash only," he said.

"Well, is there a bank nearby where I can cash this?" I asked.

"You cannot leave here until you pay the fine," the magistrate said.

I was getting mighty nervous.

"Here you go, Dave," Norm said, pulling out another $20 bill. "You can pay me back as soon as you get your check cashed."

The cop took us back to the highway on-ramp. "You boys better stay up here this time," he said.

We did. Eventually, a man who had stopped for a gas fill-up in town picked us up and took us across Nebraska, past Lincoln and Omaha and over the Iowa state line. Somewhere between Omaha and Des Moines he dropped us off at a juncture where silos rose above the flatlands and ankle-high corn stalks had sprouted all around.

Skittishly, we trudged down the scarcely used on-ramp to the scantly traveled highway. Two hours later, with the sun flickering out on the far western horizon and with approaching headlights few and far between, we reluctantly decided to call it a day. We lugged our gear back up the on-ramp and wandered into a field a quarter mile away from the two-lane country road. We unrolled our sleeping bags and climbed inside.

Except for the occasional vehicle speeding by on the highway, it was a still and quiet night – until well after midnight, that is. I heard the tires of a car squealing to a halt, doors opening and slamming shut and young men shouting up by the country road. I couldn't tell what they were saying, but they were angry voices. Duane and Norm heard them too. Maybe I heard a scuffle. Maybe not. We heard breaking glass. Maybe a beer bottle tossed on the pavement. We didn't move. We didn't talk. Slowly, carefully, silently, I reached inside the outer pocket of my backpack. Who knows what would follow the discovery of long-haired hippies sleeping in a western Iowa cornfield in the darkness of a June night? Then there was some laughter. Car doors opened and slammed shut. Tires peeled. The roar of an engine faded away. I took in a deep breath of country air. I closed my eyes. I fell into a deep, peaceful sleep.

Two African-American college professors picked us up the next morning and took us to Iowa City.

A man in a pickup pulled over there and told us he was going all the way to Dayton, Ohio, but two of us would have to ride in the truck bed. Duane and Norm hopped right in. Riding upfront, I told the driver about my travels, including our arrest in Nebraska and the $20 loan from Norm. When he let us out on Interstate 70 on the north side of Dayton, he handed me a $20 bill.

I could hardly believe it. "Thank you so much," I said.

"Not at all. Thanks for the conversation," he said.

I handed the bill to Norm and thanked him again for the loan.

The young couple that picked us up in Dayton said they were planning to visit Columbus just for the heck of it, but they were open to other options.

Duane said he and Norm had to be in New York City in three days. I said I was going home to Akron.

"OK, we'll go to Akron then," the guy in the driver's seat said.

I told Duane and Norm it would be easy for them to hitch a ride east on Interstate 80 out of Akron and take it all the way to New York.

By 10 p.m. on my fourth day out of San Francisco, my umpteenth ride took me right to the front door of my sister Vonnie and brother-in-law Al LaRue's apartment near North Main Street in Akron. I said goodbye to my hitchhiking friends, wished them good luck on their travels and thanked the young driver for the ride.

"No problem," he said. He looked at his girlfriend and asked whether she wanted to take Duane and Norm over to Youngstown and maybe even into Pennsylvania.

"Sure," she said.

Memories of hitchhike heyday

I feel blessed to have lived through and participated in hitchhike heyday. Despite the war in Vietnam – perhaps because of it – the late 1960s and early 1970s were some of the best times to grow up in America. Young people, especially, cared about each other. We reached out to each other. We gave each other a lift. We shared joints with each other. In no time at all, we became friends.

I lost count of the number of people who stopped for me along the highways. There were the guys in a VW Microbus who picked Jeff and me up in Indianapolis and took us all the way into Amarillo, after we decided it was too cold to get out in St. Louis. There was the man who treated us to the Garden of the Gods. There was the guy who welcomed me to sleep in his truck somewhere in the Rocky Mountains and then took me to Salt Lake City. There were the Native Americans who shared their beer as they drove me into the Utah desert. There was the family that took me out of that desert and all the way to California. There was the Mexican man who drove me to the border and the biker who picked me up there and gave me a knock-out joint. There was the off-duty cab driver who made sure I arrived safely at Imperial Avenue. There was the young woman who took me home for lunch at Venice Beach. There were the two hippies who hitched rides with me from Nevada to Ohio and bailed me out in Nebraska, the guy who gave me $20 to repay them and, finally, the young couple who went out of their way to take me to Akron.

Perhaps most critically, there was the truck driver who saved Jeff and me from a serious ass kicking and maybe worse in Clayton, New Mexico.

Oh, that's right, not everybody I encountered on the road was friendly, and not every night under the stars was warm and fuzzy. There was the cop who issued me a warning citation in Santa Monica, the one who kicked me out of Reno and the one who arrested me somewhere in Nebraska.

It wasn't the cops, though, who chopped the legs out from under hitchhike heyday. In 1972 and 1973, at least seven unsolved murders of female hitchhikers were reported in the area of Santa Rosa, California, north of San Francisco Bay. In June 1978, Jeffrey Dahmer, one of the country's most notorious serial killers, picked up his first victim, an 18-year-old hitchhiker, and took him to his parents' home in Bath Township, north of Akron, where he bludgeoned and dismembered the kid. Sensational crime stories from coast to coast gave hitchhiking a bad name in the decade after my cross-country journey. By the mid-1980s, it was tough to stick a thumb out just about anywhere and hope for a free ride.

Crashing in Massachusetts

After my trip, I traded my 1966 Chevy Impala convertible in for a 1969 Fiat. With my friend Ken Chrzanowski, I drove it up to Massachusetts to visit Keith and JoAnn, who had the cottage at Laurel Lake all to themselves for the week. Bill and Ruth Urban spent Saturday at the lake, where a day filled with swimming, boating, waterskiing, drinking, pot smoking and card playing left all of them pretty exhausted.

For some reason, when everybody else was ready to hit the sack, I was still raring to go. Sitting in the darkness of the main room and looking out at the moonlight sparkling off the still water of the lake, I yelled out, "Hey, Keith, I'm going to the Charlemont Inn. Do you guys want to go?"

"Shut the fuck up and go to sleep," Keith yelled from the bedroom. "It'll be closed by the time you can get there."

"How about you, Kenny?" I yelled up through the opening atop the pull-down staircase.

"No, leave me alone, Dave," he shouted down from the upper level that's furnished with single guest beds.

"Bill, do you want to go with me?" I yelled up.

"Let us go to sleep, Dave. It's too late," Ruth shouted down.

"Well, fuck it," I said to myself, as I stumbled out the door and down the stairs. I made it to my car, somehow slipped the key in the ignition and turned it on. I pulled out of the parking lot by the boat ramp and began swerving down the winding Laurel Lake Road toward Swamp Road.

It seems that the pine, spruce and birch trees are allowed to grow mighty close to the road in Erving State Forest. Too close. I didn't even notice the one that jumped out to kiss the right front fender of the Fiat. I heard the fender smash, though. I felt my forehead bounce off the windshield. I winced as chunks of broken glass from the instrument panel lacerated the insides of my thighs. Where were my pants? Where was I going in my underwear anyway? Damn, I was getting blood all over the driver's seat. What a cheap-assed car, I thought. One little bump into a tree, and it was falling apart.

At least it was still running. And it seemed to steer OK. So I whipped it around, drove it back to Ball's Acre, went inside the camp, sat myself down in a folding metal chair and moaned, "I wrecked my car."

"Shut up and go to sleep, you dumb ass," Keith shouted from the bedroom.

"No, I can't. I'm bleeding," I moaned.

"I'll give you some bleeding if you don't let us sleep," Ruth yelled from upstairs.

"I wrecked my car," I whined again.

"Stop your fucking whining and go to sleep," Keith yelled.

I sat there and pondered my situation for a while. Then I went outside and around to the cellar, swung open the wooden door, ducked into the pitch blackness, found the refrigerator, pulled out a beer and flipped off the cap with the opener on the wall. I tripped over my own foot, spilled half the beer, went back inside and moaned some more.

"Shut the hell up, Dave," Keith yelled. This went on until he finally gave in. "Damn it all, Dave," he muttered as he came out of the bedroom. "Oh, shit," he said. "You got blood all over the place."

That woke everybody up. They turned on the lights, surveyed the damage to my thighs, which wasn't as bad as it looked, and went out to assess the damage to my Fiat. We cleaned up the blood and put a couple bandages on my thighs.

Come Sunday morning, we swept the broken glass off the bucket seats of the Fiat, wrenched the quarter panel off the front tire with a pinch bar and taped up the busted headlight. Keith painted "Ouch" on the contorted fender. Keith and Bill followed Ken and me down the road to admire the injured birch tree. Somehow, despite the bent frame and warped axle, the compact Italian import got us back to Ohio in one piece. But it was beyond repair.

'Mr. Foreman … I do mind dyin'

I was broke again. I had no car. I was back living in my parents' house on Treeside Drive. My hopes for earning a college degree were dimming. My mother said I needed a job. The husband of one of her friends in the neighborhood worked in management at the Ford plant. I could start work the next week. Fortunately – for me, at least – Ken quit his job at the rubber plant and decided that he needed an air conditioner for the upstairs bedroom in his parents' house more than he needed his 1966 Impala with a three-speed stick shift on the steering column. I bought it for $100, which I borrowed from my parents. As a member of the United Auto Workers, my starting pay was more than $6 per hour, so I easily could pay them back with my first Ford check.

"Please Mr. Foreman … Slow down your assembly line. You know I don't mind workin'. But I do mind dyin'." So goes the tune written by blues musician Joe L. Carter sometime in the 1960s.

Paul Harris, the San Francisco lawyer who reinvigorated derangement induced by racism, poverty and exploitation as a defense in a 1971 bank-robbery case, used Carter's verse as the introduction to Chapter 4 of his 1997 book, "Black Rage Confronts the Law." The chapter reviews the successful insanity defense of James J. Johnson Jr., who, in 1970, was suspended for insubordination from his job at the Chrysler Corp.'s Eldon Avenue Gear and Axle plant in Detroit. Returning to the plant with a rifle, he murdered his foreman and two co-workers.

Harris made it clear that the black-rage defense must be used as a delicate ribbon, not an encompassing blanket, and that the ribbon might even be colored white.

The Johnson case was very much about the discriminatory treatment of black workers, for sure, but it also was about the hazardous conditions of auto factories, especially for low-life assembly-line workers. I became one of them.

"What was the impact of 'niggermation' on the workers?" Harris asked. "Forklifts were in a state of disrepair, light fixtures fell down, and aisles were overcrowded. There was oil on the floors, on the stairs, and on the racks workers stood on to operate the machines. Ventilation was awful … Every day, James Johnson walked into a plant with thunderous noise attacking his ears, grease from the machines covering his hands, oil on the floor lapping at his feet, and a heavy blue mist clouding his eyes."

In May 1970, 22-year-old Vietnam veteran Gary Thompson was crushed to death when his forklift overturned and fell on top of him at that same Chrysler plant in Detroit.

In the summer of 1972, a different 22-year-old Vietnam veteran nearly suffered the same fate at the Ford Motor Co.'s Cleveland Stamping Plant. It was my first day on the job. Ventilation was awful. Thunderous noise attacked my ears. Oil stuck to the soles and heals of my dad's old work boots. A heavy mist clouded my eyes. It was hotter than Nam.

I was given the simple task of squirting a white, squishy adhesive we called dum-dum around the edges of metal parts that I couldn't identify. I placed them on a belt that conveyed them to the head of an assembly line. When I emptied one 6-by-6-foot bin loaded with a ton of parts, a forklift driver would replace it with a full one. The aisles were crowded. Forklifts loaded with skids and bins stacked 12 or 15 feet high zoomed past me every which way.

I happened to glance over at the lead man on the assembly line at the right time. He happened to be looking in my direction at the right time. I saw his mouth gape wide open, but I couldn't hear his scream above the thundering presses and zapping welders. I saw him pointing above me, his index finger jabbing like a woodpecker's beak at a termite-infested tree trunk. I spun around and looked up. One of those steel bins filled with a ton of parts had been jarred loose from the top of a forklift stack and was toppling toward me. If I had been that quick and elusive in high school, I could have played halfback on the football team. The ton of parts crashed into the heavy-gauge steel worktable where I had been applying dum-dum seconds earlier. The table was smashed against the factory floor.

But for the grace of God, I would have been crushed along with it, my blood and guts mashed on the oily surface, my bones crunched like snippets of metal shunted down a scrap shoot. I have no other explanation.

It must have been God who led me away from that ammo depot in Nha Be no more than 10 minutes before it was blown to smithereens. It must have been God who made my skull miss that dry dock by 6 inches when I plunged 12 feet down from the seawall into the Saigon River. It must have been God who stopped the Viet Cong tax collectors from venturing upstairs where I was off-limits and unarmed. Well, the godlessness of communism aside, that one might be a stretch. It must have been God, though, who sent a solitary trucker through Clayton, New Mexico, to deliver Jeff Murphy and me from the clubs and fists of a group of local ruffians. I have no other explanation.

My foreman, a black man, ran over with his whistle shrieking. The line was shut down. It took 15 or 20 minutes to clean up the mess, find a replacement worktable, deliver another bin of parts and get us up and running again.

On my very first day in the stamping plant, I concluded that it was not the place where I wanted to spend my working life. I put in my time five or six or sometimes seven days a week and often 10 hours or more a day for the next six months. I bought a newer car, a 1971 Ford Torino, and I stashed away enough money to go back to college. And then, for the better part of the next two years, I was able to get into a Ford program with other college students working eight-hour shifts until midnight each Monday and Friday. That part-time job enabled me to move out of my parents' house, become self-supporting and earn my journalism degree. I owe a lot to the Ford Motor Co.

During my auto-working years, my young body withstood dozens of minor injuries, from an easily stitched forearm to a punctured foot that caused a temporary limp. Scorched jugular and pectoral regions were daily nuisances on the welding lines. But I got out of there in one piece. My brother, Danny, still likes to point out the stub of a souvenir he carries on his left hand. Most of his index finger was ripped off by a machine in the Highway Products plant when he was 18 years old. Luckily, it wasn't his arm.

Peace and love fading away

The so-called "Summer of Love," 1967, when The Mamas & the Papas urged kids of my generation, "Be Sure to Wear Flowers in Your Hair," faded into history. The Woodstock Music & Art Fair, which featured "3 days of peace & music" in 1969, became a hazy memory. "Imagine all the people living life in peace," John Lennon's dream in 1971, bled to an excruciating death before he did in 1980.

Flower children didn't elect Lyndon B. Johnson as president of the United States in 1964. They would never trust a president who cherry picked the facts about what occurred in the Gulf of Tonkin off the coast of Vietnam that year in order to accelerate the deployment of Americans to fight and die there.

Surely, my generation wouldn't grow middle aged and cynical and elect the chicken-hawk George W. Bush as president of the United States. Surely, we wouldn't trust a president who cherry picked intelligence about nonexistent weapons of mass destruction in order to deploy Americans to fight and die in Iraq.

Damn!

The courageous soldiers who saluted me and Marcus the door gunner with the two-fingered peace sign as our Huey soared over their convoy in Tay Ninh Province did not elect Richard M. Nixon as president of the United States in 1968. They would never trust a president who collaborated with a foreign government during his campaign in order to scuttle Vietnam peace talks. The riverine sailors who sang "We Gotta Get Out of This Place" in Nha Be would never trust a president who kept sending men like us to fight and die in that place for five long years after he concluded "there's no way to win the war."

Surely, my generation wouldn't grow old and crotchety and trust the draft-dodging pussy-hawk Donald J. Trump. Surely, we wouldn't trust a man who correlated his sexual escapades to the heroics of those who fought and died for their country in Vietnam. Surely, we wouldn't fall for "fake news" spread by a collaborative foreign government in order to put an autocratic serial liar in the White House, would we?

Oh, shit!

Pseudonymous Appellations

Roosevelt Barnes: Black kid I met while caddying. To the best of my recollection, that was his name.

Mark Barnett and Ron Finney: Two seniors on the Hoban High School swim team who assaulted Allan Carlini in the shower room. I changed their names.

Allan Carlini: Fellow Hoban High School student from our neighborhood whose father drove us to the bus stop each morning. I changed his name.

Dr. Carlson: The pediatrician who had bad news for me just before my 15th birthday. I don't remember his name.

Larry Chase: Buddy in Navy Supply Corps School. I remember his last name but am unsure about his first name.

Roy Cummings: HS-11 petty officer who wrote up an appeal of my discharge. I don't remember his name.

Bruce Crenshaw: Friend in the disbursing office at NAS Quonset Point. I don't remember his last name.

Jerome and Cherise Dean: My friend Aaron's children in San Diego. I don't remember their names.

"Stinky" Grayson: Fellow enlisted man in HS-11. I don't remember his name.

Rob Herdman: Shipmate on USS Forrestal. I don't remember his name.

Mrs. Hendrickson: Eighth-grade English teacher. I don't remember her name.

Bruce Horstler and his mother, **Mrs. Horstler:** Neighbors who caused my mother to raise the subject of nocturnal emissions. I changed their names.

Mr. Jenkins: Company commander in boot camp. I don't remember his name.

Mrs. Jensen: A teacher at Price Elementary School. I don't remember her name.

Cleve Jones: Sailor on USS Intrepid who died of a heroin overdose. I don't remember his last name.

Miss Kimball: English literature teacher for my final semester in high school. I changed her name.

Lt. Kline: Ranking officer among students in counterinsurgency and SERE training. I don't remember his name.

Dr. Lewis: The family physician whose office was in the plaza across the street from our house. I don't remember his name.

Mike Loomis: Petty officer with blistered face resulting from a smoke grenade. I don't remember his name.

Vince Luchetti: Sailor in my company at boot camp. I'm not sure about his first name.

Jerry Mason: Enlisted man in HS-11. I don't remember his name.

Tony Pagano: Enlisted man in HS-11. I'm not certain about his name.

Victor Perez: Supervisor in disbursing office at Quonset Point. I don't remember his first name.

Chief Petty Officer Porter: Company commander in boot camp. I don't remember his name.

Steve Powell: Fellow enlisted man in HS-11. I changed his name.

Joel Randall: Sailor on USS Intrepid who passed out tabs of Orange Sunshine. I changed his name.

Jermaine Roberts: My squad leader for SERE training. I don't remember his name.

Mrs. Rouleau: My junior-high French teacher. I don't remember her name.

John Schumm: Classmate who squealed on me for smoking in school. I changed his name.

Ricky Stemley and his mother, **Mrs. Stemley**: The seventh-grader and his mother who ratted us out over the junior-high-school lipstick initiation. I don't remember their names.

Stinson: PBR sailor who attacked a Saigon tea girl in Nha Be. I changed his name.

Rick Wilson: Friend of Mike Mooney who hung out with us a few times. I don't remember his name.

No Last Names

Becky: Girl I nearly necked with at the movie theater when I was in eighth grade. I don't remember her name.

Betsy: Girlfriend of HS-11 enlisted man Jerry Mason. I don't remember her name.

Brenda: Ron Chadwell's girlfriend. I don't remember her name.

Deborah: Girl I met at the Dome in Kent and then drove her to a cottage at Punderson State Park. I don't remember her name.

Duane and Norm: Two hippies who caught rides with me from Nevada to Ohio. I don't remember their names.

Felicia: Stanford University coed whom we met in Spain. I don't remember her name.

Gary and Greg: The brothers who picked me up hitchhiking in Utah and took me to California. I don't remember their names.

Hank: The driver who picked me and two other hitchhikers up in Nevada and dropped us off in Nebraska. I don't remember his name.

Jerry: PBR sailor who told about ARVN search-and-destroy missions. I don't remember his name.

Kathy: Girl I met at Chippewa Lake's Starlight Ballroom. I don't remember her name.

Laurie: Girl that Rick Morgan and I met at the Draught House. I don't remember her name.

Lisa and Vicky: Two girls that Mike Mooney and I met at a Lions Park dance and then nearly got them arrested. I don't remember their names.

Marcia: Tenth-grader attracted to bad boys like my friend Mike Mooney. I don't remember her name.

Marcus: Door gunner on the Slingshot Swingship. I don't remember his name.

Mark: The hippie who picked me up hitchhiking in Colorado and took me to Salt Lake City. I don't remember his name.

Nancy: Friend of my HS-11 buddy Max Winslow. I don't remember her name.

Ralph: Drunken sailor who attacked me with a razor blade in Barcelona. I don't remember his name.

Renee: Nurse whom I went dancing with in Massachusetts. I don't remember her name.

Sheila: Girl that Mike Mooney, Rick Wilson and I visited at her family's big house in Tallmadge. I don't remember her name.

Stan: Navy recruiter in Akron. I don't remember his name.

Stuart: Fifth-grade classmate I punched in the nose just as our teacher walked in the door to our room. I don't remember his name.

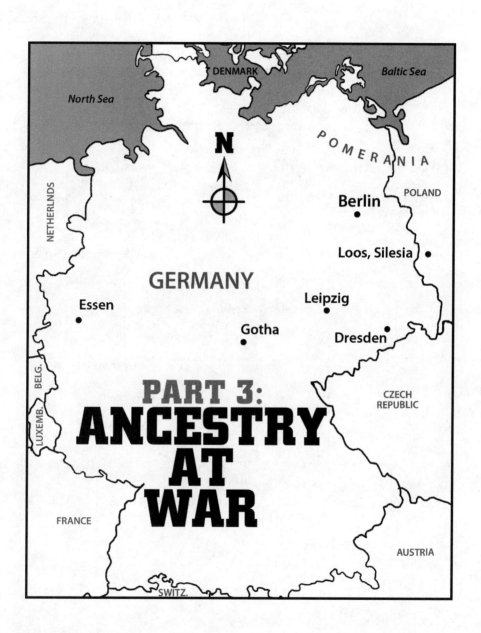

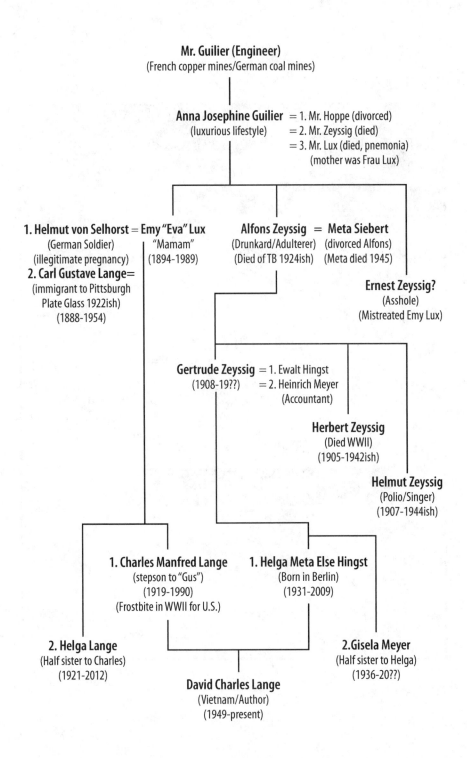

Chapter 24 | **First World War**

What's in a name? Mine is David Charles Lange.

David is Hebrew, meaning "beloved one." It's biblical, Old Testament. It's written in the Book of Samuel that a young beloved one named David slew a giant of a man named Goliath by popping him in the head with a slingshot. That David later became king of Israel and Judah. He gained everlasting infamy for his sinful seduction of a married woman by the name of Bath-Sheba.

I never killed any giants. I have tangled with some rather large, testosterone-infused acquaintances, but not all that successfully. Also, I'm no ladies' man, even though I've liked the opposite sex from my earliest recollections. I don't know whether King David ended up going to heaven or hell. "Thou shalt not kill," the Bible says. "Thou shalt not commit adultery" either. I have no idea whatever happened to Bath-Sheba, but I imagine she was pretty hot.

The encounters that David had with Goliath and Bath-Sheba occurred sometime around the 10th century B.C.

A more obscene seduction occurred about 3,000 years later, when an entire country of some 65 million Christians fell under the horrible spell of a stiff-postured Austrian with a weird, geometric mustache above his upper lip and dark hair slapped against the skin of his scalp. His name was Adolf Hitler. It was damned good fortune for me that my ancestors were not descendants of the House of David, the onetime king of Israel, at least not that I know of. There have been secrets in my family.

Both of my parents were born in Germany, Hitler's adopted homeland. Neither they nor their parents nor their grandparents could imagine it then, but the country called Germany and the madman named Hitler would become intertwined by the defining events of the 20th century, forever embedded in the annals of history.

It was the First World War, not the second one, though, that ushered my father into this world. He was conceived under mysterious circumstances at about the time that the Allies decisively defeated the Germans at the Battle of Amiens on the Western Front in August 1918, effectively ending "the war to end all wars," which may or may not explain my grandmother's uncustomary frivolity on a hot summer night. Altogether, about 18 million people died in World War I. Their bloody carcasses were scattered across many lands. Less than five months after the armistice was signed at the 11th hour of the 11th day of the 11th month of 1918, my dad was born. If he was kicking and screaming, I wouldn't blame him.

My mother arrived 12 years later, two years before President Paul von Hindenburg named Hitler chancellor of Germany, putting the star character on stage for the deadliest war of all time.

Charles, my middle name, comes from my father, Charles Manfred Lange, born April 5, 1919, in Essen, at least according to his certificate of death, which was issued 71 years later in Akron, Ohio. Based on letters addressed to him in the 1940s, Manfred might have been his first given name. I never saw his birth certificate, which might have verified that one way or another, but issuing birth certificates probably wasn't a high priority at that time and in that place. When he was alive, my father mentioned that he had been born in a smaller town called Kray, just east of Essen, a noteworthy city of culture and industry on the River Ruhr in the North Rhine-Westphalia region of far western Germany, not far from the border of Holland.

The name Charles has German origins, meaning "manly, strong, full grown." The name Manfred, which I did not inherit, also has Germanic or

Teutonic origins, meaning "man of peace." As an adult, my father stood 6 feet tall. He was broad shouldered, barrel chested and bald headed. His sturdy frame carried about 200 pounds on a lean day. His family and the people he knew growing up called him Nook, or Nookie, for some reason never explained to me. I didn't ask. My mother called him Chuck. His co-workers at the Ford Motor Co.'s Cleveland Stamping Plant called him Charlie. I called him Dad. But no one called him a man of peace.

Our surname, Lange, originates from the early Anglo-Saxon tribes. Meaning long or tall in the German language, the name emerged in the old Duchy of Saxony, circa the ninth through 12th centuries. Geographically, Saxony is situated in the northwest corner of modern Germany, bordering the Netherlands and the North Sea.

But not my father, not me, not my brother, not my sisters nor any of our children and grandchildren has a drop of Lange blood in our veins. Until after my father died, I thought I was a Lange in blood, as well as in name. I thought Carl Gustave Lange was my father's father through progeny and thus my grandfather by blood. But he was not. Gus Lange, as he was familiarly known, was my father's stepfather. Because passing along blood or depositing semen is not equivalent to fatherhood, Gus was the only father my father knew and the only true father that he ever had. He was generous in passing along his last name. I knew him as Papap, but not for long.

Gus Lange was born on Oct. 22, 1888, in Gumbinnen, East Prussia. During the unification of 1871, Gumbinnen became part of the German Empire. The city of some 30,000 inhabitants gained some historical notoriety as the site of a bloody battle on the Eastern Front near the onset of World War I, when a major German offensive was turned back by the Russian army. My grandfather, being of war-faring age, was a uniformed battler for the country of his birth, but exactly where he did his battling I do not know.

When the Second World War rolled along, Hitler made Gumbinnen and its environs a key Nazi military stronghold. In late 1944, the city was occupied by the Soviet Red Army, which, as was its inclination, inflicted severe atrocities on the civilian population. A German counteroffensive liberated Gumbinnen before it was recaptured by the Soviets in January 1945. The German people were forced to flee or die. After the war, Gumbinnen, along with the rest of northern East Prussia, was annexed to the Russian Federation and the Soviet Union. The city is now known as Gusev, Russia.

Gus Lange died in 1954 in Natrona Heights, Pennsylvania, where he was buried beneath the green grass and a small stone marker at Mount Airy Cemetery, just a few paces off Freeport Road in the northeast section of town and facing the southern terminus of Saxonburg Road. A half mile north of the cemetery, past an old dairy on the left and up a dozen steps from the roadway on the right, with the Appalachian hills sloping to higher ground behind it, sits my parents' first house. It is a one-story tract unit with two compact bedrooms moored to the cement-block walls of a damp and dungy crawl space.

The party for Papap's death, which we pretend is a celebration of the life that preceded it, is one of my earliest memories. I was 4 years old at the time and the smallest mourner at the funeral home. I foggily recall wondering about his motionless, silent disinterest amidst a few stray sobs at the rim of his casket. I didn't have a chance to ask him directly about his past, but I did question his widow, my grandmother, some 30 years later. Even then, I had trouble getting straight answers. Perhaps that was because I asked the wrong questions, maybe because her hearing and coherence weren't what they used to be, maybe because her guttural accent was thicker than my mother's. Or maybe she was just being evasive.

"How did you meet my grandfather?" I asked in my quest to record some family history while my aging Mamam was still with us.

"Huh?"

"How did you meet my grandfather?"

"Ah, wha, uh, whoot?"

"Papap," I said.

"Whoot?"

"My grandfather."

"Yaah."

"How did you meet him?"

"Your grandpuhtah wass my pahtah."

"No, I'm talking about your husband."

"How I met my husbunt?"

"Yes."

"Oh, I dunno. We hat a jub, and sum day we went out witt a tren in da morgen into da voots. We were alvays talking to zumbutty, and den he came again. An so ... "

Communication with my grandmother could be like that, even in her better years. She was a short, squat woman who projected an air of seasoned calm, at least to me, but my mother assured me that appearances can be deceiving.

Mamam, my father's mother, was born Emy Lux in 1894. She recalled that her earliest years were spent in the town of Gotha, which is in the state of Thuringia and became part of communist East Germany after World War II. Evidently, she didn't particularly care for her given name and preferred to be called Eva. Eva Lange is the name engraved on her gravestone, which is embedded in the cold ground next to her husband's at Mount Airy Cemetery.

According to Mamam's recollection, her grandfather was a mining engineer in French copper mines and later moved to take a supervisory position at coal mines in Germany, where her mother was born as Anna Josephine Guilier.

My own mother, born Helga Meta Else Hingst on March 16, 1931, in Berlin, also was familiar with Anna Josephine Guilier, because they too were related. That's right. The mining engineer Guilier was my father's great-grandfather and my mother's great-great-grandfather. And that made Anna Josephine my father's grandmother and my mother's great-grandmother. As my mother explained it, my father's mother, my Mamam, was her grandfather's half-sister and later became her mother-in-law.

My parents' marriage was not quite like procreating with your own cousin, which geneticists have determined can result in certain physical and mental deficiencies among the offspring. And I've known a lot weirder families. But it's made me wonder nonetheless.

Many years later, my mother wrote some memoirs based in part on childhood conversations she had with her grandmother, Meta Siebert, who had married Alfons Zeyssig, my father's mother's half-brother.

She said our mining engineer ancestor was "high and mighty," as people of privilege tend to be. He treated the lowly mine workers with disdain, confusing their weakness from malnourishment with laziness and considering their slave wages justly deserved.

Anna Josephine Guilier went through three husbands, at least. One of them was named Hoppe, from whom Anna was divorced. She then married a German named Zeyssig, who died after fathering Alfons. Finally, she married a man named Lux, my grandmother's father, who died of pneumonia when she was just a couple years old.

Apparently, Emy Lux's mother wasn't around much during her childhood. "My mother lost everything when her husband died," she told me. "She worked all the time, and I was always alone." Emy did spend some time with her father's mother, Frau Lux, however, and recalled, "She was good to me."

My mother's descriptions of Anna Guilier-Hoppe-Zeyssig-Lux were not complimentary. "She was neither a good nor kind person, and she made Mamam's childhood a very unhappy one," she wrote in her memoirs. "According to Mamam, there was never enough money for necessities, but Anna always rented a large and expensive apartment in order to appear to be a very important person."

My mother's mother, Gertrud Zeyssig, was born on Oct. 3, 1908, in Essen, the same vicinity where my father was born in 1919. Gertrud was the fourth and youngest child and the only daughter of Alfons Zeyssig and the former Meta Siebert.

In what seems to be a providential nexus, given the events that occurred 40 years later, Emy Lux, my grandmother on my father's side, arrived to visit Meta Zeyssig, her half-brother's wife, almost at the very moment that she gave birth to Gertrud, my grandmother on my mother's side. The 14-year-old Emy, finding the anguished and sweat-soaked Meta in bed with the gasping newborn beneath the sheets, drenched in viscous fetal membrane, ran frantically to rouse the local midwife, who saved the day.

"Meta had a hard life, because Alfons was a scoundrel who ran around with other women and spent his family's money on them," my mother wrote of her grandparents. "I don't know if he beat his wife, but he beat his children unmercifully." She told one story about Alfons dragging little Gertrud with him as he drank himself drunk at a local tavern and then gave her a vicious beating, because she had neglectfully left her tiny purse behind, which exposed the escapade to his wife.

When Emy Lux was about 16 years old, she was sent to live with Ernst, one of her half-brothers, in the city of Dresden, known as "the Florence of the Elbe." Nearly 300 miles east of Essen, Dresden lies just north of the Czechoslovakian border.

This being around 1910, it was 35 years before British and American air forces launched the single most destructive bombing in Europe during World War II. According to historical accounts, on Feb. 13, 1945, when Nazi military forces were on the threshold of total defeat, about 1,250 heavy bombers dropped more than 3,900 tons of high-explosive devastation on the city that had been best known for its historic architecture and culture, not for producing war machinery. The firestorm turned about 8 square miles of Dresden to rubble and left piles of charred corpses, many of them children, strewn along the streets. Subsequent estimates of the death toll ranged anywhere from 35,000 to 135,000. A more accurate count was said to be impossible because of the unknown number of refugees who had fled into the city from the battlefields surrounding their own towns, only to be blown to shreds.

Writing about it in his novel "Slaughterhouse Five," famed American author Kurt Vonnegut Jr., who had the misfortune of being held as a prisoner of war in Dresden at the time, said, "There must be tons of human bone meal in the ground."

My grandmother didn't have fond memories of her time in Dresden either. Her brother Ernst was about 18 years older than her. "I had it bad there," she said with a quiver in her voice. "Real bad. My brother was a mean hound. He slapped me around and everything." What did she mean by "everything"? What would make her miserable existence "real bad"? I didn't ask, just figured the worst. Ernst was a real asshole.

Back in the Essen area eight years later, the summer of 1918, a 24-year-old unmarried woman, Mamam got pregnant. Nobody bothered to share this information about my heritage with me until after she died in 1989 and after my father, the product of that illegitimate pregnancy, followed her to the grave in 1990. For the first four decades of my life, I was led to believe that Gus Lange was my grandfather by blood.

The fact of the matter, which I learned from my widowed mother, is that Emy Lux had an intimate relationship with a German soldier by the name of Helmut von Selhorst. This occurred during the final months of World War I, not long before the defeat of the Second Reich and the abdication by Kaiser Wilhelm II, who then fled to Holland. I suppose it's no surprise that the soldier von Selhorst took off as well. Who knows where? At any rate, my father was born in the spring of 1919 into a country physically shattered by war, its economy in ruins, 10 percent of its territory extracted from it by the conquering allies, 2 million of its fighting men dead and food shortages so bad, according to reports, that "Germans ate dogs, crows, zoo animals and rodents."

Historically, the use of "von," which literally means "from" or "of," was restricted to families of nobility. It actually was illegal for those without blue blood in their ancestry to use "von" before their family names. According to my mother, her father was a descendent of the von Hingst clan, but sometime in the past the family lost a good amount of the financial privilege that had been inherited with the good name. One of our ancestors sold the "von" to someone who hadn't been born with the privilege but was more adept at accumulating and retaining his fortune. Thus my mother was born merely a Hingst, and there was no "von" for me to inherit from either side.

The high and mighty privilege previously claimed by my father's engineering great-grandfather and grandmother was long gone as well. Sometime between my father's birth and the birth about three years later of his half-sister, who was given the name Helga – the same as his future wife – Mamam married Carl Gustave Lange in Essen. Like my father's father, von Selhorst, his stepfather, Gus Lange, fought on the losing side in the First World War. After the war, Gus went to Holland to find work on the railroad.

When my dad was a toddler, Mamam recalled, her half-brother Alfons, festering with the wounds of war, paid her a brief visit before moving on to Leipzig, the largest city in the eastern state of Saxony. A couple weeks later she received a letter calling her to a hospital in Leipzig. Leaving her baby, Helga, with neighbors, she took my father with her on a train trip that took all day and covered about 250 miles. That was followed by a trek on foot for several miles through the city, she said. Finally, upon their arrival, famished, filthy and wilting, the hospital barred her from entering with the child. She was directed to a local convent, where she was able to leave little "Nook" in the care of the nuns.

Returning to the hospital, Emy found her scrawny and wheezing brother in a bay crammed full of cots and moaning and coughing patients. After her long, exhausting journey with a child in tow to be by Alfons' bedside, he had but one small request. Please go fetch him a bottle of wine, he asked. That was it. No food. No earnest plea for miraculous medical care. No messages for the family. Just a bottle of wine. So she left the hospital bay, found a room for the night and purchased the cheapest bottle of wine she could find the next morning. And she returned to her brother's side. With a hint of a smile on his sputum-drenched lips and a glint in his crusty eyes, he grabbed the bottle with a quivering hand and carved out the cork with his pocketknife. As she watched him take one swig and then another and another, my grandmother recounted, "I said, 'Alfons, I talked to the doctor, and he said you got to eat.' He looked in my face, and he knew I was lying. He turned around, and he fell asleep. The next day I went back to the hospital, and he was gone."

There was little time for grief, she said. "I and that little boy had to go home. We had to walk so far. Nobody else in the family cared. I was the only one."

Mamam had better memories of Alfons Zeyssig than she did of her other half-brother, the asshole Ernst. But Alfons' wife, Meta, shed no tears after his death from tuberculosis in that Leipzig hospital. More happily moving on with little Gertrud, she was remarried to a widower named Fischer, and they rented an apartment in Tempelhof, a suburb of Berlin.

After about a year-and-a-half in Holland, Gus Lange returned to his young family in Essen, but there was no work to be found. "It was awful," Mamam said of their struggles in war-torn Germany. "Nobody had anything to eat." Fortunately, Gus had an uncle who had immigrated to the United States before the war. With the uncle's sponsorship, my dad's adoptive father again left his family, this time crossing the Atlantic for the New World, where he went to work for Pittsburgh Plate Glass. Immigrants, who were like chattel to American factory owners, would gladly supply their labor upon demand one week and collect their meager wages on payday. The next week they'd hear the empty growls in their stomachs instead of the roar of the fiery glass ovens that put food and rent money in their pockets, plus a few cents socked away for their families' eventual passage. Potato soup in Western Pennsylvania was much better than boiled rats and roasted crows in Westphalia. And before long, Gus was able to send for the wife and two little children he had left behind.

Chapter 25 | **Welcome to America**

On Dec. 19, 1923, at 6:35 in the morning, a special train for third-class passengers left the station in Bremen, where the murky Weser River empties into the frigid North Sea, for the nearby port of Bremerhaven. Having passed their final medical examinations the previous day, with German passports issued from the police station at the corner of Am Wall and Ostertorstrasse and with approval by the United States Consulate in Bremen, my grandmother, my father, then 4 1/2 years old, and his infant half-sister were among those third-class passengers to board the steamer S.S. Bremen sailing for New York City.

My grandparents came at the tail end of a long line of immigration from Germany to America that dates back to colonial times. There is a common belief that America's freedom and prosperity always have beckoned immigrants. Whether it's been political, economic or religious factors, however, the push away from native lands has been a strong force as well. For the most part, it wasn't the well-connected gentry, the well-fed citizens of money and power who left England, Ireland, France and Spain for the uncertainty of North America.

Those who were different often have been feared and generally have not been welcomed with open arms. The 2009 book by bestselling author Steven V. Roberts, "From Every End of This Earth," had this to say: "In 1753, Ben Franklin called the Germans flocking to Pennsylvania 'generally the most stupid sort of their own nation' and warned: 'They will soon outnumber us (and we) will not, in my opinion, be able to preserve our language, and even our government will become precarious.'"

It's widely understood that the German immigrants of the mid-19th century were disproportionately opposed to slavery and that Abraham Lincoln took that into account when he formulated his political platform. Evidently, it helped. Following Lincoln's election, New York Herald correspondent Henry Villard made a stunning pronouncement in his Dec. 9, 1860, report: "In Ohio, Illinois, Indiana, and Wisconsin, native Republicans now openly acknowledge that their victory was, if not wholly, at least to a great extent, due to the large accessions they received in the most hotly contested sections from the German ranks."

During the Civil War, some 177,000 German immigrants joined the Union Army, many of them motivated by the parallels they saw between slavery in the New World and the serfdom they themselves escaped in the old one.

Undoubtedly, cheap labor – actually free labor, in the case of imported Africans – has been the greatest motivator for opening up American borders to foreigners. About 12 million African laborers prodded by spears and intimidated by futile resistance to gunfire, were chained and shipped across the Atlantic during the heyday of slavery. The vast majority of them slaved in the Caribbean sugar colonies. About 600,000, just 5 percent of those uprooted black men, women and children, toiled on plantations in the States.

About 5 million Germans arrived in the United States between 1850 and 1930. With industrialization creating a demand for factory workers, some 2.66 million German-born people were counted in the 1900 U.S. Census, more than from any other country. Even after the so-called Great Wave of immigration shifted to Southern and Eastern Europe in the early 20th century, the 1930 Census counted more than 1.6 million German arrivals, second only to Italians at about 1.8 million.

Although American industrialists welcomed the labor supply, women and children included, Americans themselves, many of them witnessing competition for jobs grow and wages stagnate, were not so welcoming toward those foreigners, or aliens, as the derogating ilk would have it.

Nativism has been especially acute during wartime. That surely was the case when America was drawn into two world wars against Germany in the 20th century.

Historical scholar John Higham noted in his book, "Strangers in the Land, Patterns of American Nativism 1860-1925," that enemy alien regulations during World War I were applied much more aggressively to German immigrants than to those from Austria-Hungary and other central European enemy states. Higham pointed out that American writers of the era revised historical records to eliminate "references to early American settlers as Teutonic declaring that most present-day inhabitants of Germany are Alpines rather than Nordics. A physician, William S. Sadler, wrote a whole book to prove the latter point, arguing that 90 percent of the German Nordics had been killed off in the wars of the previous 300 years. This indicated, according to a lurid report in the Hearst press on the views of Professor Henry Fairfield Osborn, that the modern German population was actually descended from Asiatic barbarians."

Transitioning between an extensive exploration of mythical attitudes toward American Indians and a revealing cross reference to the Apache chief Geronimo by way of the mission that eradicated the jihadist Osama bin Laden, editor and author Jesse Walker devoted several pages in his meticulously researched 2013 book, "The United States of Paranoia: A Conspiracy Theory," to German-American fallout during World War I.

"The domestic struggle against the alien octopus was sometimes horrifying, sometimes comic, sometimes a bit of both," Walker wrote. "Some towns prohibited performances of German music. Pittsburgh banned Beethoven. There was a vigorous crackdown on German-owned breweries. The comic strip 'The Katzenjammer Kids' retconned the title characters' national origins, reassuring readers that the boys were really Dutch."

German books were burned. German-Americans were tortured. One of them, a poor miner, was lynched by a mob in Collinsville, Illinois. His killers were acquitted of committing the "patriotic murder." Lutheran parochial schools, with their predominantly German-American student bodies, were labeled as subversive. Public schools were ordered to stop teaching the German language. After a flu pandemic killed some 675,000 Americans,

Bayer, a German company, was accused of contaminating aspirin.

President Woodrow Wilson created the Committee on Public Information to propagandize against phantom German agents infiltrating every niche of American society to undermine its fighting men in Europe. Several thousand German-Americans were taken to concentration camps. The intolerance directed at them was justified by an editorial in the Washington Post, which said, "In spite of excesses such as lynching, it is a healthful and wholesome awakening in the interior of the country."

Not so unlike the way American Indians were portrayed earlier, Germans, during the First World War, were depicted as savages capable of inflicting unthinkable atrocities. "Show the Hun that we can beat him at his own game," President Wilson's propaganda agency implored.

When my grandmother and her two children joined her husband in the Allegheny River valley northeast of Pittsburgh a half-dozen years after the end of the war, she didn't feel like a barbarian, a savage or even a Hun. She didn't know she had subhuman blood flowing in her German veins. What she did know was that somehow, some way, her new land had to be better than the one she left.

Fortunately, the suspicions, the fears, the guilt by heredity, the hate and the ignorance instilled by war were subsiding. Her new neighbors, many of them with Eastern European roots, were good people, my grandmother said.

The opportunity to rise up from the clinching muck of subservience wasn't so good. The so-called American dream did not pave many streets with gold, certainly not for the majority of immigrants.

Gus, Eva, Charles and Helga Lange settled in a section of Harrison Township called Campton, which, along with the likes of Birdville, Ducktown and Pughtown, eventually became Natrona Heights. Natrona Heights is located about 18 miles as the crow flies northeast from where the Allegheny and Monongahela rivers converge to form the mighty Ohio River at a point known as the Golden Triangle. It is situated just north of and at a higher elevation than the town of Tarentum, where modest houses and local shops line narrow streets along the banks of the Allegheny.

In his brief history about Birdville, Bob Barrage wrote that bald eagles and other birds of prey were abundant in the wilderness when the first white men set foot in the area around 1670. Birdville, however, takes its name not from soaring eagles or even from scavenging pigeons but from an English-born carpenter by the name of Richard Bird, who purchased the land in 1889. The people who moved into the homes he built there called them "Bird houses."

Bird, the builder, had been dead and buried for nearly 20 years by the time my grandparents arrived in the area and Gus Lange set out to build his own little stick house. The Pittsburgh Plate Glass Co., later renamed PPG Industries, had been founded in 1883 in Creighton, an industrial town 3 miles downstream. Along with the steel mills that surrounded it, the glass factory where my grandfather was employed ran much like many of the brooks that feed the Allegheny River – fast and furious on tumultuous days but trickling slow during dry spells. "When he got work and got paid, he could buy lumber to put into the house," Mamam told me. "When there was no pay, he couldn't work on the house. It was bad."

While my father was growing up and his family struggled to get by in western Pennsylvania, some 4,000 miles away, on the other side of the Atlantic Ocean, the other side of my ancestry struggled to pick up the pieces in a land crushed by the bombs of war, a nation emasculated by the Treaty of Versailles and an economy smothered by punitive reparations payable to the victors. As part of that World War I treaty, the region of Alsace-Lorraine was returned to France, which had relinquished it to Germany a half century earlier as its punishment for losing the Franco-Prussian War. That could explain the French name Guilier of my mining engineer great-great-grandfather on my father's side and great-great-great-grandfather on my mother's side and possibly for the French name Lux of my great-grandfather on my father's side.

In 1929, 10 years after the Treaty of Versailles was signed, Gertrud Zeyssig, my mother's mother and my father's half cousin, turned 21. Upon reaching the age of adulthood, she left her family, which operated a small grocery store inside the train station in Essen, where postwar inflation swelled the cost of a loaf of bread to a million marks and replaced pocket books with wheelbarrows. She headed for Berlin, Germany's capital and largest city, where her disarming smile and gift for conversation, a "sparkling personality," as my mother put it, landed her a job as a waitress in a fancy restaurant. It was at the restaurant that she met a smooth-talking, hard-drinking waiter named Ewald Hingst, who became my grandfather.

"They fell in love, hormones took over, and I was conceived before the wedding in October 1930," my mom explained. Five months after the marriage, on March 16, 1931, Helga Hingst was born in Berlin. "Wedded bliss did not last much beyond my birth because of my father's increased heavy drinking," she said. "When he came home drunk one night and smacked me, because I was crying – I was only 9 months old – my mother ended the marriage."

After the divorce, my grandmother and my mother went to live in an apartment that my great-grandmother shared with her second husband and his two children.

In 1934, Gertrud Zeyssig Hingst married her second husband, Heinrich Meyer. They moved to Tempelhof, the suburb of Berlin, and, in February 1936, my mother was joined by a half-sister, Gisela Meyer. Heinrich Meyer treated my mom like his own daughter, and she became known as Helga Meyer to her friends and neighbors. According to the legalities by which surnames are conveyed, however, she remained a Hingst.

With a big city park and playground just across the street from their first-floor apartment, my mother remembered a wonderful early childhood. She recalled swimming in the summer, ice skating and sled riding in the winter and long walks through the forests surrounding the capital city that was home to the Reichstag and the Brandenburg Gate. She loved the sandy beach at one of the two lakes of Wannsee in southwest Berlin, where the shooting competitions of the 1936 Olympics were held.

She was too young to pay much attention to the Olympic Games or comprehend the political circumstances that drew intense international scrutiny to her country and hometown that summer. The shining star of the Berlin Olympics was the pride of Cleveland East Technical High School and Ohio State University, Jesse Owens, who won four gold medals for the United States in the track and field events. After his victorious performances, much was made about the significance of this black man showing up Chancellor Adolf Hitler and his illusions about Aryan supremacy. There were news reports back in the States about Hitler purposely leaving the Reichsport stadium so that he wouldn't have to shake Owens' hand.

In a 1972 interview, Owens said, "I didn't know I had been ignored until the Olympics were over. I got a phone call from somebody asking

402 | Dave Lange | Virginity Lost in Vietnam

me about it. I didn't know what they were talking about." The winner of the 100-meter and 200-meter dashes, the broad jump and four-by-100-meter relay was treated to thunderous cheers from the stadium crowd of 100,000, most of them Germans, and he was mobbed by autograph-seeking Berliners.

Katie Kasper, who was a teenage German gymnast at the time and who became my mom's best friend throughout their adult years in America, remembered those Olympics well. It was one of the best memories of her lifetime to be able to travel to the big capital city and perform as part of the festivities, she said. The biggest talk of the town, she said, was that fleet athlete from the United States. All the young, white Germans were eager to catch sight of the young, black Jesse Owens.

Regardless of whether Hitler snubbed the greatest track star in the world or accepted the reality of minority achievements in the 1936 Olympics, he earned his odorous repute.

Back in the United States, racism was overtly evident to Jesse Owens, who said, "I couldn't ride in the front of the bus. I had to go to the back door. I couldn't live where I wanted." There were no congratulations from President Franklin D. Roosevelt. "Hitler didn't snub me," Owens said. "It was FDR who snubbed me."

Incredibly, after the war broke out, Jesse Walker wrote in "The United States of Paranoia" that there were claims in the South about black churches "receiving Nazi propaganda." As the rumors went, "Hitler has told the Negroes he will give them the South for their help" and "make the white people slaves and the Negroes the leaders."

Jesse Owens proved that he was the fastest man in the world in the 1936 Olympics. But he didn't prove anything about Hitler, who soon would do so much to reveal his ignominious self. The fact that German athletes won more gold, silver and bronze medals than any other country in those Olympics didn't prove anything about racial or ethnic superiority.

Those may have been joyous times for Germany, and it may have been a happy childhood for my mother. But it was a mirage. The Great Depression was consuming the American economy. The European economies were sinking along with it. Benito Mussolini's "corporative state" was imposing its fascist hold over the people of Italy but making the trains run on time. Adolf Hitler, the former Austrian house painter, capitalizing on Germans' anti-Versailles resentment and anti-communist mindset and scapegoating the country's Jewish minority, was fortifying his stranglehold.

Even by the time of my mother's birth in 1931, the prelude to World War II already was underway in the Far East with Japan's march into Manchuria. In January 1942, leading Nazi officials held the Wannsee Conference to discuss plans for the "Final solution to the Jewish question."

My parents' paths, which were connected by ancestry but had not yet crossed, were being drawn by a fate beyond their control and a world out of control.

Chapter 26 | **World War II Winners**

It's been said that hindsight is 20/20, that we can look back through the lens of time and see things clearly. Fat chance. Historians know better.

On June 28, 1914, in Sarajevo, now the capital of Bosnia and Herzegovena but then part of Austria-Hungary, Archduke Francis Ferdinand, heir to the Austro-Hungarian throne, was assassinated by a young Bosnian, with support from high Serbian officials. That incident is widely cited as the key prelude to World War I, with Austria-Hungary and its ally, Germany, on one side and Serbia, with its patron, Russia, on the other. Unfortunately for Germany – and perhaps for hundreds of millions of people who wound up behind the Soviet Union's iron curtain three decades later – France, Belgium and Britain got in the way. After nearly three years of pleading neutrality, the United States joined the fray when President Woodrow Wilson got around to signing a declaration of war against Germany on April 6, 1917.

Germany surrendered on Nov. 11, 1918. The terms of the Treaty of Versailles, which was signed in France the following June, called for the dismemberment of Germany, including the return of Alsace and Lorraine to France and most of West Prussia to Poland. Another thing that pissed the Germans off was what they considered exorbitant monetary reparations to be paid to the Allies. Also, Germany was disarmed, which really didn't work out so well.

The Germans thought they got a raw deal. They couldn't swallow the blame for the war. But they lost, there's no doubt about that, and it's not the losers who get to write history with authority.

On March 16, 1935, Hitler denounced the Treaty of Versailles mandate for German disarmament, and America watched from a comfortable distance. That September, his German government made persecution of Jews an official policy, causing little discomfort across the deep, blue sea. In March 1936, Germany reoccupied the demilitarized Rhineland. Five months later, with Jesse Owens leading the pack, the United States joined the rest of the world to celebrate the Summer Olympics in Berlin.

In October 1936, establishing the Berlin-Rome Axis, Hitler and good buddy Italian dictator Benito Mussolini affirmed their countries' common affection for fascism, a simpatico they extended to Francisco Franco's government in Spain a month later.

While communists, homosexuals, Jews, Gypsies, disabled people and others deemed anathema to right-wing fanaticism were the internal victims of gnawing violence, the actual outbreak of war in Europe might be pinpointed to the German Army's occupation of Austria in March 1938, with no resistance and minimal international reaction. Or it could be tied to the Nazi-Soviet nonagression pact of strange bedfellows in August 1939, which made passive Poland easy pickings to be torn apart by two hungry wolves. Britain and France declared war on Germany that September, but the flaccid French Army had no backbone to support that boldness. By the time Belgium, the Netherlands and then France fell to the frenzied German invaders in 1940, culpability was crystal clear.

Even the Soviets recognized it when 3 million Axis troops invaded their territory on June 22, 1941. Communists on the left and fascists on the right both wield razor-sharp blades from which naked spines should never be exposed. But only liars and fools suggest that the two edges of the political spectrum bear any semblance of compatibility. Communists, of course, build their authoritarianism with the silly notion that men, being created equal, should share the benefits of property and production. Fascists, among whom Mussolini and Hitler were the shining stars, shunned such Marxist notions, collaborating with wealthy corporate leaders to trap laborers into low wages, long hours and hazardous working conditions.

In the summer of 1941, most Americans still watched from a safe distance as the second great horror of the century was unmasked. The immigrant Lange family, of Natrona Heights, Pennsylvania, though, was less disconnected.

The so-called "peacetime" draft ended abruptly on Dec. 7, 1941, "a date which will live in infamy," as FDR put it after Japanese planes from aircraft carriers attacked the U.S. Navy's Pacific Fleet in Honolulu, Hawaii, as well as our bases in the Philippines, Guam and Midway. The president called for a declaration of war the next day and got it with an 87-0 vote by the U.S. Senate and a 388-1 vote by the U.S. House. Supporting their Asian ally, Germany and Italy declared war on the United States three days later, to which the United States reciprocated.

By early 1942, my father was writing letters home from Fort Kobbe in the Panama Canal Zone. If the Japanese could inflict catastrophic damages on America's naval forces in Hawaii, it surely made sense to be on high alert to protect our vital maritime connection between the Atlantic and Pacific, both for military maneuverability and for the transportation of civilian goods.

As everybody knows, talk is cheap. Patriotism is a very easy concept to claim as your own, especially when your country goes to war. But there really are only two ways to validate that claim. The most apparent one is to sign up for the military, wear a uniform and put your life on the line. My father was one of nearly 1.5 million Americans who served their country during World War II.

The other way to prove your support for war is to make sacrifices for it, especially to help pay the huge costs of defending your country. For World War II, tax increases raised revenues from $8.7 billion in 1941 to $45.2 billion in 1945. That patriotic tradition began during the Civil War, when Congress imposed a variety of income and excise taxes to preserve the nation. During World War I, with passage of the Revenue Act of 1916 and the War Revenue Act of 1917, taxpayers' support for the country increased from $761 million in 1916 to $3.6 billion in 1918. According to a 2009 report by former Treasury Department economist Bruce Bartlett in Forbes Magazine, "In 1950 and 1951 Congress increased taxes by close to

4 percent of GDP to pay for the Korean War, even though the high World War II tax rates were still largely in effect. In 1968, a 10 percent surtax was imposed to pay for the Vietnam War, which raised revenue by about 1 percent of GDP." President George H.W. Bush raised taxes in 1990 to help pay for the first Gulf War in the Mideast.

After the 21st century rolled around, with the first President Bush's eldest son, George W. Bush, occupying the Oval Office, though, the sense of shared sacrifice was turned on its head. Not only did he send the sons and daughters of mostly working-class families to wars in Afghanistan and Iraq, but he reduced taxes, mostly on the wealthiest Americans, which drove up the national deficit to unprecedented levels.

A sense of the civilian sacrifice back home, above and beyond taxes, came through in my dad's New Year's Eve letter of 1942. "So you are going to get some more gas after all – I'm certainly glad to hear that," he wrote. "Gee, Mum, I can't imagine it being 10 below back home – that's much too cold, but I think I could enjoy it myself. So the batteries in both cars are dead. I only hope that you can get the new ones without waiting long for them."

There were communications about sacrifices being made by the citizens for the war effort, rationing of everything from the coal that heated their homes and gasoline that powered their cars to shoes for their feet and food for their bellies. The price for potatoes skyrocketed from 25 cents to a buck apiece. On March 23, 1943, my father wrote, "I suppose that, by this time, the point system, or should we call it the modern methods of starvation, has begun. Boy! I hate to think how it'll be a year from now if conditions are so bad already. I read the column by Elsie Robinson which you sent, and it must be just so. That piece about the soldier coming home wounded and finding his family on the verge of being thrown out of their home is the last straw. So it proves very clearly that this Soldiers' and Sailors' Act isn't any help at all."

There was news about friends and relatives who answered the call of duty. After one of the families in the old neighborhood heard from their son, my dad wrote on March 12, "That certainly must have been wonderful news to the Sadeskys – just imagine if, after all this time since the Philippines were taken – good news to them, but I hear that poor Eddie often wishes that he was dead rather than be under such conditions, don't you think so? I think I would. Before this hell is over, he'll probably starve to death or they'll maybe kill all prisoners. If only we knew when this would end, if ever, and is it worth all that has to be sacrificed? I wonder. And it all seems to be at a standstill right now. I hate to think of how long it will last should the Russians be forced to give in."

Eddie Sadesky might have missed out on the Bataan Death March in April 1942, when the Japanese forced some 66,000 Filipino and 12,000 American prisoners – starving, thirsting and beaten – to hike 65 miles up the coast of the Bataan Peninsula to Fort San Fernando, where they were packed like sardines into rail cars and transported to prisoner-of-war camps. If Eddie had been there, he very well could have been one of the tortured, tormented, debilitated, fevered and bayonetted thousands who never again wrote a letter home to loved ones.

My father left the Canal Zone on Dec. 14, 1943. After a year back in the States, during which time we have no written account, he shipped out on Jan. 31, 1945. He arrived in Scotland a week later. His military records listed his occupational specialty as "interpreter," taking advantage of the language he learned as a toddler and which often was spoken in his home. He was qualified as a sharpshooter and marksman with the M1 rifle and assigned to the 42nd Rainbow Combat Infantry Division.

According to the World War II history of the 42nd published in 1946, the Rainbow Division was "the most famous fighting organization of World War I." It was reactivated in July 1943 under the command of Maj. Gen. Harry J. Collins. On Oct. 14, 1944, Collins received orders from Washington, "Get your three infantry regiments ready to go overseas."

Unbeknownst to them, they were heading toward the Battle of the Bulge on the Western Front, including the dense and rugged Ardennes Forest of Belgium, Luxembourg and parts of France and Germany. The Rainbow regiments arrived at Marseilles on Dec. 8 and 9 and officially became known as Task Force Linden. The surprise attack by the Germans began on Dec. 16. Task Force Linden was assigned to the Seventh Army in the vicinity of Strasbourg and arrived on Dec. 23. From there, the Rainbow infantrymen established defensive positions along the Rhine River to the north.

By the time the Battle of the Bulge, the bloodiest one fought by the United States in World War II, ended on Jan. 25, 1945, the Americans had suffered some 89,000 casualties, including 19,000 killed. German losses were put at about 85,000. Their advance was halted, and they were on the run. The Allies prevailed. "Thus it was that the Rainbow infantrymen repulsed what later proved to be the last offensive action ever launched by the German army on the Western Front," the division history recorded. "The German had hoped to regain Alsace, but he had failed."

My father just missed the Battle of the Bulge, but the war was far from over when he arrived along with other reinforcements, weapons and fodder shortly thereafter.

Task Force Linden was dissolved on Feb. 6. On Feb. 14, the Rainbow Division was ordered to the front lines in the Hardt Mountains near the French border with Germany. The infantrymen dug into foxholes and conducted reconnaissance and combat patrols against the battle-tested German 6th Mountain Division, whose defenses were fortified with thousands of land mines. In a matter of 11 days, the Americans carried out 139 patrols, penetrating 2,000 yards into enemy lines. They killed 74 Germans, wounded 22 and captured eight. The Rainbow suffered 11 dead, 45 wounded and 11 missing in action. Most of the American casualties were caused by mines.

Division artillery and 83rd Chemical Mortar Battalion support was critical in crushing the morale of the enemy. One German prisoner told his captors, "The artillery was so bad that we would rather retreat than fire upon your men when we saw them coming. It got so bad that we were afraid to fire, for, if a machine gun opened up, you would locate the position and blast it with your terrible artillery." Upon advancing to the town of Melch, where reports had indicated a German command post was positioned, the infantrymen found nothing but rubble and bodies.

All in all, it was a fine introduction to war for my dad.

The Rainbow Division pushed on to the Siegfried Line, called the Westwall by the Germans for its location along the country's western border. The advance was described as "probably the most rugged on the entire front."

The fighting was intense and brutal, and the casualties were high. Fortunately for my father, his only physical damage was a serious case of frostbite in his feet and lower legs. It was a temporary setback on the push into northwestern Germany and southward to Munich, but it contributed to lifelong pain and eventual leg amputation in his later years.

By mid-March 1945, the Rainbow's 222nd, 232nd and 242nd infantry regiments were racing for the German border, with the 3rd Battalion of the 232nd crossing near the town of Husselkopf at 2:34 p.m. on the 18th, four minutes ahead of the 3rd Battalion of the 242nd. The German retreat came grudgingly.

Crossing the Rhine River on March 31 and entering the city of Worms, the site where Martin Luther took a stand before the Diet of Worms in 1521 and launched the Protestant Reformation, the Rainbow Division found entire blocks of buildings leveled by Allied bombing and nary a house left under roof.

Then it was eastward to northern Bavaria and the industrial city of Wurzburg on the Main River, where, on March 16, British Royal Air Force bombers killed some 5,000 civilians and obliterated the medieval town center. The words, "Heil Hitler!" painted on the wall of Marienburg Castle were replaced by rainbows and the inscription, "42nd Infantry Rainbow Division." With the bridges destroyed, the Americans met German machine-gun fire as they crossed the river on pontoon boats but disposed of that resistance, as well as a counterattack by two lonely tanks that followed. The occupation of Wurzburg did not come easily. Every block of the narrow streets had to be cleared of mounds of rubble, and nearly every crumpled house and building concealed snipers, many city police and firemen among them, firing guns and lobbing mortars at the infantrymen. Finally, the Rainbow's persistence and courage were rewarded with another captured city and 2,500 prisoners, not to mention a bountiful stash of bubbly Wurzburg champagne.

Similar scenarios played out in places like Arnstein, Werneck, Mulhausen, Ettleben, Nordheim and Schweinfurt, where 5,000 German defenders were ordered to fight to the last man – or teenager, as the case often was – just before the commander giving the orders high-tailed it out of there. Most of them, some 3,000, defied the orders and surrendered as prisoners. As the victorious Rainbow troops moved in, scores of slave laborers in the Schweinfurt factories, mostly Polish and Russian women, rushed out of bomb shelters to kiss and hug the liberators. The city was secured just in time for a solemn prayer and flag ceremony on a war-torn square in honor of President Roosevelt, who died on April 12, 1945.

There were more towns to take – Furth, Nurnburg, Donauworth – and more rivers to cross – the Aisch, the Danube, the Regnitz, the Lech. Time after time, the Rainbow Division was up to the challenge. On April 24, at Donauworth on the Danube, in the Schwaben, or Swabia, region of Bavaria, it was a fight to the death as the entrenched German troops battled the American tanks and infantrymen. When it was over, only 17 prisoners were taken.

And then there was Dachau, one of the most horrifying, most feared and most reviled places on Earth. Opened in 1933 about 10 miles northwest of Munich, Dachau was the first Nazi concentration camp in Germany. Until 1938, most of its occupants were Germans imprisoned for political reasons. Between 1933 and 1945, more than 3.5 million of them were locked up, and about 77,000 were executed for subversion, conspiracy and otherwise resisting the Nazis. Many of them were plucked from government, military and civil positions. Communists, socialists and other "enemies of the state" were prime suspects. At Dachau, they were joined by Jehovah's Witnesses, homosexuals and emigrants, as well as more than 11,000 German and Austrian Jews. There were 32,000 documented deaths at Dachau, and thousands more were undocumented.

Dachau served as a model for other concentration camps. But those that are most notorious for the Nazis' extermination of some 6 million Jews during World War II were located outside of Germany, including Auschwitz, Treblinka, Sobibor and Majdanek in Poland and Maulthausen in Austria. The death toll at Dachau paled in comparison to the 1.1 million who perished in the gas chambers of Auschwitz, 800,000 slaughtered at Treblinka or 200,000 killed at Sobibor, but that did not diminish the revulsion of Rainbow Infantry officers and men who arrived at the gate there under the leadership of Brig. Gen. Henning Linden on April 29, 1945.

As recorded in the Rainbow history, "Drawn up on sidings outside the camp itself, they found 50 boxcars, each one filled with about 30 men who had either starved to death in these cars or had been killed by the machine guns of the guards when they tried to escape. Many of the bodies were naked, the men who survived the longest having stripped them in an effort to keep warm." Those tormented Jews, perhaps 1,500 in all, had recently arrived from Buchenwald, which was abandoned by the Nazis in January. Only one skeleton of a man was found alive.

With the unstoppability of the American advance becoming evident over the previous days, most of the Nazi SS guards and administrative staff had fled the camp. A young German junior officer, 2nd Lt. Heinrich Wicker, recently brought in from the Eastern Front, was left to conduct the formal surrender. According to the Rainbow account, the liberators were met by sniper fire from the few remaining guards and promptly wiped them out.

Sixty-seven years later, in 2012, one of those liberators, 91-year-old Don Ritzenthaler, broke his long silence on the terrible day that he could never shake from his memory. As reported by his grandson, John Deem, in North Carolina's Lake Norman Citizen, Ritzenthaler and his fellow infantrymen were overcome by the gruesome scenes they encountered, from the crush of bodies in the boxcars, to the gas chamber disguised as a shower room, to corpses piled in the crematorium building and strewn about outside, to hundreds more diseased and dying in the infirmary. "After what we saw, we shot any German guards we saw on sight," he told his grandson, who, in turn, wrote, "What I pray, though, is that he dies knowing he was nothing like the Germans who acted as Satan's lackeys at Dachau. If he had been like them, he wouldn't have shot them, because he wouldn't have given a damn."

The secret of the Dachau slaughter had been out since the 1980s, though. The guards were all gone. Like the young officer Wicker, those who met the Americans were German and Hungarian troops sent in from the battlefield to assist with the surrender. They were ordinary soldiers. They were not resisting, nor were they part of the extermination machine. Guilt by association is a mighty strong stimulator under unimaginable circumstances. Even the photographs of the Dachau carnage in my father's copy of the "Rainbow Infantry Division World War II History" left a sickening, indelible impression on his son, who surreptitiously leafed through its pages as a boy.

Before fleeing the camp, the guilty guards had slaughtered some 2,000 inmates. The infantry arrived in time to liberate 33,000 prisoners at Dachau, but many of them were so far gone that their freedom was short-lived.

From there, the Rainbowmen trudged onward through Munich, the Bavarian capital. There they raided the cellar where Hitler began his beer-hall putsch in 1923 then was charged with treason and served nine months in prison. After 114 days of combat and a 450-mile trudge through mud and guts and blood, they reached the Austrian border in time for the German surrender on May 7, 1945. They had seized 6,000 square miles of territory, taken 51,000 prisoners and sustained 5,949 casualties.

One of those prisoners, a Nazi general, was captured by my dad. The circumstances of that capture are unknown. Mostly, my father's fluency in German was put to good use in the interrogation of prisoners following their surrender. Quite possibly, his conversation, as well as his carbine, played a role in the general's surrender. At any rate, my dad's soldierly action was rewarded with the Bronze Star Medal, which was engraved with the words, "Heroic or Meritorious Achievement," on its backside. Charles Manfred Lange was separated from the U.S. Army on Nov. 9, 1945, and returned home to Natrona Heights. He kept that Bronze Star in a box in a drawer in his bedroom dresser. He didn't talk about it. Nor did he speak about the Siegfried Line, Wurzburg, Schweinfurt, Donauworth, Munich or Dachau.

Among his other souvenirs of the war, my father kept a beautifully crafted and maintained 12-gauge shotgun and a military rifle, both of them German made, in the bedroom closet. In the aftermath of their hard-fought victory over fascism, American soldiers collected countless weapons from German civilians.

Not only was there good reason to disarm the enemy, but there also were reasons why gun ownership was common there. Following Germany's defeat in World War I, the Treaty of Versailles mandated the confiscation of guns from the population. In 1919, the Weimar government passed Regulations on Weapons Ownership and required that "all firearms, as well as all kinds of firearms ammunition, are to be surrendered immediately." The law was partially relaxed 10 years later with the issuance of firearms permits.

After Hitler bulled his way into power, gun ownership was encouraged among the general population, which no longer needed permits for shotguns and rifles and for whom handgun permits became more readily available. For painfully apparent reasons, though, Regulations Against Jews' Possession of Weapons were passed in November 1938.

Not surprisingly, the names of Hitler and Nazism became synonymous with hatred and evil and just about everything else that is despised in this world. Probably it's no wonder that, long after Hitler and his reign were extinguished by the collaborating forces of humanity, the less-collaborative forces of ideology readily connect them to those with whom they disagree.

Well into the 21st century, Wayne LaPierre, executive vice president of the National Rifle Association, and his followers repeatedly associate the advocacy of any sort of gun-control legislation with Hitler and the Nazis. The fact is that Hitler and the Nazis eased up on the gun controls that had been legislated by their democratically elected predecessors.

Neither were the Nazis liberals, progressives, socialists or communists. They hated wealth redistribution every bit as much as American conservatives do today. They certainly were shitty conservatives, but they were right-wing assholes nonetheless.

Furthermore, the Nazis were not atheists. Most of them attended Protestant or Catholic churches. They believed in God and in Jesus Christ and in life after death. Some of them cruelly believed that Christianity called upon them to inflict pain, suffering and death on Jews and others they considered beneath them. I believe they were not true Christians. I can only hope they got what they truly deserved upon their deaths.

None of this is to say that all is well with left-wing fanaticism, with communists who believe that religion is the opiate of the masses and with autocrats who really do take away people's guns.

Like most Americans who wanted to get on with their lives after World War II, my dad paid little attention to world-changing occurrences in the Far East. In September 1945, a man by the name of Ho Chi Minh declared an independent republic in French Indochina. Ho was no stranger to the brutal French colonialists who had ruled over the Vietnamese people from 1858 until they were routed by the Japanese during World War II. The Japanese conquerors were no less ruthless than the French, but they taught the Vietnamese a lesson they would not forget. From then on, the Vietnamese people knew that Asians don't have to take shit from Caucasians. Following the defeat of Japan by the United States, the French were determined to re-establish their colonial dominance. But Ho Chi Minh had other ideas.

Chapter 27 | **World War II Losers**

There was a time when grassy, green parks were safe havens where children in the big cities of Europe and North America could escape the confines of apartment life. Neighbors could be trusted. Strangers were not watched with suspicious eyes. The 1930s were such a time in the Tempelhof section of Berlin, where my mother lived happily for her first eight years.

And the park across the street from her family's first-floor flat was such a place. Like other little girls in the neighborhood, Helga Meta Else Hingst spent many carefree hours there playing dolls with friends, sledding down a gentle hill in the winter and letting her hair fly through the wind as she kicked her sandaled feet toward the blue sky on a sturdy swing set. It was where she experienced her first innocent kiss in the shade of a tree on a warm summer day.

My mom attended an all-girls school and took to learning with a passion, including the English language. She loved visiting her grandmother, Meta Siebert Zeyssig Fischer, who lived nearby, cooked tasty lunches and told fascinating stories.

On Sept. 1, 1939, the day that German warplanes and troops invaded Poland, Helga heard the news from an older neighborhood girl that their country was at war. There was no disruption of peace for Berliners at first. With that undisturbed sense of wellbeing, her stepfather, Heinrich Meyer, took the family on vacation to the mountains of Pomerania. A few days later, though, Heinrich, who was an accountant, received a telegraph from home with the news that he was being drafted and must return to Berlin at once.

Deciding that the highlands 100 miles or so northeast of Berlin provided a healthier, safer environment, my grandmother, Gertrud Meyer, decided to stay there with 8-year-old Helga and her 3-year-old sister, Gisela. Derived from the Slavic "po more," meaning "land at the sea," Pomerania, divided between today's Germany and Poland, rises up south of the Baltic Sea, with a jagged coastline in the west and sandy shore in the east. Inland, the Baltic Ridge is punctuated with glacial moraines that catch seasonal snows blowing from the Scandinavian north. It was on that Christmas Day, the first wartime one for my mother, that she received the most memorable gift of her life. It was her "poesie album," as she called it, an autograph book.

She packed it along with her textbooks after she enrolled in a two-room schoolhouse, where she began to collect signatures and short notes or poems from her friends and classmates. "Each room contained four grades," she recalled. "I loved that school, especially in the winter, when we walked to school on a mountain and skied back home."

My grandmother, my Oma, had two older brothers, Herbert Zeyssig, born in 1905, and Helmut, born in 1907.

For Herbert, right or wrong, willingly or not, war meant serving his country. German conscription began in March 1935, a year in advance of the Nazis' actual military advances.

Herbert entered the tank force, known as Panzers in German. With the Nazi propaganda machine directing attention toward Joseph Stalin's atrocities against the Russian people and the horrors of communism, plus Hitler's somewhat less-mentionable belief in the inferiority of Slavic peoples, the Panzers were engaged in the eastern push toward Moscow in June 1941. The early going resulted in major German victories and massive Soviet losses but also a fateful underestimation of the Russian resolve. By late fall, the advance was slowed by stiffening resistance and was halted 5 miles short of Moscow. With Soviet reinforcements arriving from Siberia and with winter supplies cut off from the west, the Germans, still in their warm-weather uniforms, were pounded by enemy guns, blasted by temperatures that plummeted to 50 degrees below zero and had to scrounge for food.

According to historical estimates, although the Germans inflicted somewhere between 650,000 and 1.28 million losses on the Soviets, they themselves suffered between 248,000 and 400,000 casualties in the Battle of Moscow. The Battle of Stalingrad that followed in late 1942 and early 1943 is credited with turning the tide on the Eastern Front for the Soviets.

My great-uncle Herbert Zeyssig was never seen nor heard from again.

His younger brother, Helmut, was afflicted by a bout of poliomyelitis, an acute infectious infantile paralysis commonly known as polio, when he was a child. Although 90 percent of the victims exhibited no symptoms whatsoever, the paralysis suffered by others could be permanently disabling and sometimes deadly. Helmut was somewhat fortunate in that his paralysis resulted in the crippling of his hand.

Physical deformities were among the conditions considered counterproductive by the Nazis' promulgation of racial purity. According to the United States Holocaust Memorial Museum, the persecution of these "unfit" Germans was one component of their societal filtration, which more consequentially was inflicted upon "biological enemies," especially Jews and Gypsies. Strategies against the supposed scourge escalated from forced sterilization to eliminating "life unworthy of life" and "useless eaters." At least 5,000 disabled children are believed to have been starved or lethally medicated by the Nazis.

Helmut Zeyssig may have been afflicted by polio, but he also was blessed with a mellifluous voice. It was the songs that he chose to sing with that voice, rather than the disability of his limb, that attracted the attention of the Nazis.

By most accounts, open German resistance to Hitler's regime was small and unorganized. Some Christians, notably Jesuit priests Alfred Delp and Augustin Rosch and the Lutheran Dietrich Bonhoeffer, were active in clandestine opposition. There were conspiracies within the German Army, including a 1944 Hitler assassination attempt. Many Jews were hidden from the Nazis by their Christian friends and neighbors. In early 1943, hundreds of unarmed German women successfully stood their ground against the Gestapo on Berlin's Rosenstrasse to prevent their Jewish husbands from being dragged away. Approximately 77,000 German citizens were put to death for various forms of resistance.

Helmut, my great-uncle, expressed his opposition by singing protest songs on the streets of Berlin. For that, he was hauled off to the Majdanek concentration camp near Lublin, Poland. He was never seen nor heard from again. But the Nazis returned his belongings, just the clothes off his back, actually, to his mother. They told her that her son had died from a hemorrhage. She washed his clothes in the bathtub. The water turned blood red.

Aside from the fighting forces and victims of the Nazis' extractions from society, by and large, the German people, from the spacious green parks of Berlin and Hamburg to the ridges of Pomerania and mountains of Bavaria, kept their peace as the war gathered steam. But in August 1940, after Luftwaffe bombers targeting Royal Air Force fields outside London drifted off course, hitting houses and killing civilians in the city, British Prime Minister Winston Churchill retaliated with bombs on Berlin the next night. Welcome to the war, German people.

Beginning on Sept. 7, the blood of British civilians flowed time and time again as German bombers inflicted a rein of booming terror. London endured 57 consecutive sleepless nights during which a million houses were damaged and 40,000 people were killed.

Gertrud, Helga and Gisela were in for a rude awakening when they returned to Berlin to care for their ill mother and grandmother, Meta. It wasn't long before the British bombs made Berliners feel the same pain as Londoners did.

"When the first explosions shook our apartment building, we children hid in corners and under chairs," my mother wrote in her memoirs. "Some older kids even wet their pants. After a while we got used to the bombings. It became our way of life. Every night now we heard that miserable siren that made us go to the reinforced basements.

"As the bombing increased to more than one alarm at night, our mothers placed mattresses in the basement and put us to bed there every night, which meant that we would not have to get up, get dressed and go to the basement night after night. When my mother sensed the danger of our building collapsing on us, we were enrolled in a children's bunker. However, after a horrible attack one night, we all enrolled in a family bunker."

Five huge public shelters were established in the city, including one at the Berlin Zoo, capable of protecting 65,000 people from the bombs, and many others were set up below government buildings, in subway stations and elsewhere.

Berlin was hit by 363 air raids during the war. The British policy of only bombing military targets and infrastructure was abandoned in 1940 in favor of area bombing, which did not spare civilians or their homes. Berlin's Tempelhof Airport was fair game before and after the targeting expansion. Death and destruction in Berlin came courtesy of the Royal Air Force until 1943, when the U.S. Air Force joined in. Sir Arthur Harris, who headed the British air command put it in perspective. "The Nazis entered this war under the rather childish delusion that they were going to bomb everyone else, and nobody was going to bomb them," he said. "At Rotterdam, London, Warsaw and half a hundred other places, they put their rather naive theory into operation. They sowed the wind, and now they are going to reap the whirlwind." Childish indeed.

By late 1943, with more than 800 long-range bombers at his disposal, Harris was able to wreak havoc on Berlin night after night. Hundreds were killed on each raid, 1,000 and even 2,000 on the deadliest nights. Some 450,000 homes were destroyed in the relentless assault on civilians, mostly women and children.

Not coincidentally, the Germans decided it was a good idea to evacuate the capital city of its nonessential inhabitants, especially the children. Some 1.2 million people, about a quarter of the population, were relocated to rural areas before even heavier bombings obliterated my mom's hometown.

In early 1944, Hitler closed the schools and ordered all school-age children out of the city, with or without their mothers. Just as she was about to be packed up with classmates on an awaiting bus, Helga saw her mother, grandmother and sister running toward her. They had made arrangements to move out to the country together, as opposed to letting the government make arrangements to move them out separately to who knows where.

Their first destination was a town called Meesow, back in Pomerania. The owners of a large estate there were ordered by the government to take in refugees from the cities. Needless to say, the landowners didn't fully appreciate the intrusion, but it was a treat for young intruders. "We children had a great time there," my mother said, "riding horses across the fields or riding in a horse-drawn carriage with the inspector." She made friends and collected more signatures in her album.

The adults got the message that they were unwelcome guests, though, and the family moved on to a place called Regenwalde, also in Pomerania, where my grandmother had some friends who owned a grocery store. She helped out around the store. Helga got a taste of peaceful small-town life, the bombs of Berlin echoing in the recesses of her still young but rapidly maturing mind. Regenwalde produced more signatures and notes in her autograph album.

At the end of summer, they moved to a town called Loos in Silesia, which gave them an opportunity to see Heinrich Meyer, my grandmother's husband and my mother's stepfather, who was at a nearby outpost to train military recruits from the Ukraine.

Silesia, southwest of Berlin, is one of those regions that's bounced around among victorious states throughout history – from Greater Moravia to Bohemia and to Poland in the 10th century. It was back in Bohemian hands under the Holy Roman Empire and then part of the Austrian Habsburg Monarchy in the early 1500s. Prussia conquered most of Silesia in 1742, connecting it to Germany for the next two centuries. A piece of it was sliced off and returned to Poland after Germany's loss in World War I. Following World War II, most of Silesia went to Poland, former Austrian parts went to Czechoslovakia, and a small section was retained by East Germany.

It was in full control of Nazi Germany when my mom, then 12 years old, arrived and enrolled in the nearest high school, which was an hour's train ride away from Loos. The daily commute and classroom interaction gave her an opportunity to bond with fellow displaced Berliners and transplants from other cities. It was on the train that she met her first boyfriend, who had been evacuated from Hamburg on the North Sea to a different Silesian village. His signature and sweet poetry were the most prized additions to her album.

Sometimes, she said, she and a girlfriend would walk part of the way and pass a prisoner-of-war camp where captured American airmen were being held. "We would stop when the prisoners were outside to try out our English," she said. "It usually did not take long before we were chased away. The POW camp and our dads being soldiers on the Russian front were our only reminders of war."

Hundreds of POW camps were dispersed throughout Germany and its occupied territories. Stalags generally were for captured enlisted men, and Oflags held officers. They were organized in districts, one of them being headquartered in the Selesian city of Breslau. Its Stalags were located in places like Gorlitz, Teschen and Neuhammer. Oflags were in Kreuzburg, Silberberg, Tittmoning and elsewhere.

In the summer of 1944, peaceful life again began to fade away for my displaced ancestors. After becoming a teenager that spring, my mother and her classmates got drafted into the service of the Nazi regime. Some of them were assigned to dig ditches, presumably as obstacles to slow down the advancing Russians and to provide cover for their own soldiers. Others, including my mom, were dispatched to farms, where they helped with the harvest. Within a week, overcome with homesickness, she hitched a horse-drawn wagon ride to a train station and made her way back to Loos. The schools didn't reopen that fall. My grandmother, mother and even little Gisela helped local farmers pick potatoes in the fields. It was back-breaking labor that left them stooped over for hours after each workday, but food wasn't free, and they had to do something if they wanted to eat.

Thundering in the distance and a red glow on the eastern horizon at night began to cast a gloom over the faces of villagers and refugees alike. With the ground shuddering more ominously by the day, farmers loaded up their wagons, hitched their horses and headed west. Helga, Gisela, Gertrud and Meta were among those left behind, waiting and hoping for a train to carry them to safety before the dreaded arrival of the Russian tanks.

"God has always taken care of us. Why would he stop now?" Meta assured her granddaughters. She was right. "At the last minute, we were able to board a train to safety," my mother said. "It was a very close call. When our train pulled out, the Russian tanks moved in no more than 200 yards away on a street beyond a heavily wooded area. They made so much noise that they did not detect us. We children were not afraid, because all of the adults on board kept reassuring us. I have no idea how my mother was able to stay strong." Amidst the turmoil and their scramble for survival, she realized that she had left her beloved autograph book behind. With it were the names and cherished messages of young friends she would never see again, not knowing whether they lived or died.

After several days on the train, they arrived at a small station and hiked on foot, suitcases in hand, about 3 miles to a small Czechoslovakian village, which remained under control of the Nazi occupation. They were directed to an upstairs sleeping area with straw spread over the floor serving as bedding. "Already the next morning we were covered with bedbug bites," my mother recalled. "Later we added head lice, which was horrible for me with my long hair. The people were so poor that they had no running water, let alone plumbing, in their homes." They had to walk more than 2 miles to the nearest bathing facility.

Resentment of the German occupation, which ran high in the village from the get-go, became more menacing as word spread that Hitler's credibility and quest for European domination were going up in smoke. On May 6, 1945, Gen. George S. Patton Jr., commander of the U.S. 3rd Army, ordered his units to discontinue their advance and allow the Russians, who had routed the Germans from Prague the previous day, to occupy the rest of Czechoslovakia.

With cowering turned to bravado, one of the men in the village went into the sleeping area of the displaced German women and children with his pistol drawn, lined them up against a wall and waved the weapon in their faces. Except for the clothes they were wearing, all of their belongings were taken from them. After Russian soldiers arrived, the Germans were escorted out of town. Shouting villagers lined up to pelt them with stones and shower them with phlegmy spittle. "We were glad to turn our backs on the people of that village," my mother said.

The group of Germans drifted through Czechoslovakia, not knowing for sure whether they were heading toward home or what was awaiting them around the next bend in the road. As they passed through one village, a drunk stumbled out of a pub and threatened them with a knife. "I kept walking and closed my eyes tight, expecting to be stabbed," Helga said, recalling the experience of a 14-year-old German girl. Responding to the screams of her family, a Russian soldier arrived in the nick of time, knocked the drunk on his ass and led them to safety.

Not all the Russians they encountered were of that nature. "They had not had leave from the army since the beginning of the war. They were starved for the warmth of a woman," my mother said, fully understanding that warmth is not what horny warriors tend to starve for from their defeated enemies. "We had to try to avoid them in order not to become their victims." On one occasion, a stalking Russian soldier sensed the presence of females who had sought seclusion in the attic of an abandoned building, stepped inside and called for a woman, any woman. My great-grandmother told the others to be silent and still as her quivering legs carried her scrawny old body down the creaking staircase in response to his demand. With her false teeth tucked away in the pocket of her filthy dress, she managed a gummy smile as the man approached and squinted through the shadowy hallway. "Arghh!" he spouted, his lusty enthusiasm suddenly neutralized by the unenticing rendezvous. He stomped off in search of other prey.

That incident was worth a good laugh later, but the wandering, the begging for food from resentful Czechs, the nightly search for shelter, the fear of the unknown and the horror of the known took an unhappy toll on the German women and children. Skeletal bodies of starved babies and toddlers were deposited in shallow graves on the roadsides. Anguished mothers refused to go on, some of them slitting their wrists or throats, choosing to meet their dead offspring in the hereafter rather than meet their conquerors from the east.

Finally, word spread about trains beginning to roll again, and my mother's family managed to find a station. Several days later they were able to board a freight train heading west. When that train came to a halt, they got out, begged for food and followed the rails on foot. They caught other trains when they could, as long as they were heading west, north or south.

Eventually, they arrived at the station in Sagan, Silesia, where my mother had gone to school the previous year. They made the 15-kilometer trek to Loos but found it deserted by its former inhabitants and mostly in ruins. They arrived at the house where they had felt safe and at peace not so long ago by the way the calendar measures time but so much further by the way history changes things.

"Mattresses were slashed and defecated on," my mother said. "Clothes were ripped and photos crumbled. I could not cry. I had seen too much horror and death that I had lost my ability to cry." By the light of the next day, she took a better look through the piles of trashed treasure. "I rejoiced over every picture that had not been destroyed," she said. Just as she was ready to leave, something caught her eye under a pile of feathers from torn pillows. "It was blue leather and in fairly good shape – my autograph book!" she said with delight. "I sat on the floor and caressed it as I read the wonderful familiar pages." There they were. Her friends, their feelings for each other, their hopes of growing up, their fears about the war, their rosy impressions of the fair countryside around them and, yes, their prickly observations about the ugliness unfolding over the hills in the diminishing distance. "I still could not cry. War does that to children," she said. "But there was a ray of sunshine inside of me. The world would be right."

The Russian soldiers who occupied the village were disciplined and organized. They put the refugees to work. There were potatoes and other crops to be harvested from the fields and even some cows to be milked. My mom and her family filled their bellies, found fresh clothes in abandoned homes, regained their strength and then resumed their journey toward Berlin.

Mostly they walked, they rode on freight trains when they could and once were given a ride by Russian soldiers on the back of their truck. The two women and two girls were dropped off in a residential section of a town, where they began knocking on doors and looking for somewhere to spend the night, but nobody answered. The Russians returned after a while, my mother said, and were surprised to find them still in the street as darkness approached. "One of them climbed over a barbed-wire fence and pounded at the door," she said. "He got us a place to stay in their garage. Then he went out to get some food. He could not speak German, and I could not speak Russian, but we both had learned English in school. There we were, a German and a Russian conversing in English. It went quite well in spite of our different accents."

Their long days on the road, slowed by the struggling pace of my aging great-grandmother, and shivering spring nights in abandoned buildings finally were rewarded by the somber sight of what was left of their hometown. "I looked around at the bombed-out houses and the rubble that covered the streets," my mother said. "There were no buses or streetcars running. There was no public transportation of any kind. Berlin was a disaster, but it looked beautiful to me. All I could think of was, 'Berlin, Berlin, oh, you, my beloved, wonderful city.'"

By the time the bombing ended, Berlin had been targeted by more than 9,000 Allied sorties that dropped some 45,000 tons of exploding carnage on the capital city. Approximately 50,000 civilians were killed. Ninety percent of the buildings were leveled. Its rich architectural heritage – palaces, museums and cathedrals – lay in heaps of historic proportion.

What 14-year-old Helga, 9-year-old Gisela, their mother, Trude, and grandmother, Meta, knew about the horrors inflicted upon their fellow human beings in the name of the German people is hard to say. Many years later, reacting to a news account about a Holocaust survivor broadcast on the black-and-white television set in our American living room, my mother expressed some skepticism about the enormity of the monstrous extermination. Before she could finish a sentence, my father interjected with uncharacteristic finality. "I saw what they did," he said. "Anyone who says otherwise is wrong. We should be the last ones to deny it." That was the end of that.

The Potsdam Conference from July 17 to Aug. 2, 1945, divided what was left of Germany into four occupation zones administered by the United States, Great Britain, France and the Soviet Union. Although Berlin was wholly within the Soviet zone, because of its political and symbolic significance, the city was subdivided into four sectors as well.

Fortunately, Tempelhof became part of the American sector. The apartment where my mother had spent her early years was occupied by Allied soldiers, so the extended family, 12 of them in all, crowded into my great-grandmother's small apartment. There was no heat and little food to be found.

Meta Siebert Zeyssig Fischer had survived her early marriage to my great-grandfather Alfons Zeyssig, the scoundrel who took my grandmother with him to a bar and beat the crap out of the little girl when she left her purse there. Meta persevered after the untimely death of her second husband. One of her sons died on the Eastern Front, the other in a concentration camp. She lived through the relentless bombing of Berlin. She comforted her grandchildren as Russian tanks closed in on their safe haven in Czechoslovakia. She did her best to shield them from the stones and spit hurled at them by their loathing hosts as they were marched out of the village. Her wrinkled face and toothless advance spoiled the appetite of a sex-starved Russian soldier as my grandmother, then 36 years old with well-defined feminine attributes, huddled in the darkness with my blossoming teenage mother and her pre-pubescent sister. And she made it home.

But her frail body, weakened by a scarcity of food and worn by months on the road, lost the war. Not long after their return to Berlin, she sat down on a dreary November day, fainted and never came to. While many other German corpses were wrapped in blankets or rugs and plopped into the cold, hard earth, Trude found a coffin-like box for her beloved mother, and they ceremoniously laid her to rest below the frosted grass in a cemetery plot. Again, my mother knew what it meant to be a child of war. "I could not cry for my treasured grandmother," she said. "There were no tears left in me."

Despite their mourning, the Christmas Eve of 1945, a time of peace instead of war, was special indeed. My mother and her cousin managed to find a small, crooked spruce tree on the outskirts of town and bartered a few fragrant branches for a box of dried fruit and dumplings from a grocer. In the basement, they retrieved some colorful, dusty but shiny ornaments and a broken star, which they glued back together, and decorated that tree. They lit homemade candles and tuned in Christmas carols on the radio. The gifts they exchanged included blouses made out of sheets and tablecloths, mittens made from the wool of an old sweater and a winter coat made out of an old army blanket. "We were ready to celebrate Christ, who had brought us through this horrible war," my mother said. "Then the doorbell rang. It was my dad, who had finally returned from the war. We were together again, and we all felt truly blessed."

From time to time throughout her life, my mom would dig out her autograph album. "I read it every so often, and I get a catch in my throat. It makes me remember the war – the good times and the bad," she said. "I mourn all of the young men – boys, really – that had to die on both sides, but I still cannot cry."

I don't think she ever did. I heard her yell a lot, too often at me. I saw and heard her argue with my dad more often than I cared to. But I never saw her cry.

About the Author

Dave Lange is a 1975 graduate of Kent State University with a bachelor of arts in journalism news. He also studied political science in graduate school at the University of Akron.

His 40-year newspaper career included positions as features editor and then Sunday Paper editor for the daily Lake County Telegraph, editor of the daily Geauga Times Leader and editor in chief of the weekly Greater Cleveland Real Estate News.

For most of his career, Lange was editor of the weekly Chagrin Valley Times and its sister publications, the Solon Times and the Geauga Times Courier. The Times was honored with the Ohio Newspaper Association's General Excellence Award as the state's best weekly newspaper 19 times during his 25 years of leadership. Individually, the ONA awarded him first place in editorial writing 15 times and first place in column writing eight times.

Lange was named the best columnist among all Ohio newspapers in 2011 by the Cleveland Press Club and has received numerous Ohio Excellence in Journalism Awards for editorial and column writing. He also was awarded first place statewide for column writing in 2000 by the Society of Professional Journalists.

Lange served in a support capacity with the Brown Water Navy's riverine forces in Vietnam from February 1969 to February 1970. As a member of Helicopter Anti-Submarine Squadron 11 from February 1970 until his discharge in December 1971, he made Mediterranean Sea and North Atlantic deployments. He was awarded the Vietnam Service Medal with four campaign stars, Republic of Vietnam Campaign Medal, National Defense Service Medal plus Navy Unit Commendation and Meritorious Unit Commendation ribbons.

He is a member of Vietnam Veterans of America, Veterans of Foreign Wars and American Legion.